Athos
in
America

Athos
in
America

by JASON

FANTAGRAPHICS BOOKS

All stories written and drawn by Jason and colored by Hubert

FANTAGRAPHICS BOOKS
7563 Lake City Way NE
Seattle WA 98115
fantagraphics.com

Translated by Kim Thompson
Series Designed by Jason and Covey
Cover Design by Alexa Koenings
Production and lettering by Paul Baresh
Associate Publisher is Eric Reynolds
Published by Gary Groth and Kim Thompson

Special thanks to Jerome Martineau.

To receive a free catalog of comics, call 1-800-657-1100, write us at the address above, or visit our website at www.fantagraphics.com. Visit the website The Beguiling, where Jason's original artwork can be purchased: www.beguiling.com

Distributed in the U.S. by W.W. Norton and Company, Inc. (1-212-233-4830)
Distributed in Canada by Canadian Manda Group (1-800-452-6642 x862)
Distributed to comic book stores by Diamond Comics Distributors (1-800-452-6642 x215)
Distributed in the United Kingdom by Turnaround Distribution (44-020-8829-3002)

First printing: December, 2011

ISBN: 978-1-60699-478-8

Printed in China

CHAPTERS

PRESENTING:

THE SMILING HORSE

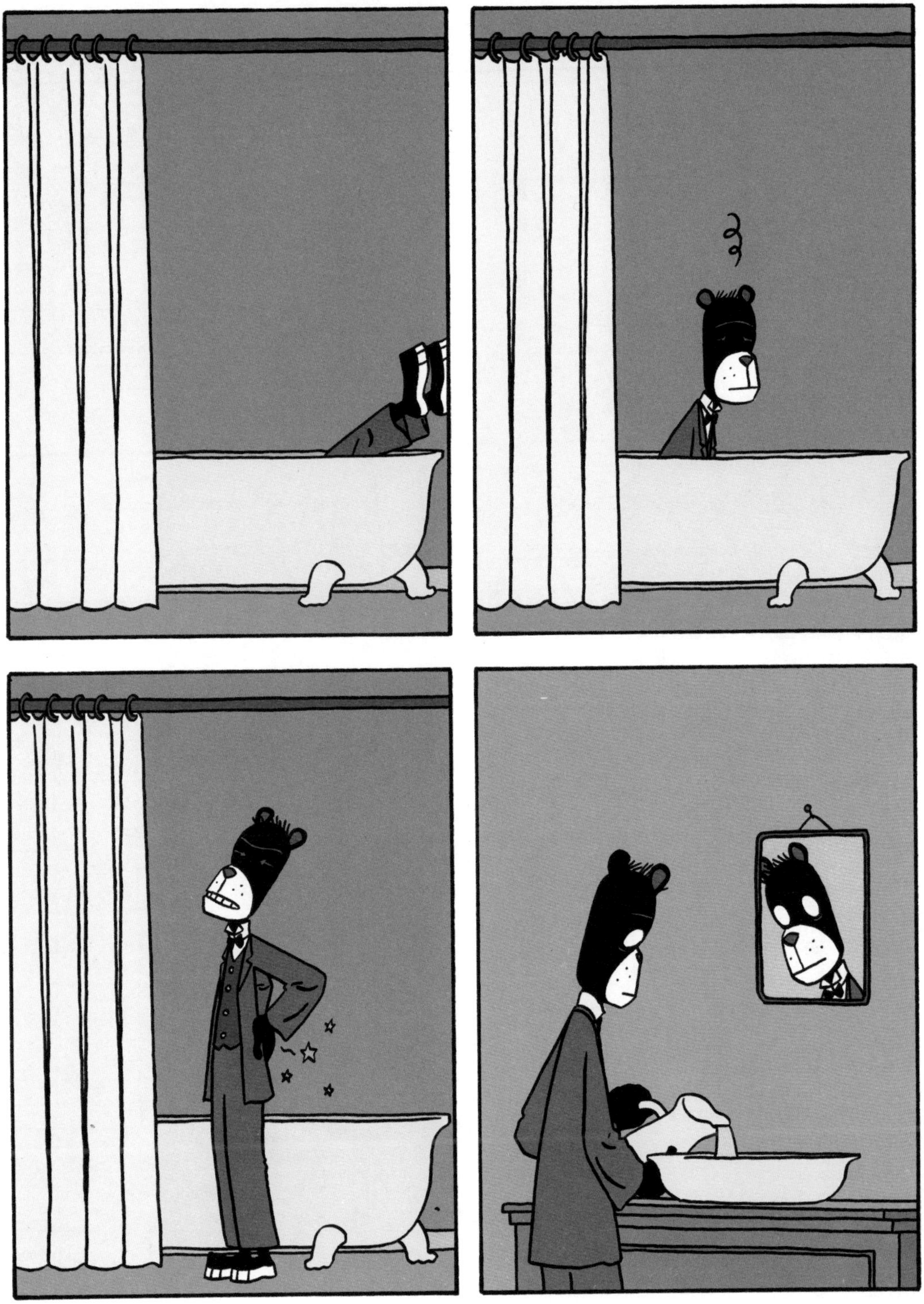

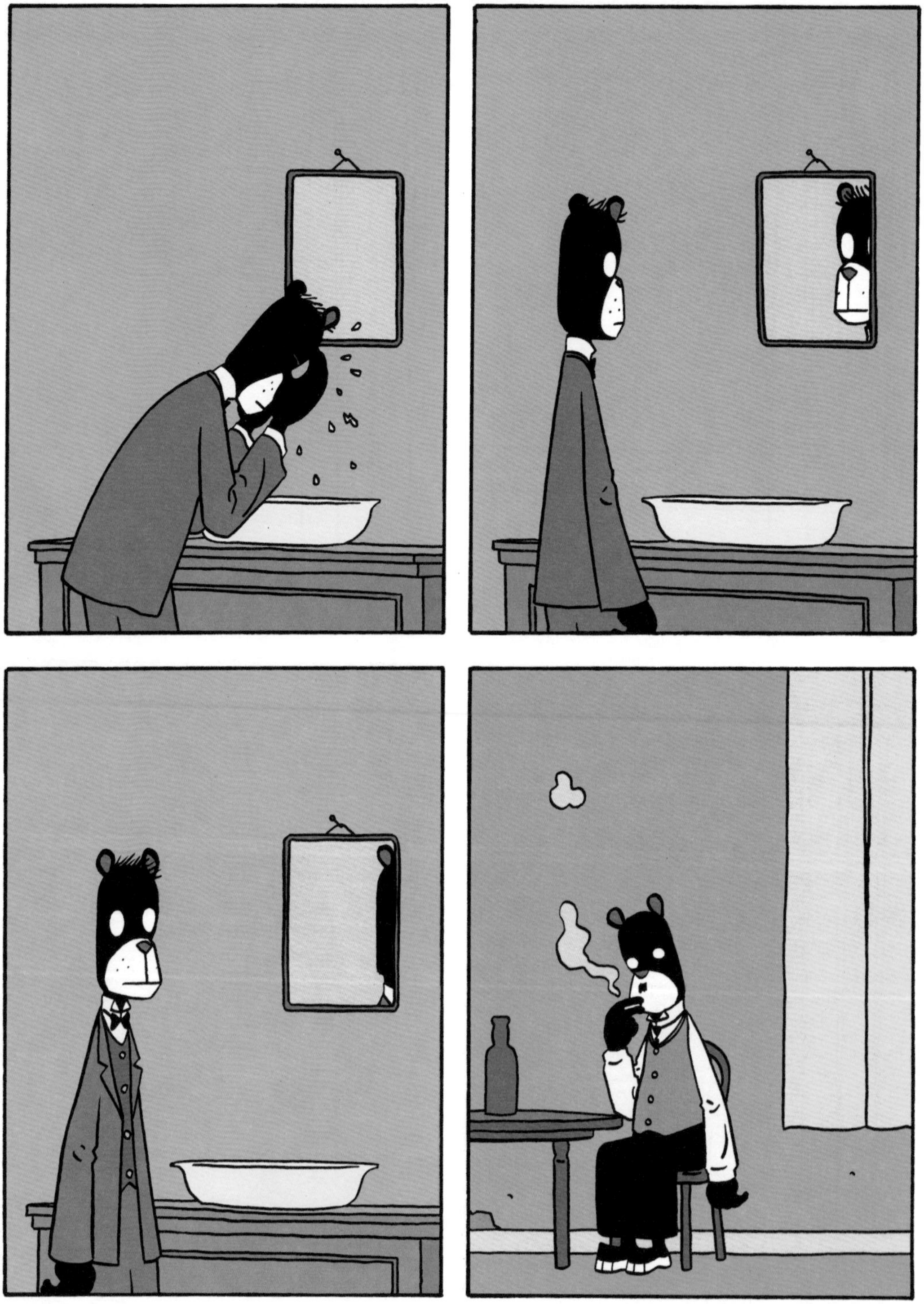

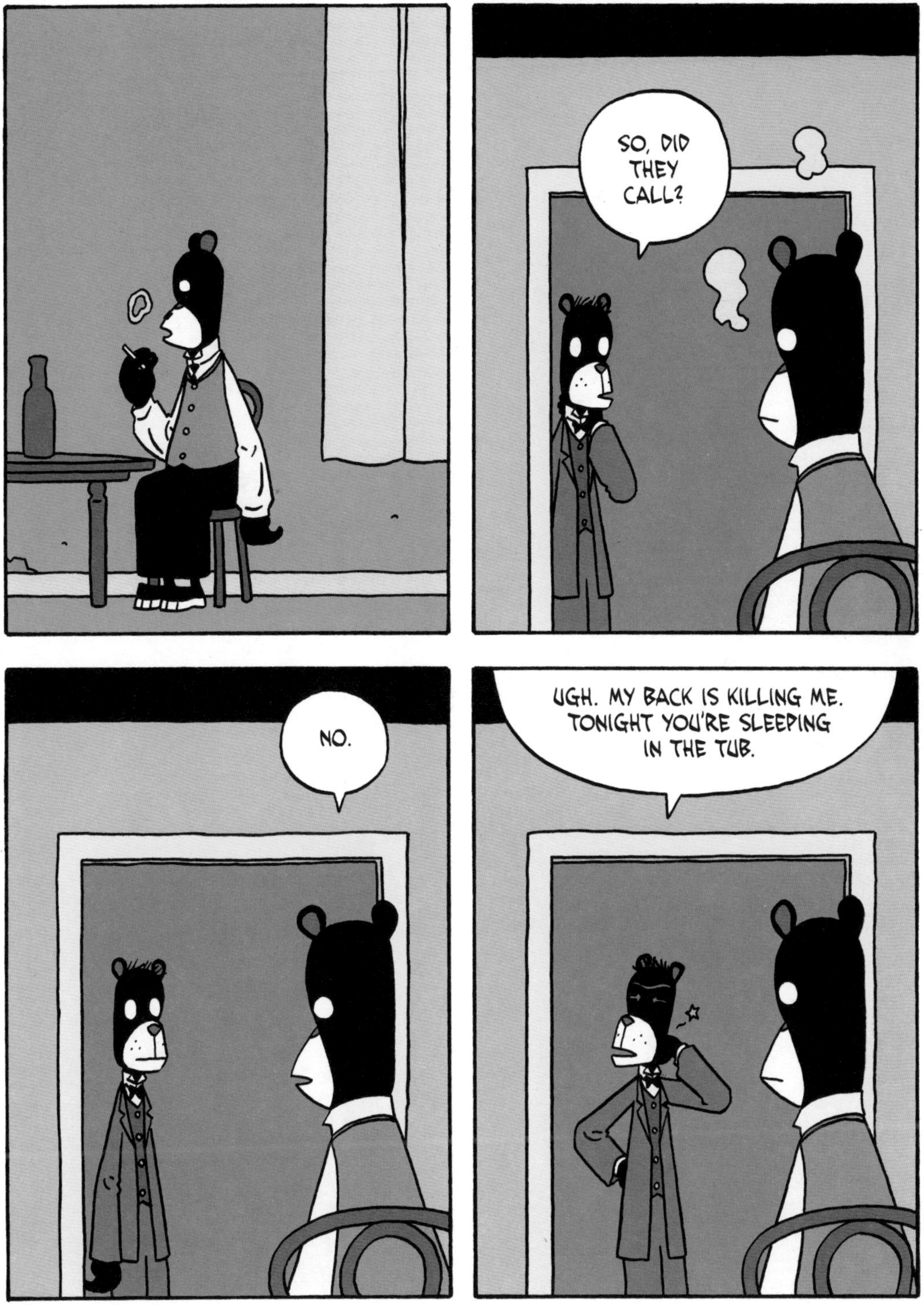
SO, DID THEY CALL?
NO.
UGH. MY BACK IS KILLING ME. TONIGHT YOU'RE SLEEPING IN THE TUB.

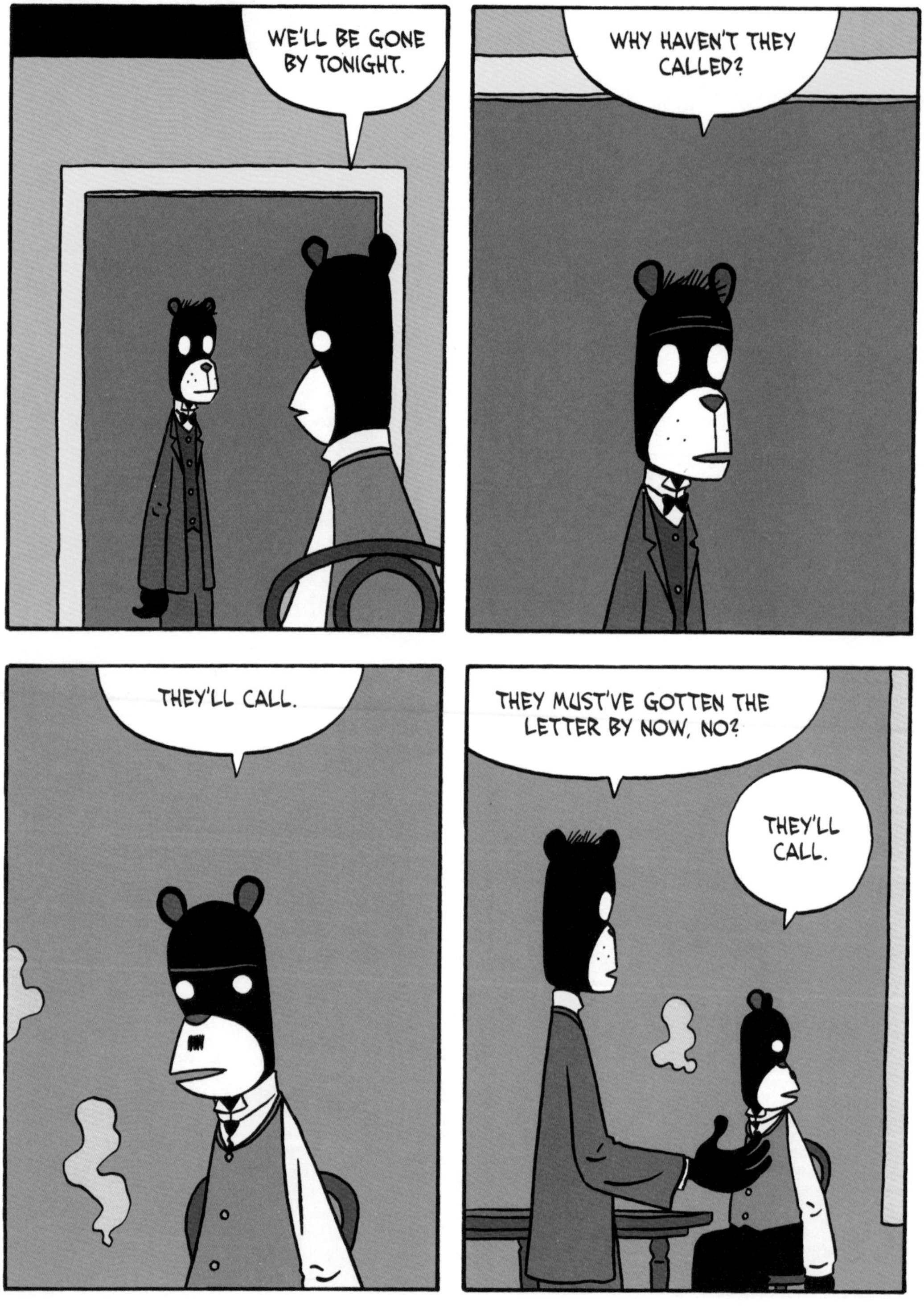
WE'LL BE GONE BY TONIGHT.
WHY HAVEN'T THEY CALLED?
THEY'LL CALL.
THEY MUST'VE GOTTEN THE LETTER BY NOW, NO?
THEY'LL CALL.

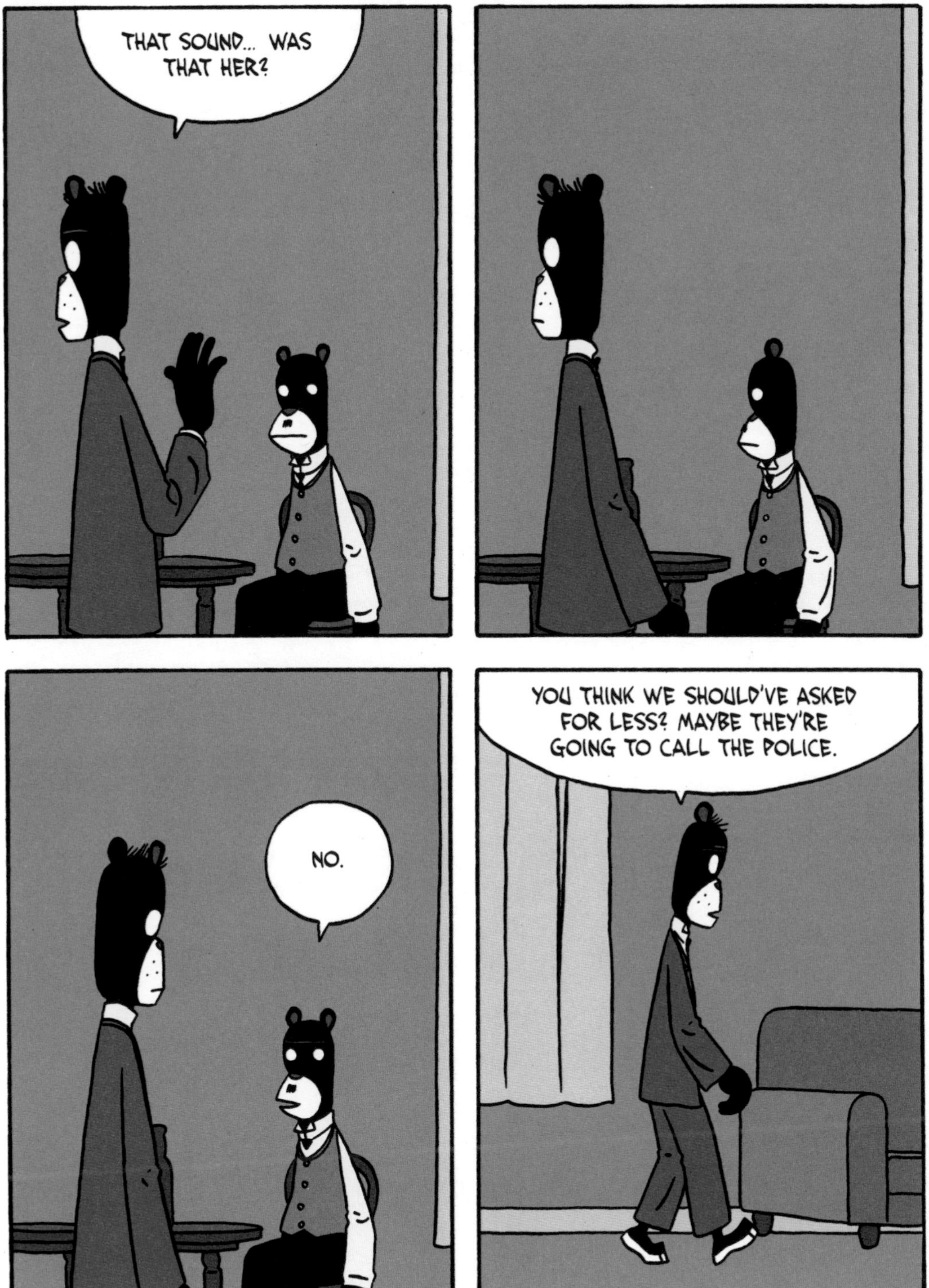
THAT SOUND... WAS THAT HER?
NO.
YOU THINK WE SHOULD'VE ASKED FOR LESS? MAYBE THEY'RE GOING TO CALL THE POLICE.

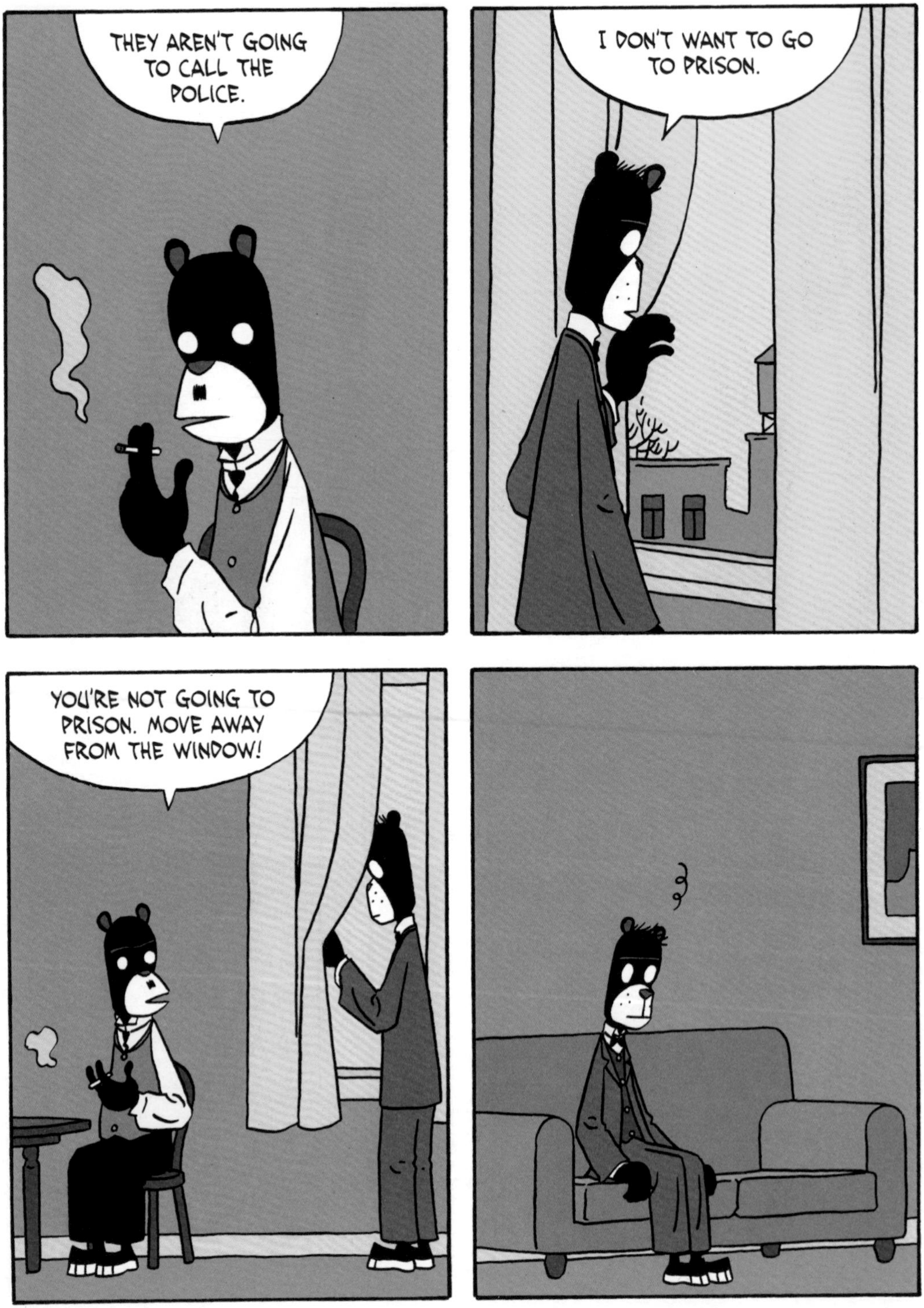
THEY AREN'T GOING TO CALL THE POLICE.
I DON'T WANT TO GO TO PRISON.
YOU'RE NOT GOING TO PRISON. MOVE AWAY FROM THE WINDOW!

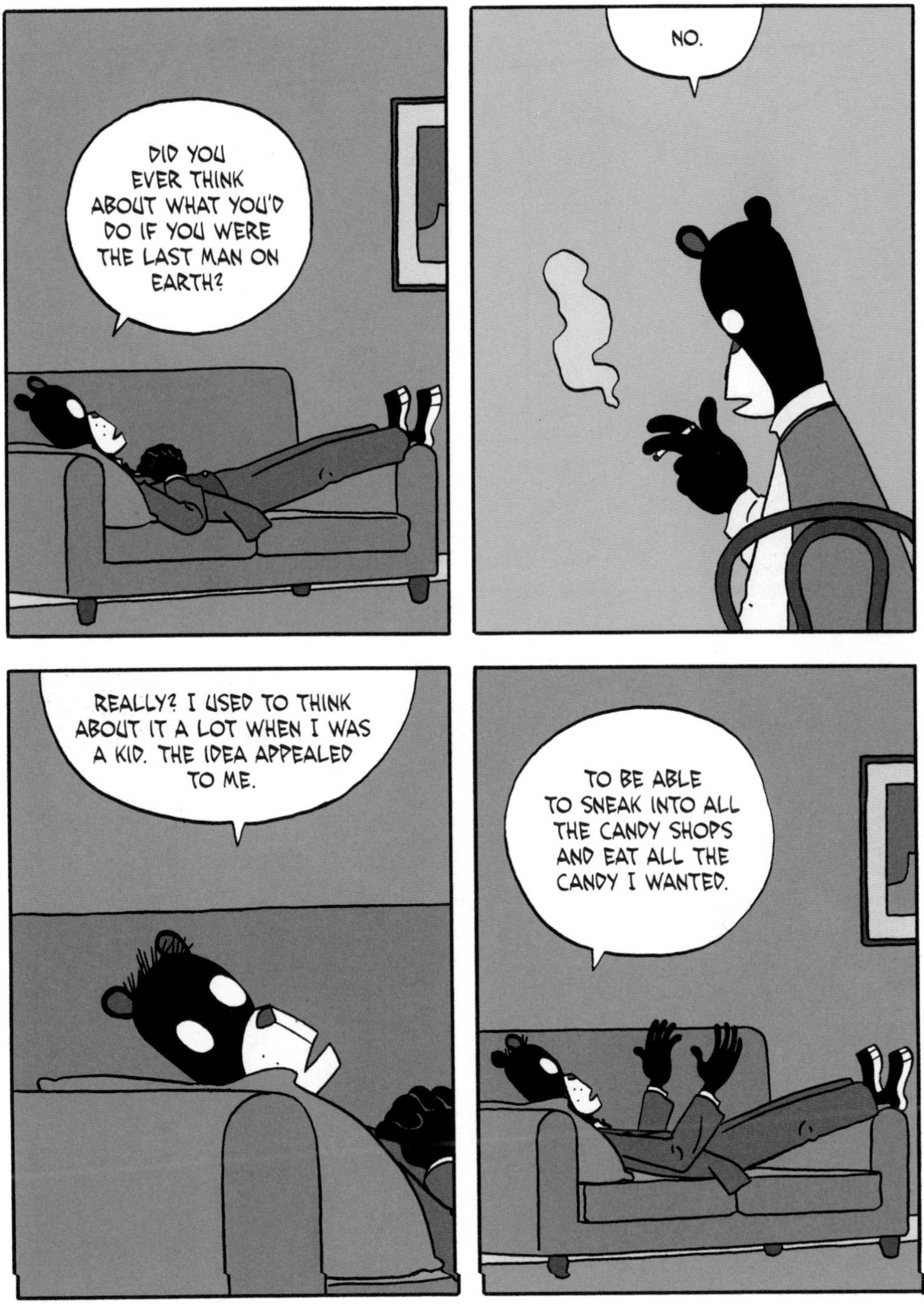
DID YOU EVER THINK ABOUT WHAT YOU'D DO IF YOU WERE THE LAST MAN ON EARTH?
NO.
REALLY? I USED TO THINK ABOUT IT A LOT WHEN I WAS A KID. THE IDEA APPEALED TO ME.
TO BE ABLE TO SNEAK INTO ALL THE CANDY SHOPS AND EAT ALL THE CANDY I WANTED.

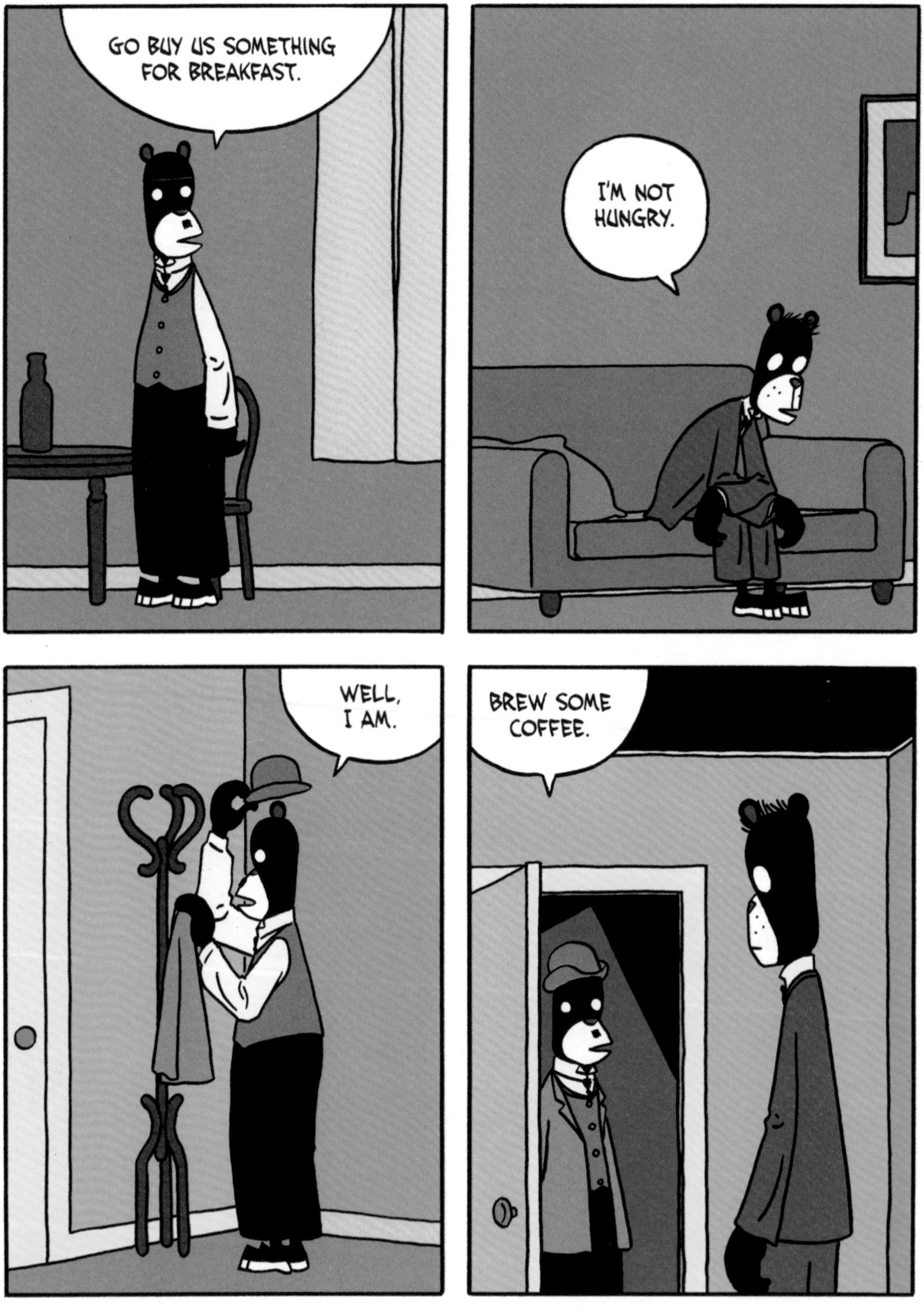
GO BUY US SOMETHING FOR BREAKFAST.
I'M NOT HUNGRY.
WELL, I AM.
BREW SOME COFFEE.

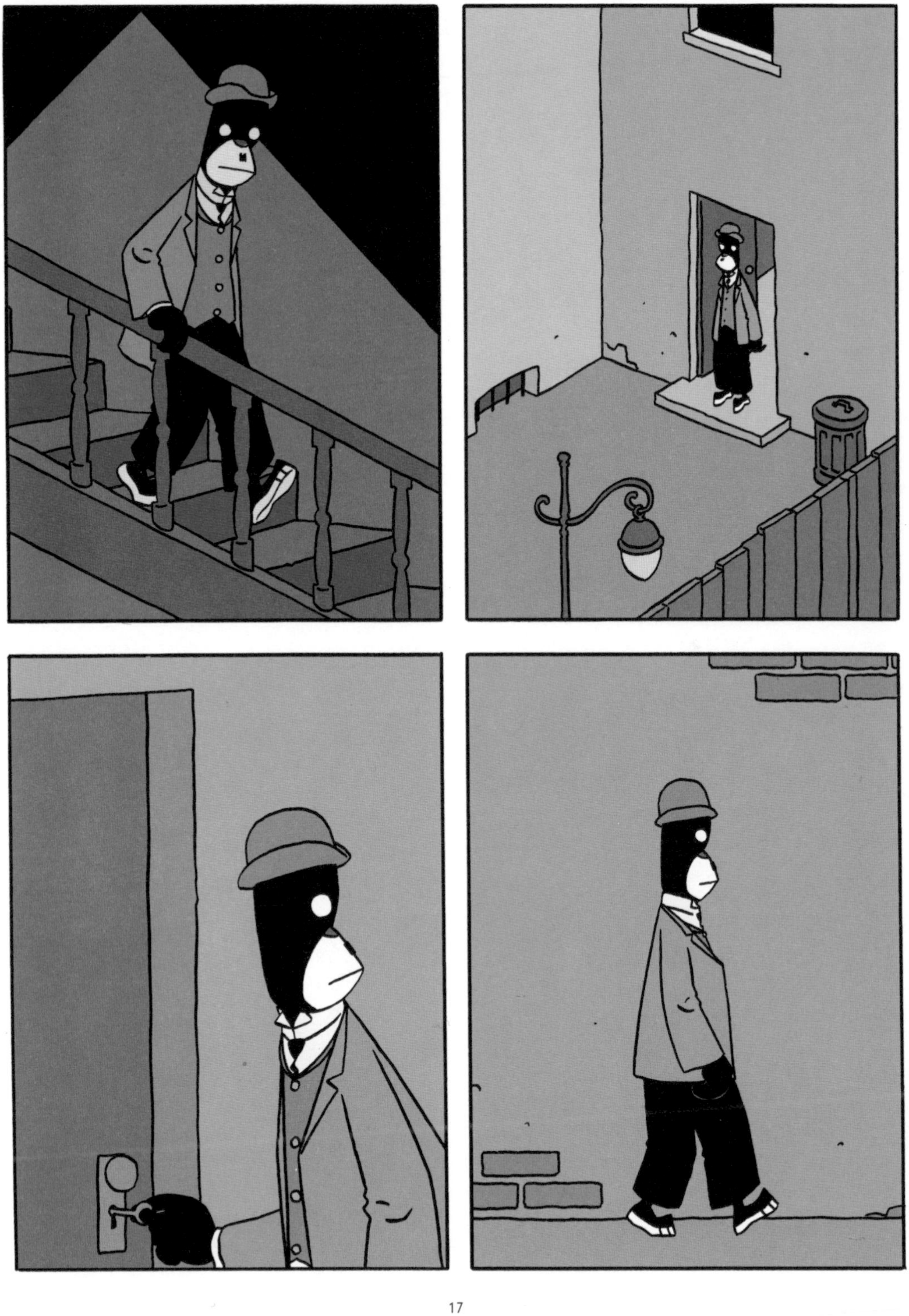

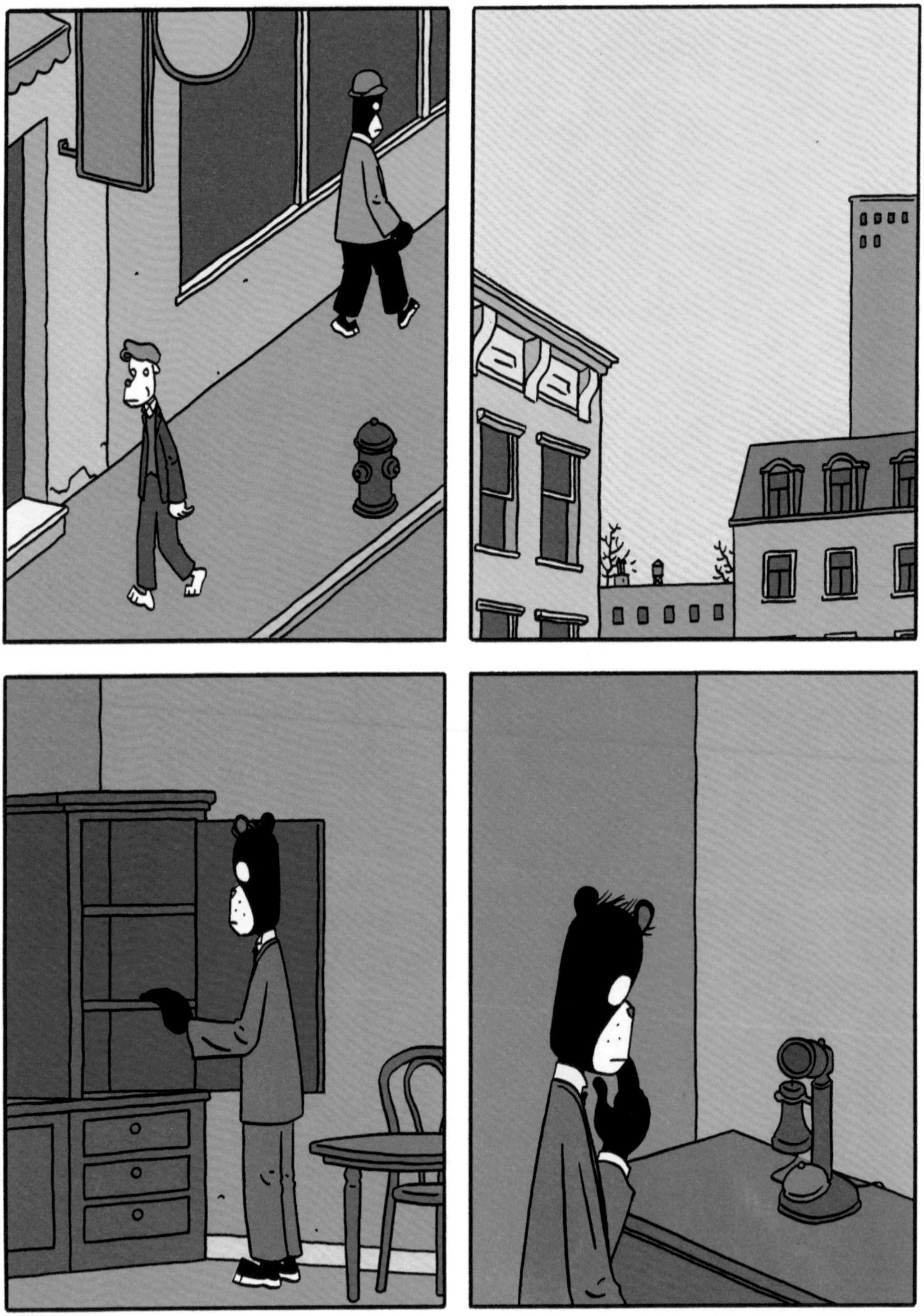

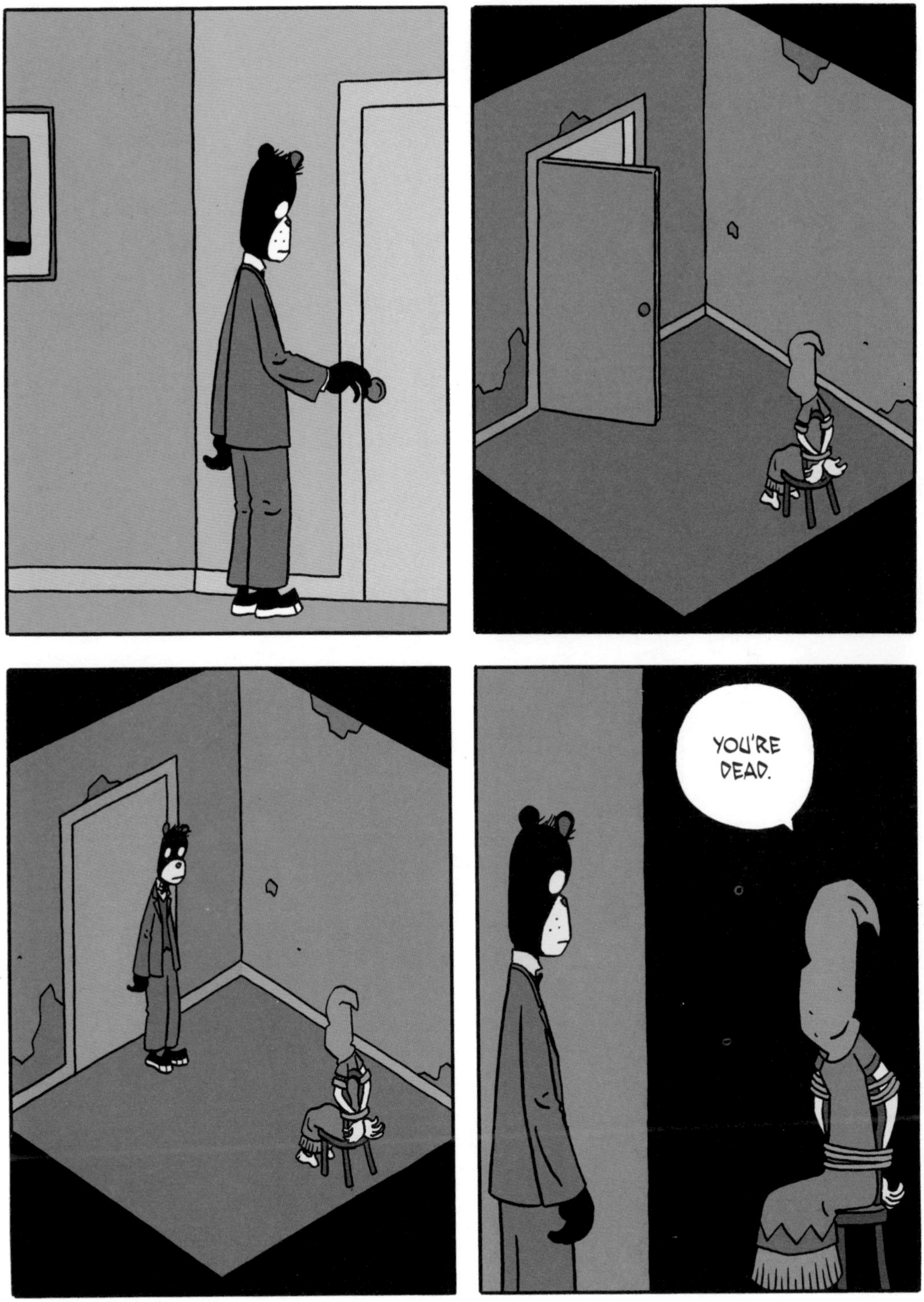
YOU'RE
DEAD.

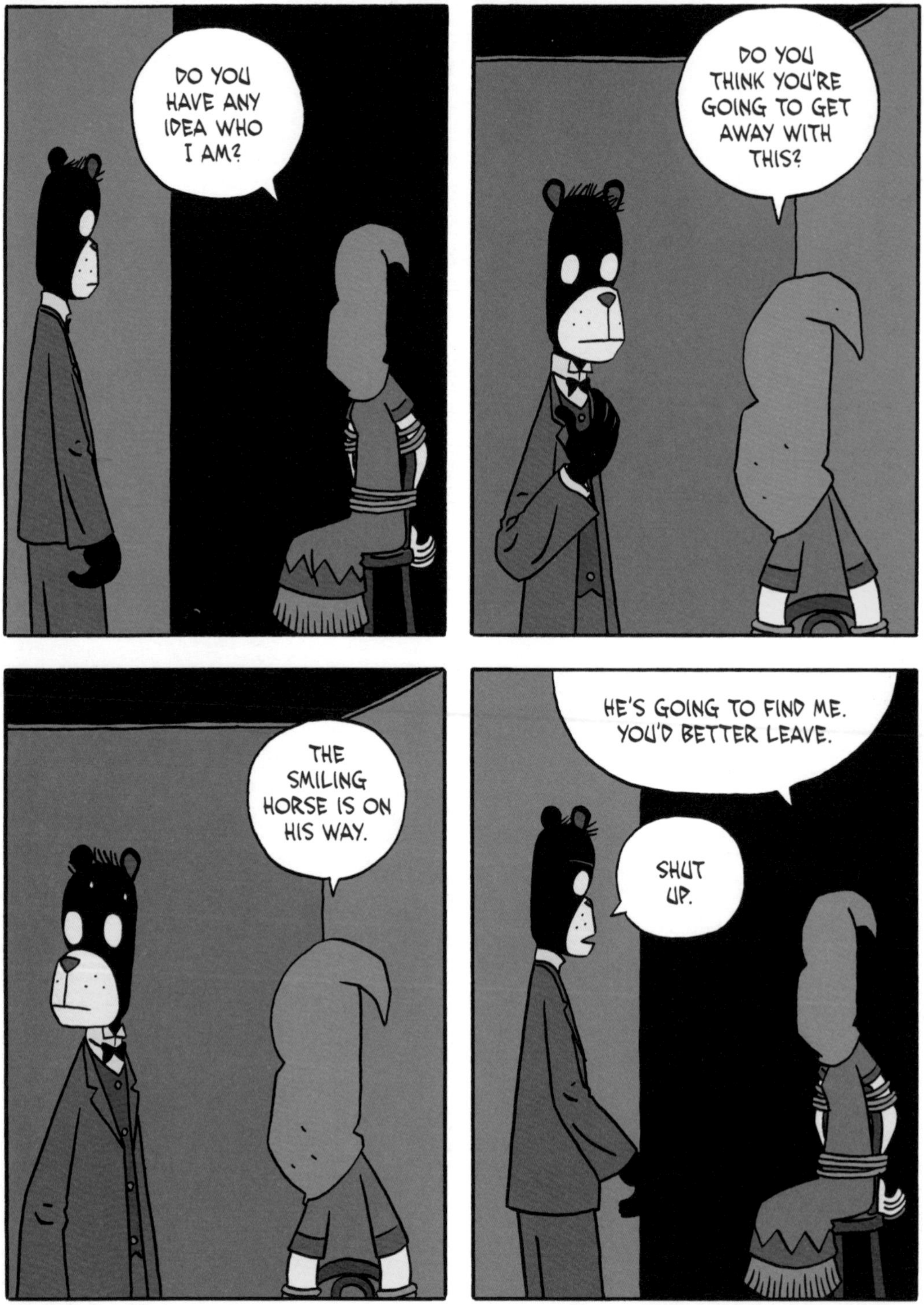
DO YOU HAVE ANY IDEA WHO I AM?
DO YOU THINK YOU'RE GOING TO GET AWAY WITH THIS?
THE SMILING HORSE IS ON HIS WAY.
HE'S GOING TO FIND ME. YOU'D BETTER LEAVE.
SHUT UP.

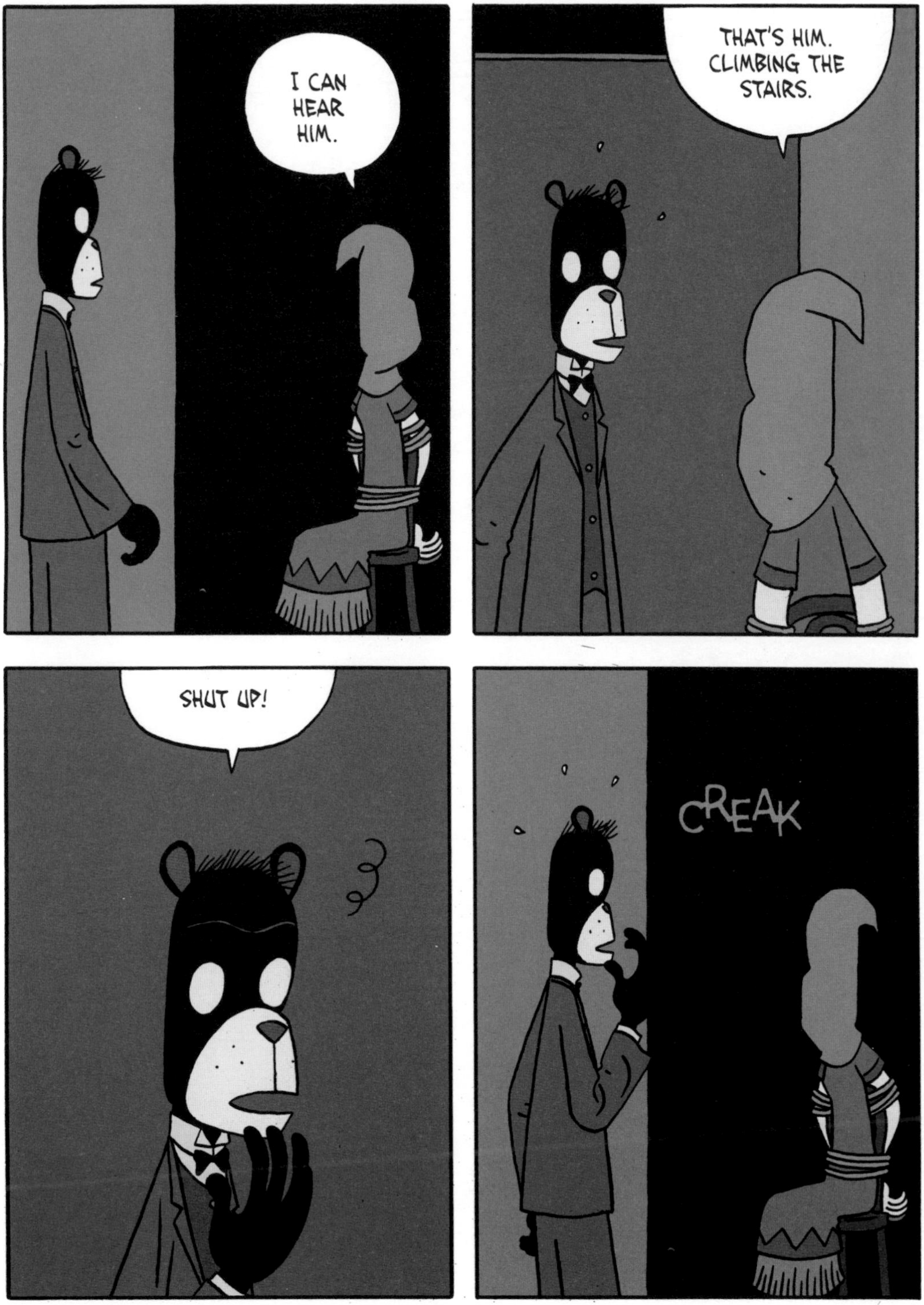
I CAN HEAR HIM.
THAT'S HIM. CLIMBING THE STAIRS.
SHUT UP!
CREAK

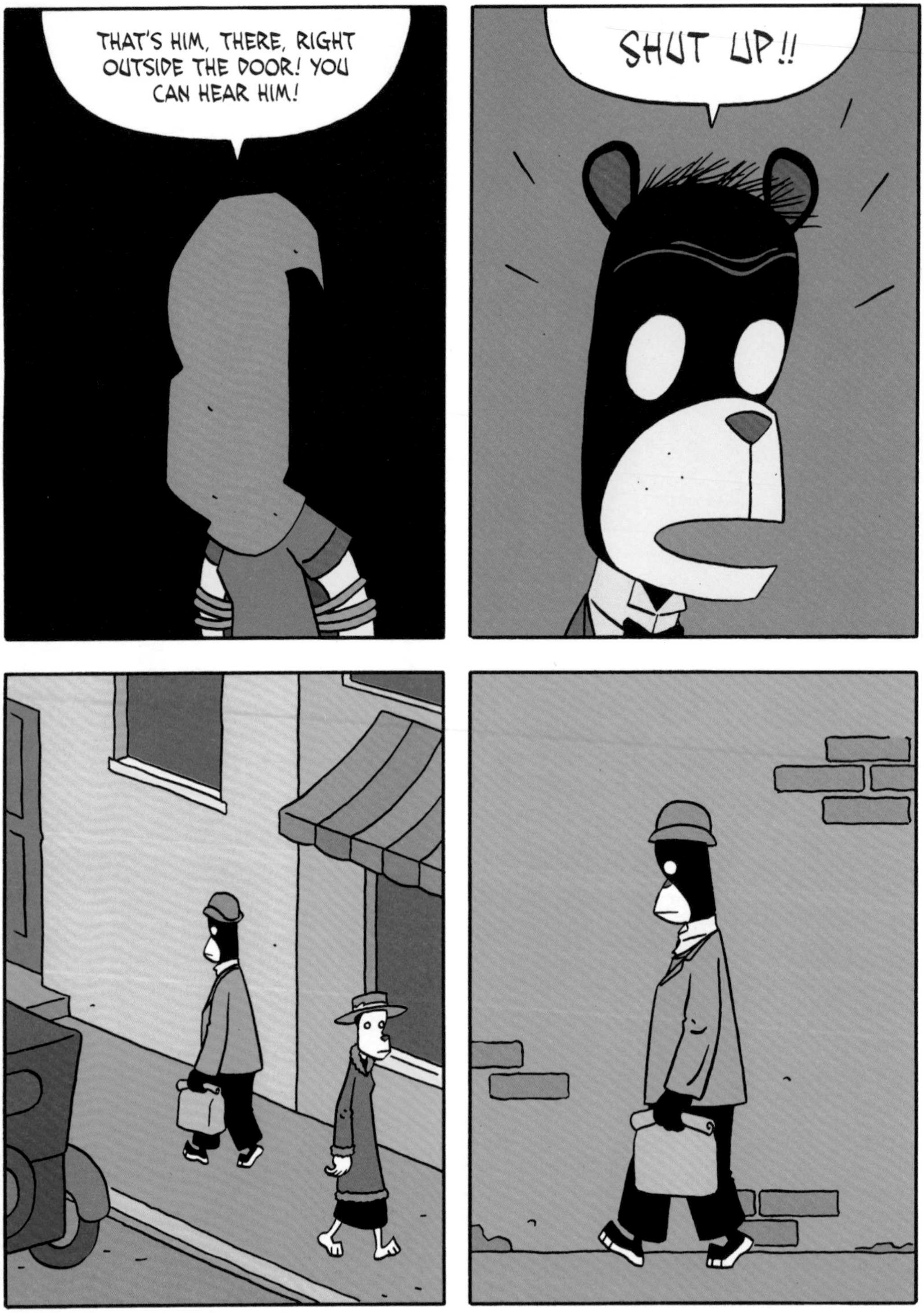
THAT'S HIM, THERE, RIGHT OUTSIDE THE DOOR! YOU CAN HEAR HIM!
SHUT UP!!

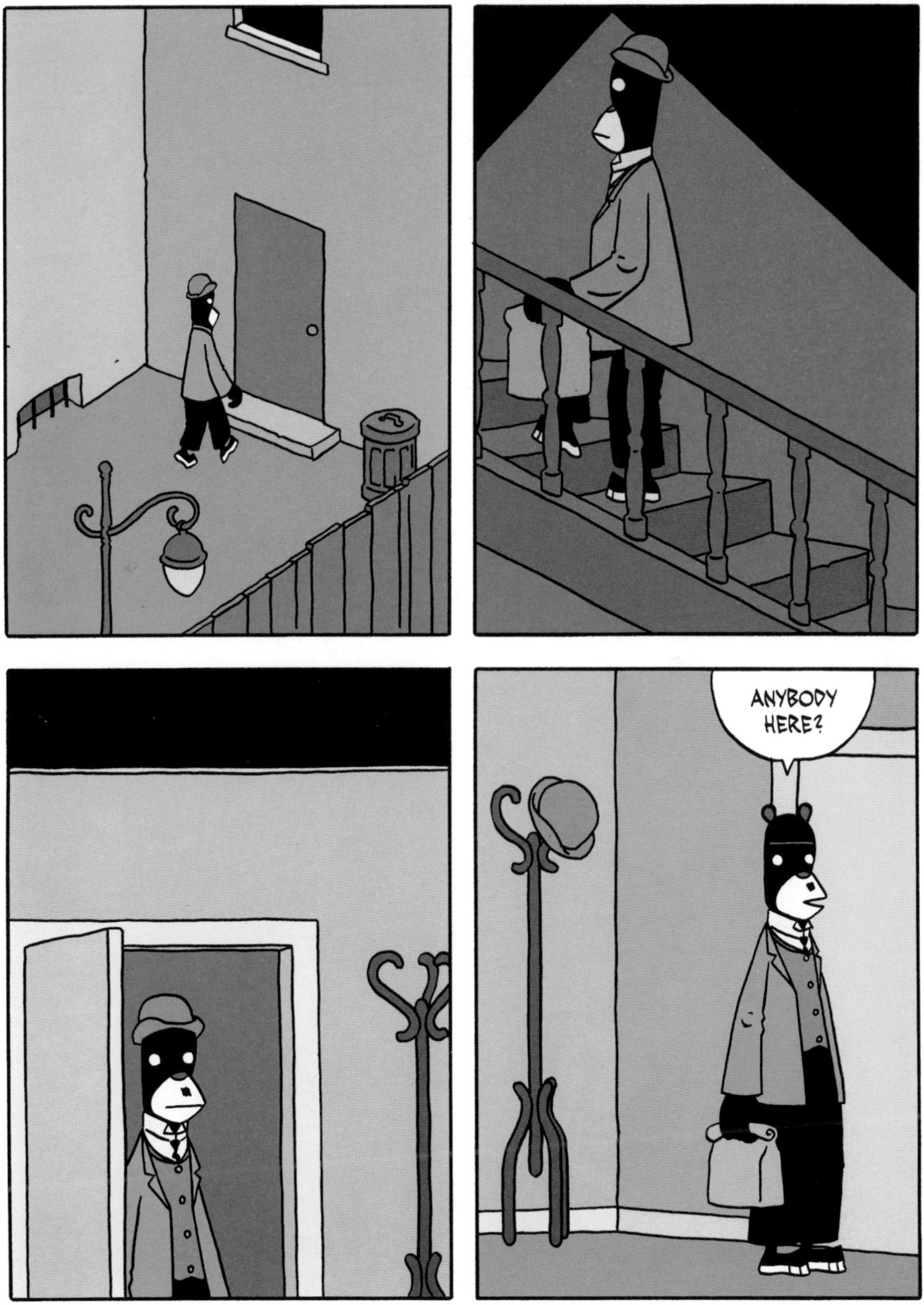
ANYBODY HERE?

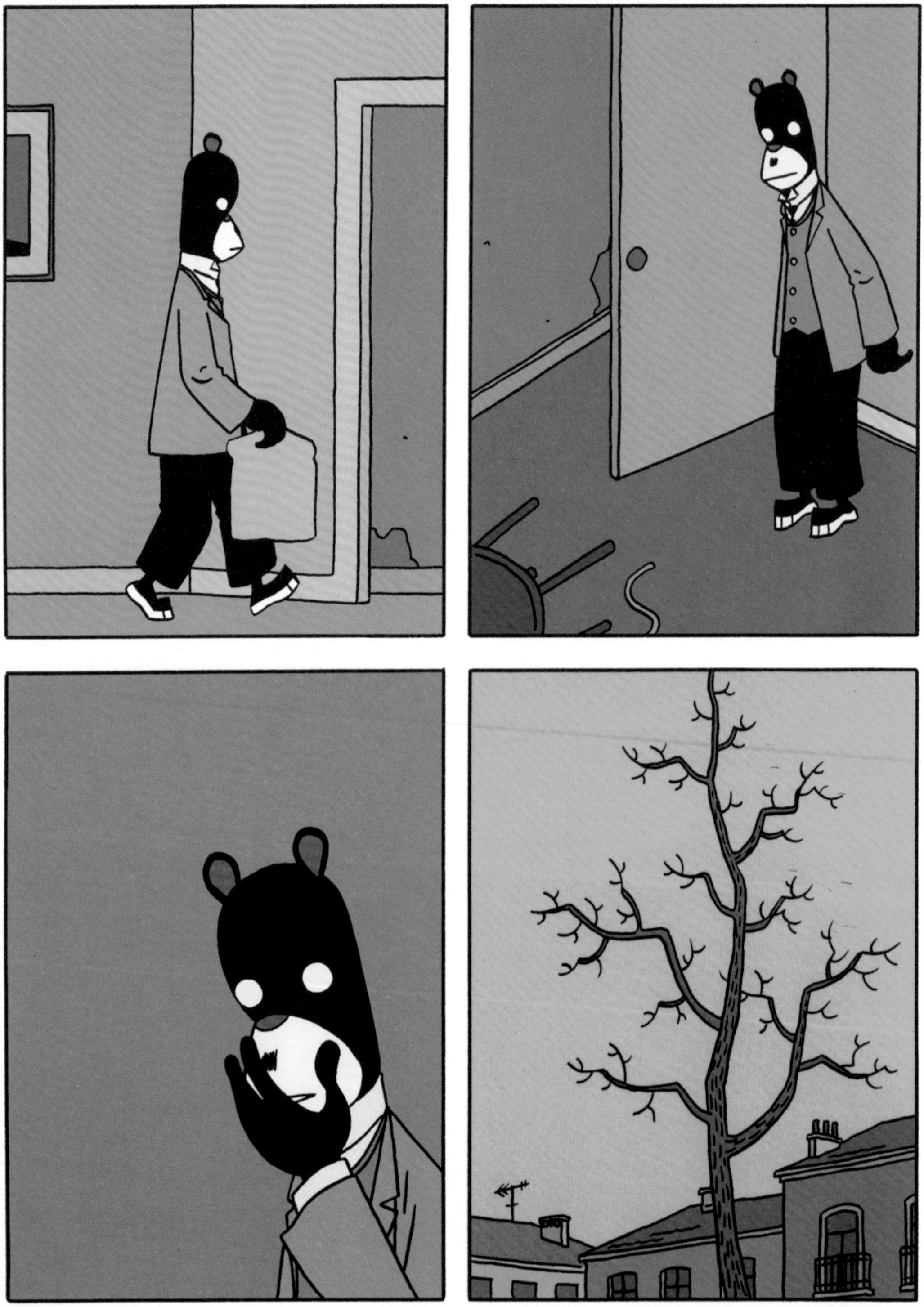

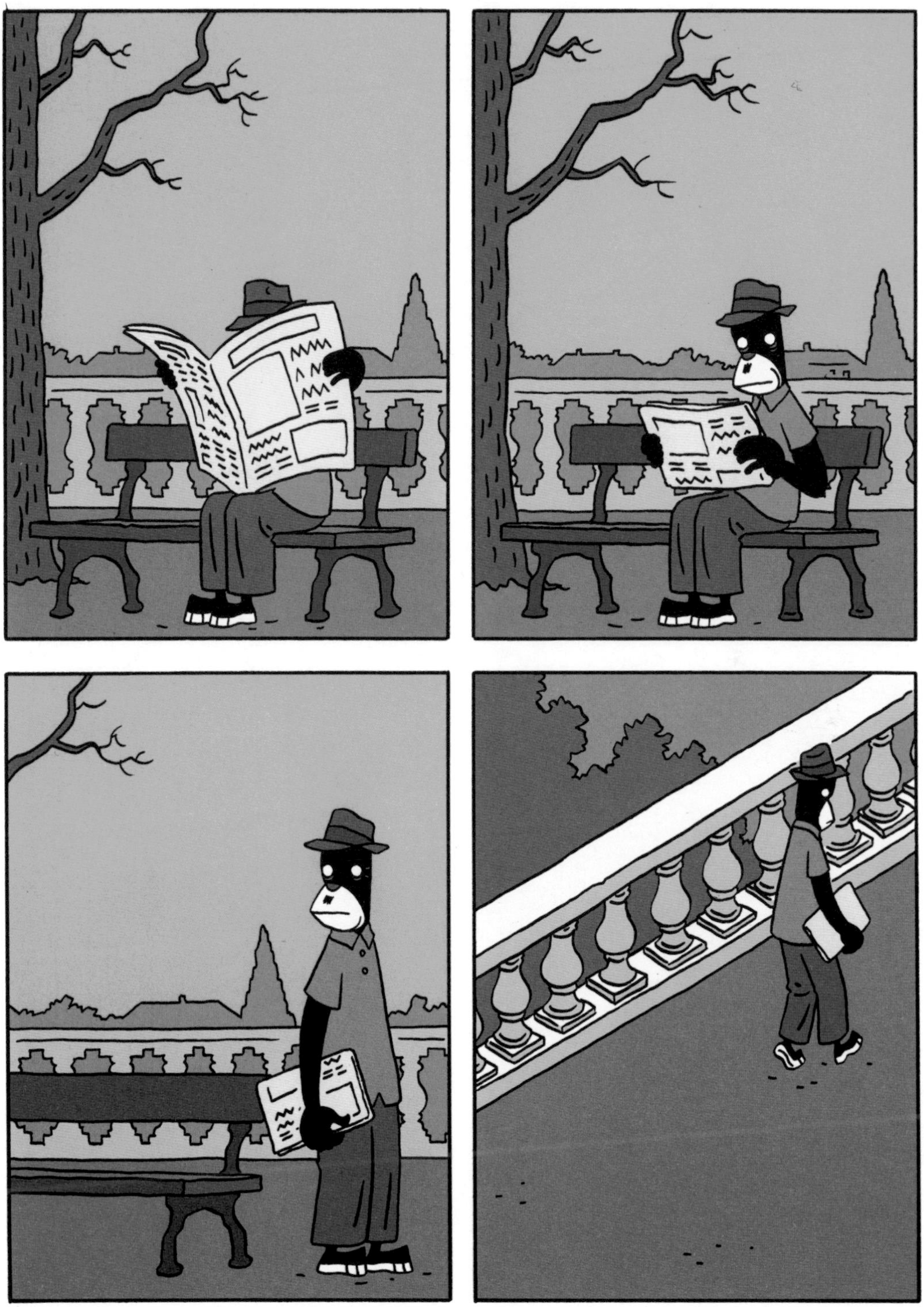

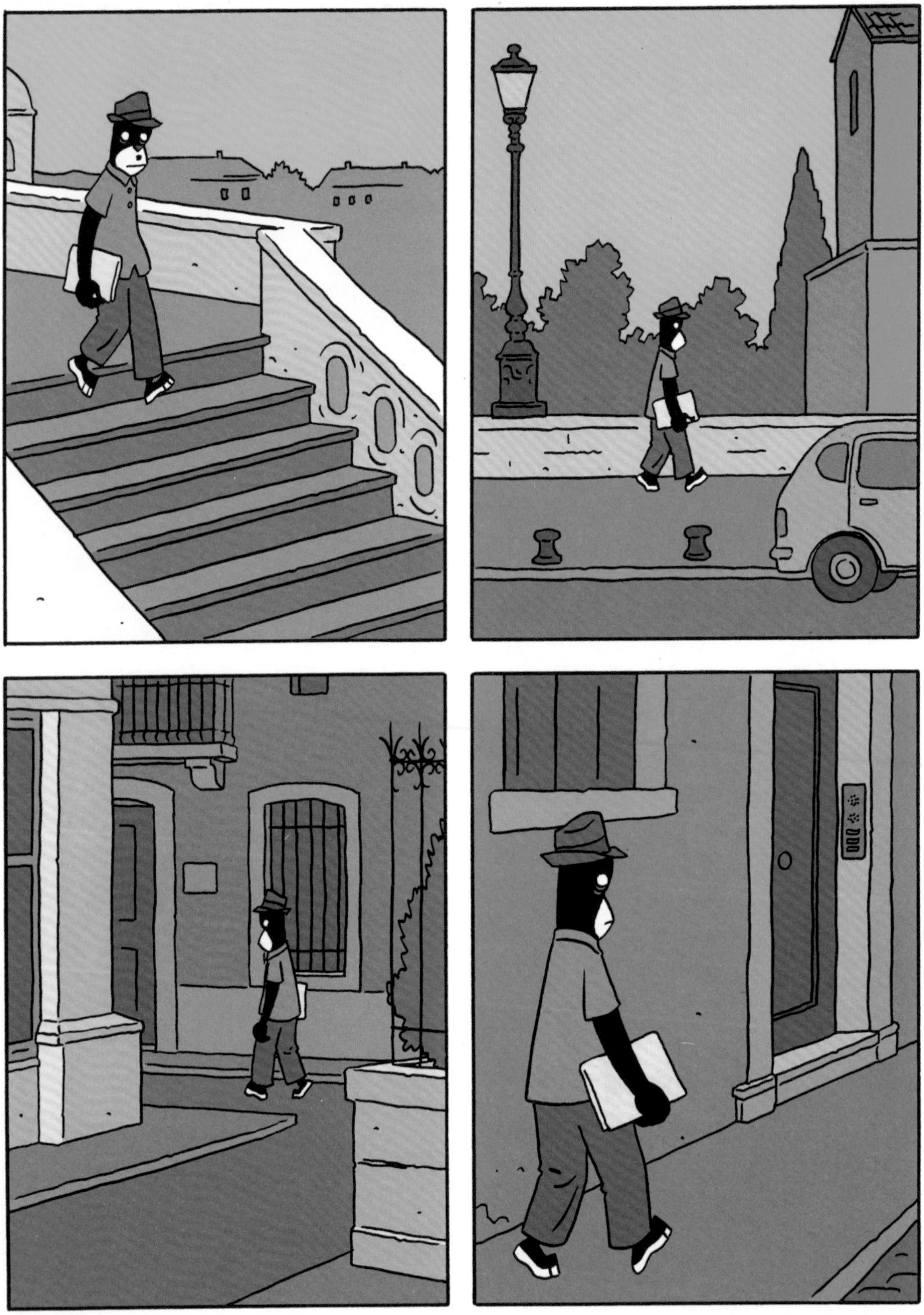

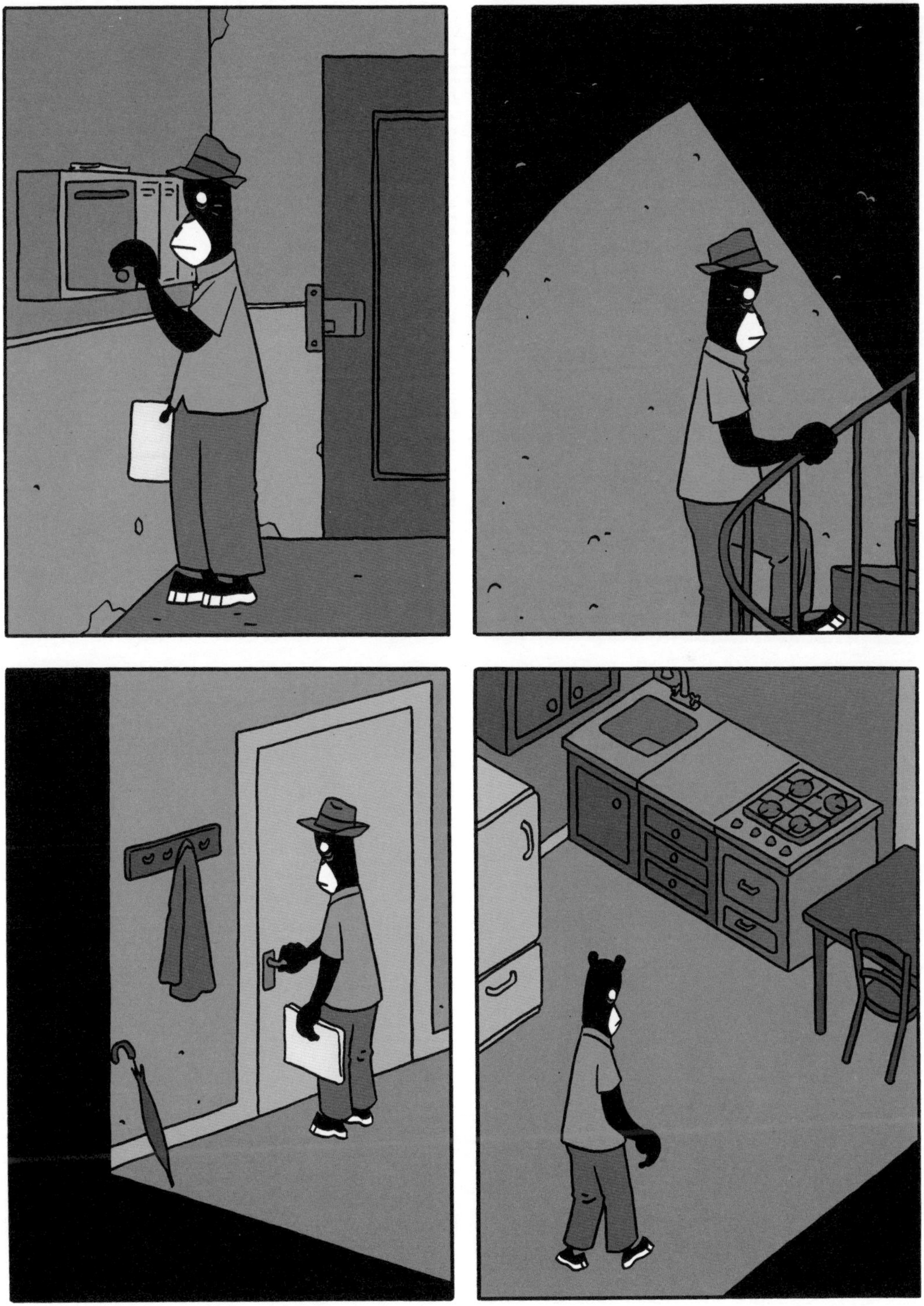

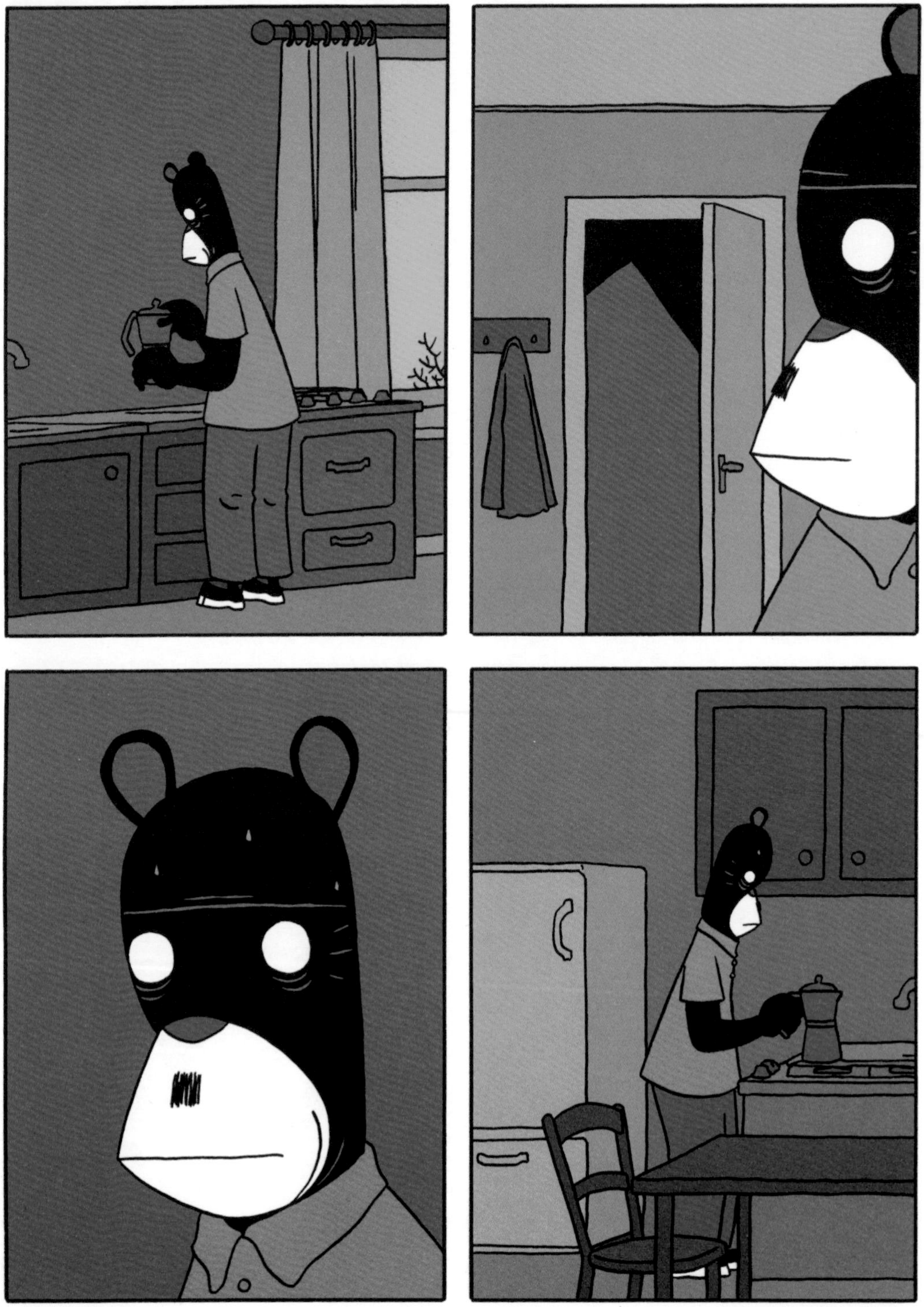

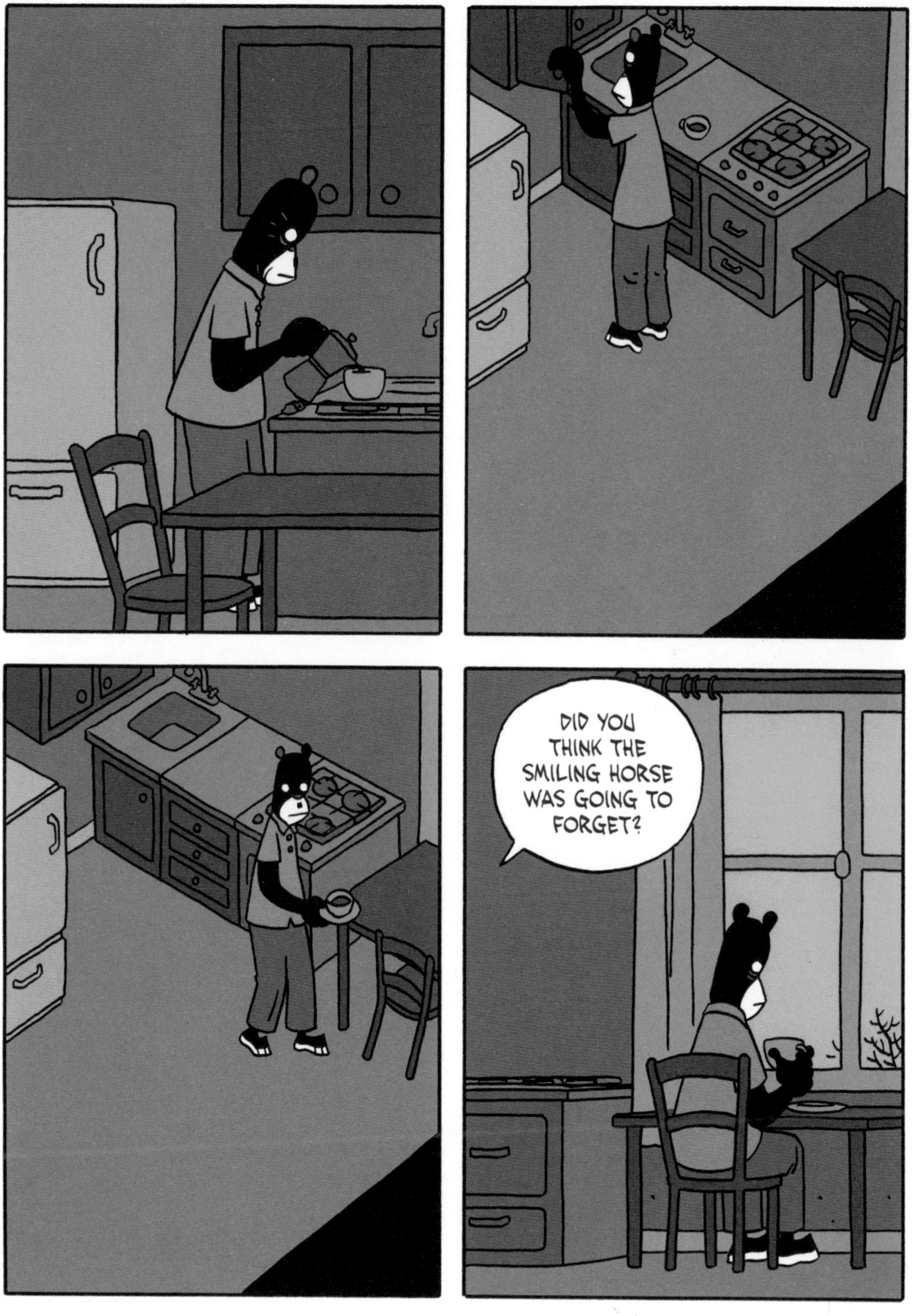
DID YOU THINK THE SMILING HORSE WAS GOING TO FORGET?

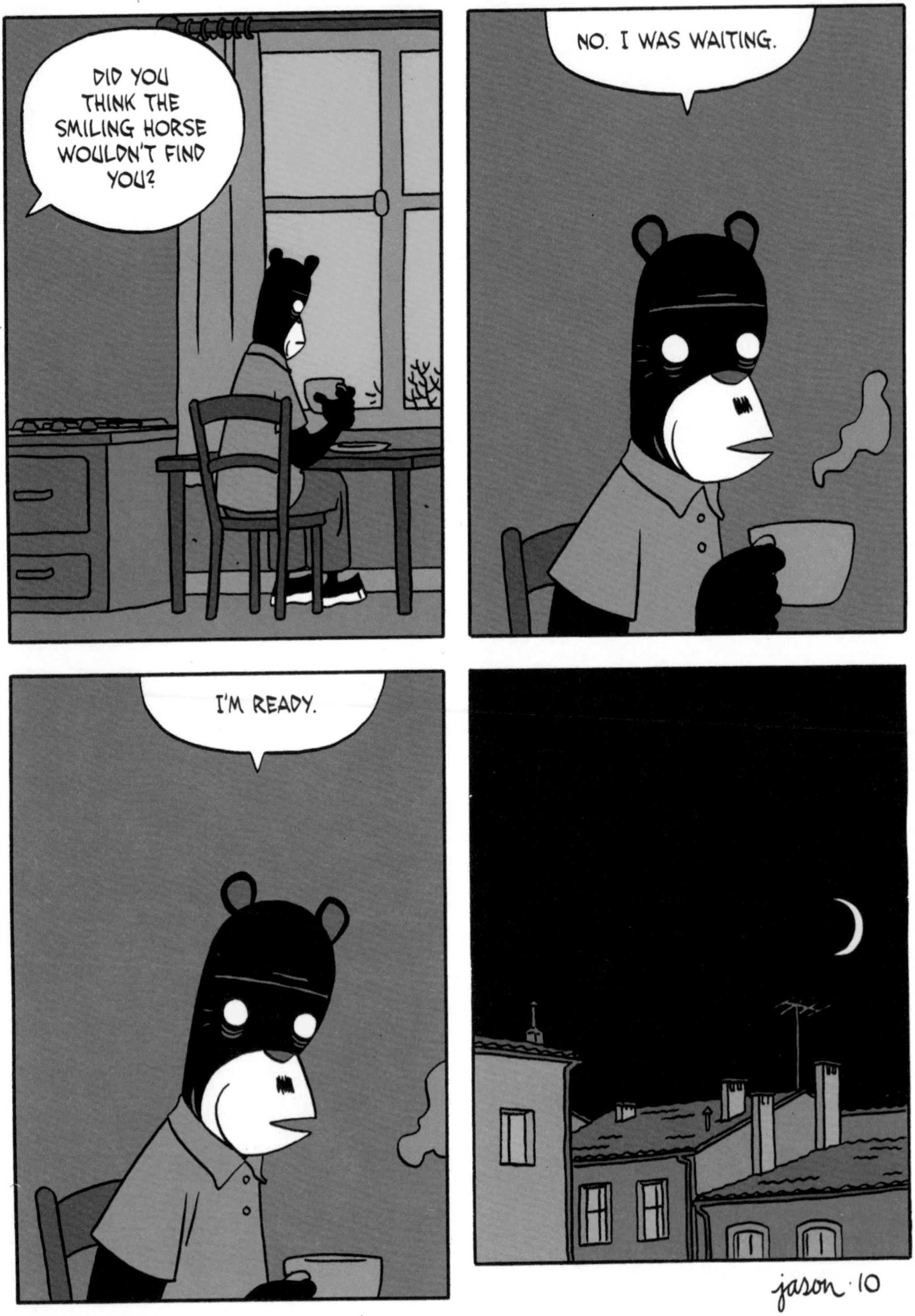
DID YOU THINK THE SMILING HORSE WOULDN'T FIND YOU?
NO. I WAS WAITING.
I'M READY.
jason · 10

———

A CAT FROM HEAVEN

HEAVEN

———

BASTARD!

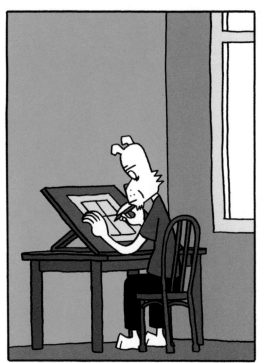

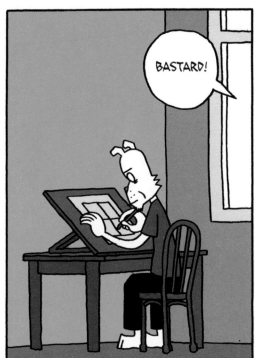

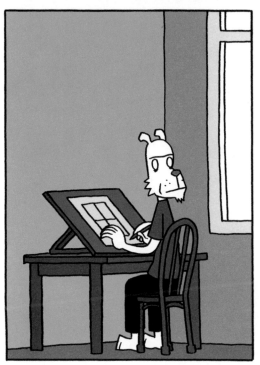

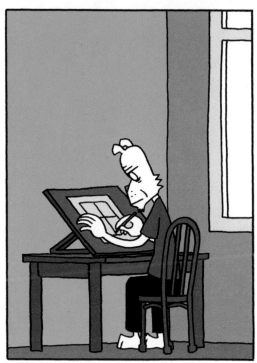

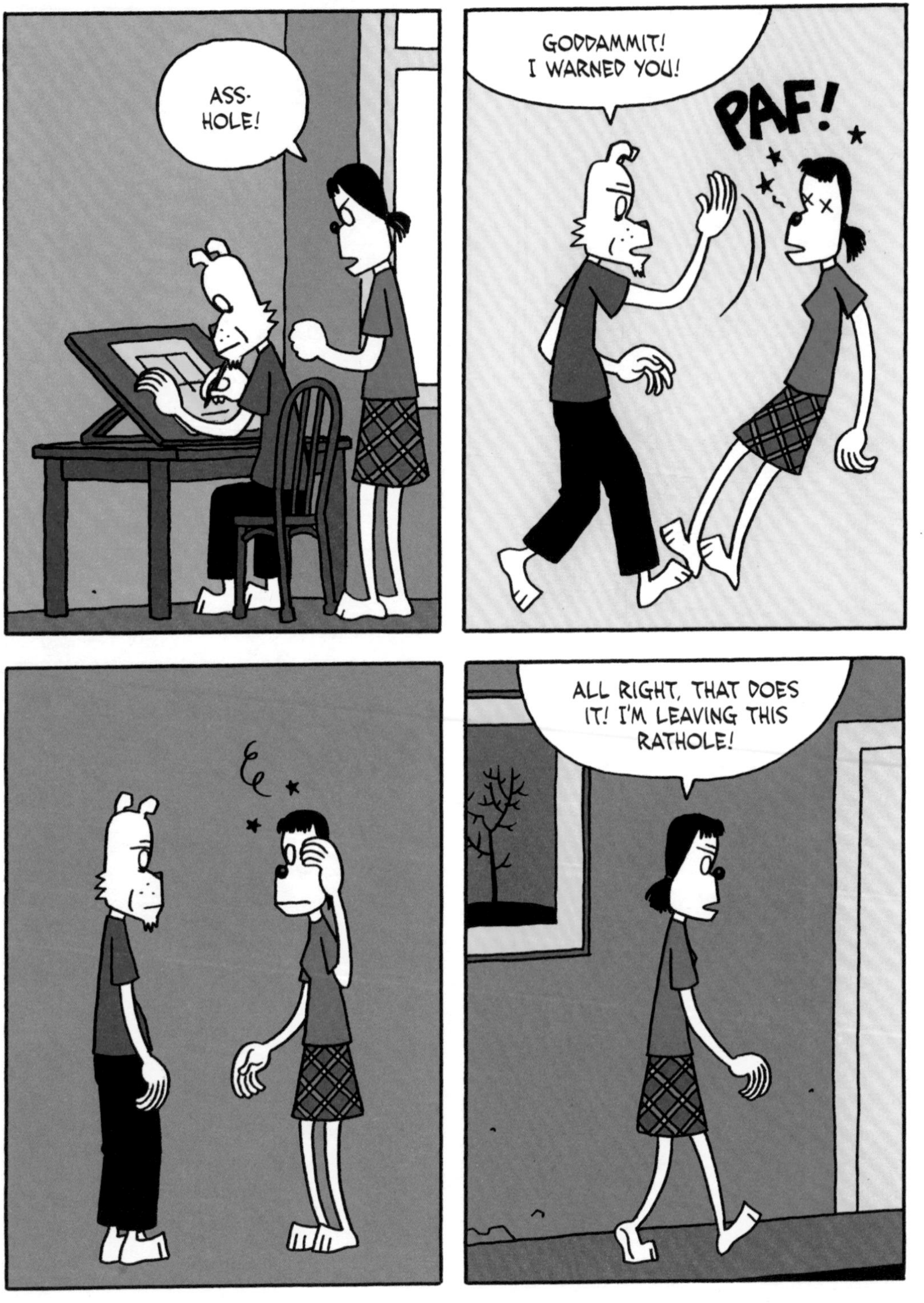
ASS-HOLE!
GODDAMMIT! I WARNED YOU!
PAF!
ALL RIGHT, THAT DOES IT! I'M LEAVING THIS RATHOLE!

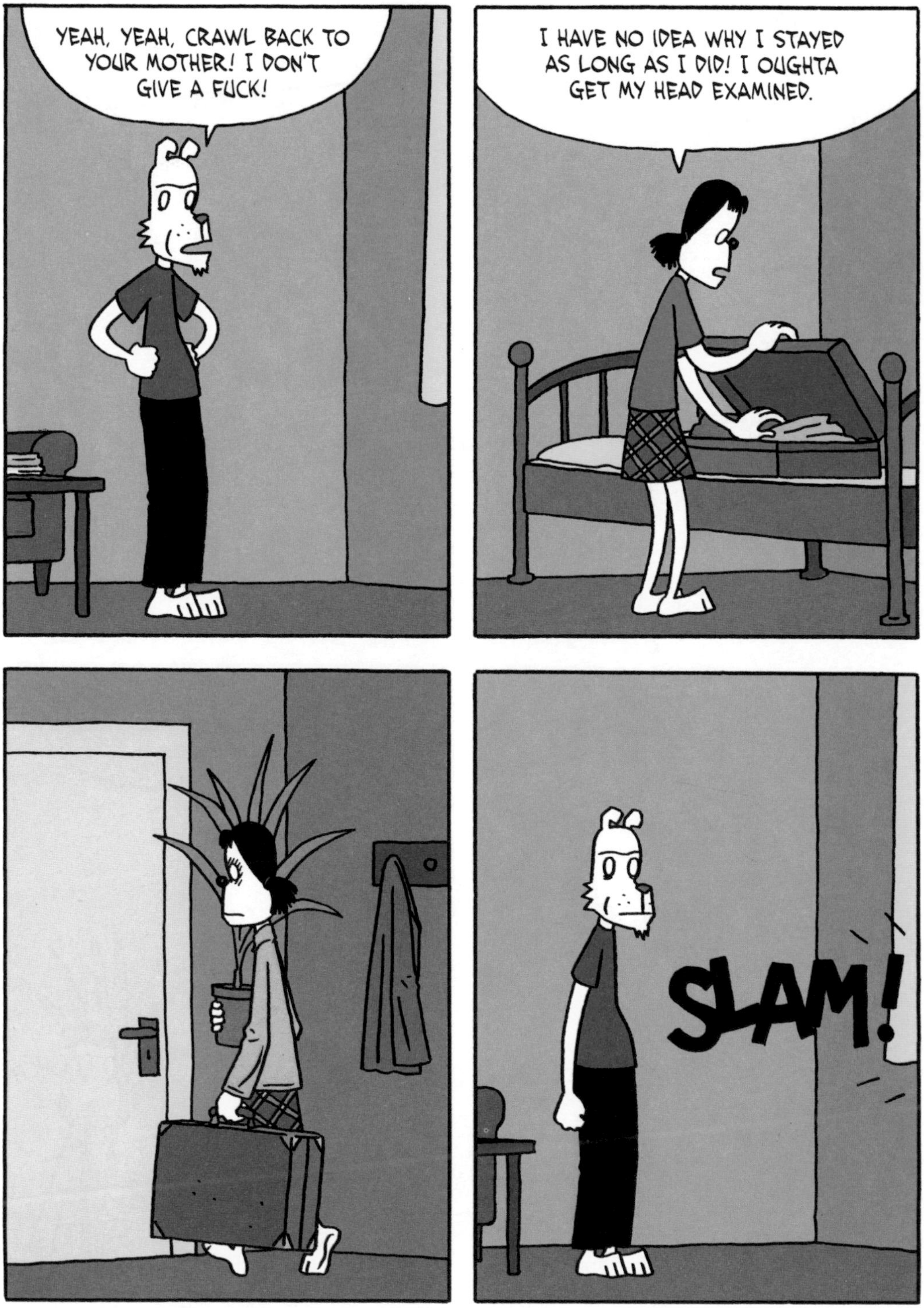
YEAH, YEAH, CRAWL BACK TO YOUR MOTHER! I DON'T GIVE A FUCK!
I HAVE NO IDEA WHY I STAYED AS LONG AS I DID! I OUGHTA GET MY HEAD EXAMINED.
SLAM!

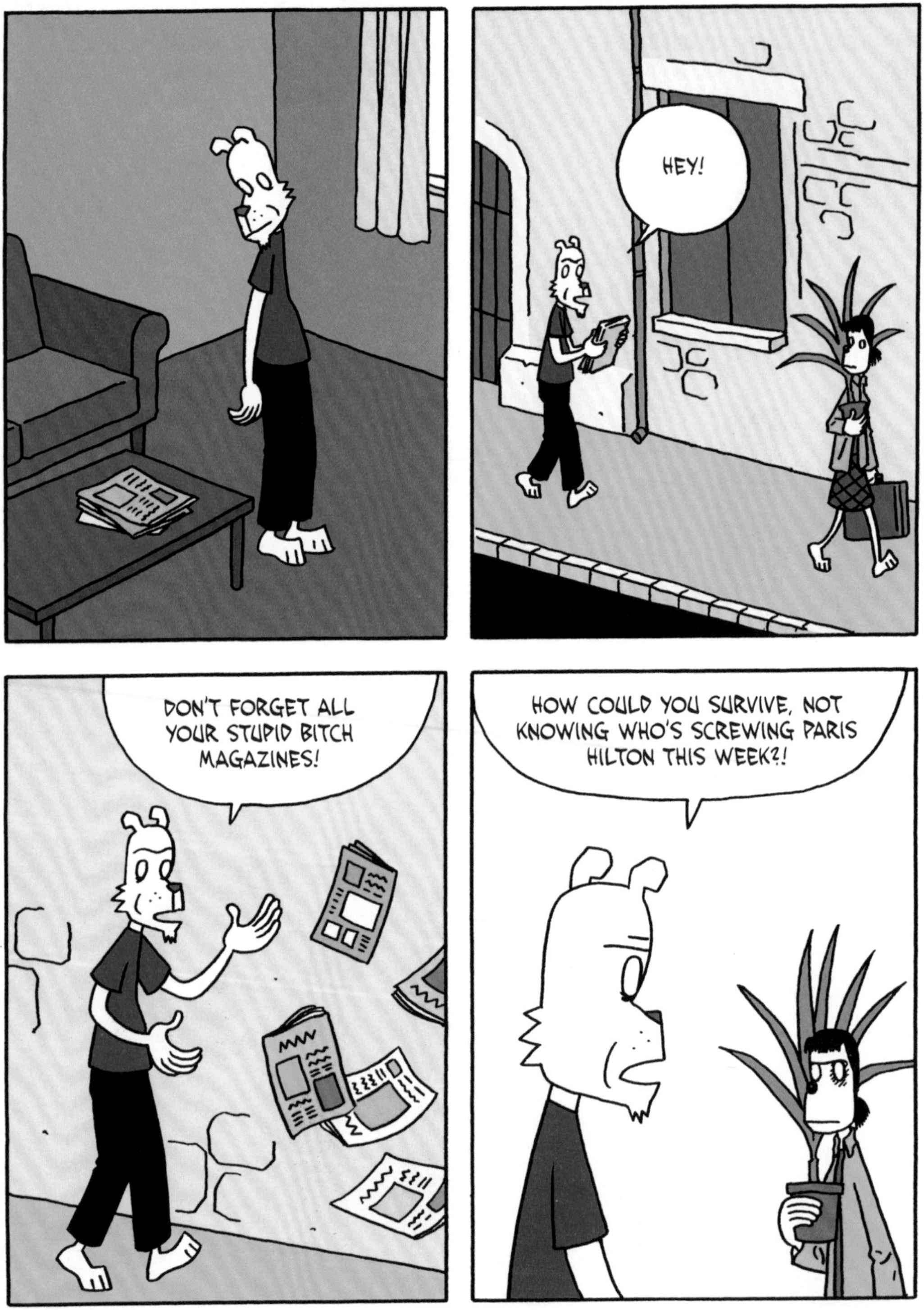
HEY!
DON'T FORGET ALL YOUR STUPID BITCH MAGAZINES!
HOW COULD YOU SURVIVE, NOT KNOWING WHO'S SCREWING PARIS HILTON THIS WEEK?!

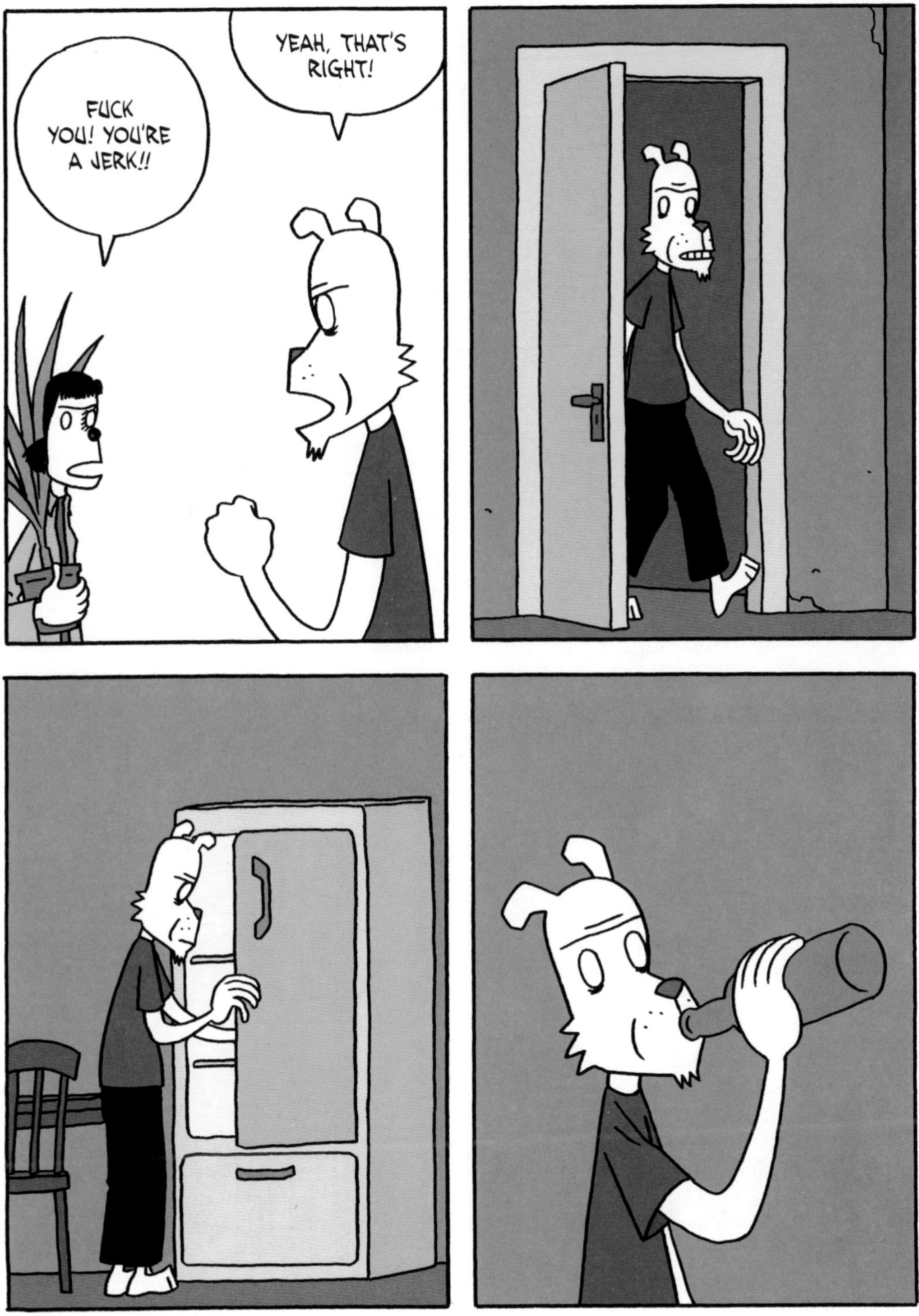
FUCK YOU! YOU'RE A JERK!!
YEAH, THAT'S RIGHT!

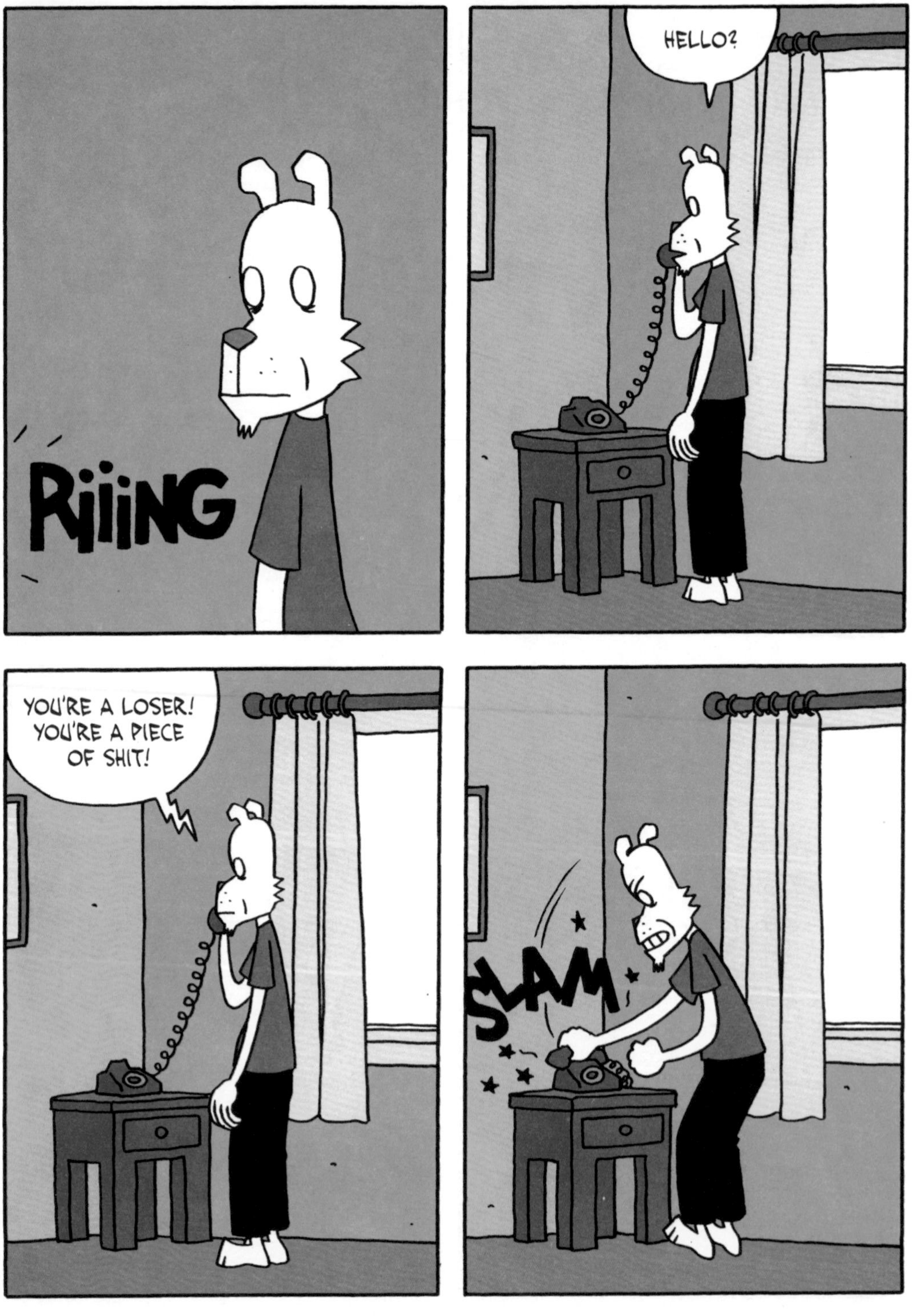
RIIING
HELLO?
YOU'RE A LOSER! YOU'RE A PIECE OF SHIT!
SLAM

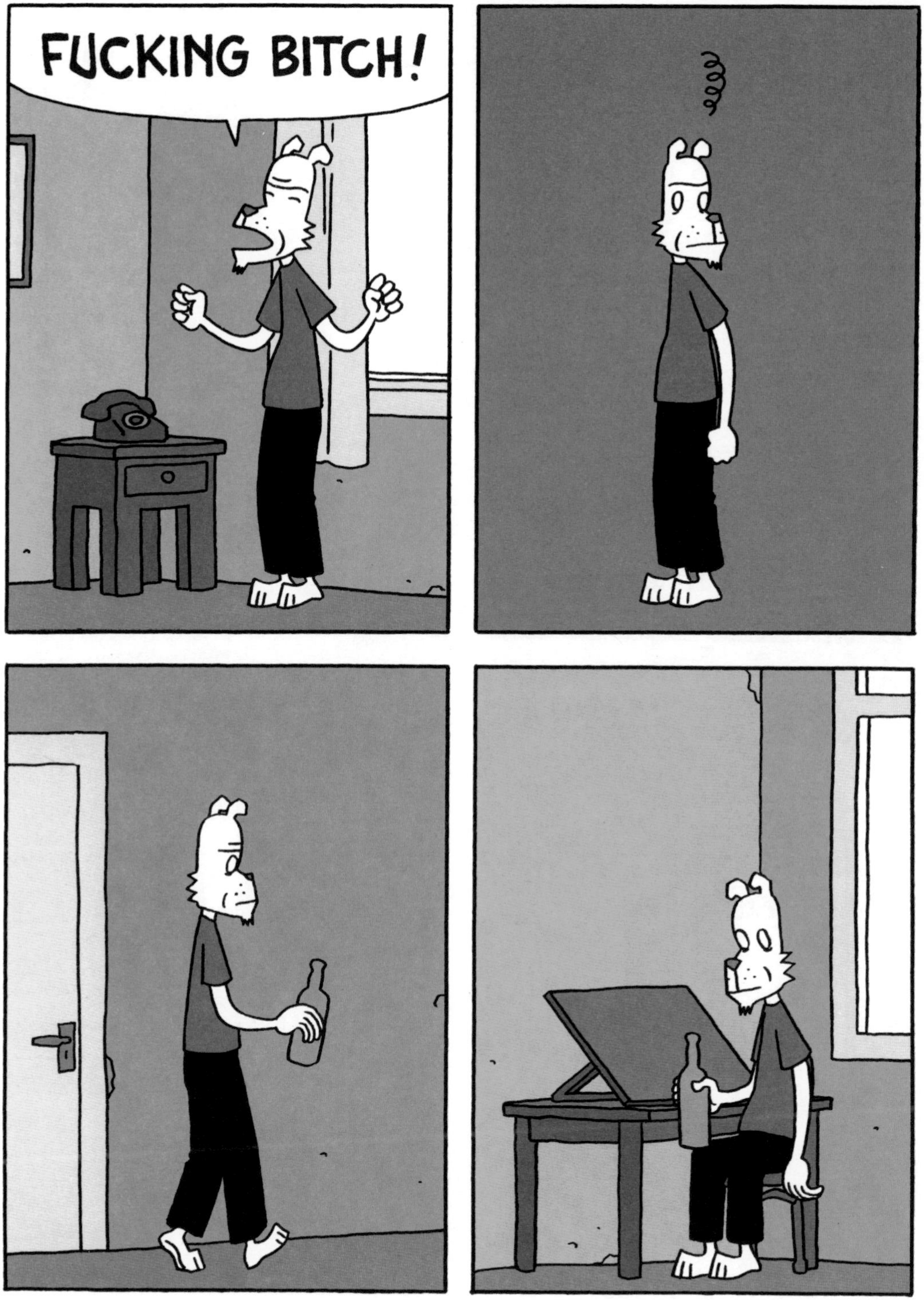
FUCKING BITCH!

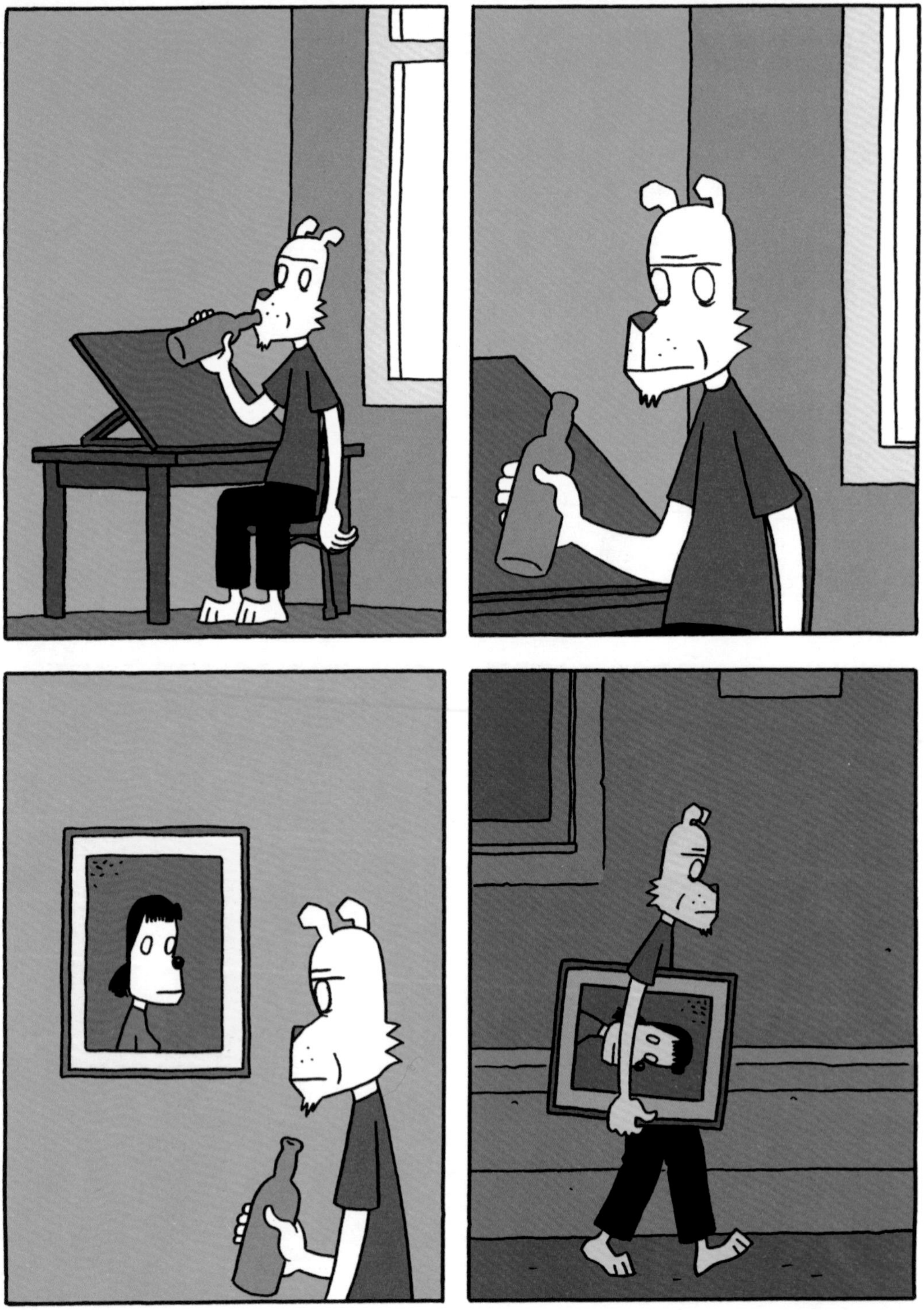

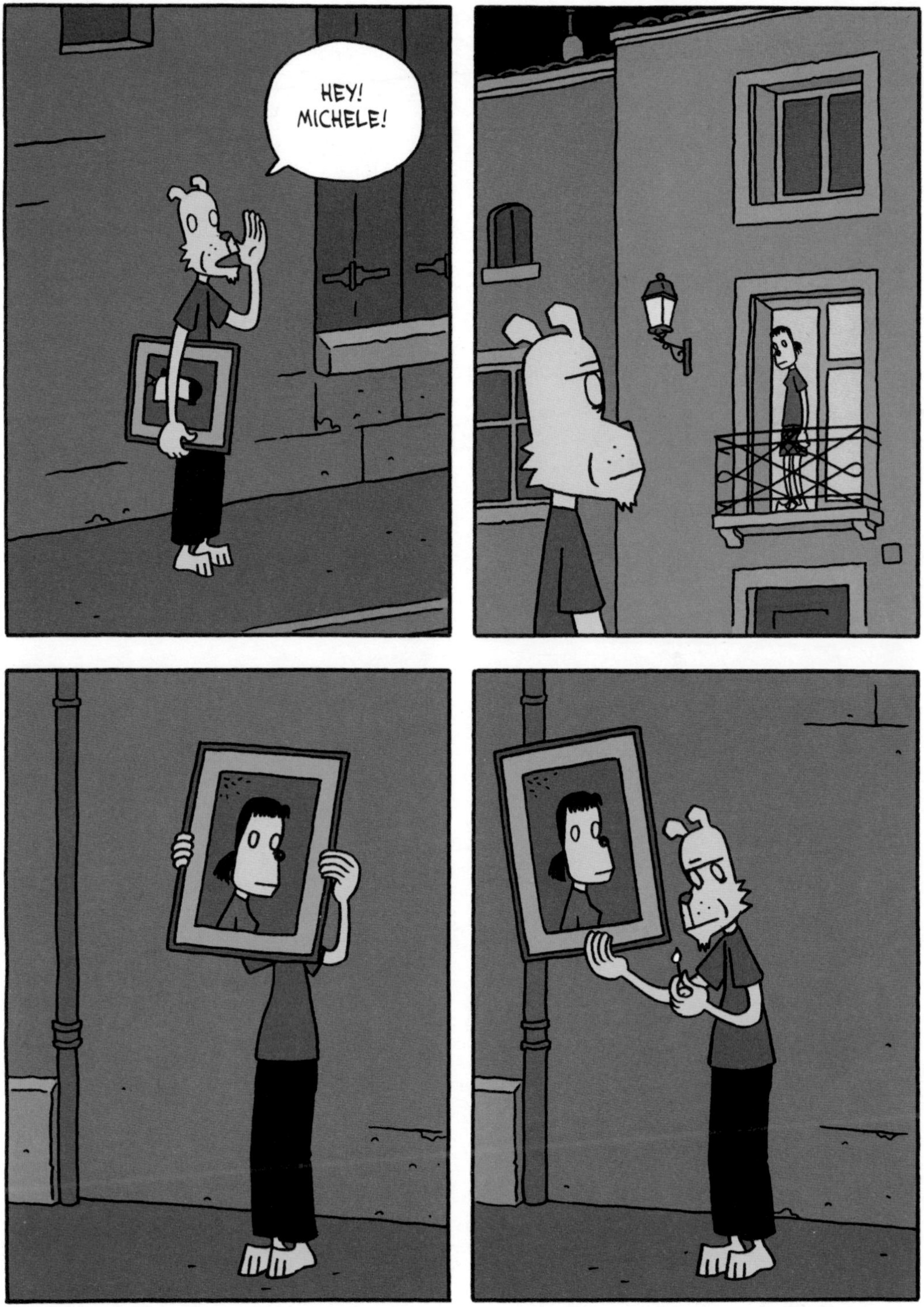
HEY! MICHELE!

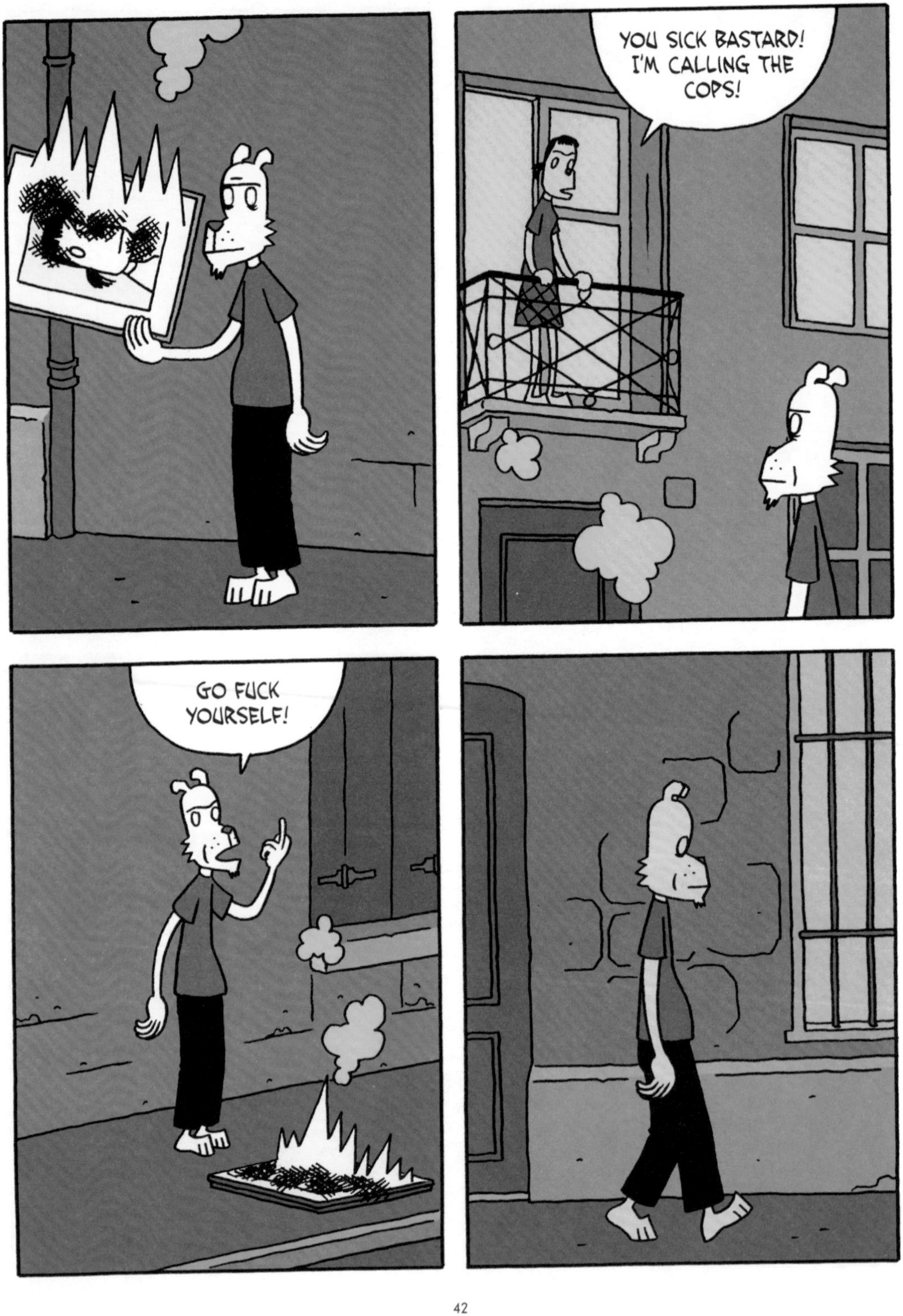
YOU SICK BASTARD! I'M CALLING THE COPS!
GO FUCK YOURSELF!

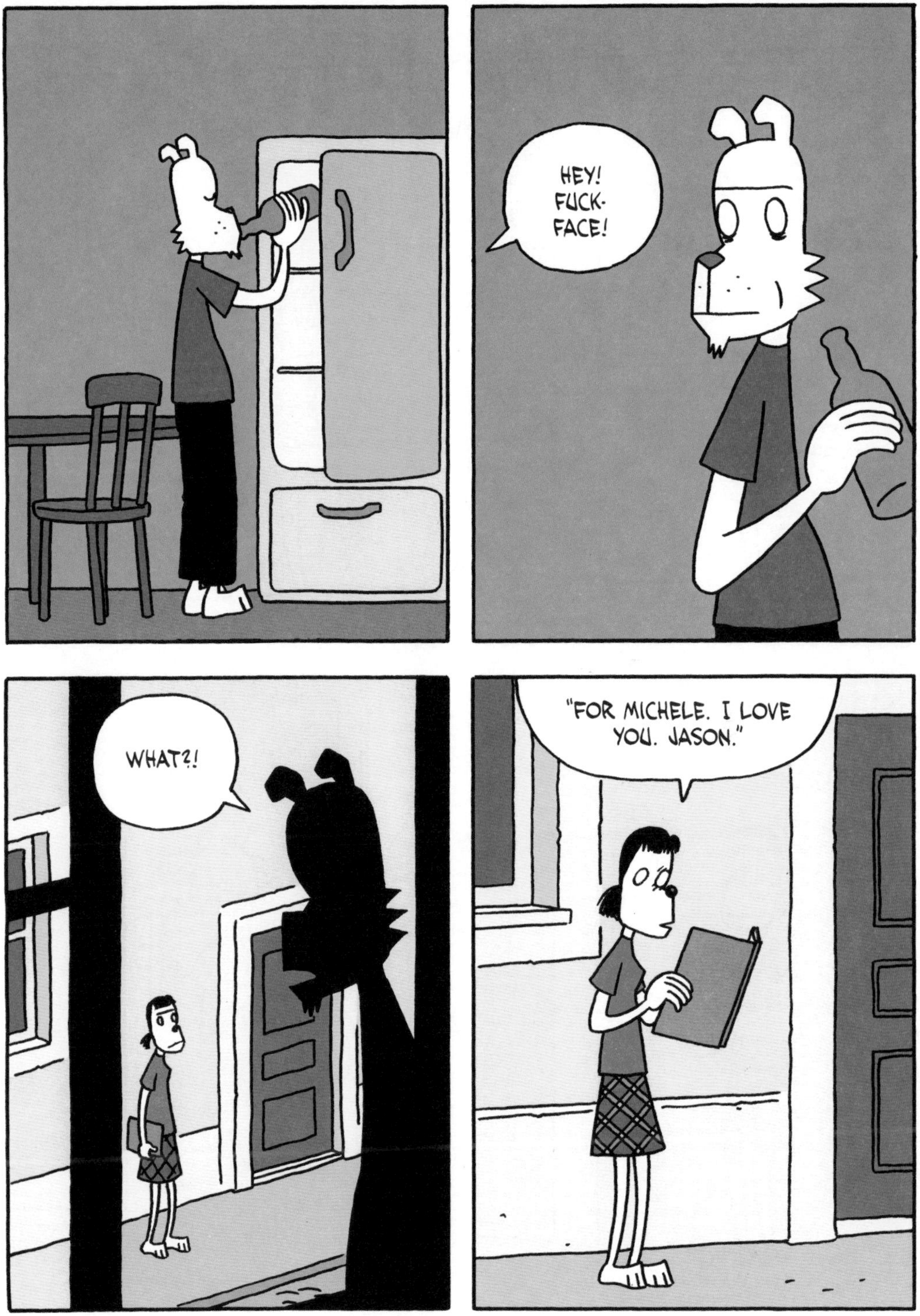
HEY! FUCK-FACE!
WHAT?!
"FOR MICHELE. I LOVE YOU. JASON."

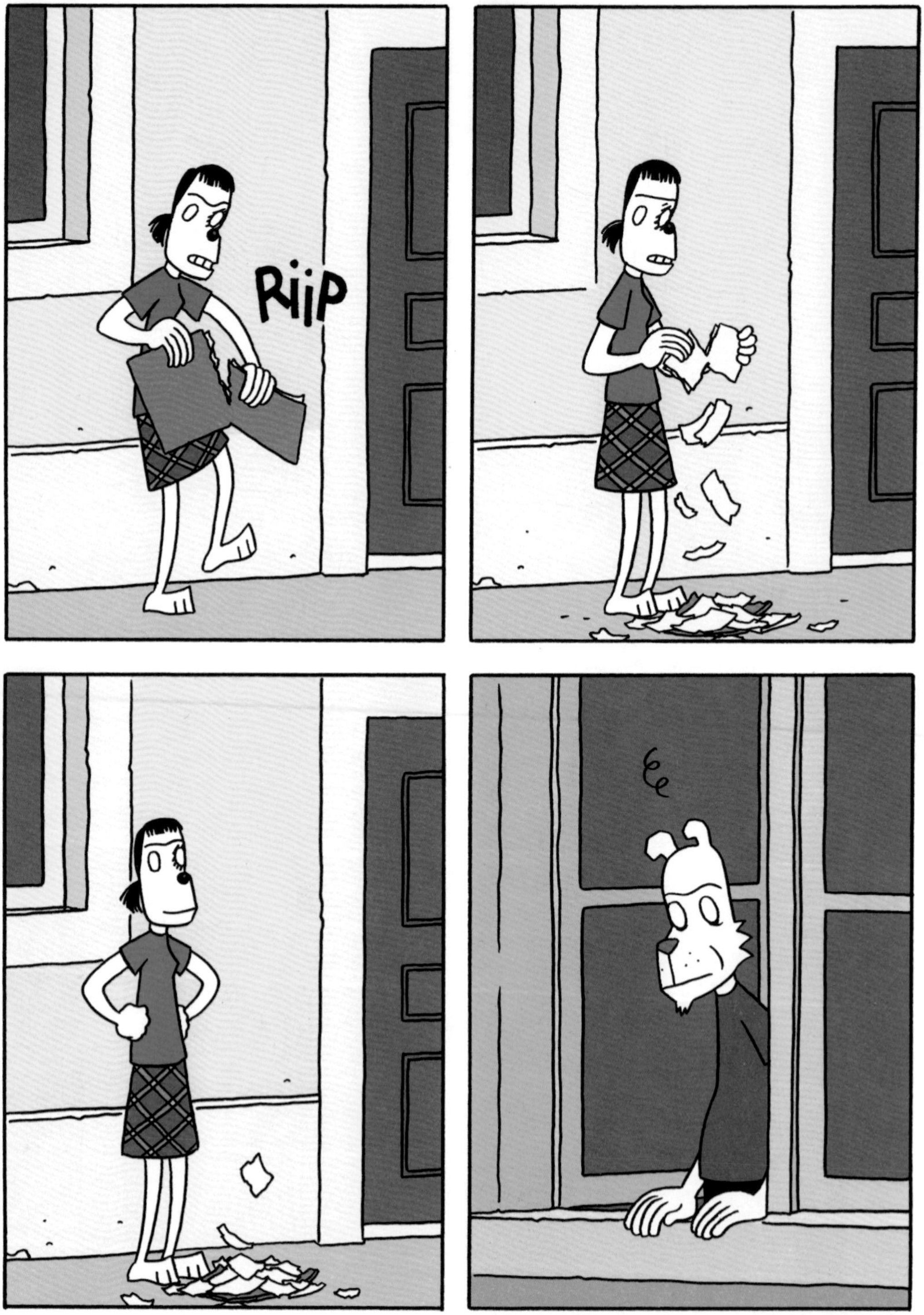
RIIP

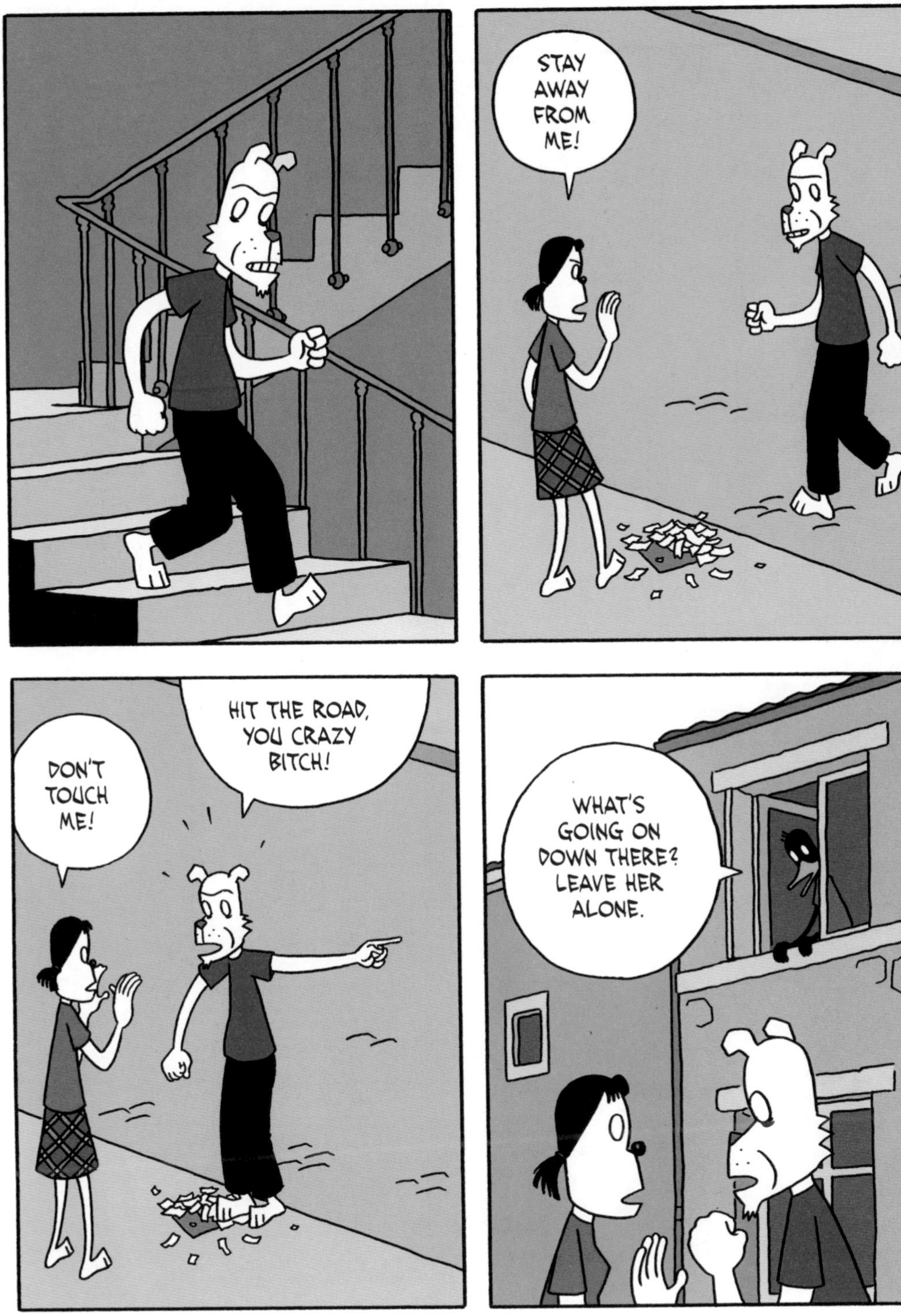
STAY AWAY FROM ME!
DON'T TOUCH ME!
HIT THE ROAD, YOU CRAZY BITCH!
WHAT'S GOING ON DOWN THERE? LEAVE HER ALONE.

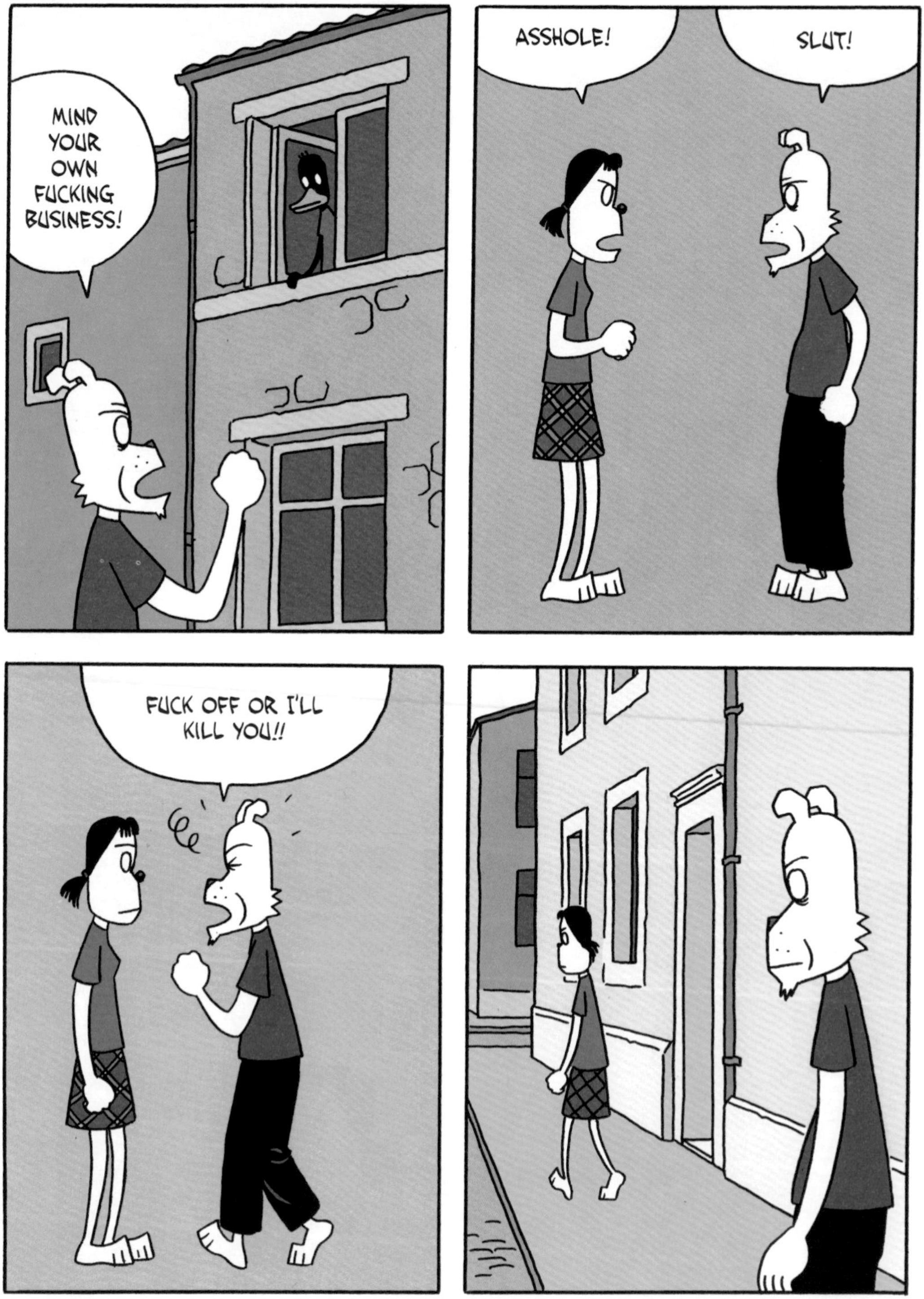
MIND YOUR OWN FUCKING BUSINESS!
ASSHOLE!
SLUT!
FUCK OFF OR I'LL KILL YOU!!

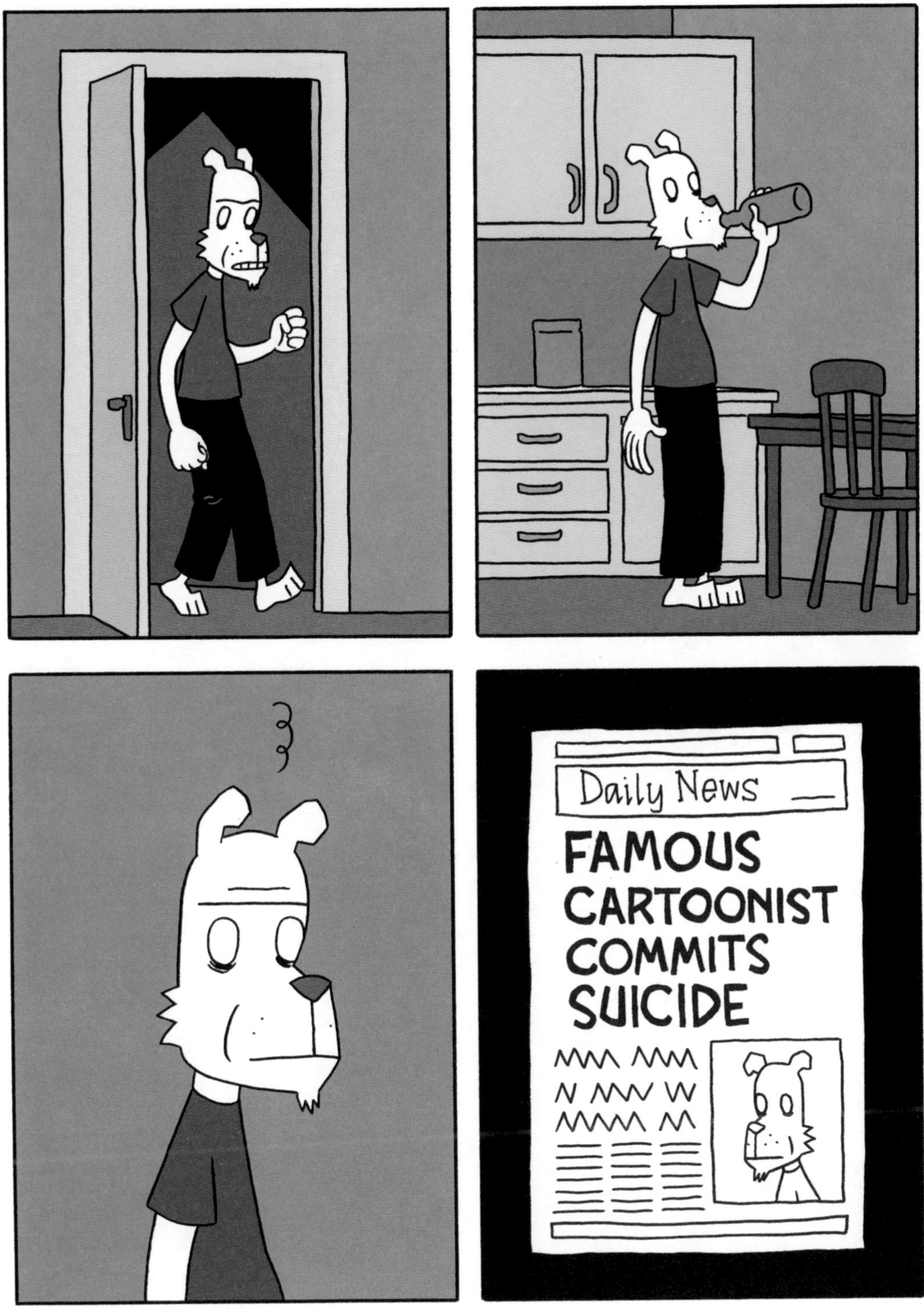
Daily News
FAMOUS CARTOONIST COMMITS SUICIDE

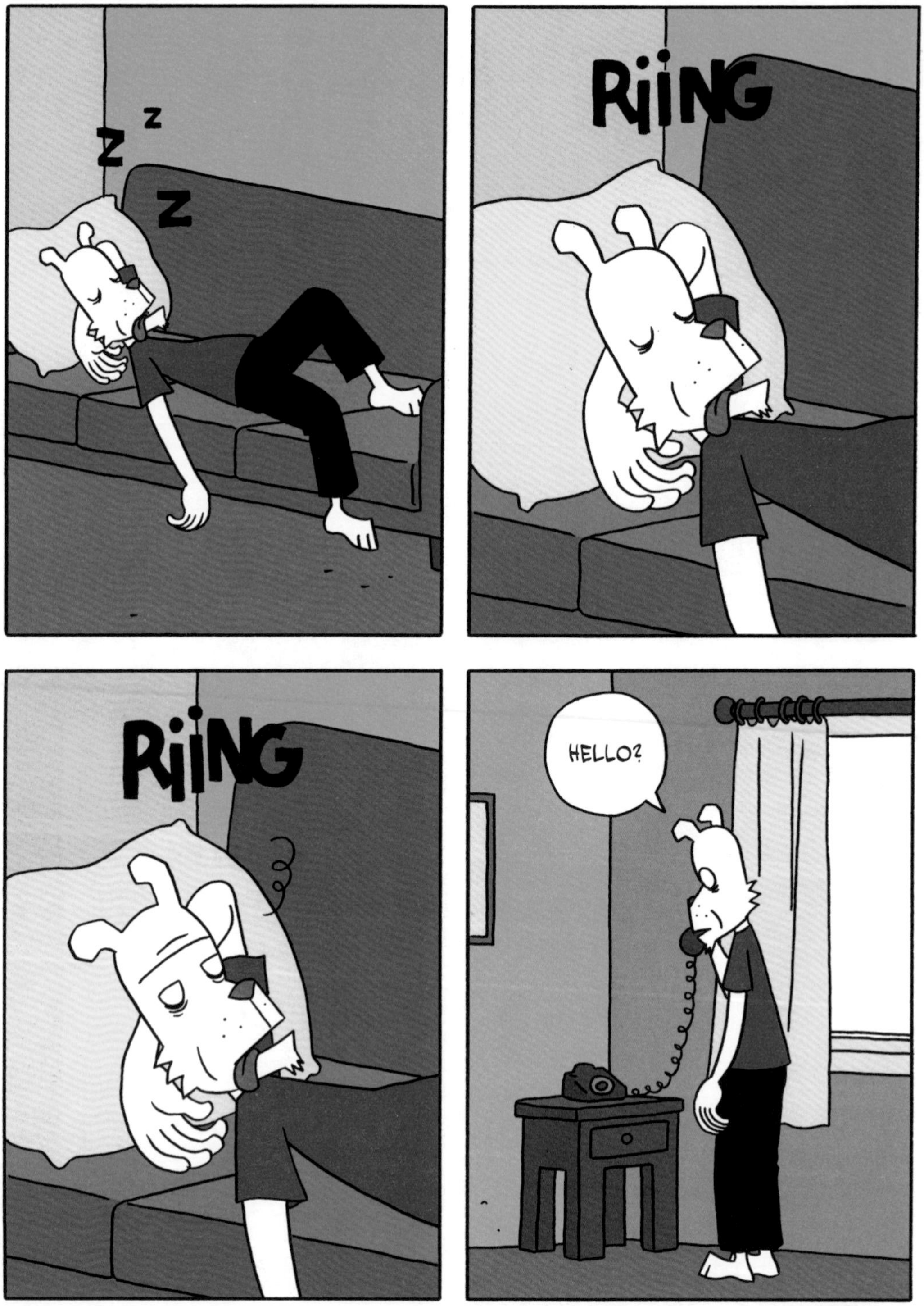
Z
Z
Z
RIING
RIING
HELLO?

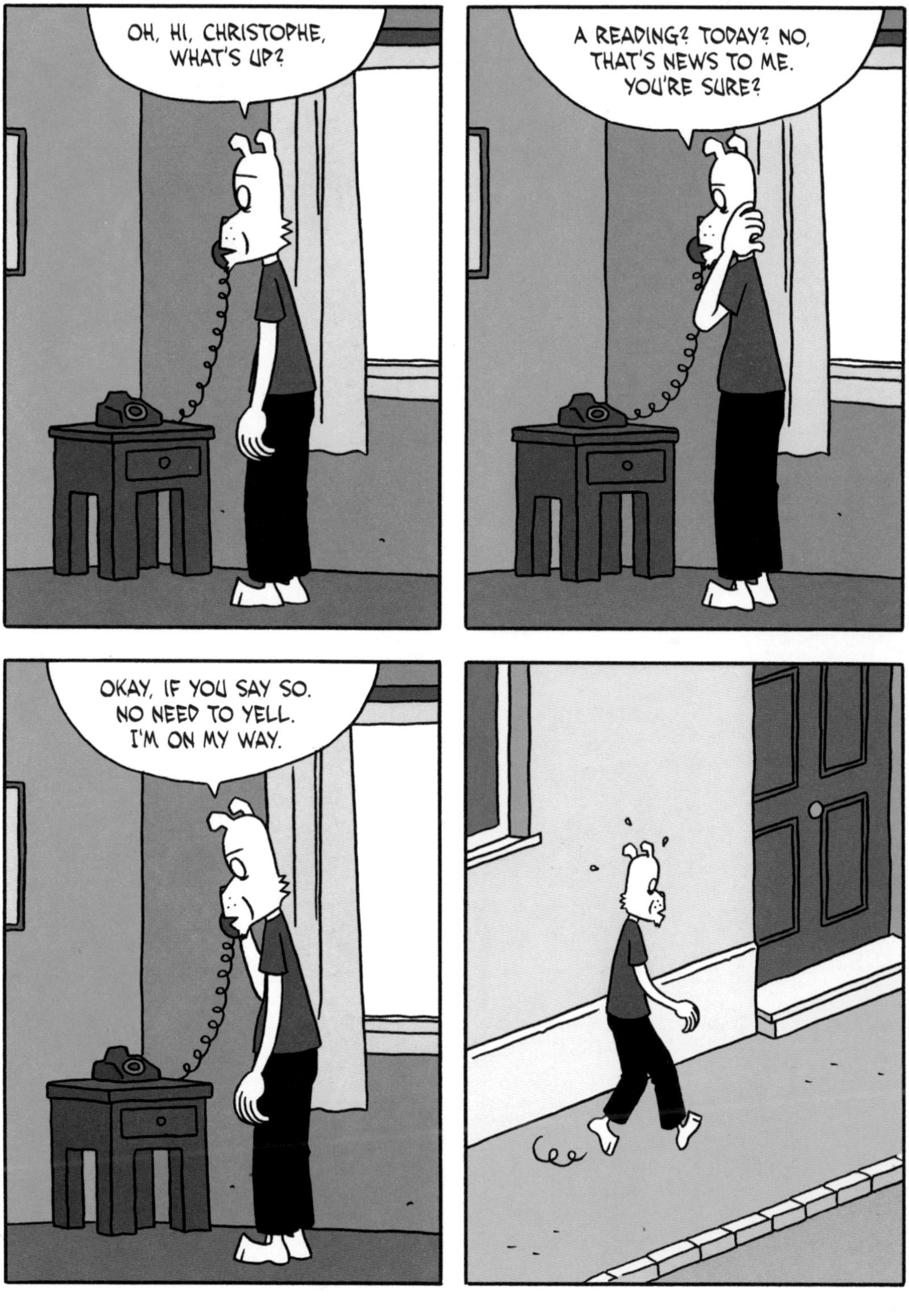
OH, HI, CHRISTOPHE, WHAT'S UP?
A READING? TODAY? NO, THAT'S NEWS TO ME. YOU'RE SURE?
OKAY, IF YOU SAY SO. NO NEED TO YELL. I'M ON MY WAY.

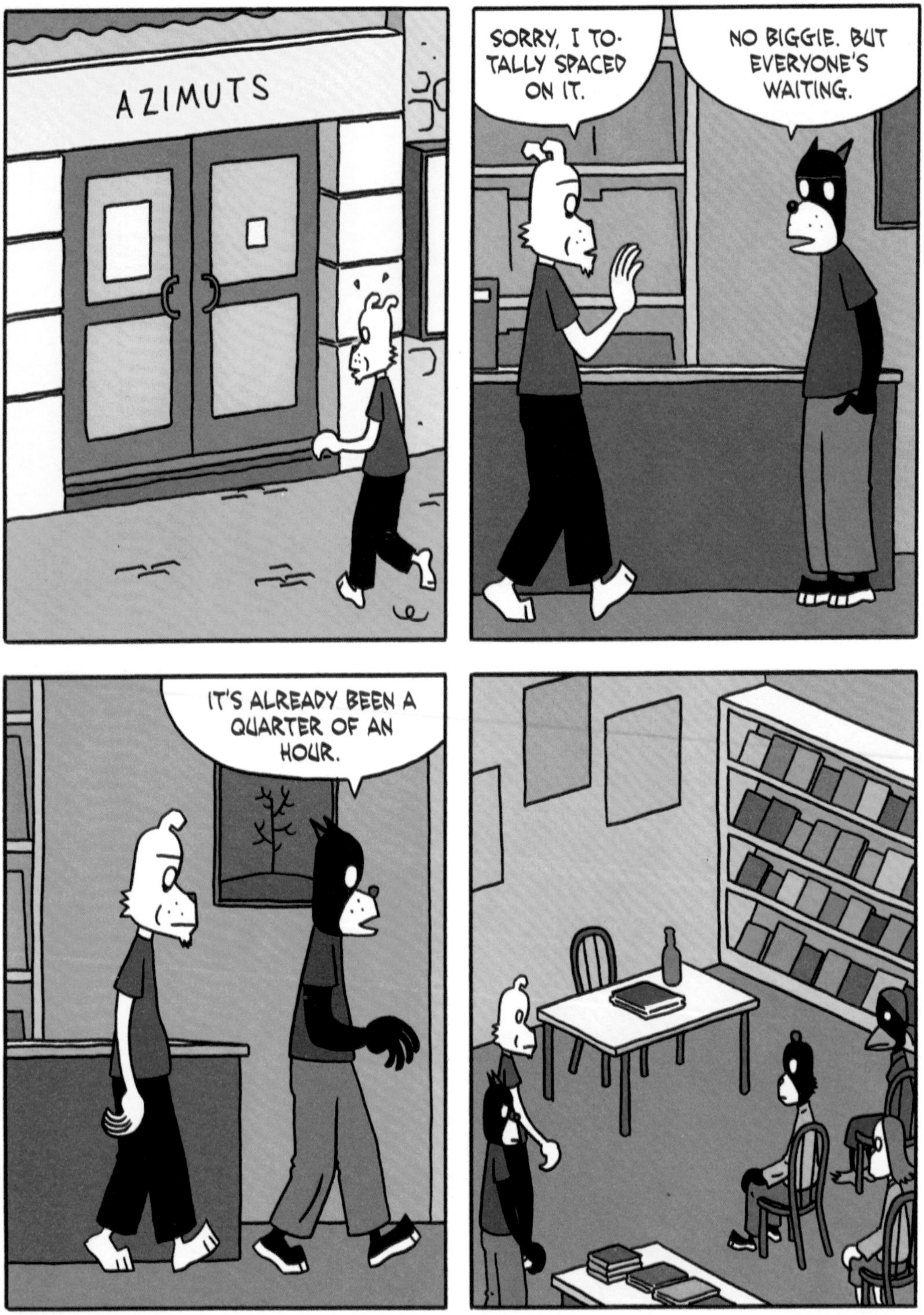
AZIMUTS
SORRY, I TOTALLY SPACED ON IT.
NO BIGGIE. BUT EVERYONE'S WAITING.
IT'S ALREADY BEEN A QUARTER OF AN HOUR.

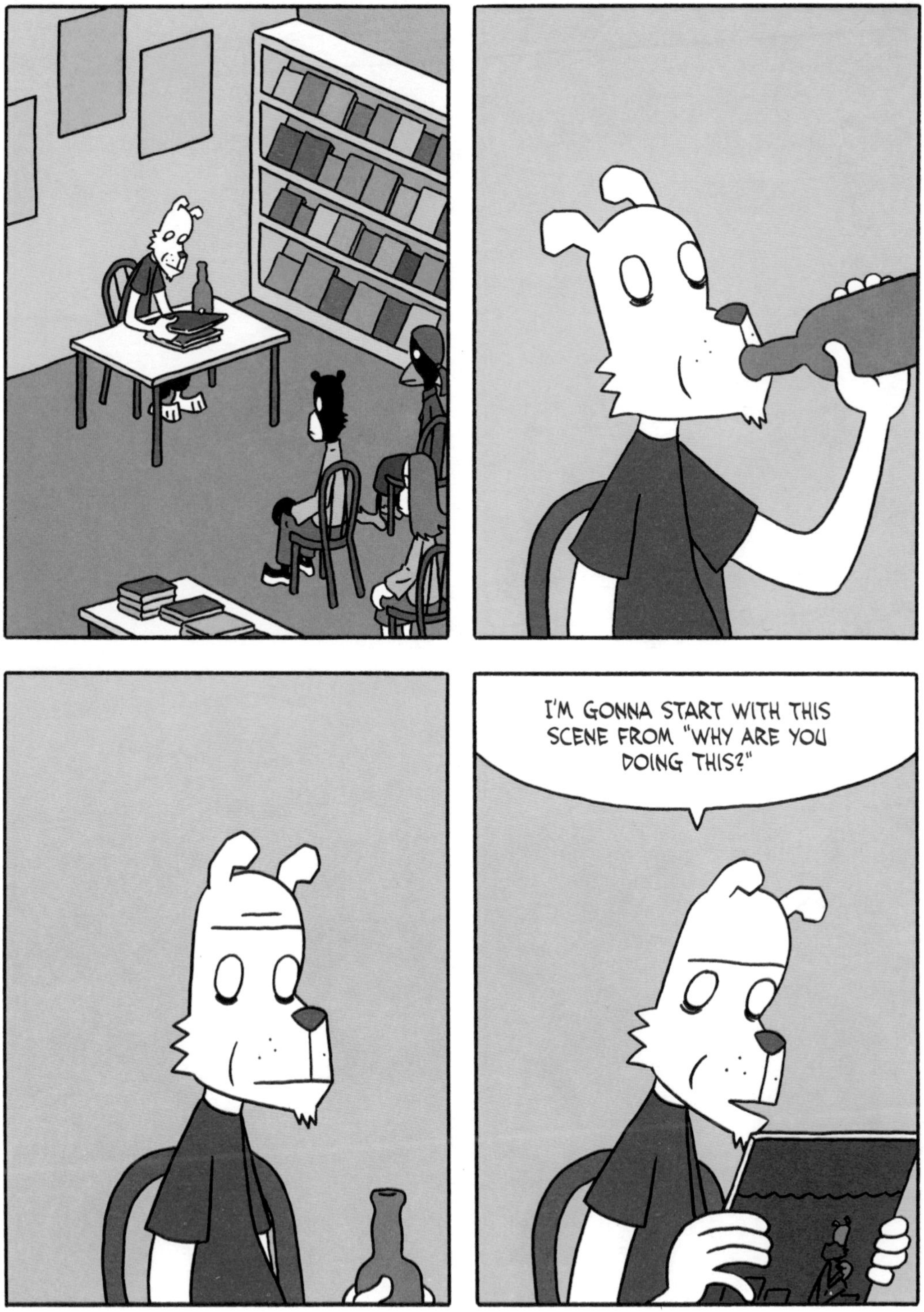
I'M GONNA START WITH THIS SCENE FROM "WHY ARE YOU DOING THIS?"

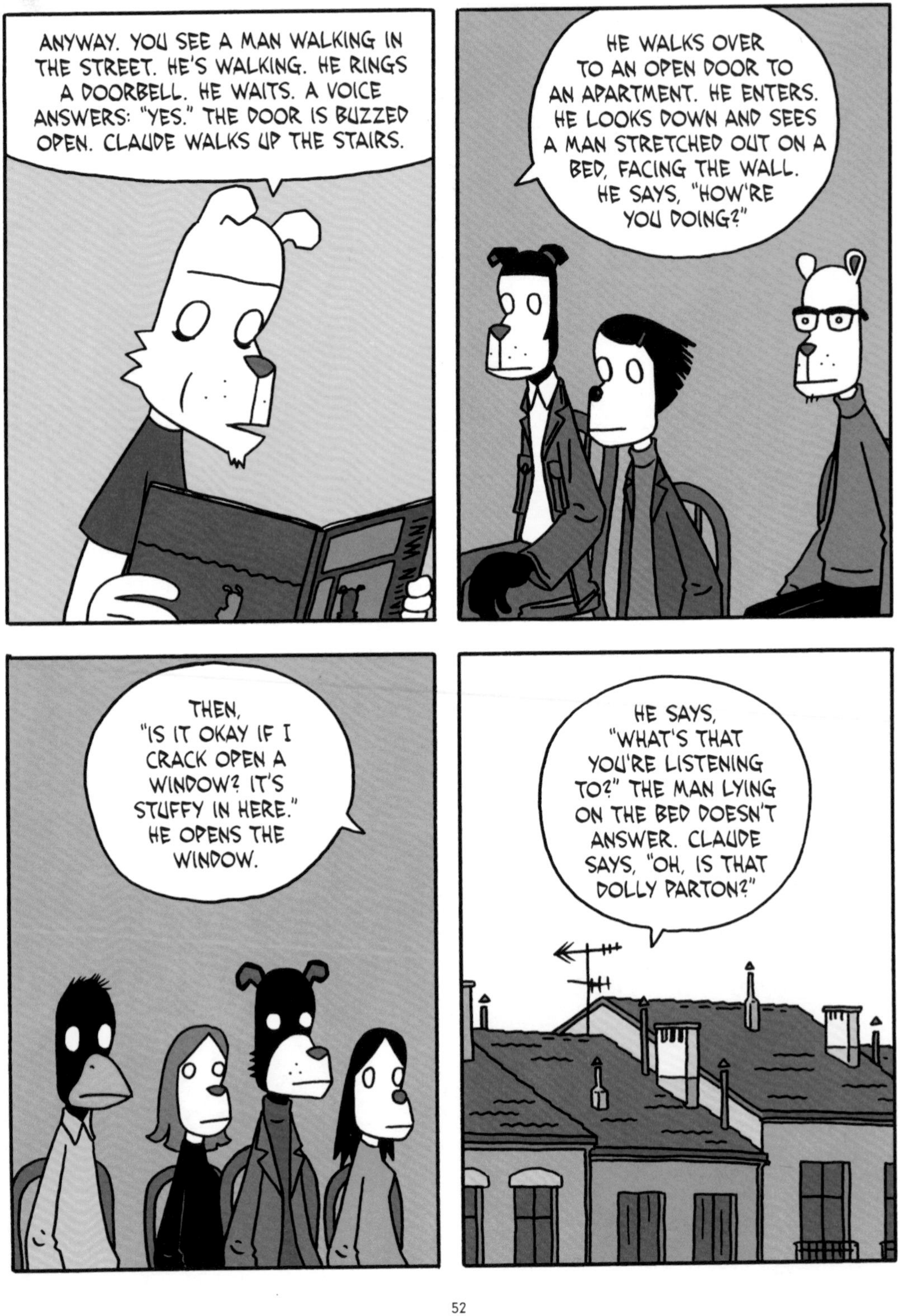
ANYWAY. YOU SEE A MAN WALKING IN THE STREET. HE'S WALKING. HE RINGS A DOORBELL. HE WAITS. A VOICE ANSWERS: "YES." THE DOOR IS BUZZED OPEN. CLAUDE WALKS UP THE STAIRS.
HE WALKS OVER TO AN OPEN DOOR TO AN APARTMENT. HE ENTERS. HE LOOKS DOWN AND SEES A MAN STRETCHED OUT ON A BED, FACING THE WALL. HE SAYS, "HOW'RE YOU DOING?"
THEN, "IS IT OKAY IF I CRACK OPEN A WINDOW? IT'S STUFFY IN HERE." HE OPENS THE WINDOW.
HE SAYS, "WHAT'S THAT YOU'RE LISTENING TO?" THE MAN LYING ON THE BED DOESN'T ANSWER. CLAUDE SAYS, "OH, IS THAT DOLLY PARTON?"

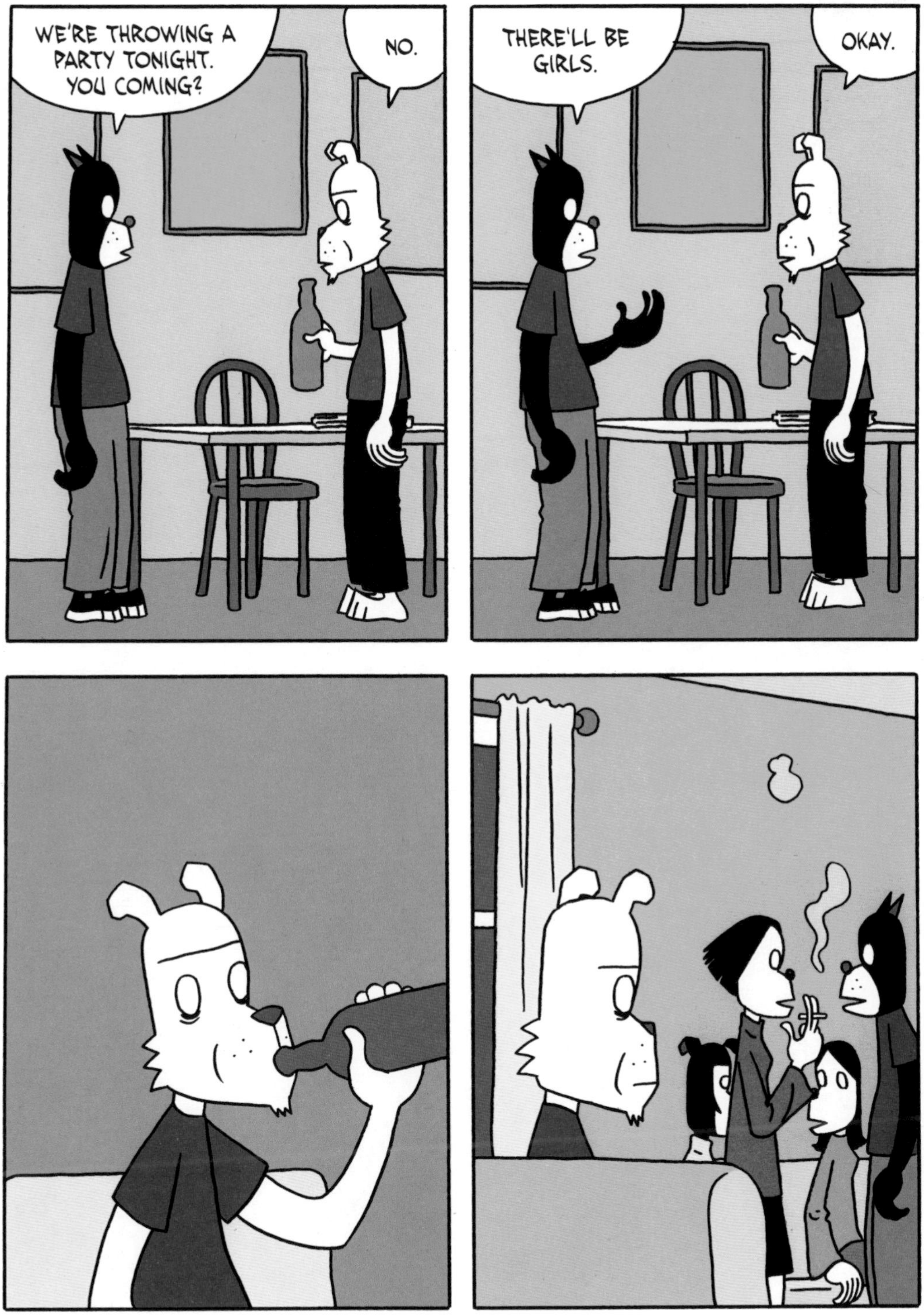
WE'RE THROWING A PARTY TONIGHT. YOU COMING?
NO.
THERE'LL BE GIRLS.
OKAY.

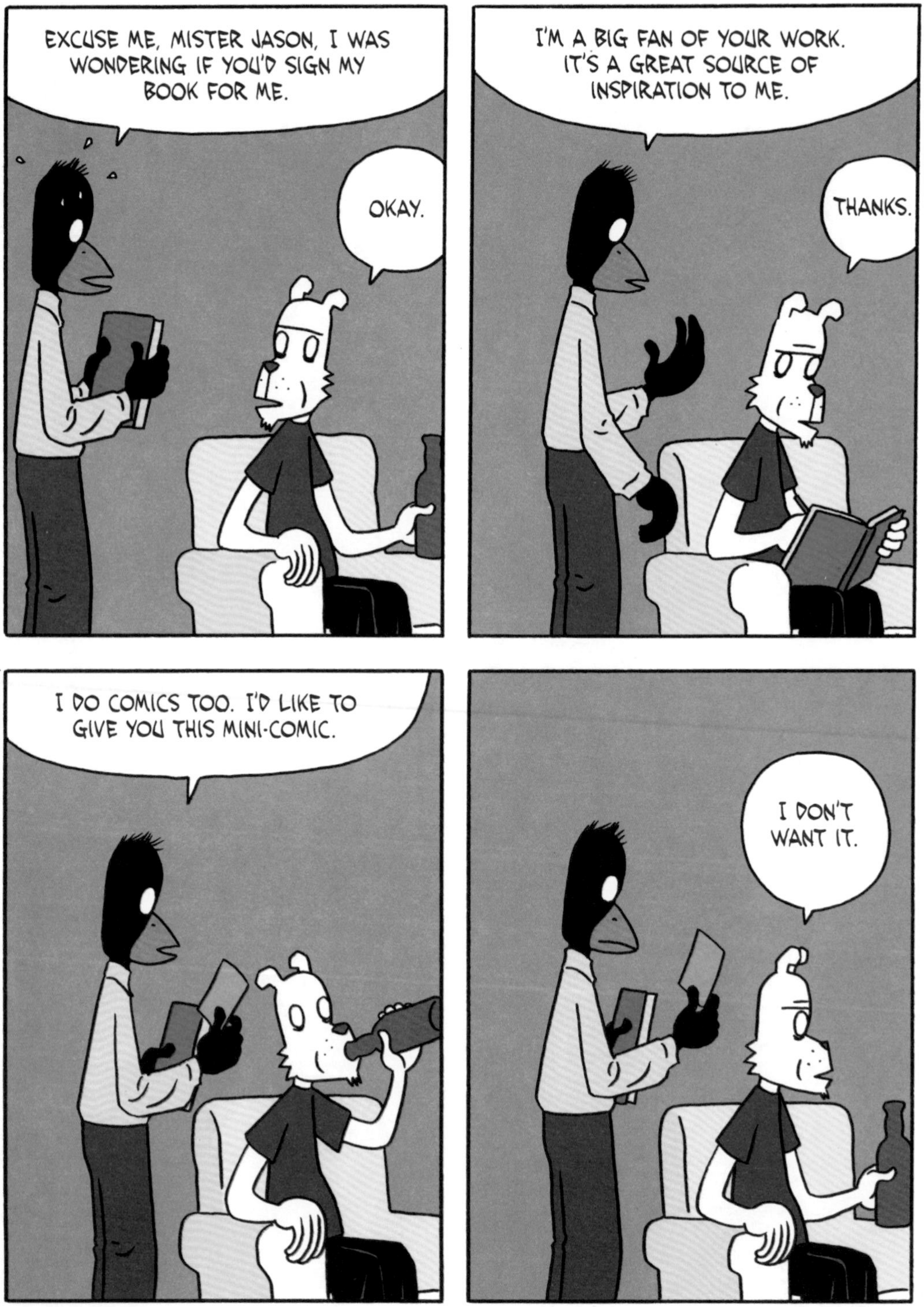
EXCUSE ME, MISTER JASON, I WAS WONDERING IF YOU'D SIGN MY BOOK FOR ME.
OKAY.
I'M A BIG FAN OF YOUR WORK. IT'S A GREAT SOURCE OF INSPIRATION TO ME.
THANKS.
I DO COMICS TOO. I'D LIKE TO GIVE YOU THIS MINI-COMIC.
I DON'T WANT IT.

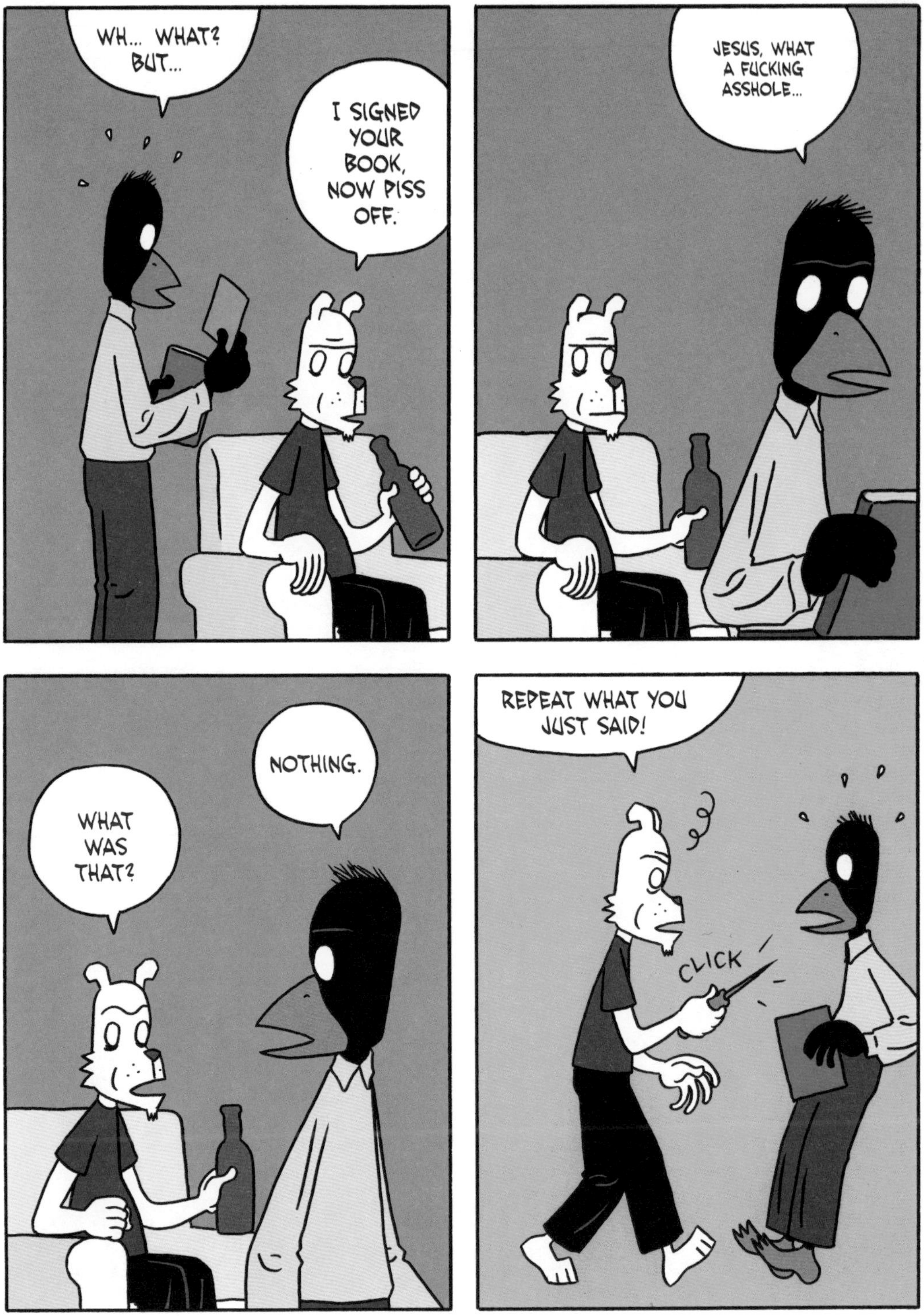

WH... WHAT? BUT...
I SIGNED YOUR BOOK, NOW PISS OFF.
JESUS, WHAT A FUCKING ASSHOLE...
WHAT WAS THAT?
NOTHING.
REPEAT WHAT YOU JUST SAID!
CLICK

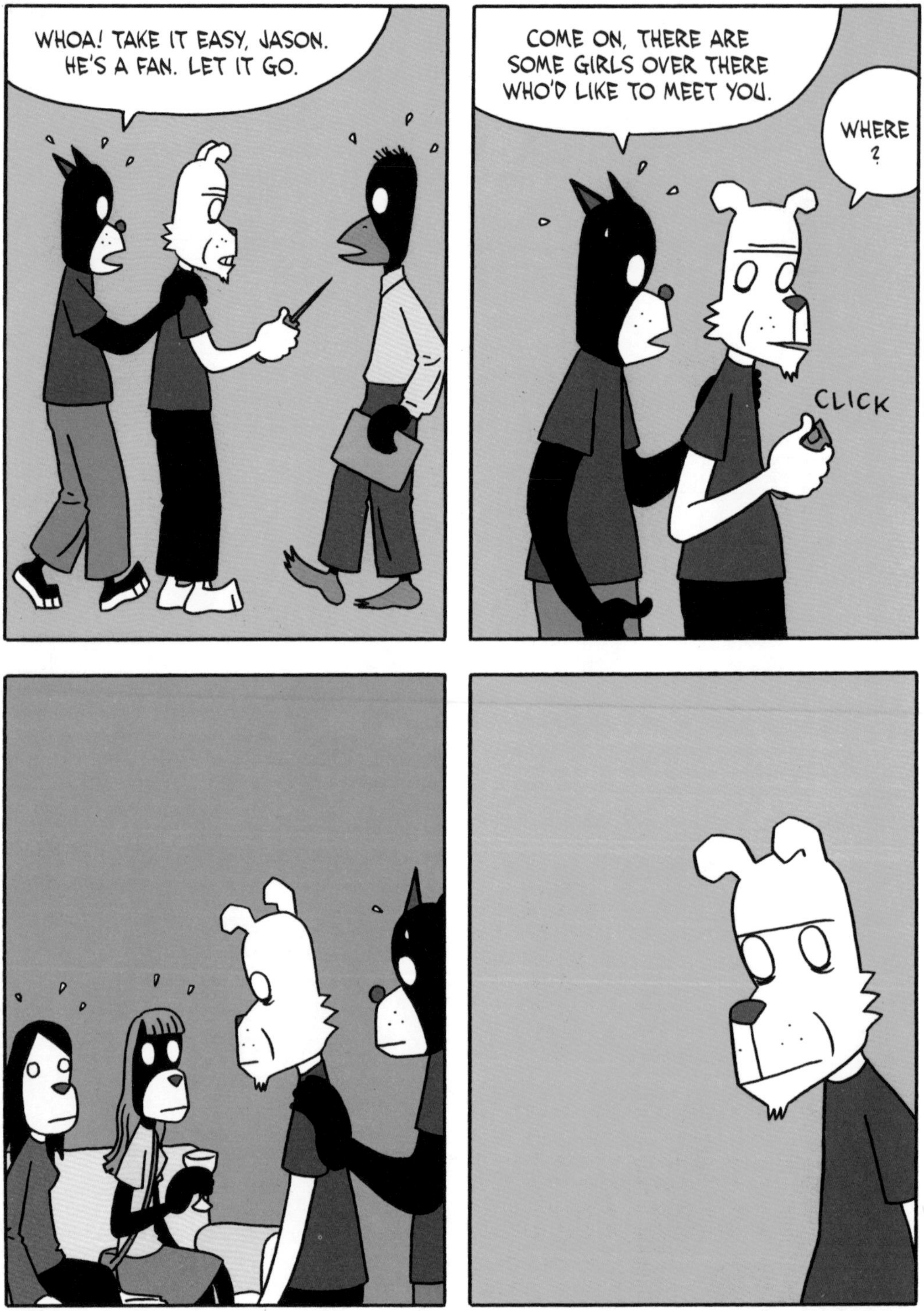
WHOA! TAKE IT EASY, JASON. HE'S A FAN. LET IT GO.
COME ON, THERE ARE SOME GIRLS OVER THERE WHO'D LIKE TO MEET YOU.
WHERE?
CLICK

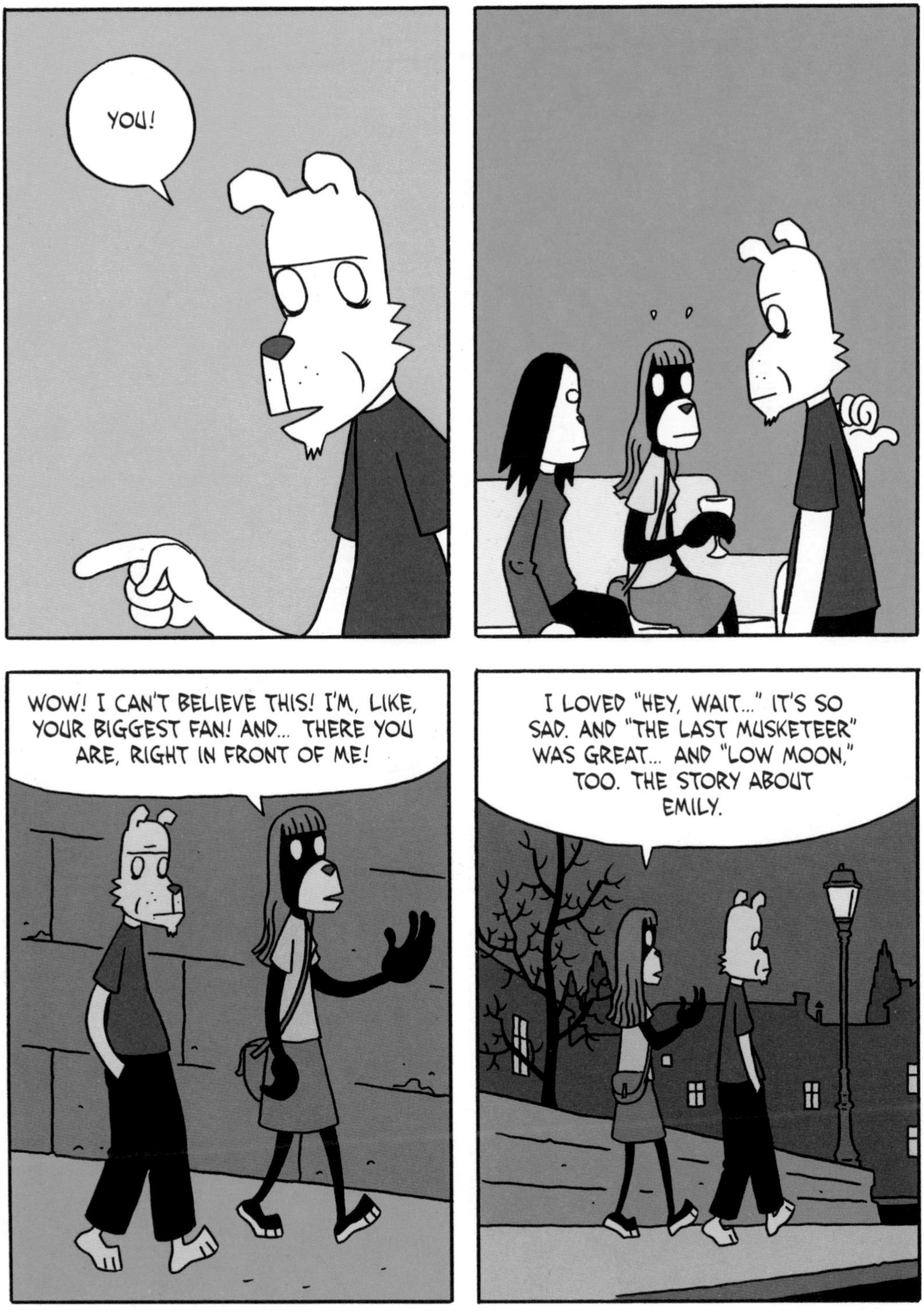

YOU!
WOW! I CAN'T BELIEVE THIS! I'M, LIKE, YOUR BIGGEST FAN! AND... THERE YOU ARE, RIGHT IN FRONT OF ME!
I LOVED "HEY, WAIT..." IT'S SO SAD. AND "THE LAST MUSKETEER" WAS GREAT... AND "LOW MOON," TOO. THE STORY ABOUT EMILY.

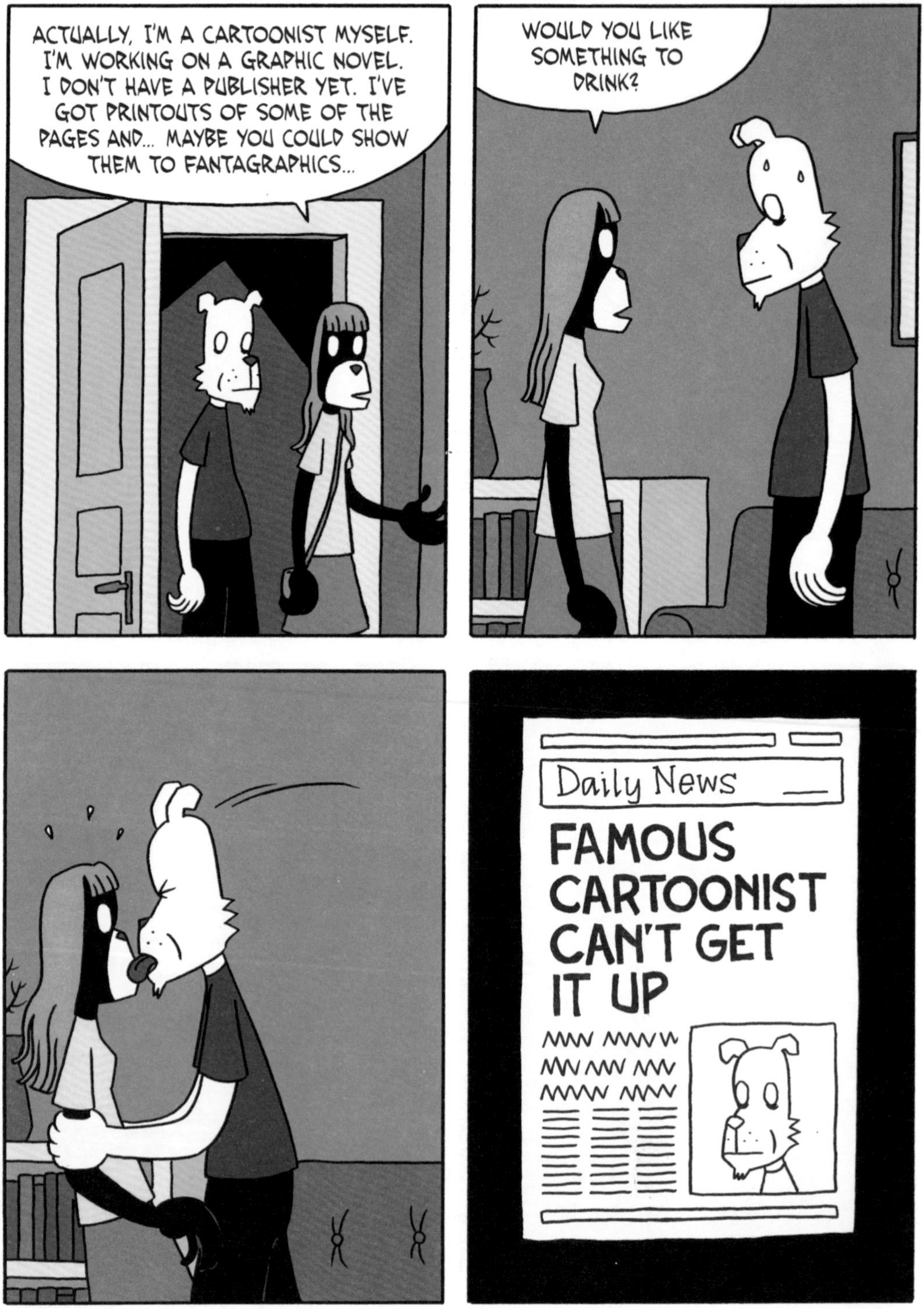
ACTUALLY, I'M A CARTOONIST MYSELF. I'M WORKING ON A GRAPHIC NOVEL. I DON'T HAVE A PUBLISHER YET. I'VE GOT PRINTOUTS OF SOME OF THE PAGES AND... MAYBE YOU COULD SHOW THEM TO FANTAGRAPHICS...
WOULD YOU LIKE SOMETHING TO DRINK?
Daily News
FAMOUS CARTOONIST CAN'T GET IT UP

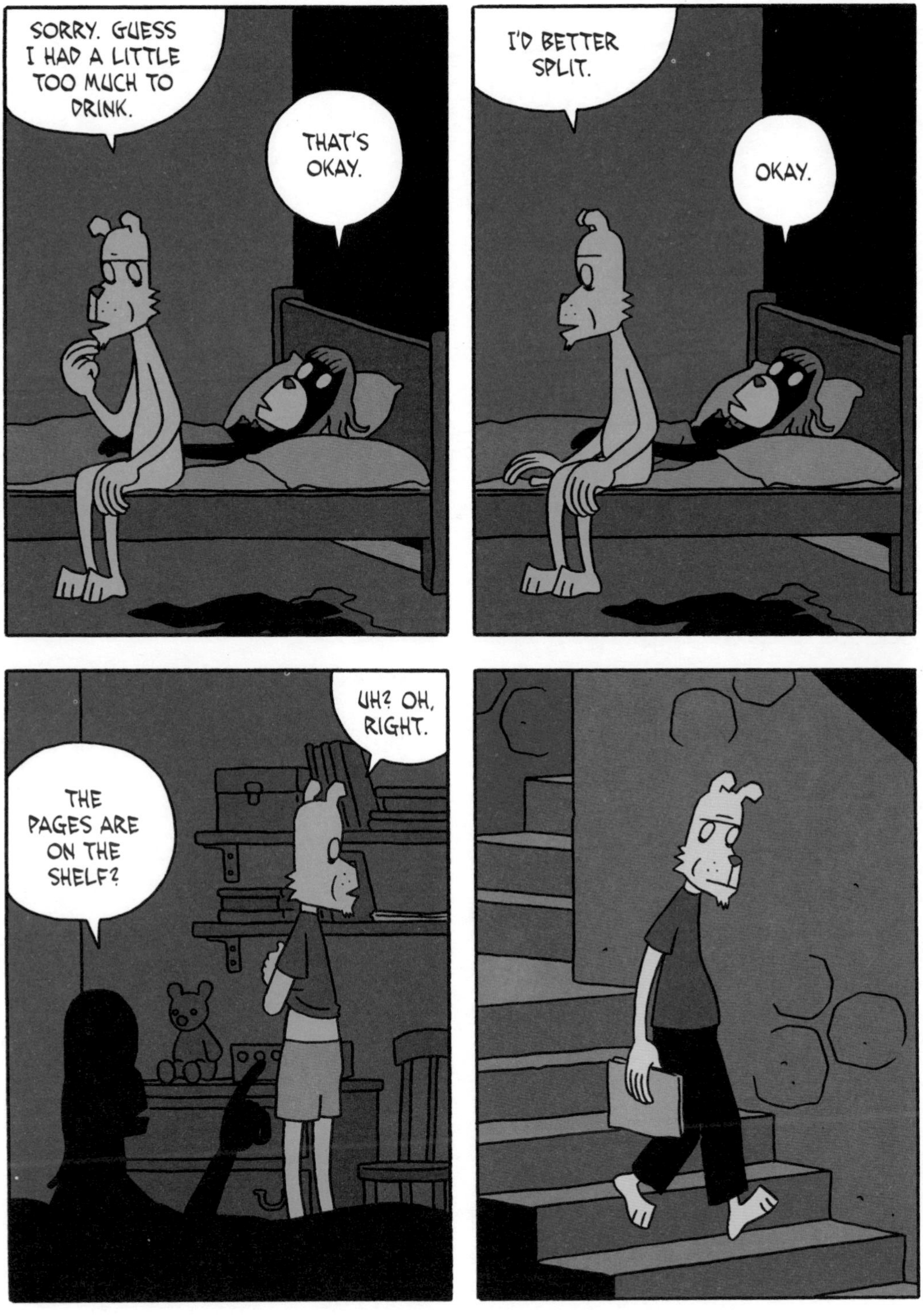
SORRY. GUESS I HAD A LITTLE TOO MUCH TO DRINK.
THAT'S OKAY.
I'D BETTER SPLIT.
OKAY.
THE PAGES ARE ON THE SHELF?
UH? OH, RIGHT.

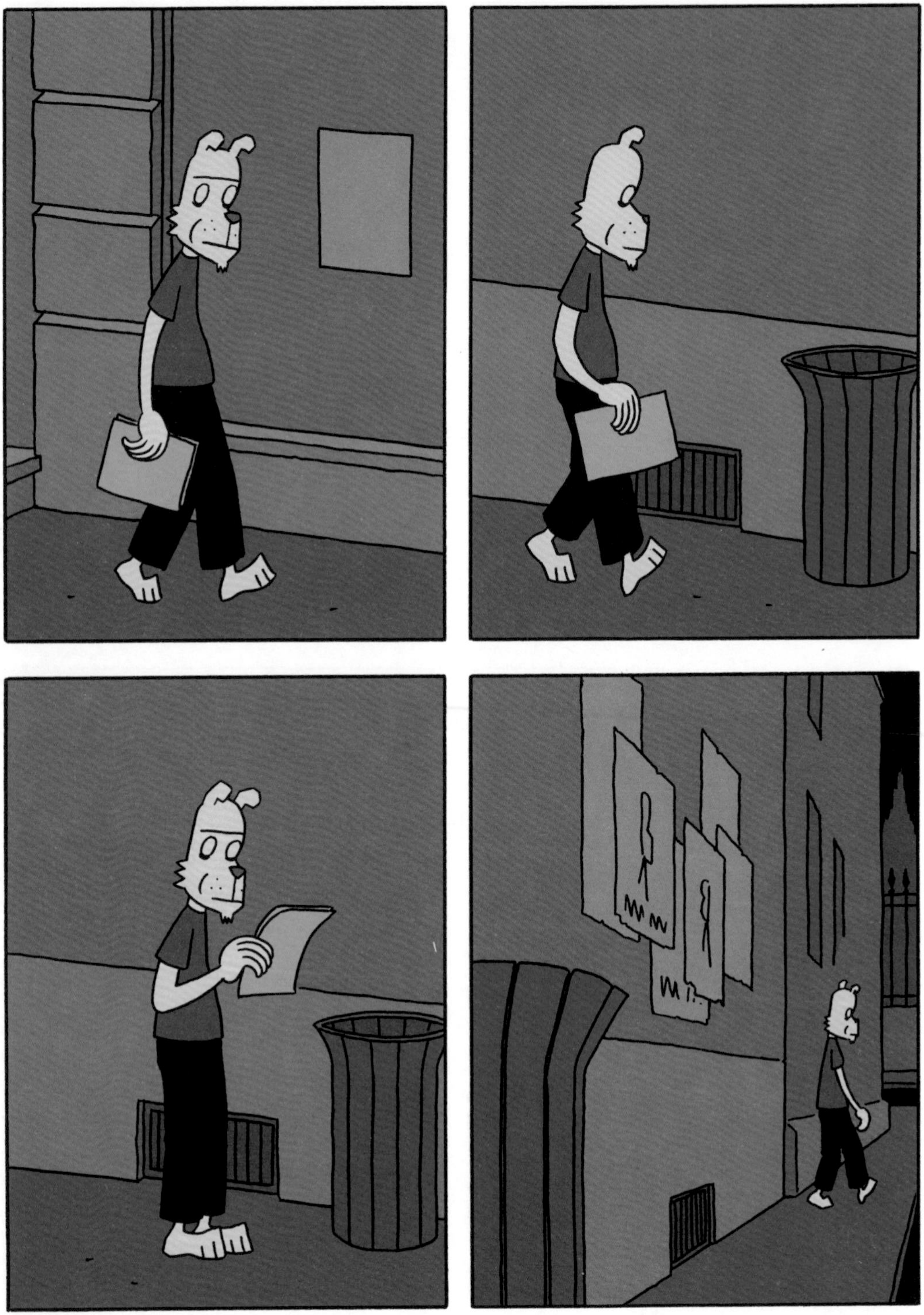

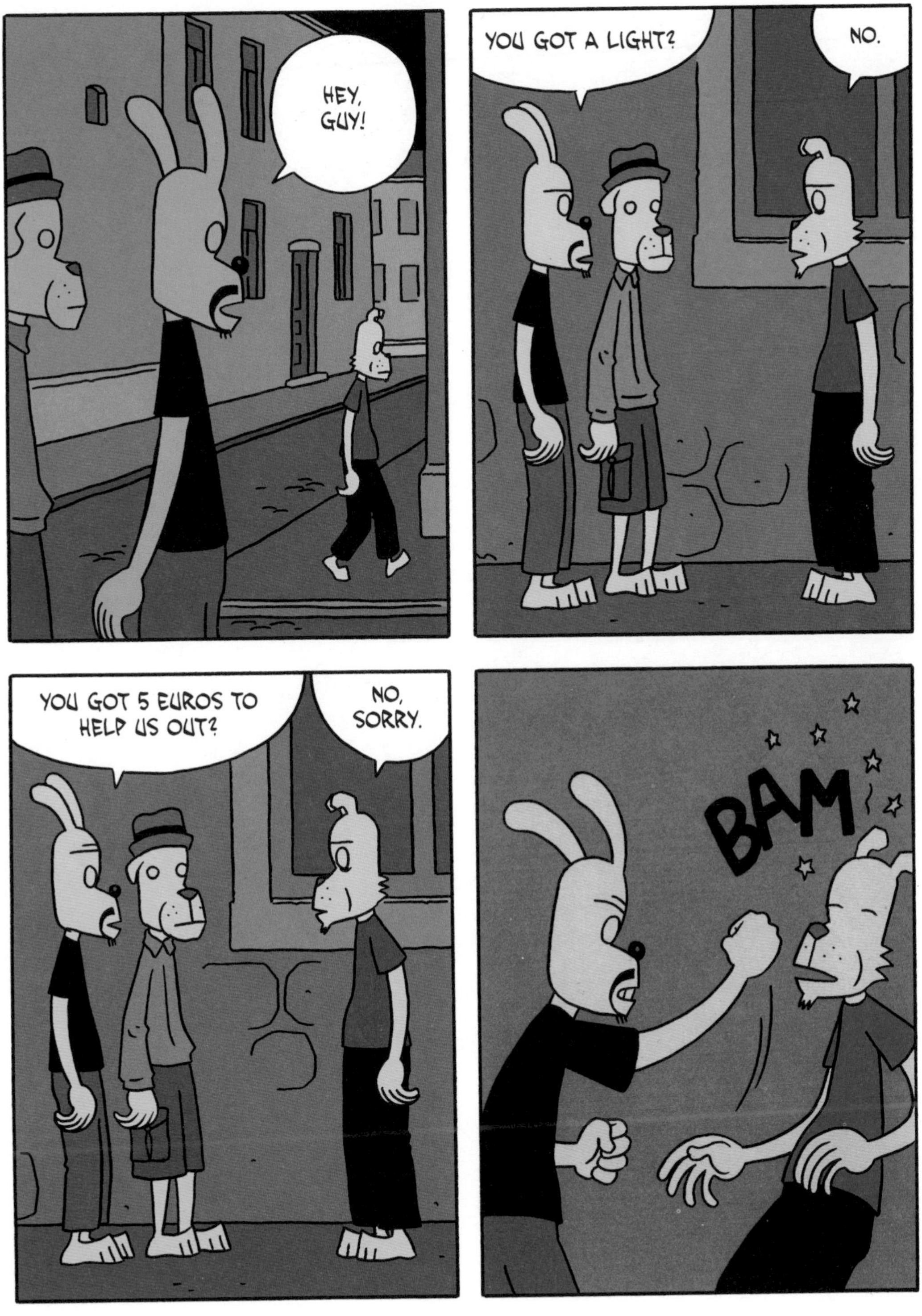
HEY, GUY!
YOU GOT A LIGHT?
NO.
YOU GOT 5 EUROS TO HELP US OUT?
NO, SORRY.
BAM

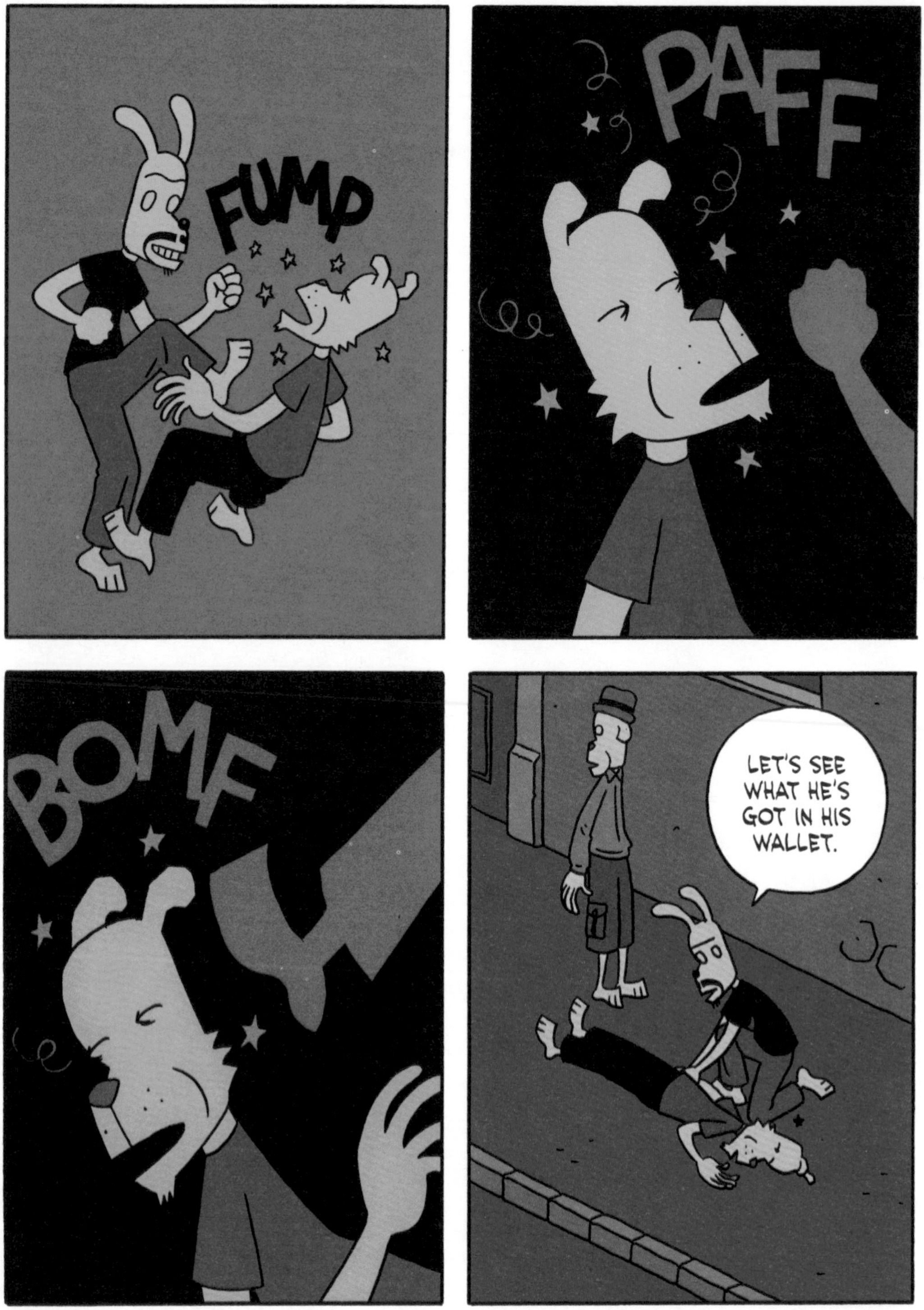
FUMP
PAFF
BOMF
LET'S SEE WHAT HE'S GOT IN HIS WALLET.
JC

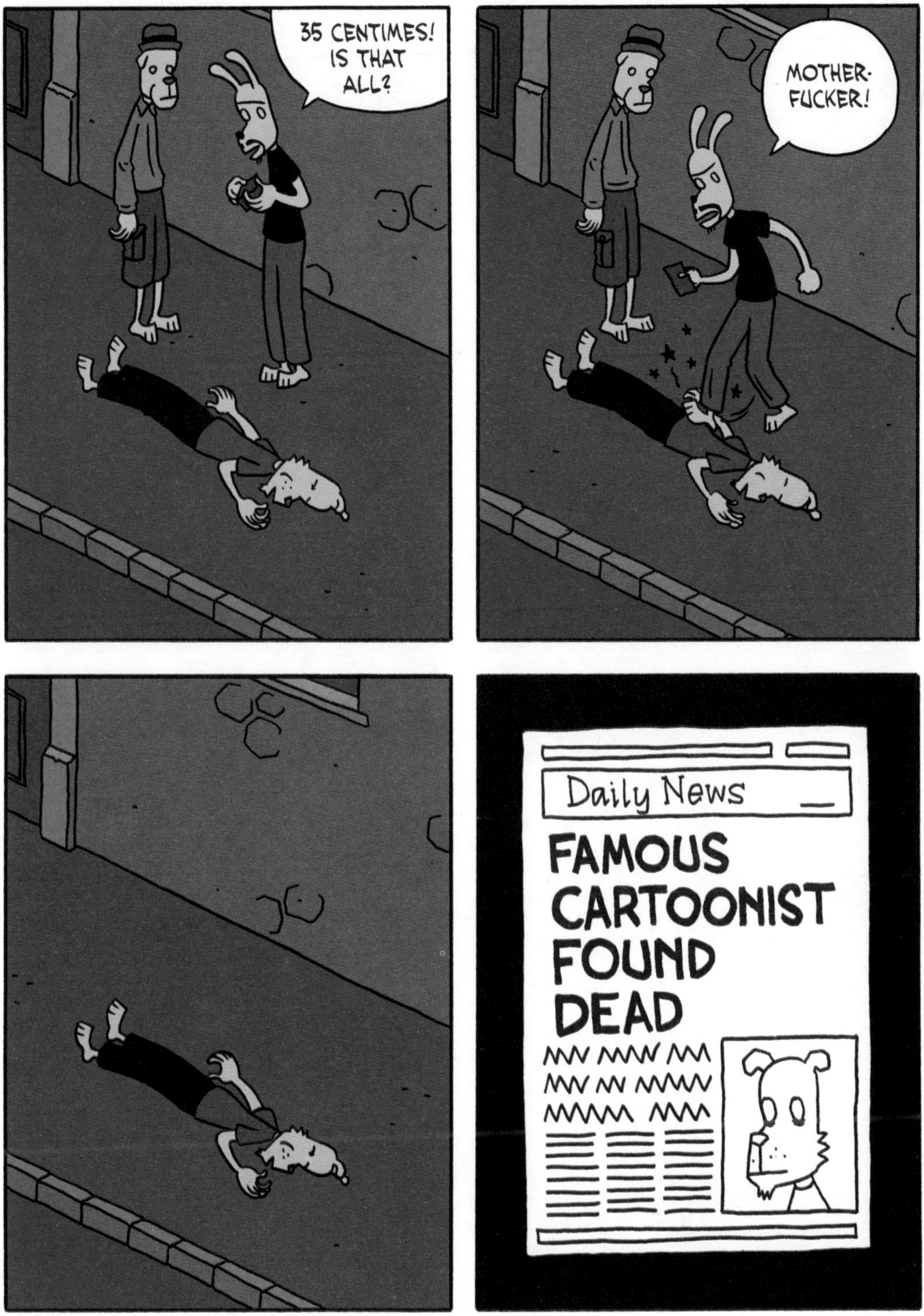
35 CENTIMES! IS THAT ALL?
MOTHER-FUCKER!
Daily News
FAMOUS CARTOONIST FOUND DEAD

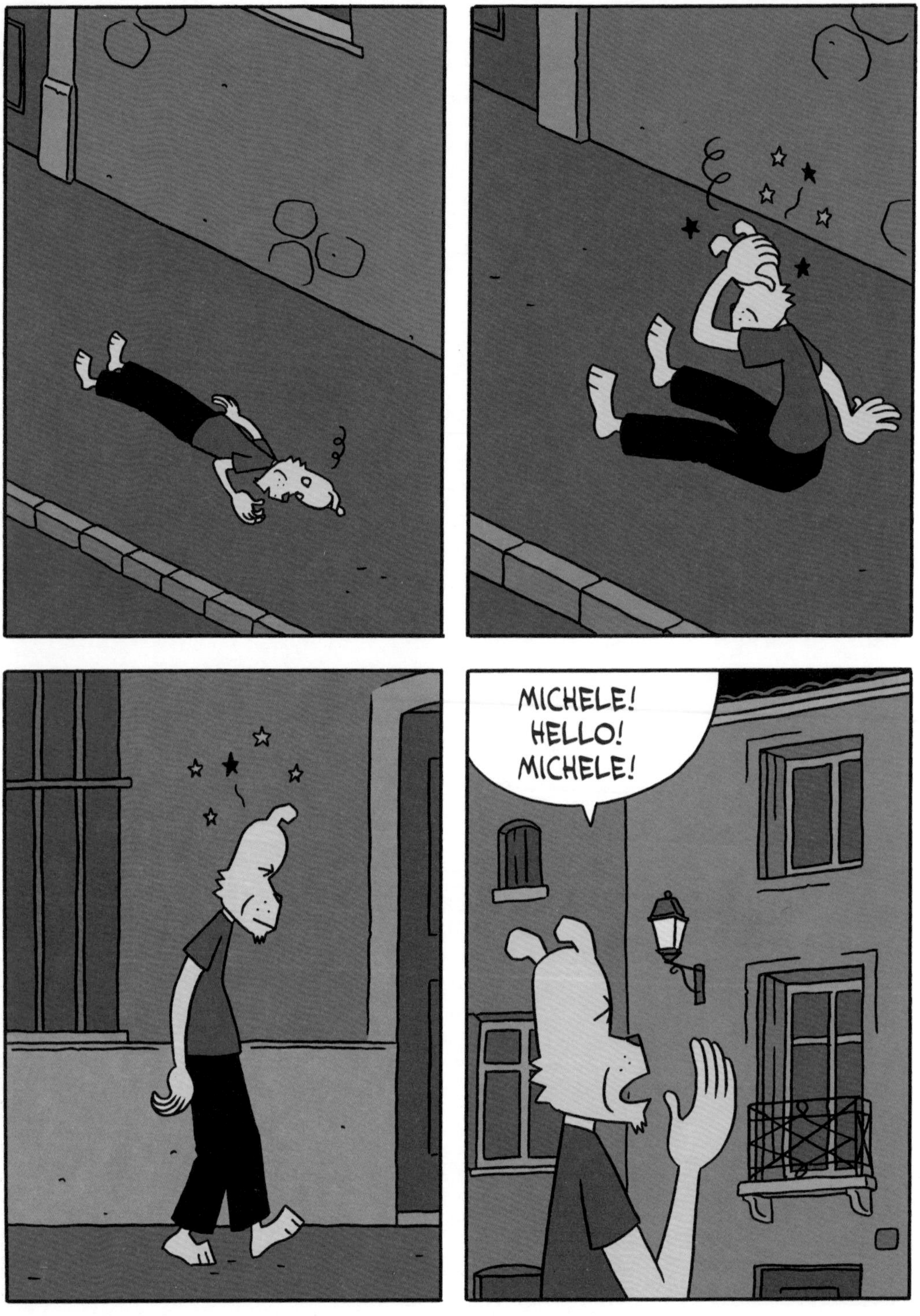
MICHELE!
HELLO!
MICHELE!

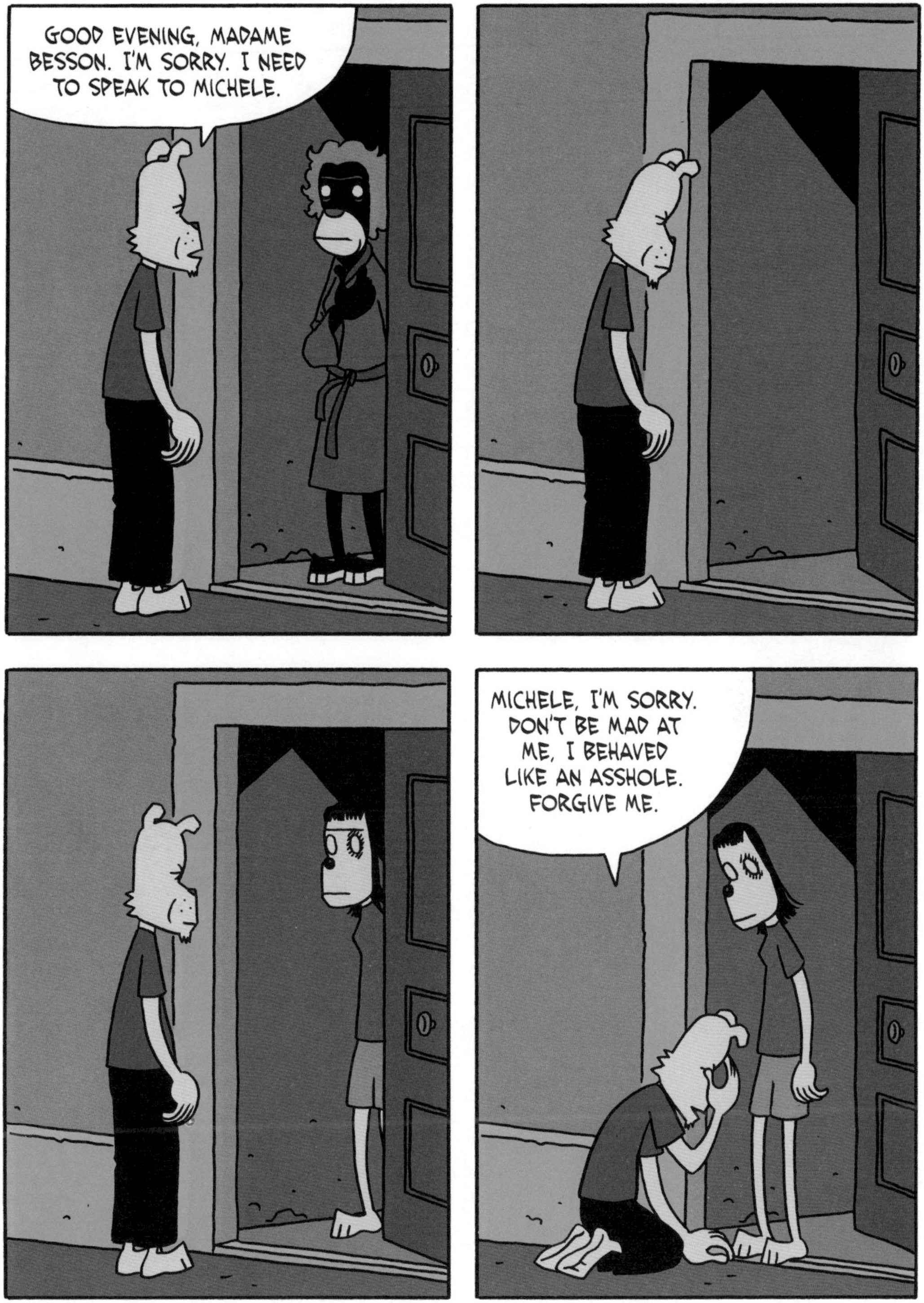
GOOD EVENING, MADAME BESSON. I'M SORRY. I NEED TO SPEAK TO MICHELE.
MICHELE, I'M SORRY. DON'T BE MAD AT ME, I BEHAVED LIKE AN ASSHOLE. FORGIVE ME.

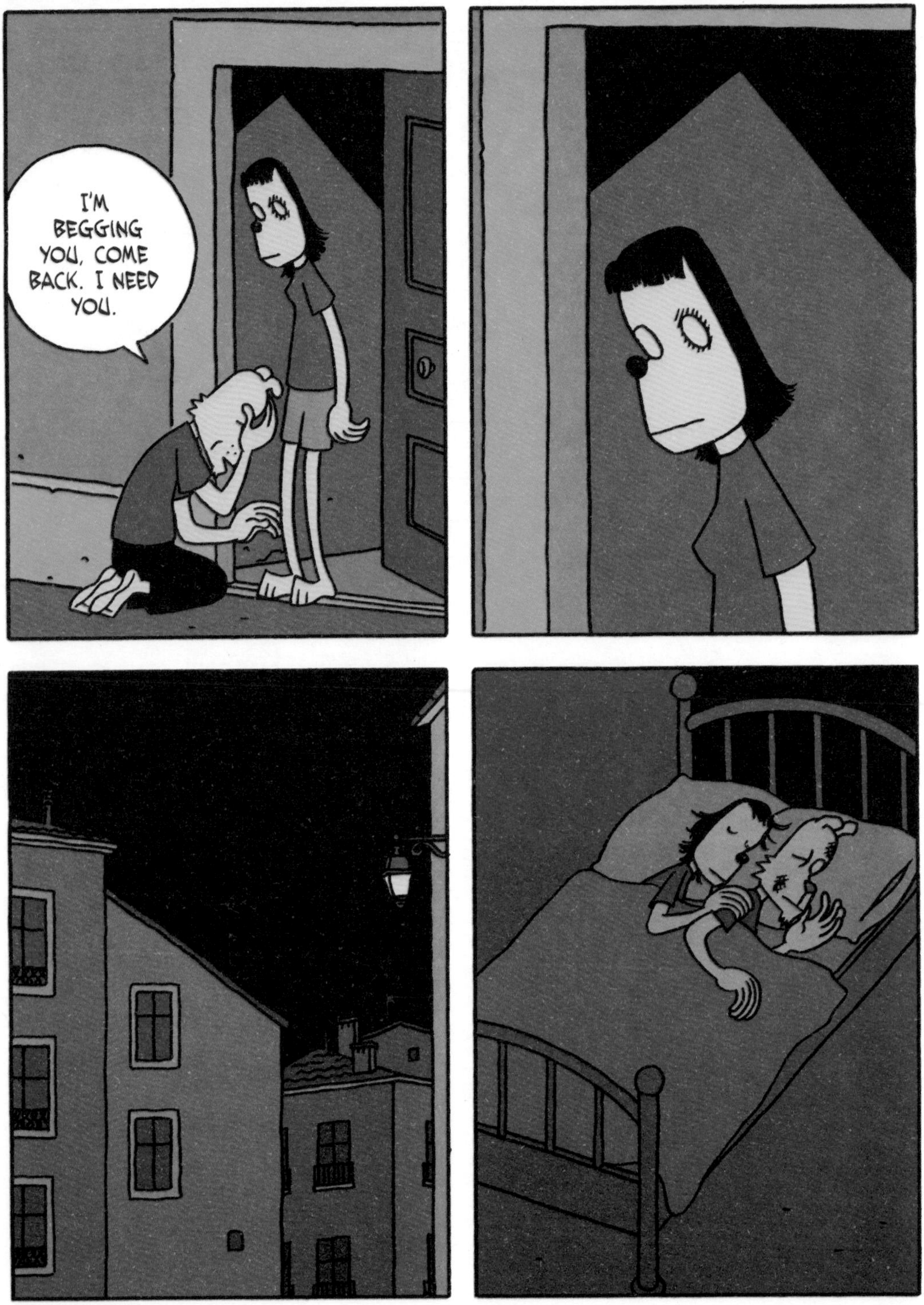
I'M BEGGING YOU, COME BACK. I NEED YOU.

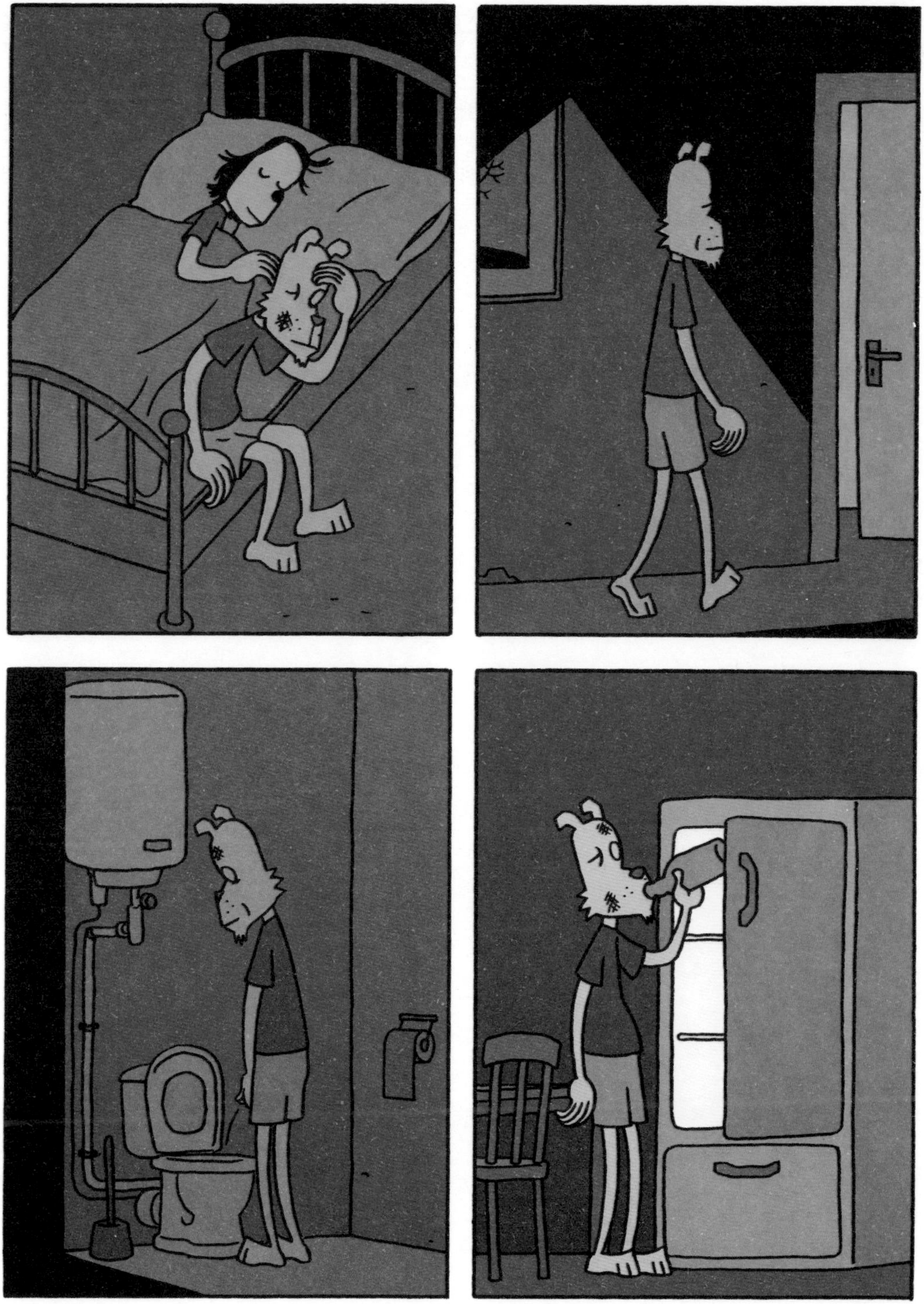

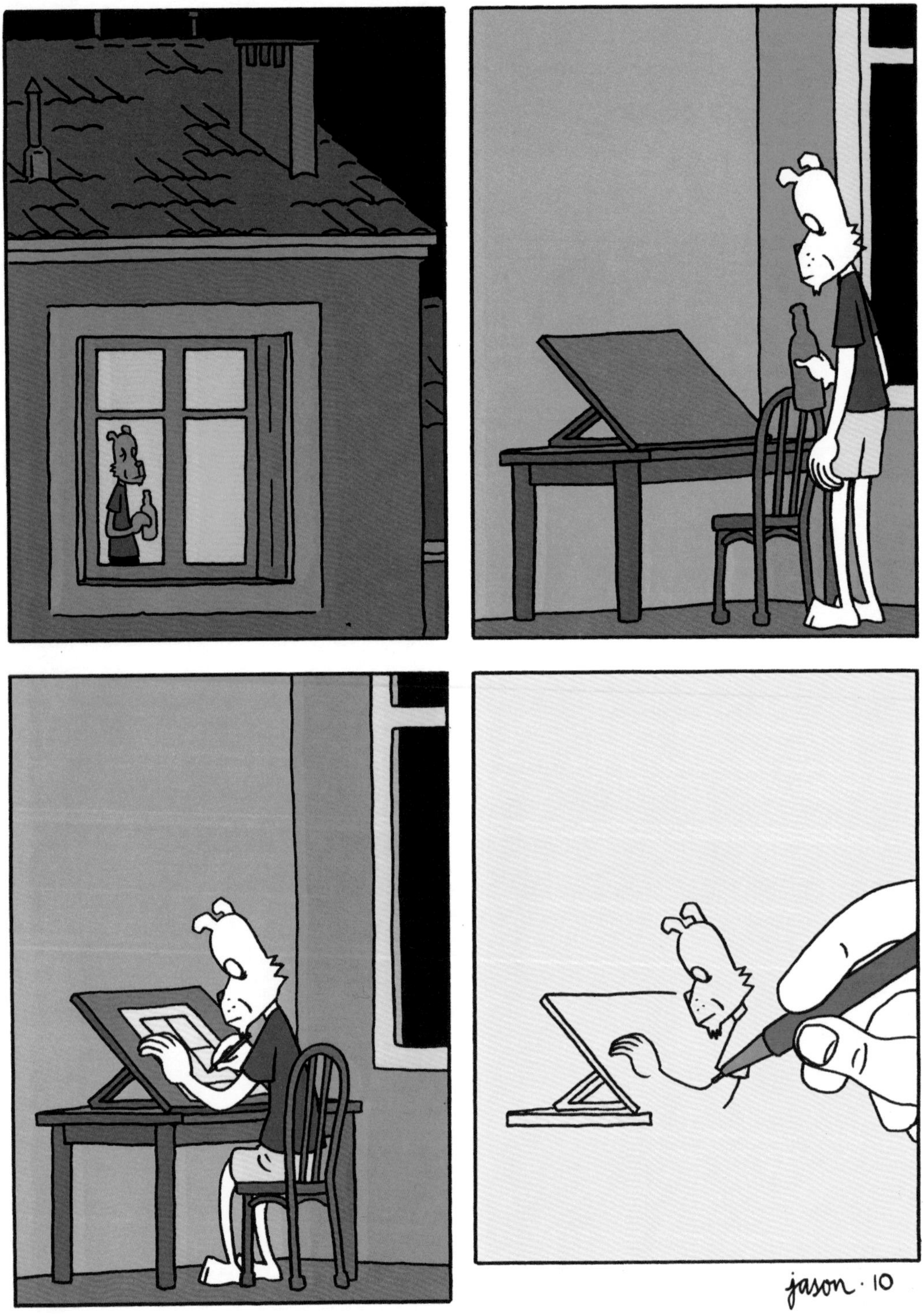
jason · 10

PRESENTING:

———

THE BRAIN
THAT WOULDN'T
VIRGINIA WOOLF

———

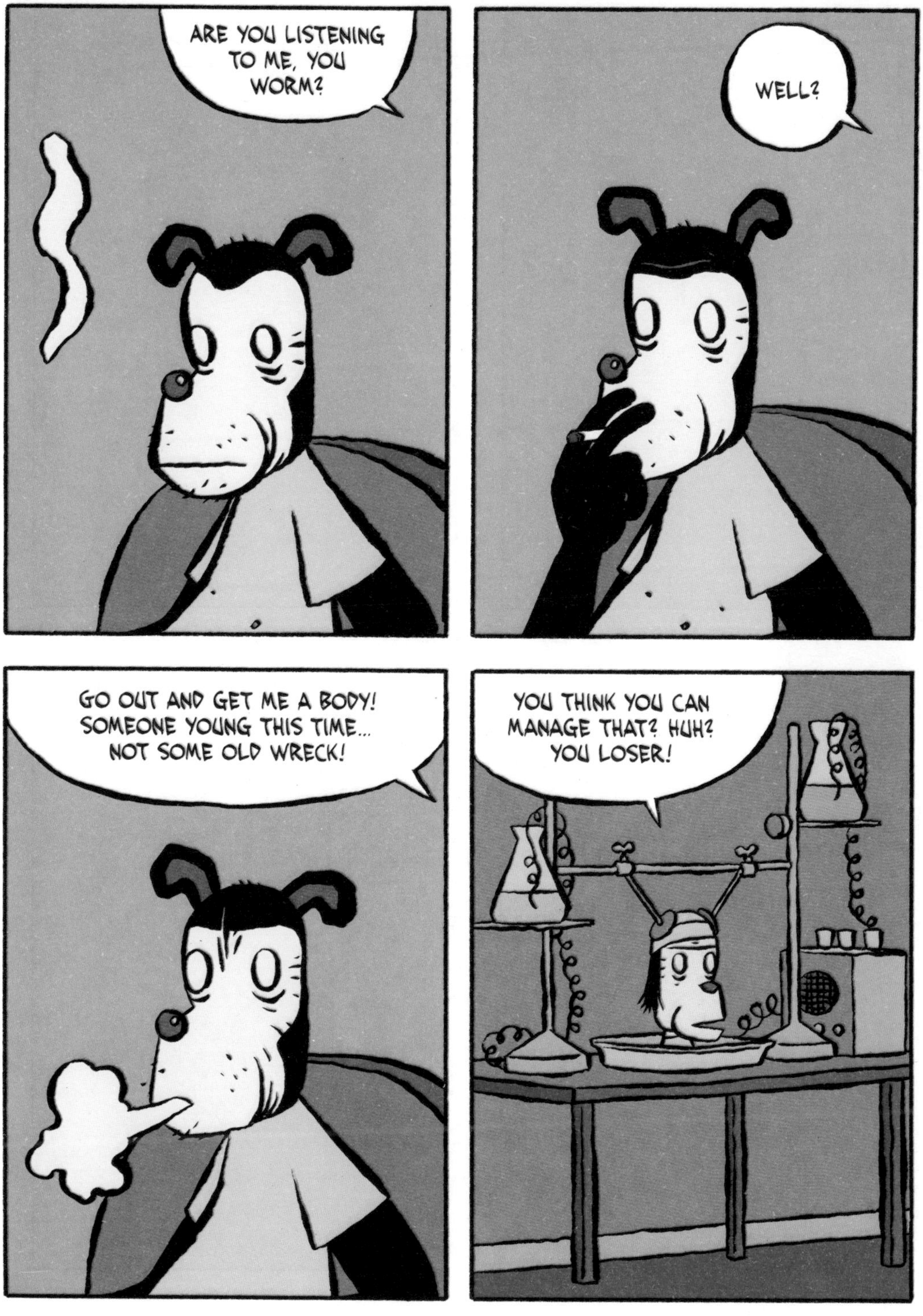
ARE YOU LISTENING TO ME, YOU WORM?
WELL?
GO OUT AND GET ME A BODY! SOMEONE YOUNG THIS TIME... NOT SOME OLD WRECK!
YOU THINK YOU CAN MANAGE THAT? HUH? YOU LOSER!

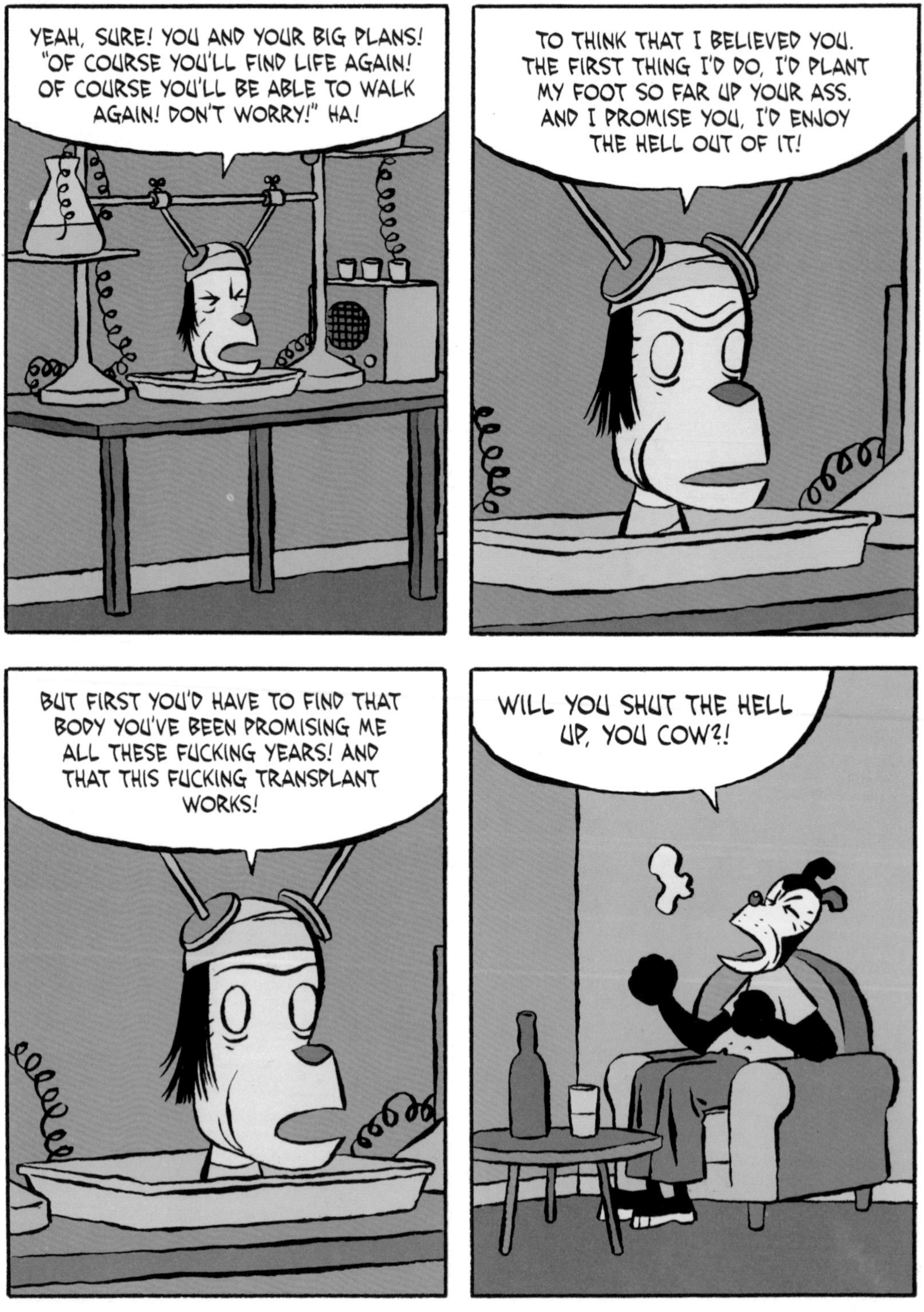
YEAH, SURE! YOU AND YOUR BIG PLANS! "OF COURSE YOU'LL FIND LIFE AGAIN! OF COURSE YOU'LL BE ABLE TO WALK AGAIN! DON'T WORRY!" HA!
TO THINK THAT I BELIEVED YOU. THE FIRST THING I'D DO, I'D PLANT MY FOOT SO FAR UP YOUR ASS. AND I PROMISE YOU, I'D ENJOY THE HELL OUT OF IT!
BUT FIRST YOU'D HAVE TO FIND THAT BODY YOU'VE BEEN PROMISING ME ALL THESE FUCKING YEARS! AND THAT THIS FUCKING TRANSPLANT WORKS!
WILL YOU SHUT THE HELL UP, YOU COW?!

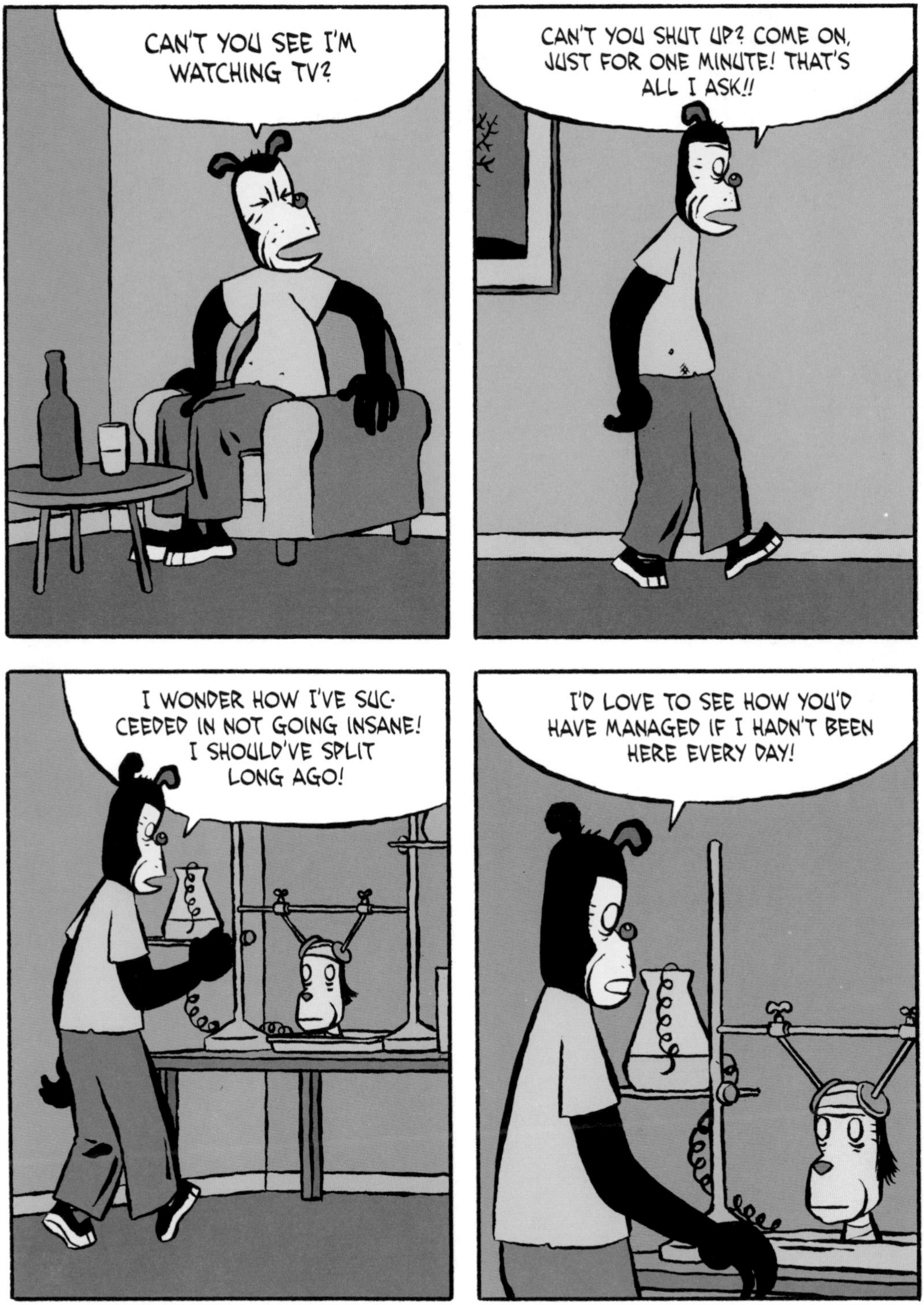
CAN'T YOU SEE I'M WATCHING TV?
CAN'T YOU SHUT UP? COME ON, JUST FOR ONE MINUTE! THAT'S ALL I ASK!!
I WONDER HOW I'VE SUC-CEEDED IN NOT GOING INSANE! I SHOULD'VE SPLIT LONG AGO!
I'D LOVE TO SEE HOW YOU'D HAVE MANAGED IF I HADN'T BEEN HERE EVERY DAY!

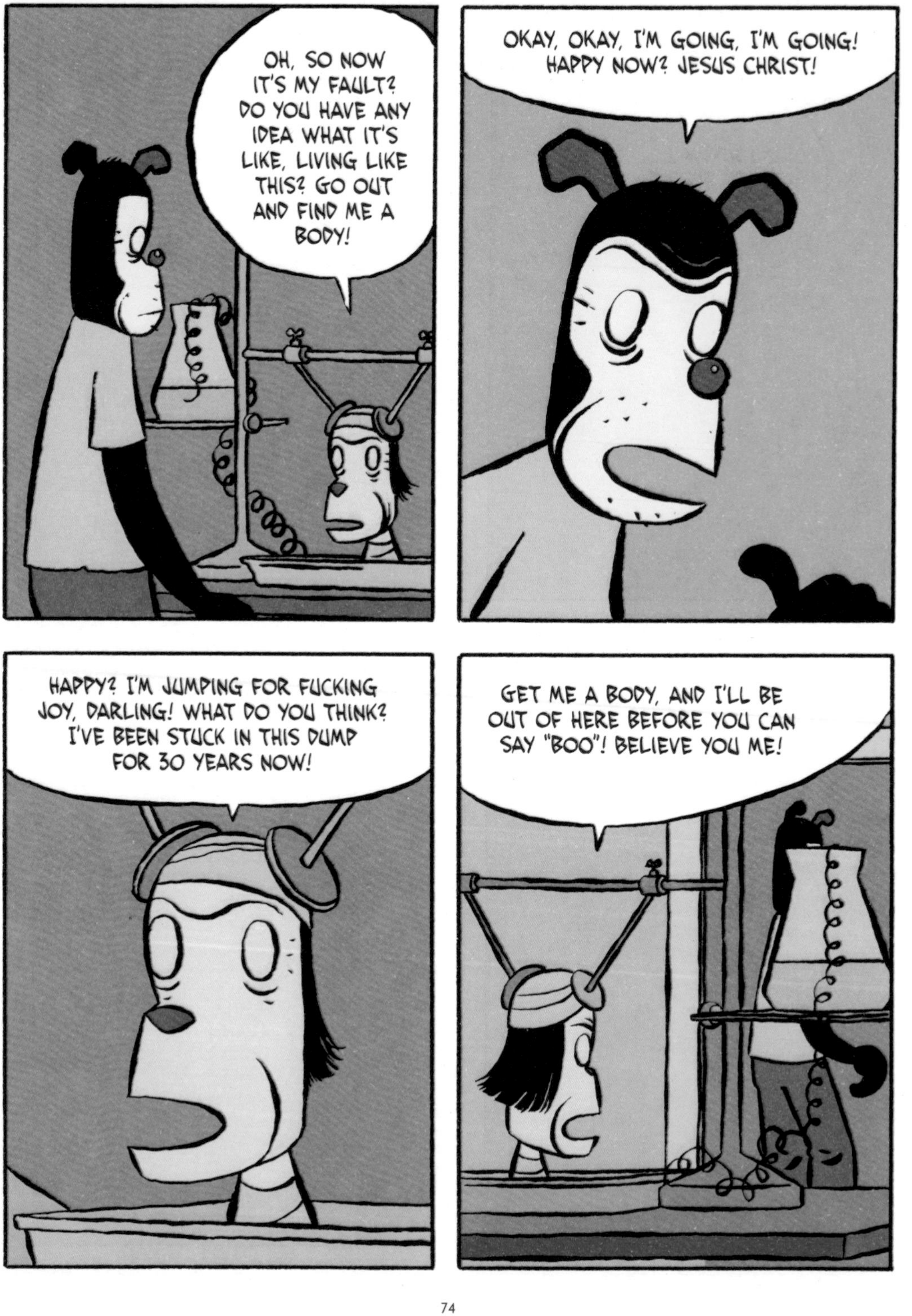
OH, SO NOW IT'S MY FAULT? DO YOU HAVE ANY IDEA WHAT IT'S LIKE, LIVING LIKE THIS? GO OUT AND FIND ME A BODY!
OKAY, OKAY, I'M GOING, I'M GOING! HAPPY NOW? JESUS CHRIST!
HAPPY? I'M JUMPING FOR FUCKING JOY, DARLING! WHAT DO YOU THINK? I'VE BEEN STUCK IN THIS DUMP FOR 30 YEARS NOW!
GET ME A BODY, AND I'LL BE OUT OF HERE BEFORE YOU CAN SAY "BOO"! BELIEVE YOU ME!

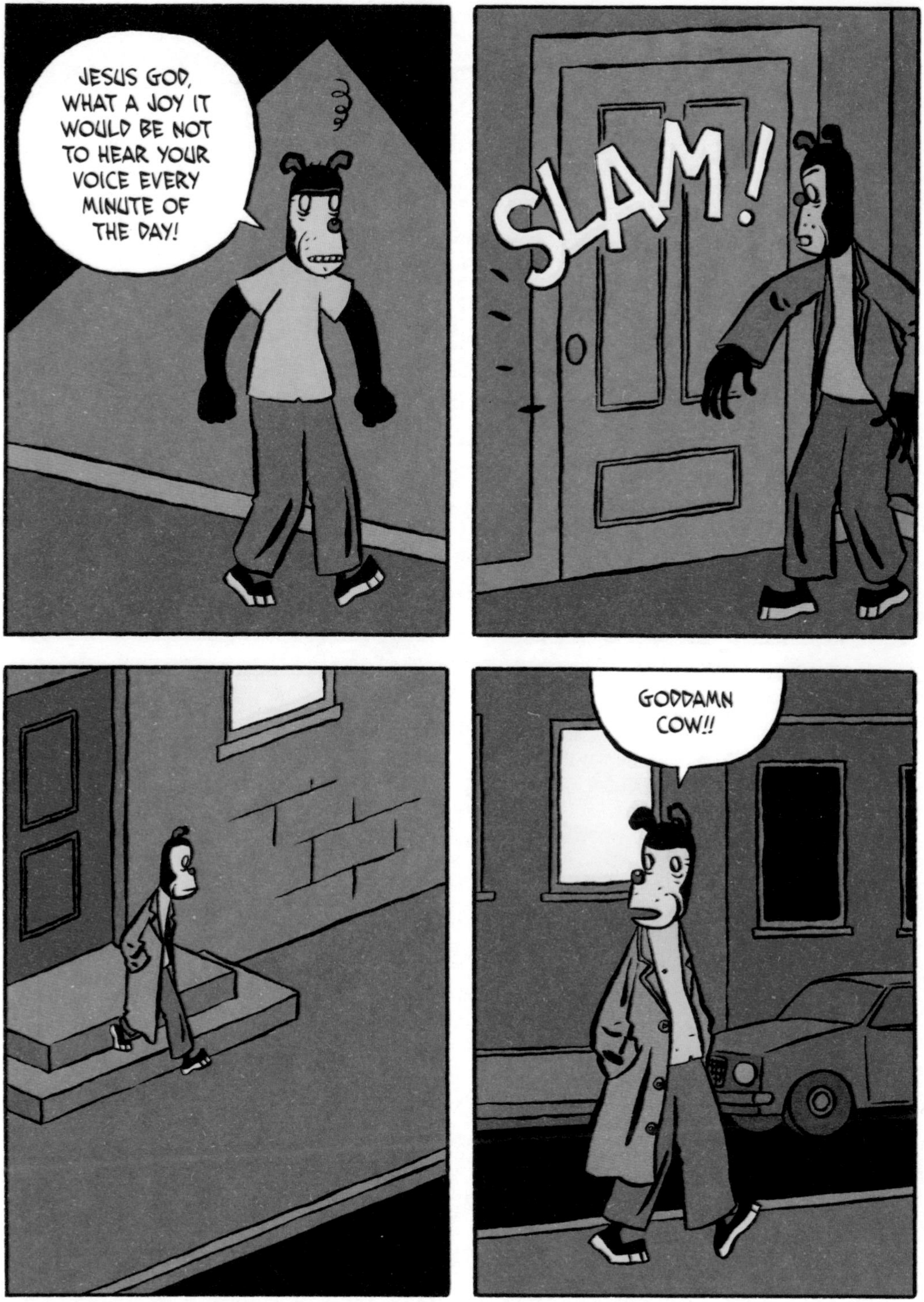
JESUS GOD, WHAT A JOY IT WOULD BE NOT TO HEAR YOUR VOICE EVERY MINUTE OF THE DAY!
SLAM!
GODDAMN COW!!

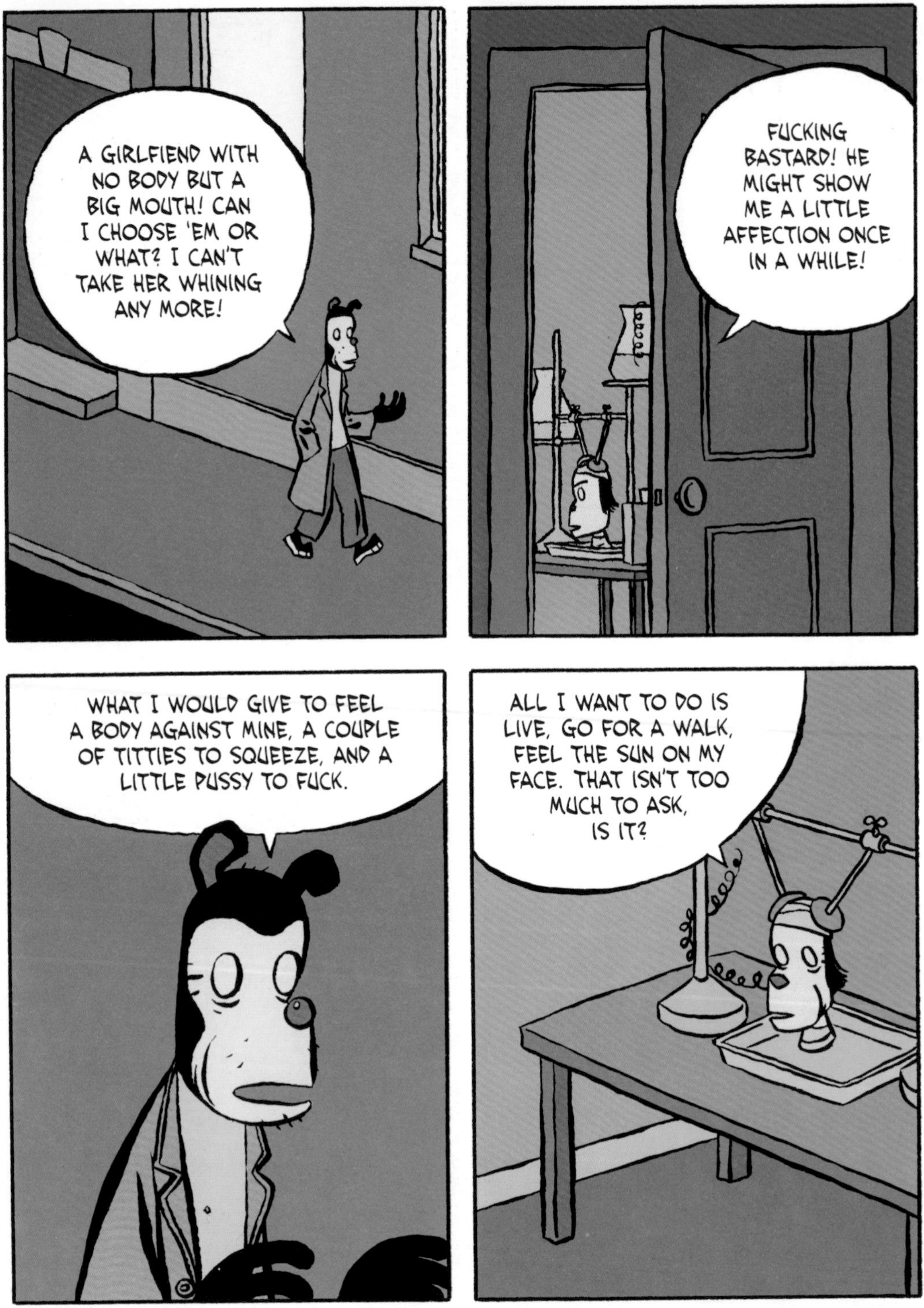
A GIRLFIEND WITH NO BODY BUT A BIG MOUTH! CAN I CHOOSE 'EM OR WHAT? I CAN'T TAKE HER WHINING ANY MORE!
FUCKING BASTARD! HE MIGHT SHOW ME A LITTLE AFFECTION ONCE IN A WHILE!
WHAT I WOULD GIVE TO FEEL A BODY AGAINST MINE, A COUPLE OF TITTIES TO SQUEEZE, AND A LITTLE PUSSY TO FUCK.
ALL I WANT TO DO IS LIVE, GO FOR A WALK, FEEL THE SUN ON MY FACE. THAT ISN'T TOO MUCH TO ASK, IS IT?

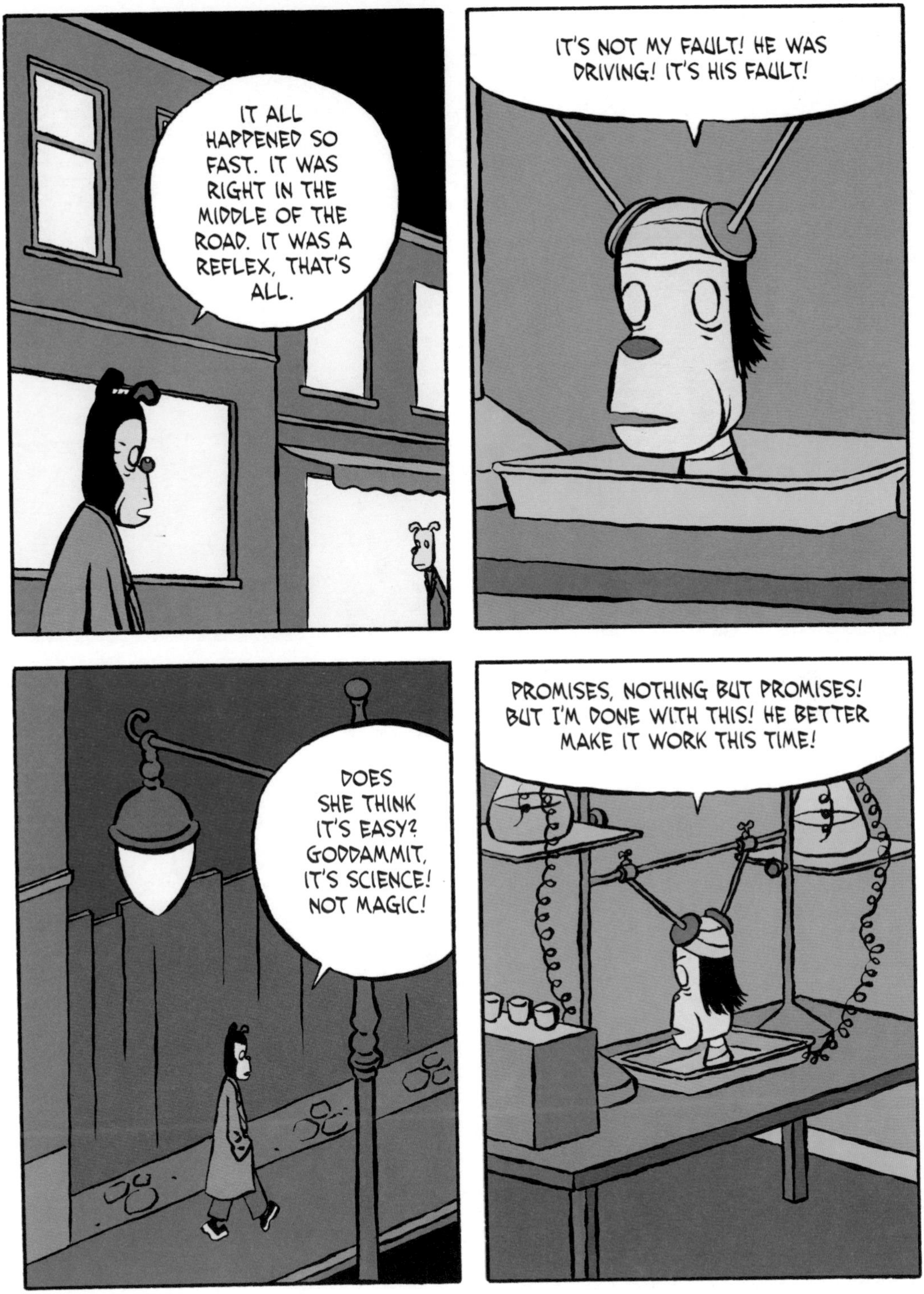
IT ALL HAPPENED SO FAST. IT WAS RIGHT IN THE MIDDLE OF THE ROAD. IT WAS A REFLEX, THAT'S ALL.
IT'S NOT MY FAULT! HE WAS DRIVING! IT'S HIS FAULT!
DOES SHE THINK IT'S EASY? GODDAMMIT, IT'S SCIENCE! NOT MAGIC!
PROMISES, NOTHING BUT PROMISES! BUT I'M DONE WITH THIS! HE BETTER MAKE IT WORK THIS TIME!

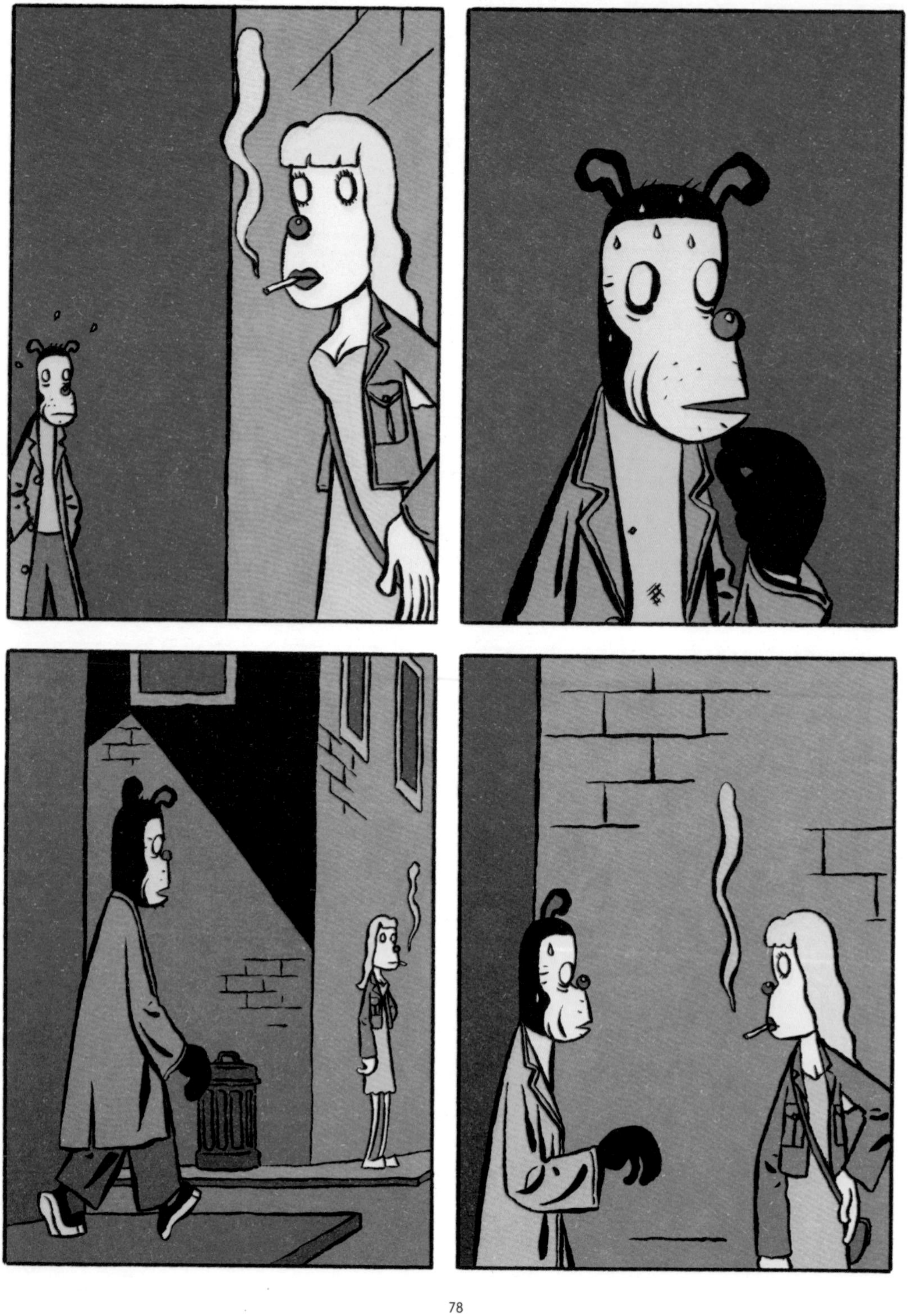

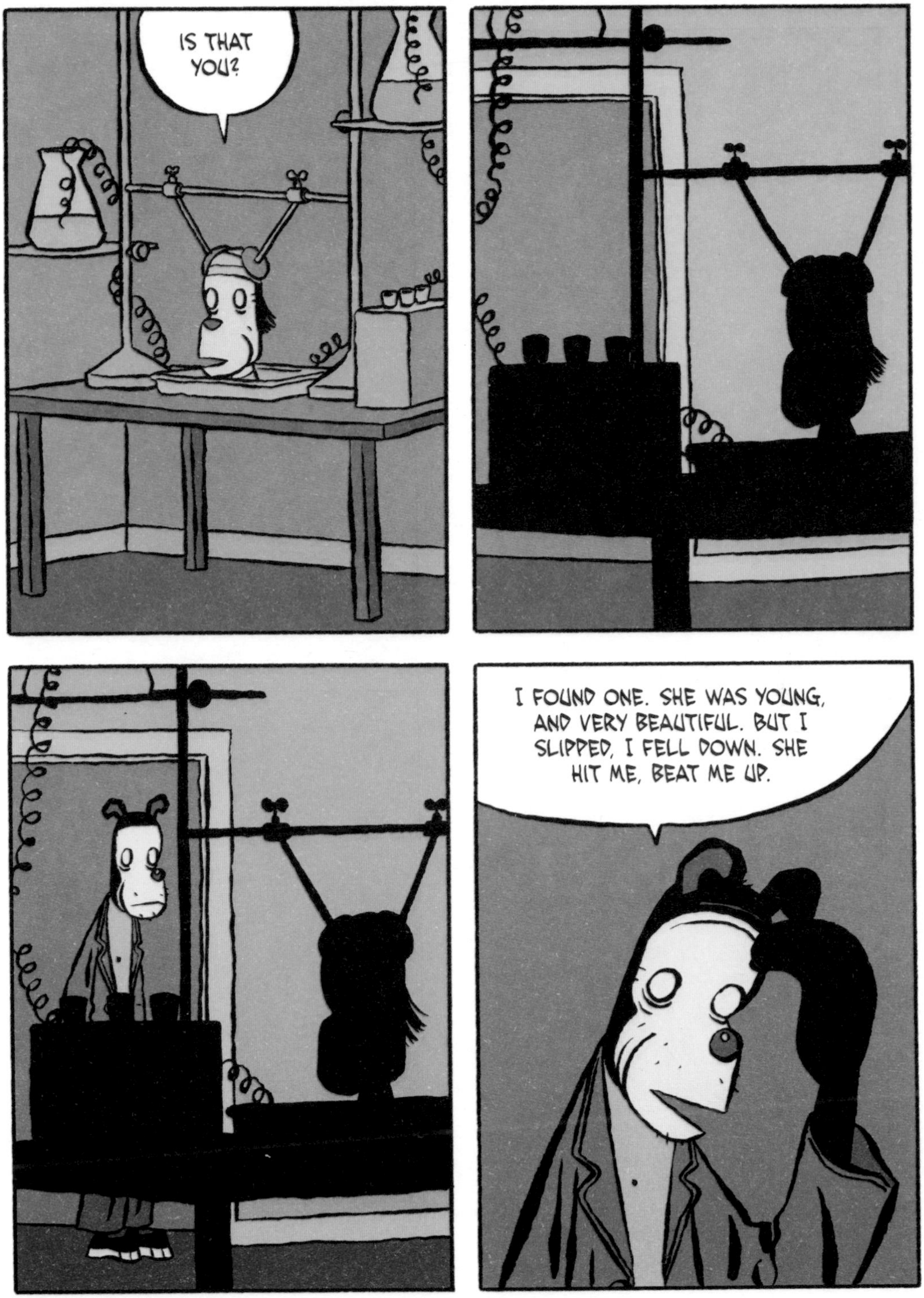
IS THAT YOU?
I FOUND ONE. SHE WAS YOUNG, AND VERY BEAUTIFUL. BUT I SLIPPED, I FELL DOWN. SHE HIT ME, BEAT ME UP.

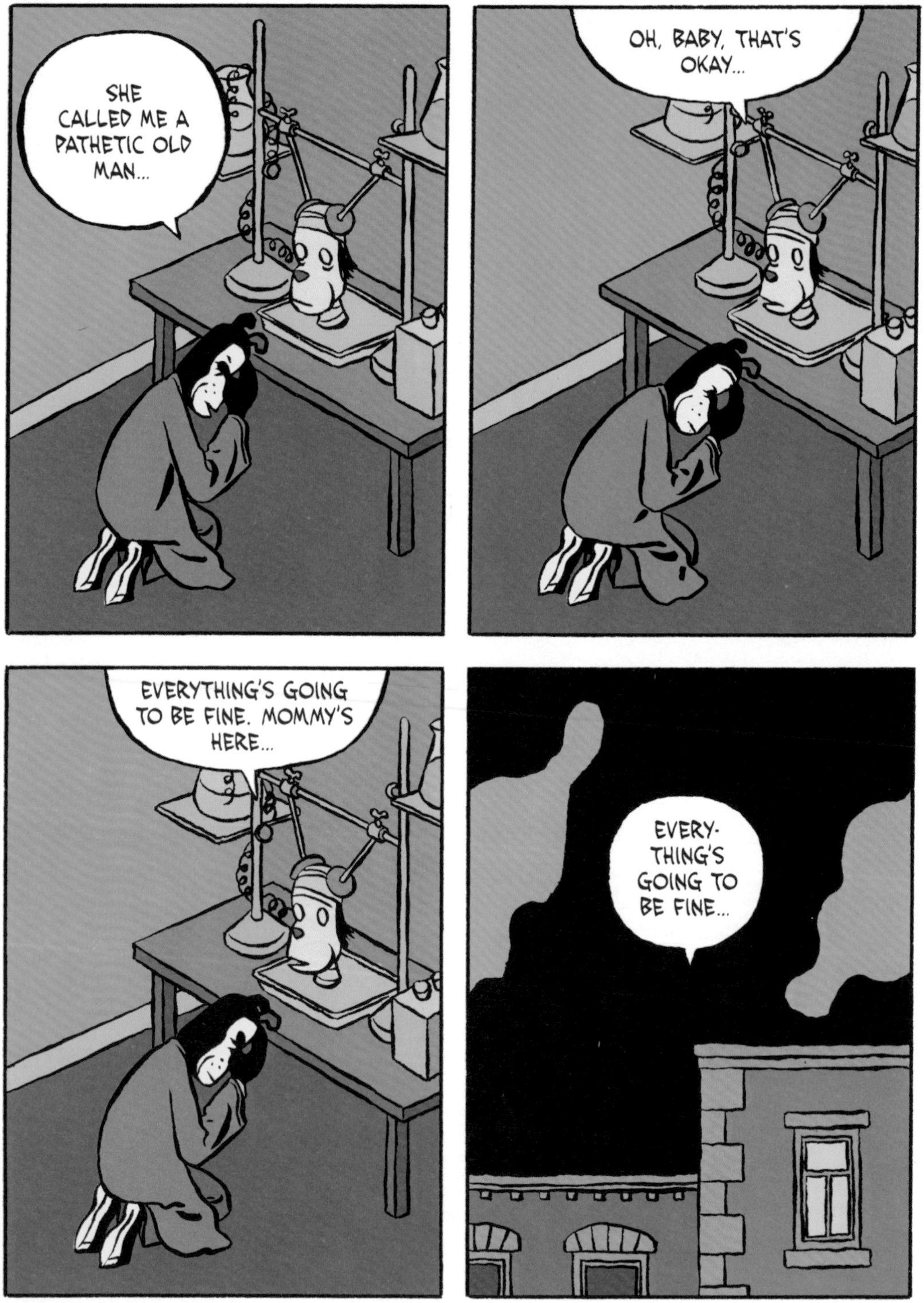
SHE CALLED ME A PATHETIC OLD MAN...
OH, BABY, THAT'S OKAY...
EVERYTHING'S GOING TO BE FINE. MOMMY'S HERE...
EVERY-THING'S GOING TO BE FINE...

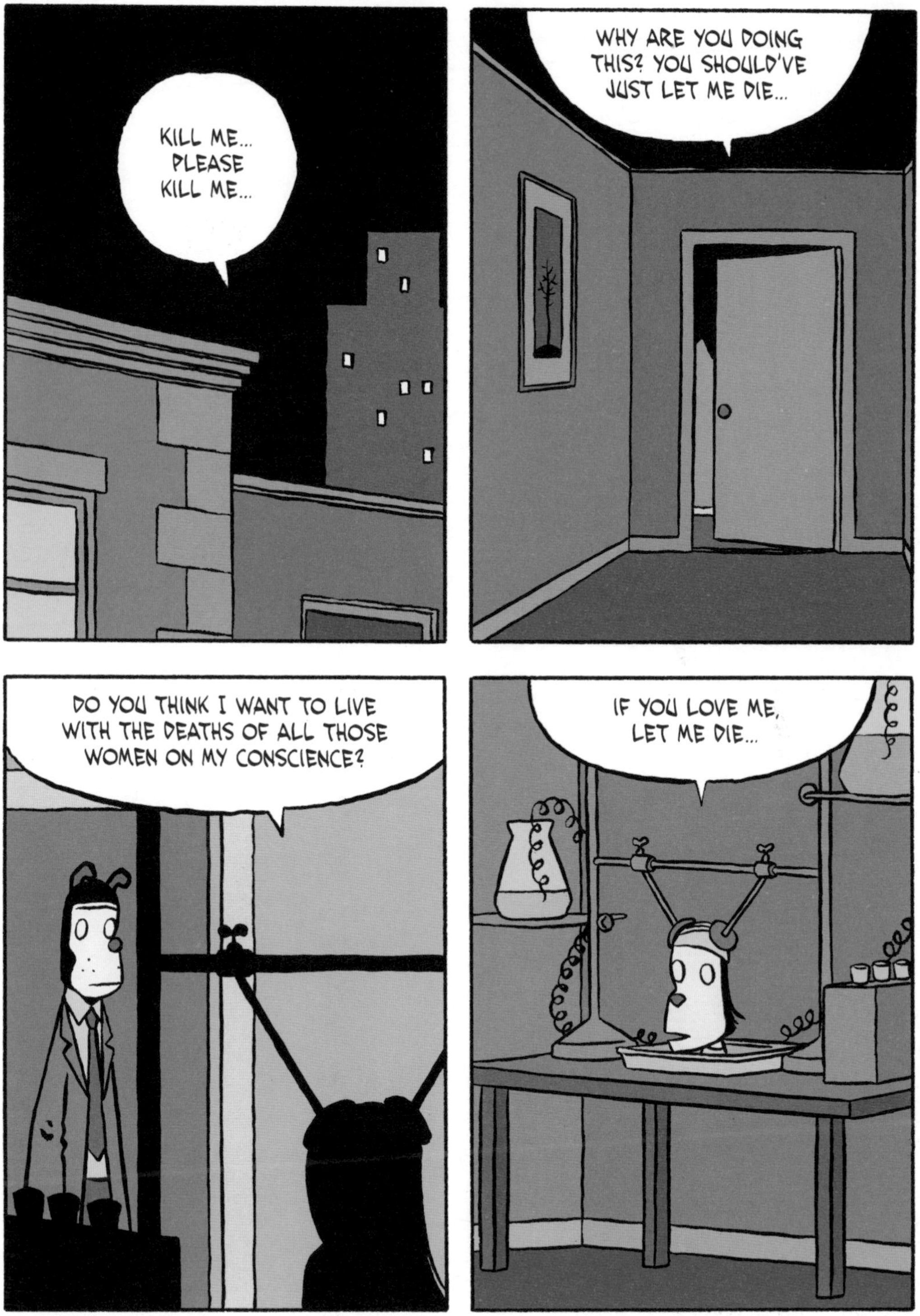
KILL ME... PLEASE KILL ME...
WHY ARE YOU DOING THIS? YOU SHOULD'VE JUST LET ME DIE...
DO YOU THINK I WANT TO LIVE WITH THE DEATHS OF ALL THOSE WOMEN ON MY CONSCIENCE?
IF YOU LOVE ME, LET ME DIE...

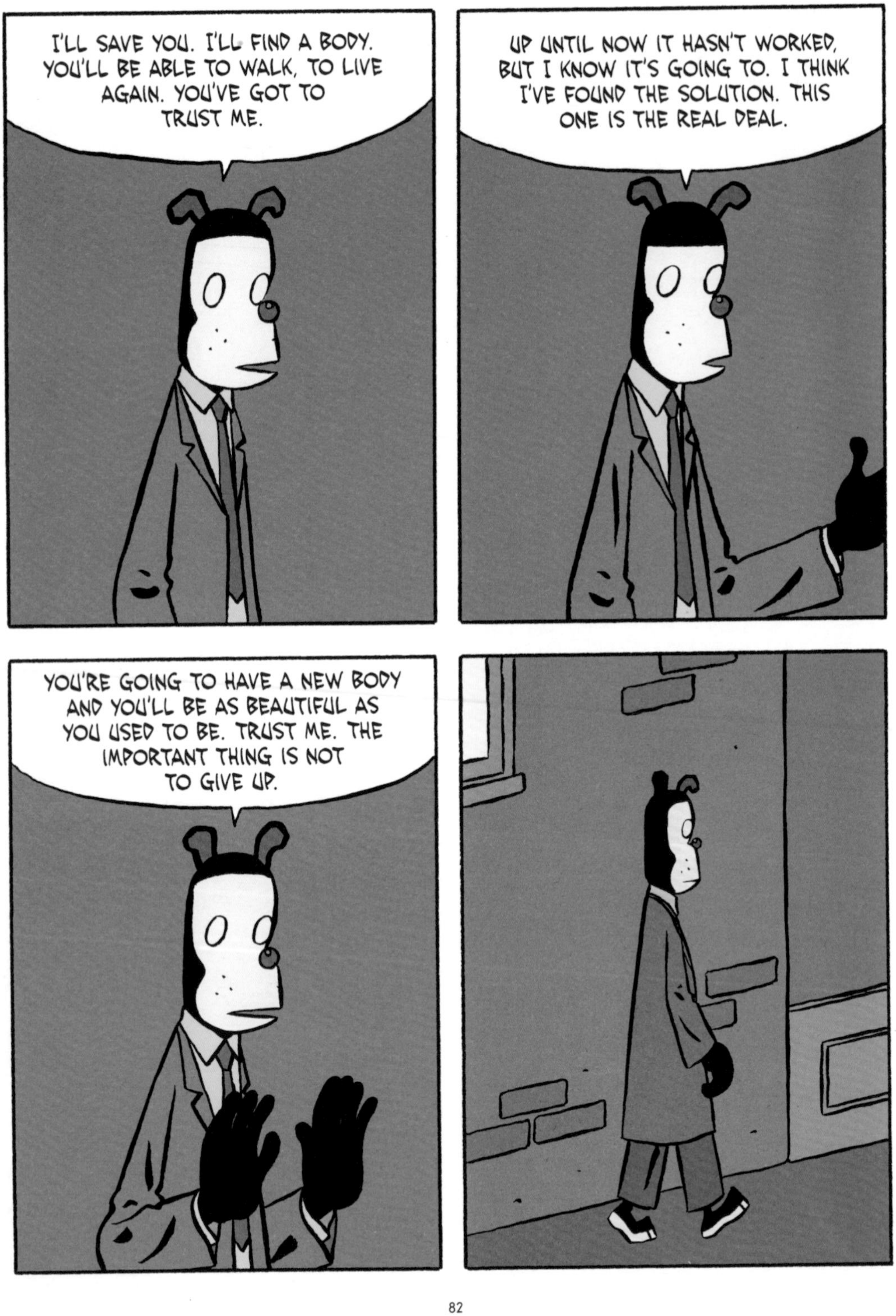
I'LL SAVE YOU. I'LL FIND A BODY. YOU'LL BE ABLE TO WALK, TO LIVE AGAIN. YOU'VE GOT TO TRUST ME.
UP UNTIL NOW IT HASN'T WORKED, BUT I KNOW IT'S GOING TO. I THINK I'VE FOUND THE SOLUTION. THIS ONE IS THE REAL DEAL.
YOU'RE GOING TO HAVE A NEW BODY AND YOU'LL BE AS BEAUTIFUL AS YOU USED TO BE. TRUST ME. THE IMPORTANT THING IS NOT TO GIVE UP.

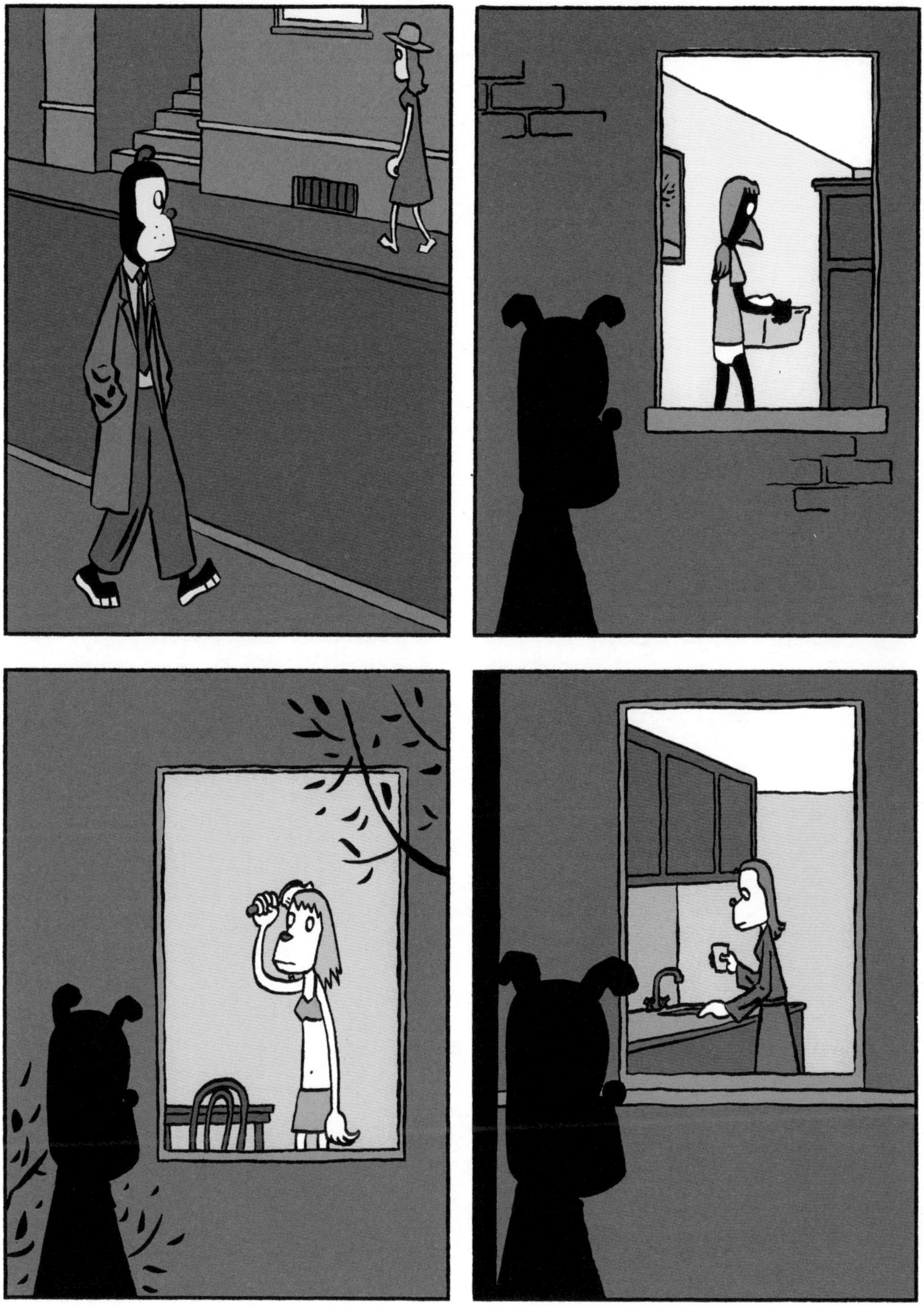

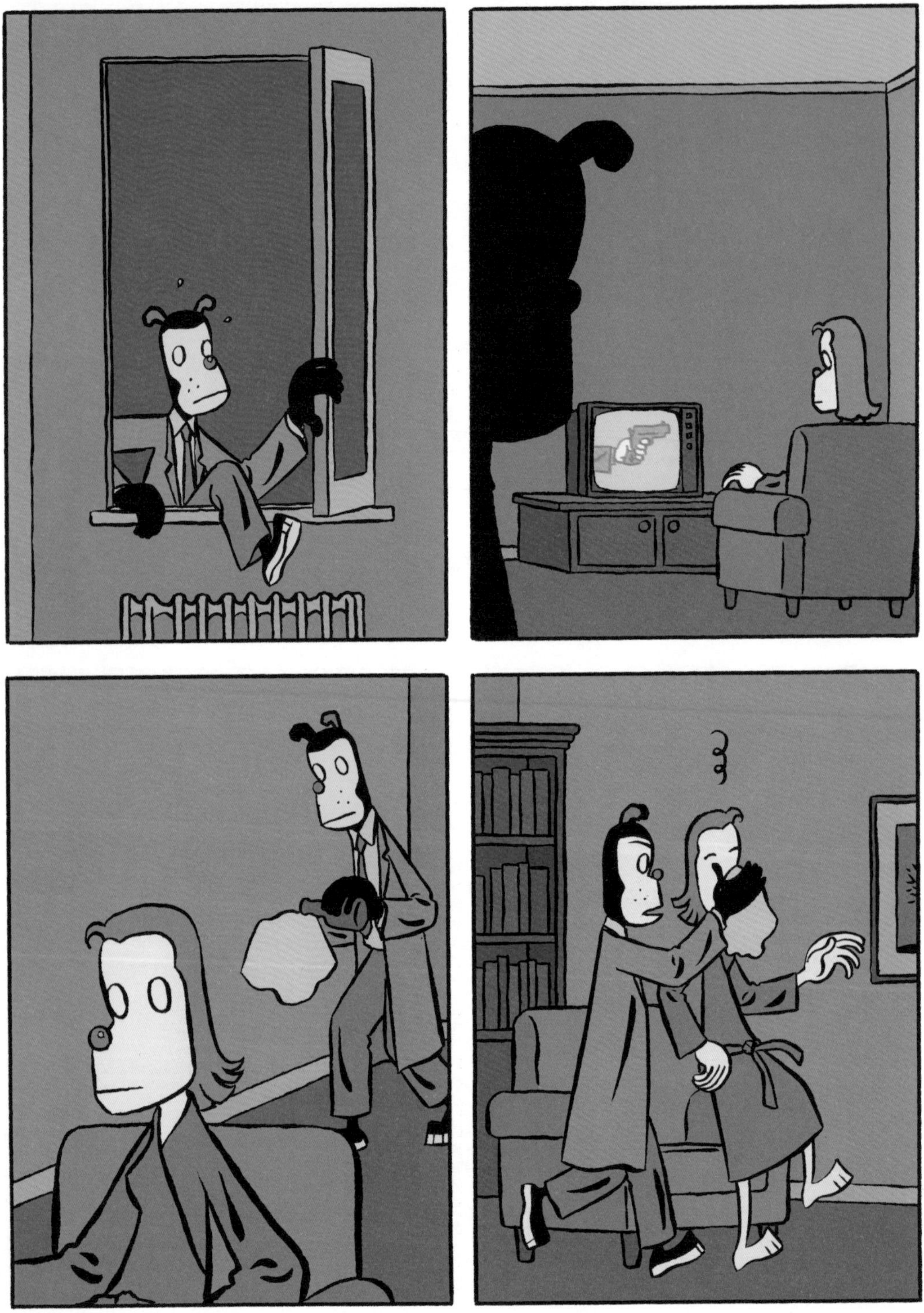

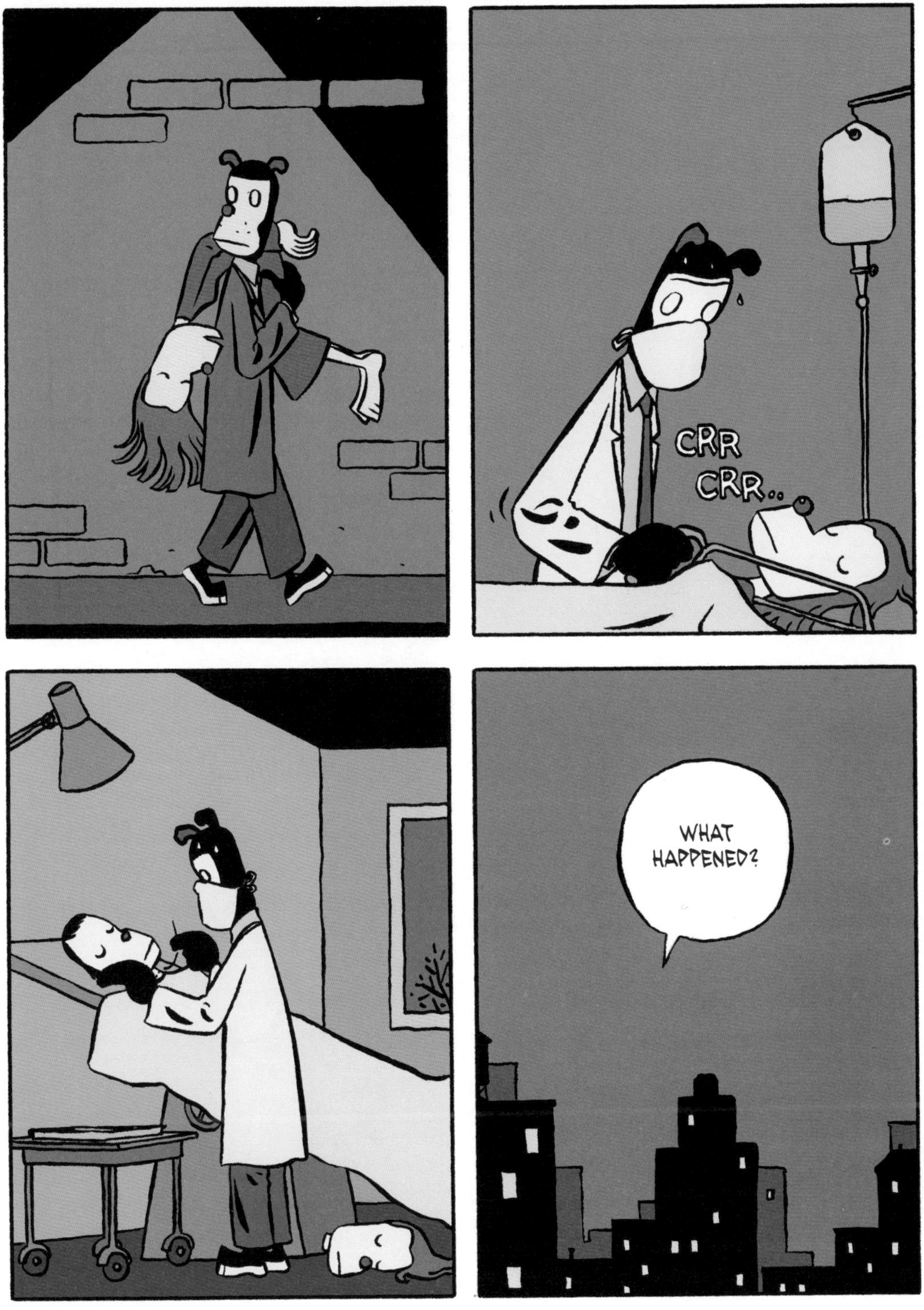
CRR
CRR..
WHAT HAPPENED?

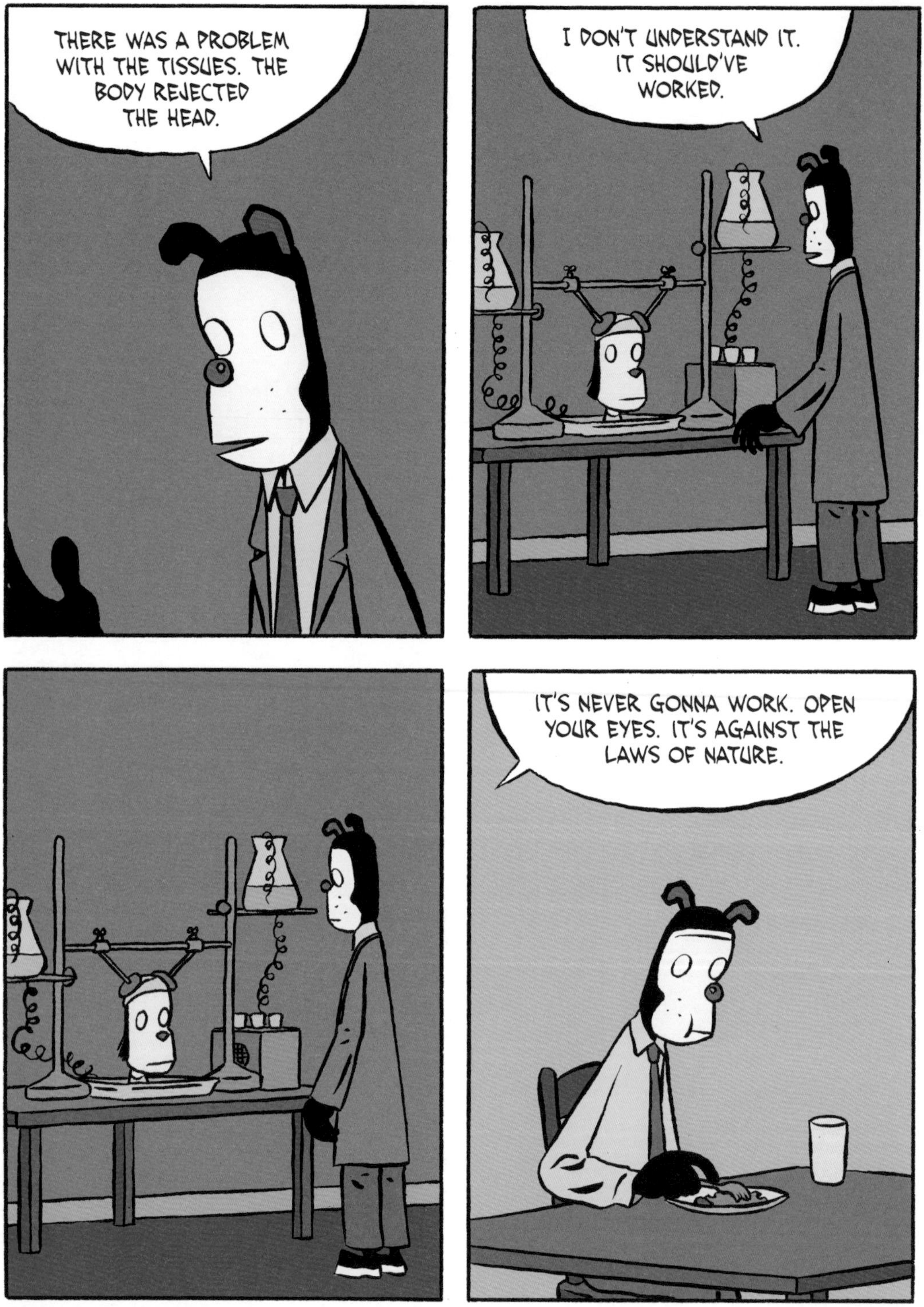
THERE WAS A PROBLEM WITH THE TISSUES. THE BODY REJECTED THE HEAD.
I DON'T UNDERSTAND IT. IT SHOULD'VE WORKED.
IT'S NEVER GONNA WORK. OPEN YOUR EYES. IT'S AGAINST THE LAWS OF NATURE.

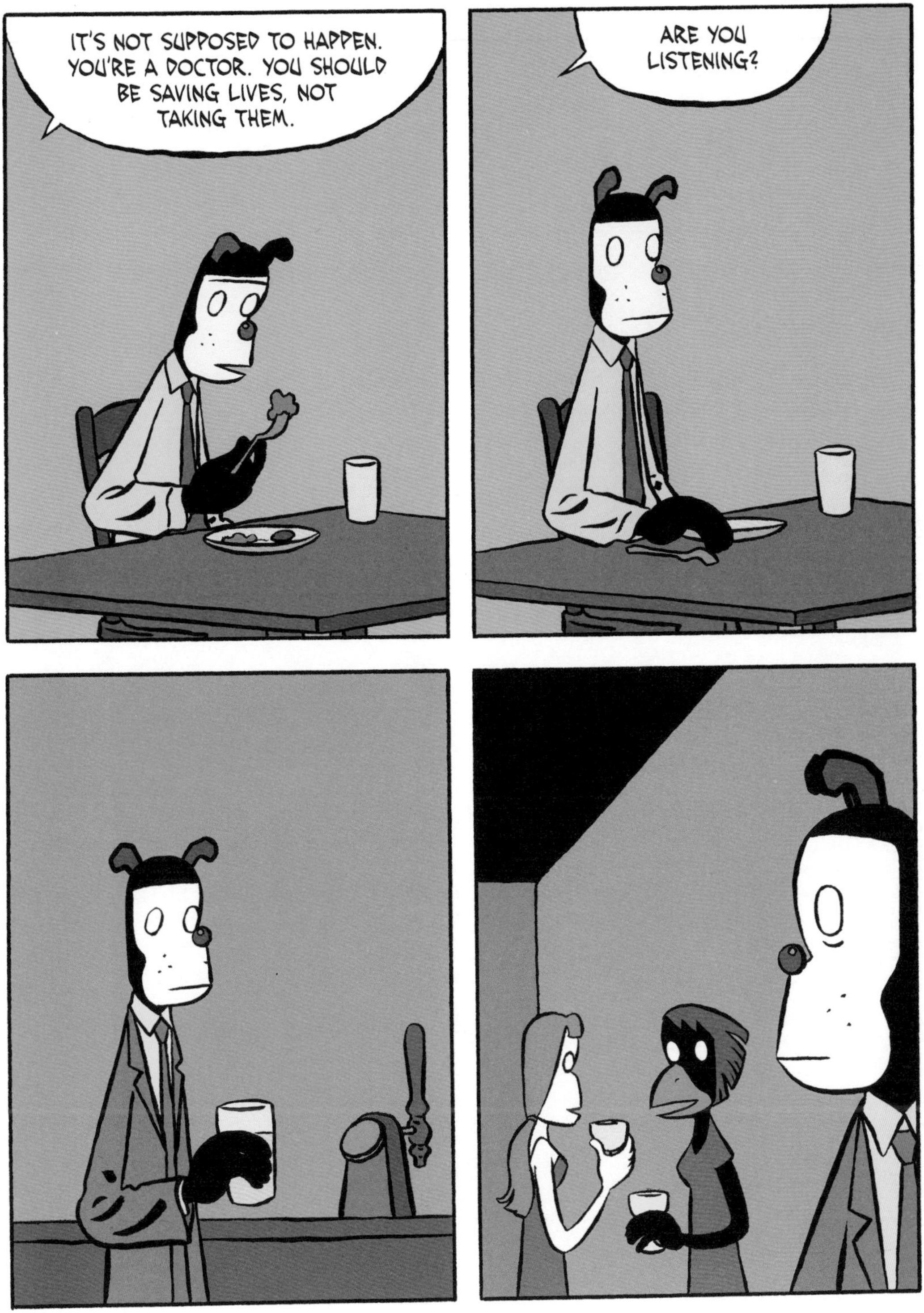
IT'S NOT SUPPOSED TO HAPPEN. YOU'RE A DOCTOR. YOU SHOULD BE SAVING LIVES, NOT TAKING THEM.
ARE YOU LISTENING?

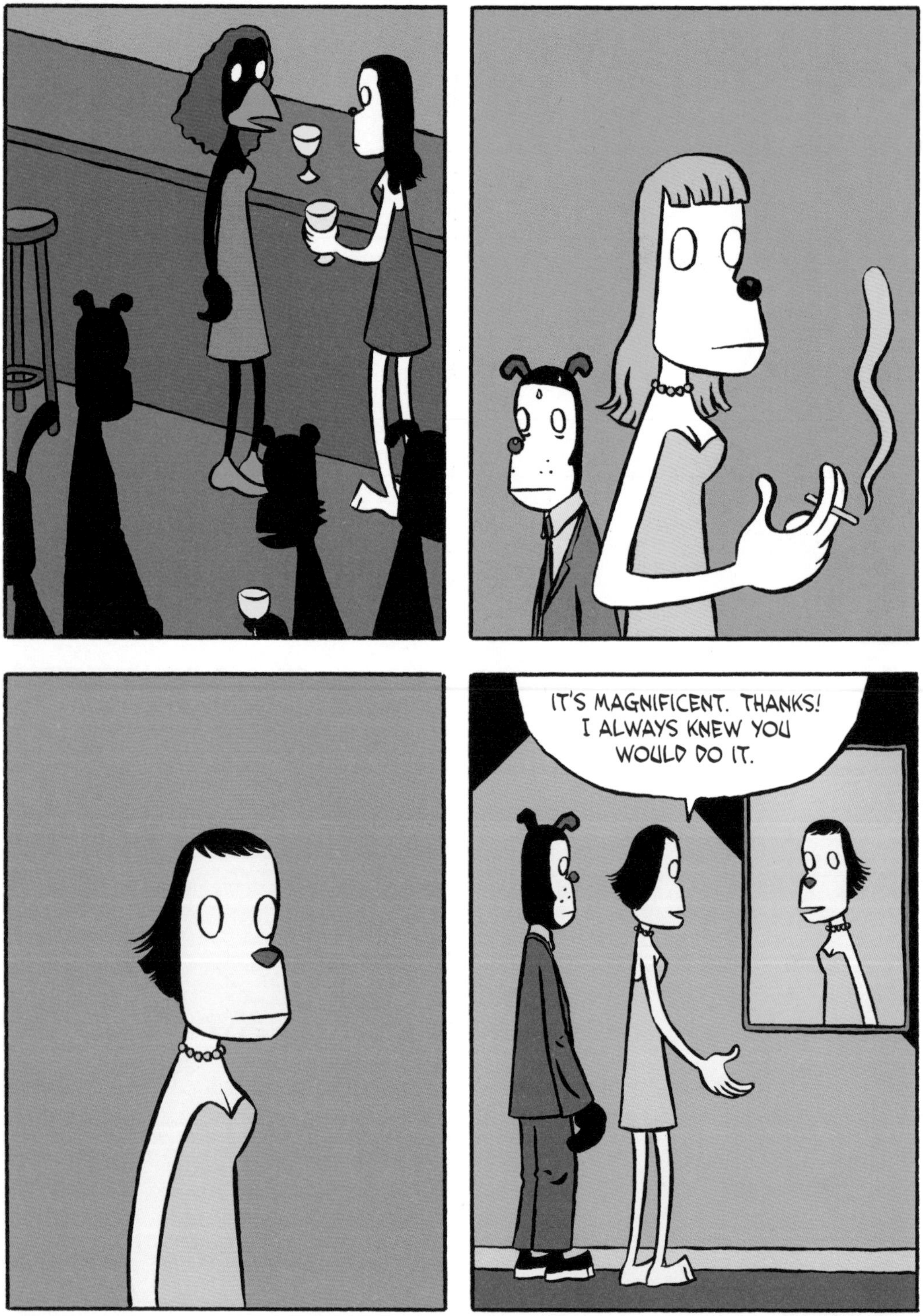
IT'S MAGNIFICENT. THANKS! I ALWAYS KNEW YOU WOULD DO IT.

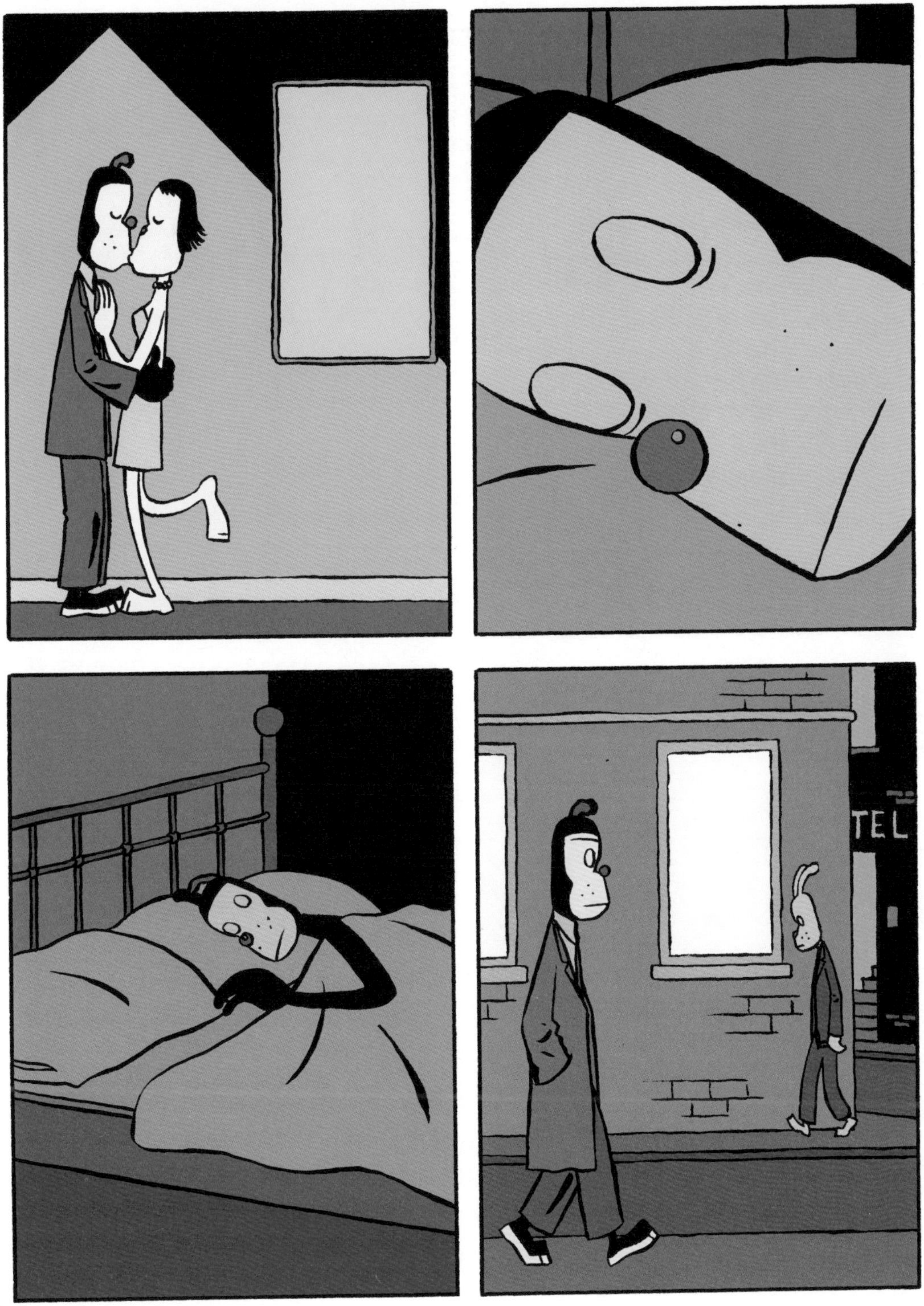
TEL

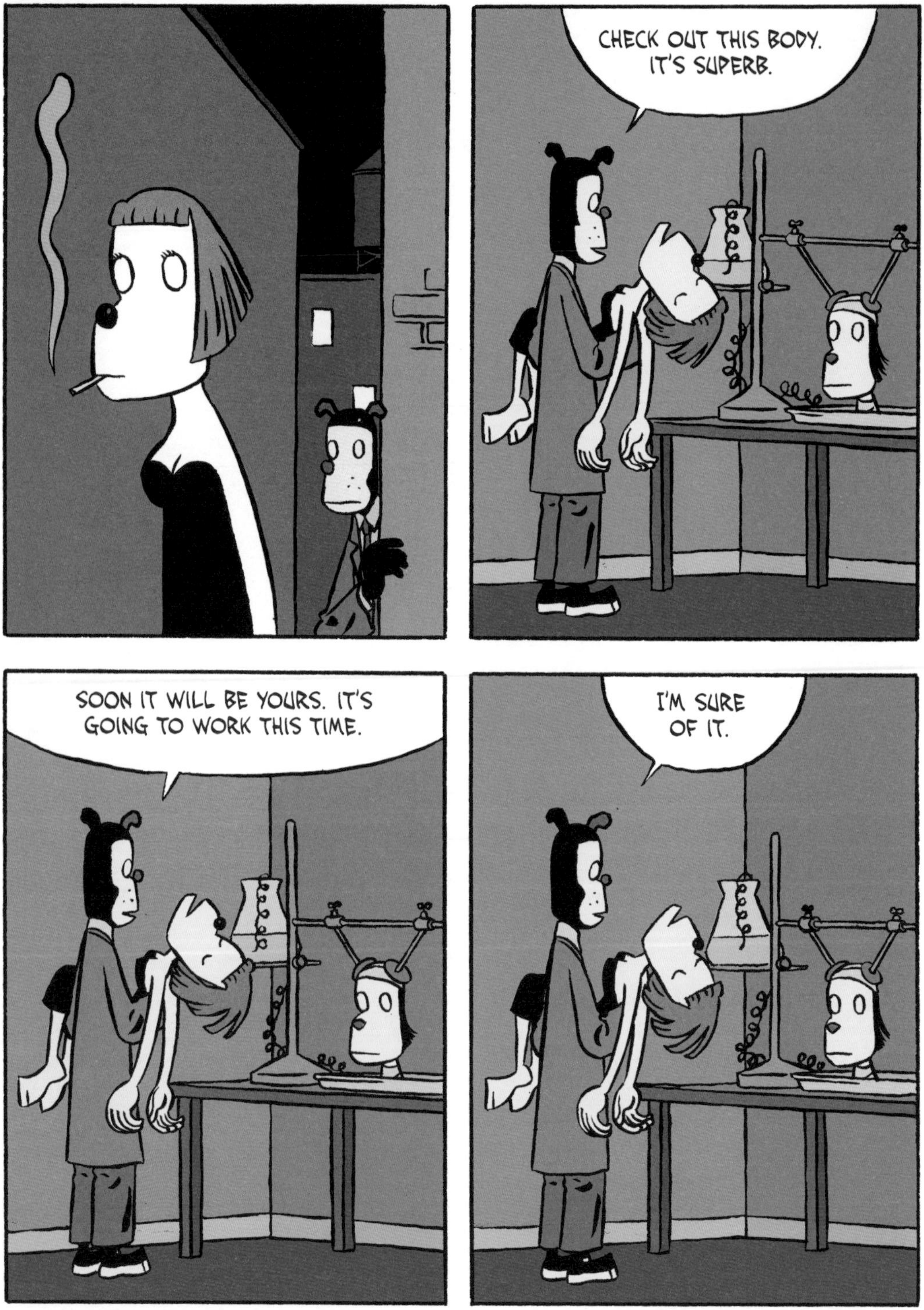
CHECK OUT THIS BODY. IT'S SUPERB.
SOON IT WILL BE YOURS. IT'S GOING TO WORK THIS TIME.
I'M SURE OF IT.

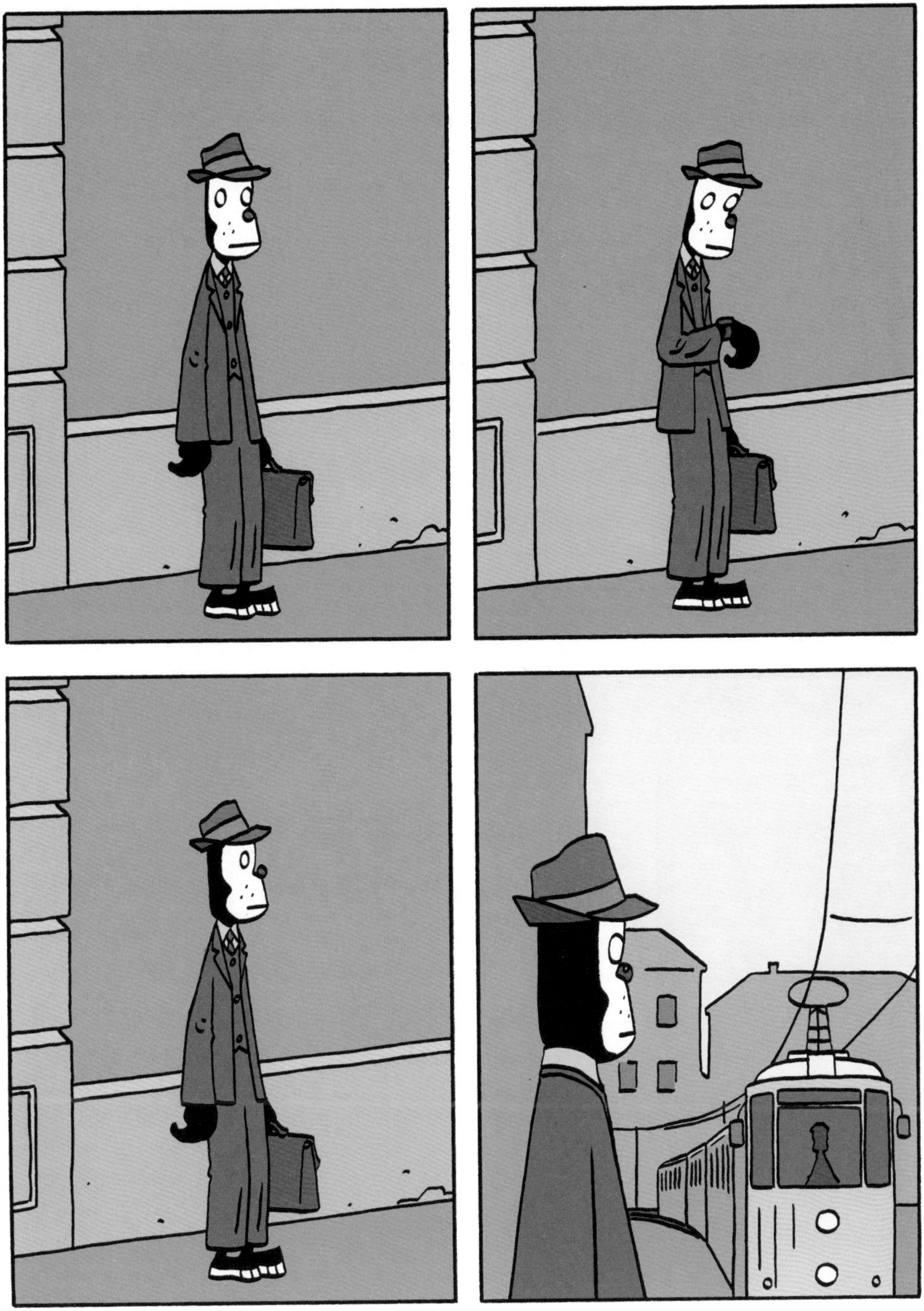

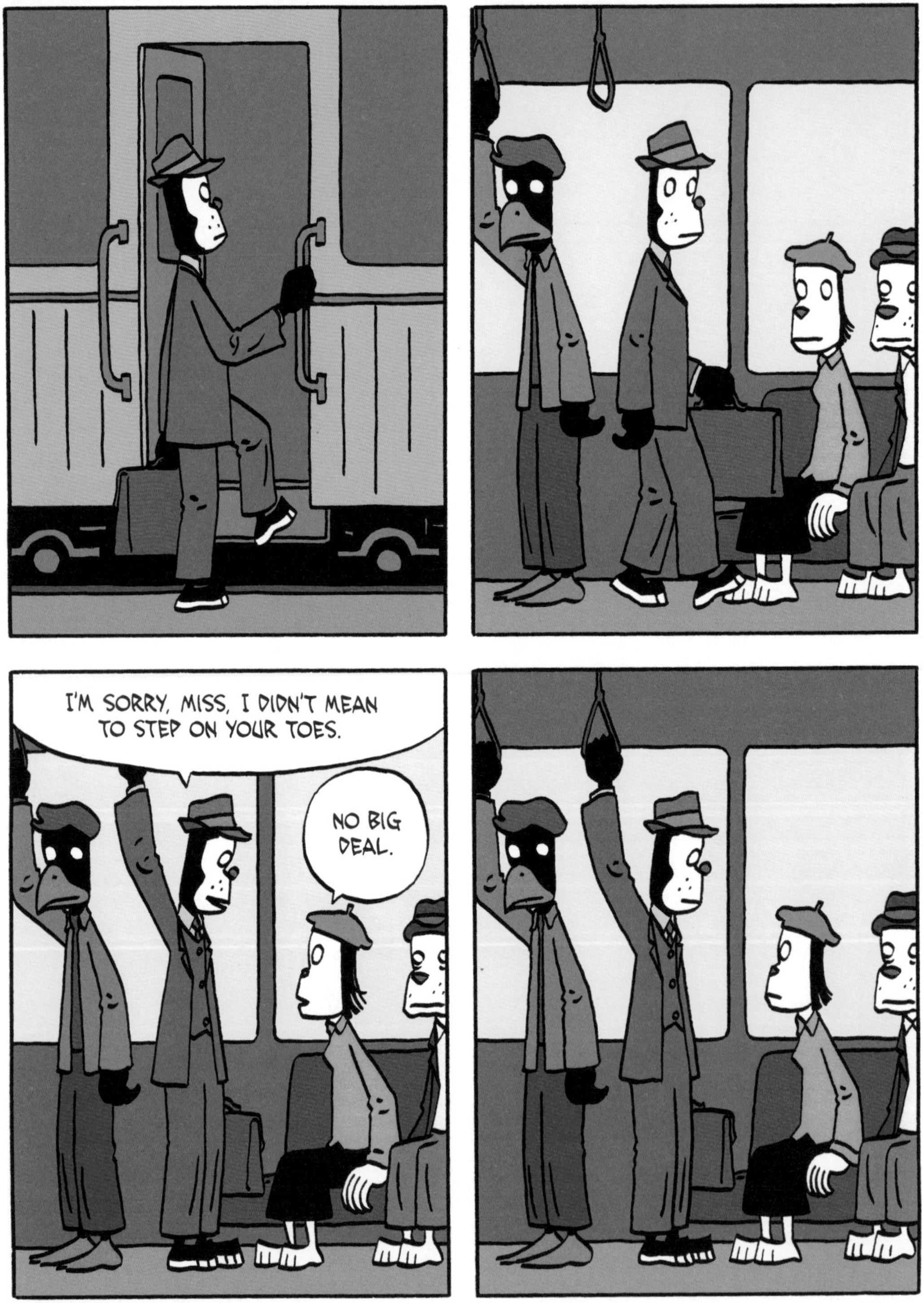
I'M SORRY, MISS, I DIDN'T MEAN TO STEP ON YOUR TOES.
NO BIG DEAL.

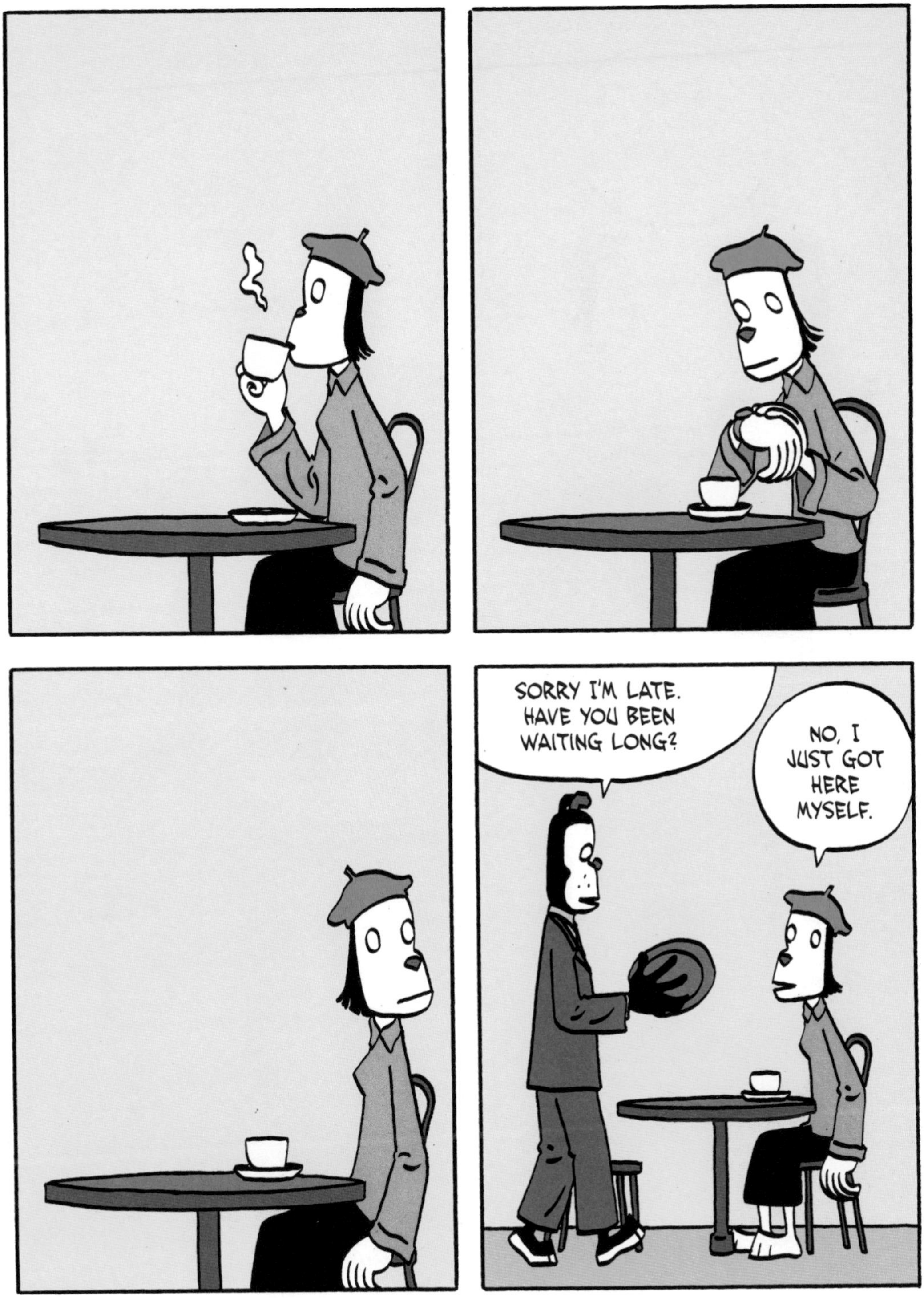
SORRY I'M LATE. HAVE YOU BEEN WAITING LONG?
NO, I JUST GOT HERE MYSELF.

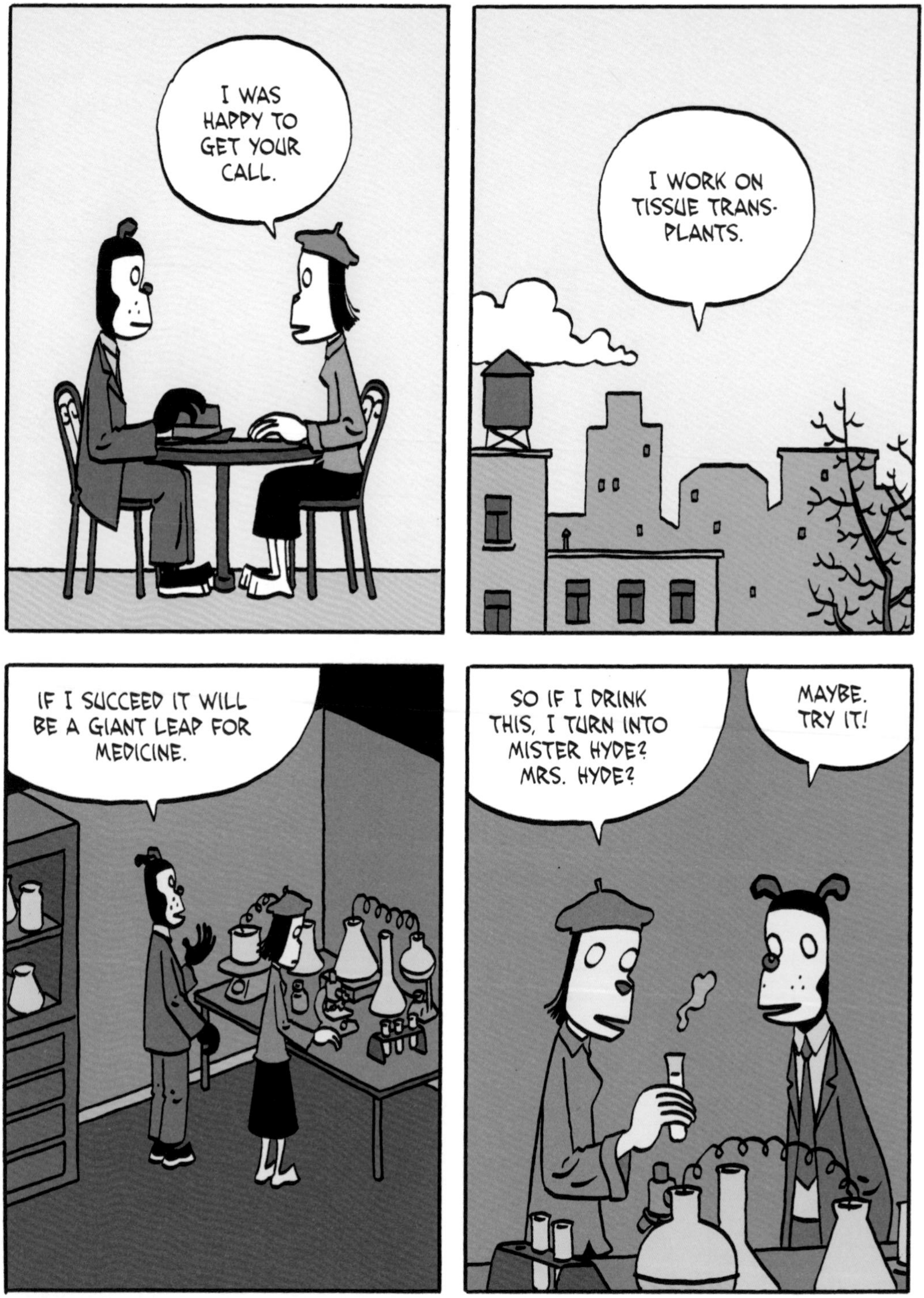
I WAS HAPPY TO GET YOUR CALL.
I WORK ON TISSUE TRANS-PLANTS.
IF I SUCCEED IT WILL BE A GIANT LEAP FOR MEDICINE.
SO IF I DRINK THIS, I TURN INTO MISTER HYDE? MRS. HYDE?
MAYBE. TRY IT!

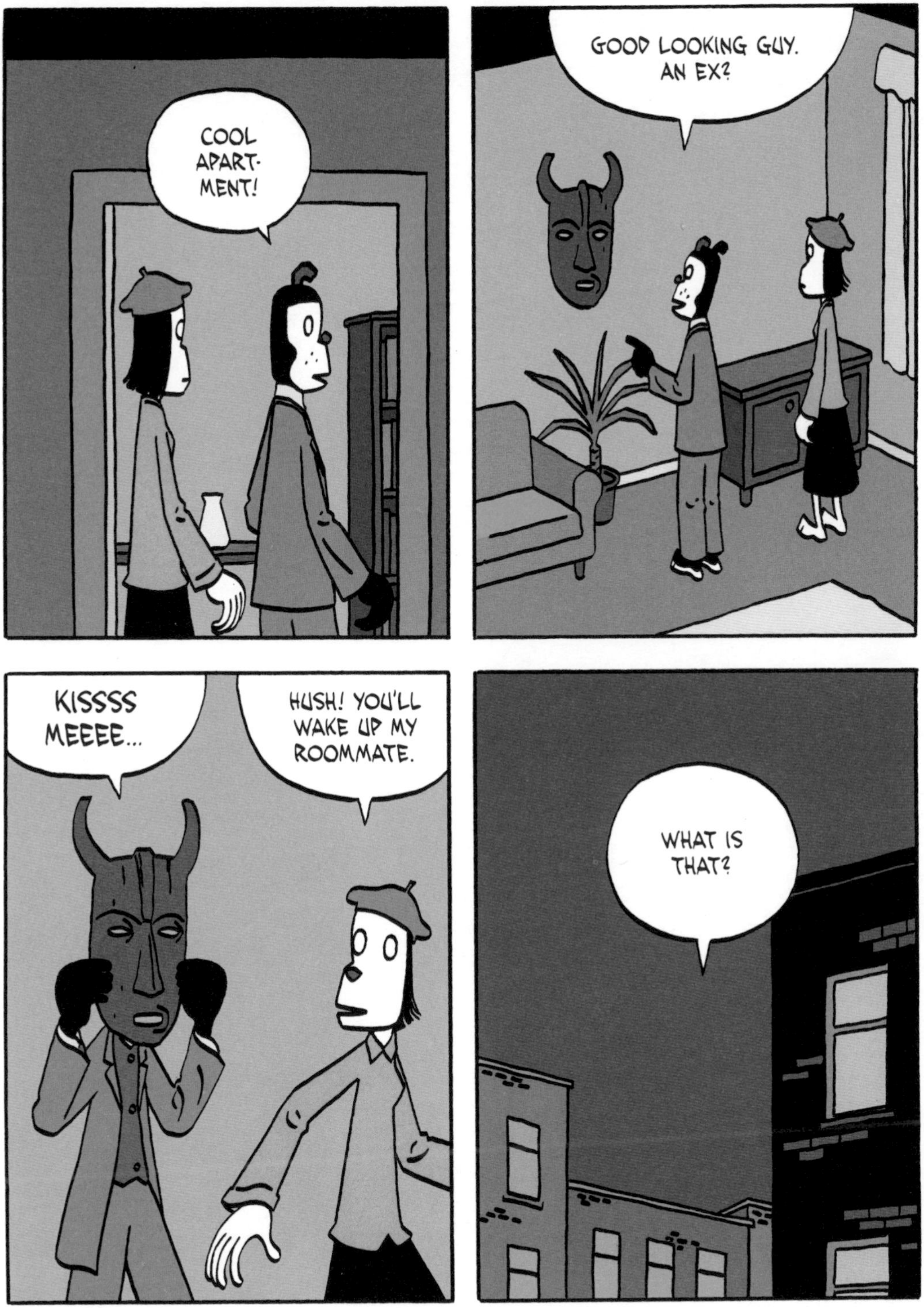
COOL APART-MENT!
GOOD LOOKING GUY. AN EX?
KISSSS MEEEE...
HUSH! YOU'LL WAKE UP MY ROOMMATE.
WHAT IS THAT?

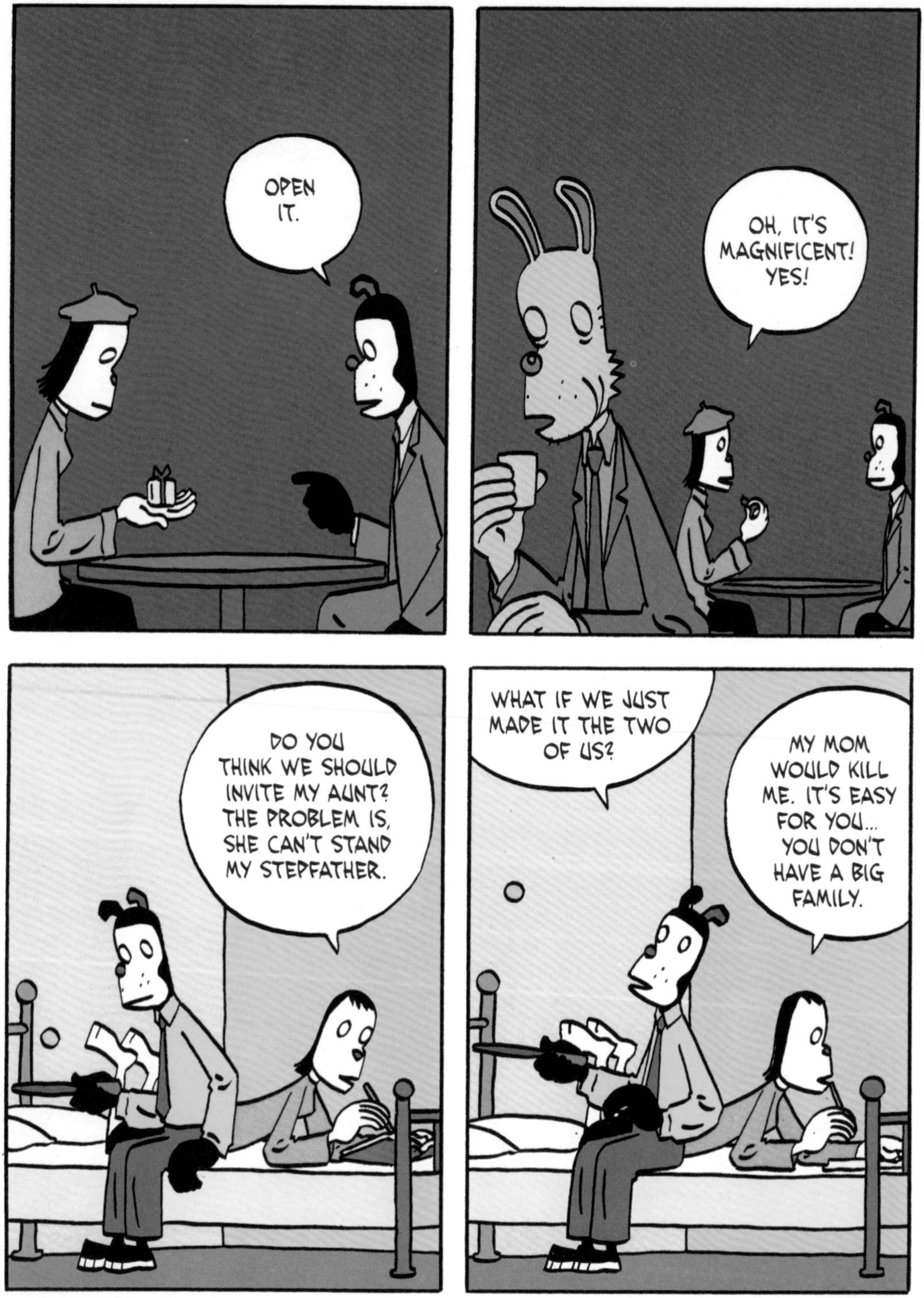
OPEN IT.
OH, IT'S MAGNIFICENT! YES!
DO YOU THINK WE SHOULD INVITE MY AUNT? THE PROBLEM IS, SHE CAN'T STAND MY STEPFATHER.
WHAT IF WE JUST MADE IT THE TWO OF US?
MY MOM WOULD KILL ME. IT'S EASY FOR YOU... YOU DON'T HAVE A BIG FAMILY.

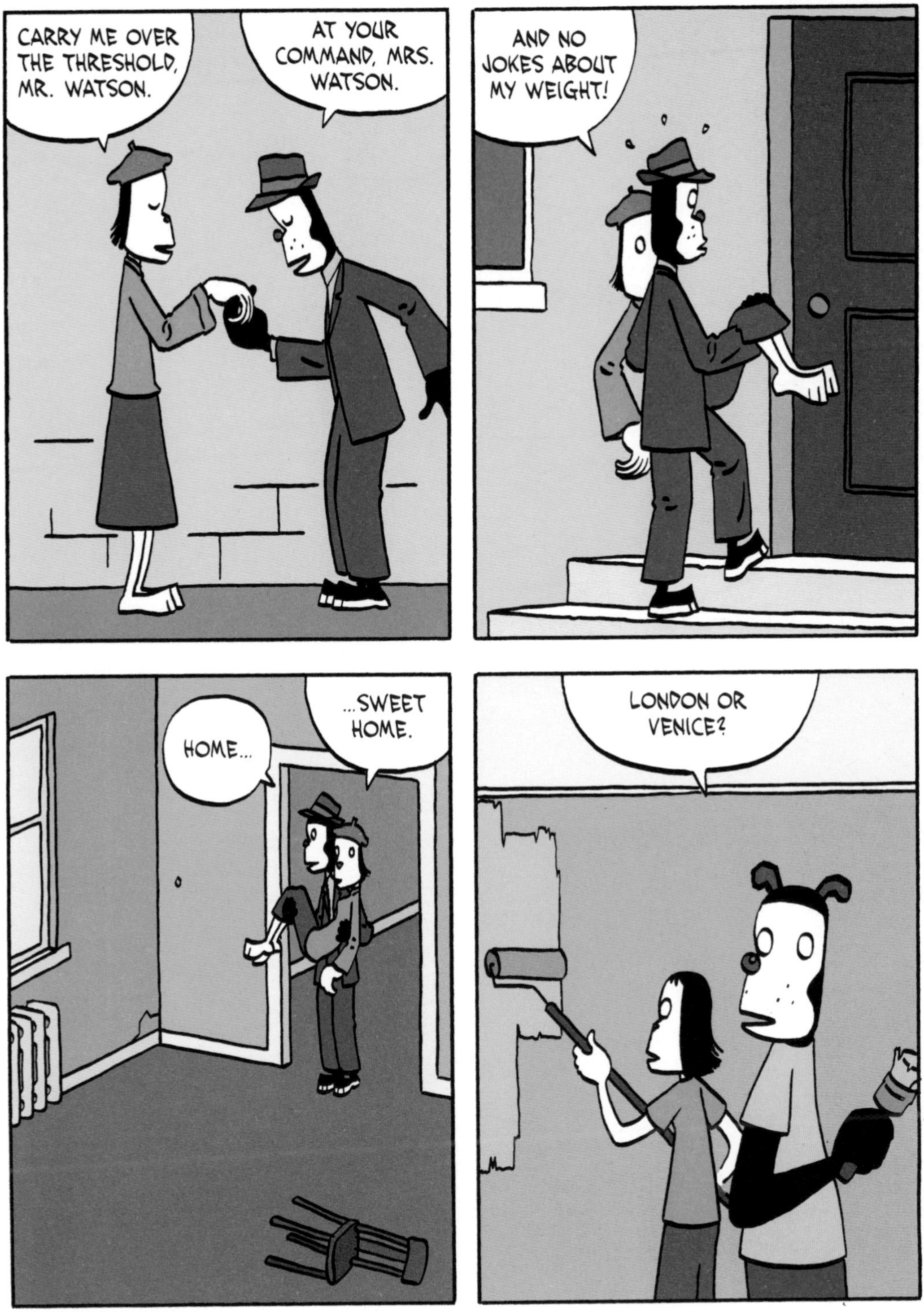
CARRY ME OVER THE THRESHOLD, MR. WATSON.
AT YOUR COMMAND, MRS. WATSON.
AND NO JOKES ABOUT MY WEIGHT!
HOME...
...SWEET HOME.
LONDON OR VENICE?

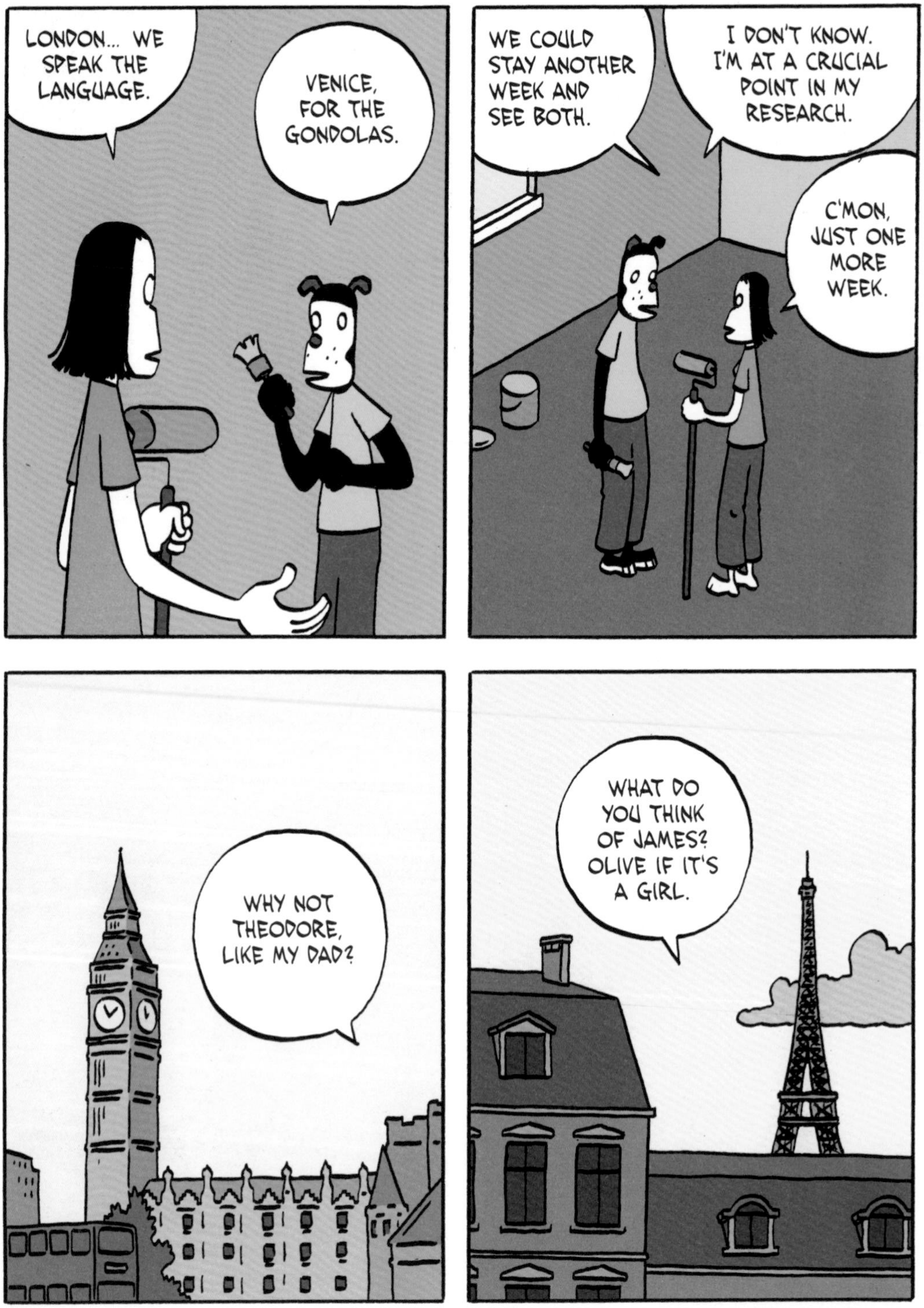
LONDON... WE SPEAK THE LANGUAGE.
VENICE, FOR THE GONDOLAS.
WE COULD STAY ANOTHER WEEK AND SEE BOTH.
I DON'T KNOW. I'M AT A CRUCIAL POINT IN MY RESEARCH.
C'MON, JUST ONE MORE WEEK.
WHY NOT THEODORE, LIKE MY DAD?
WHAT DO YOU THINK OF JAMES? OLIVE IF IT'S A GIRL.

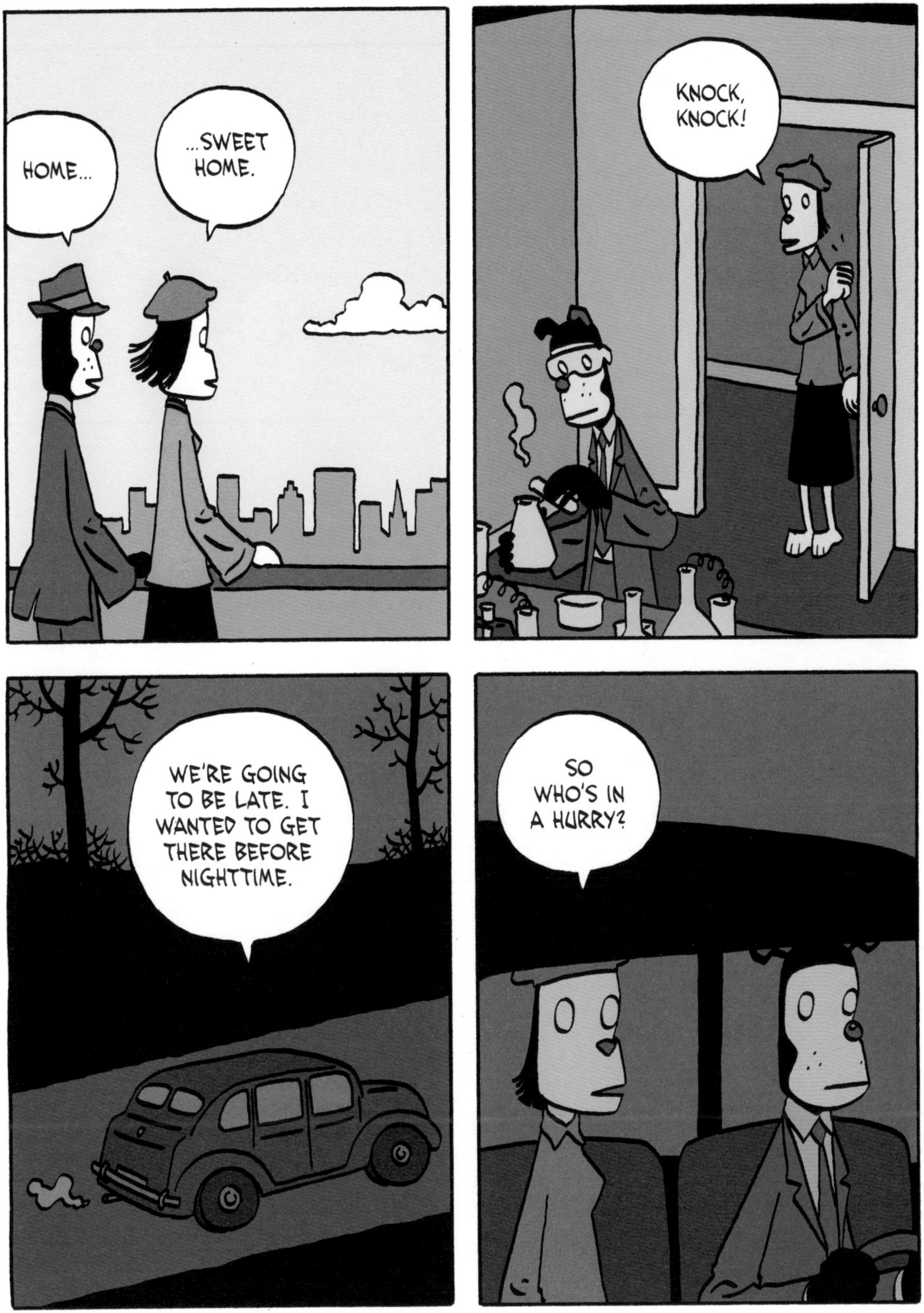
HOME...
...SWEET HOME.
KNOCK, KNOCK!
WE'RE GOING TO BE LATE. I WANTED TO GET THERE BEFORE NIGHTTIME.
SO WHO'S IN A HURRY?

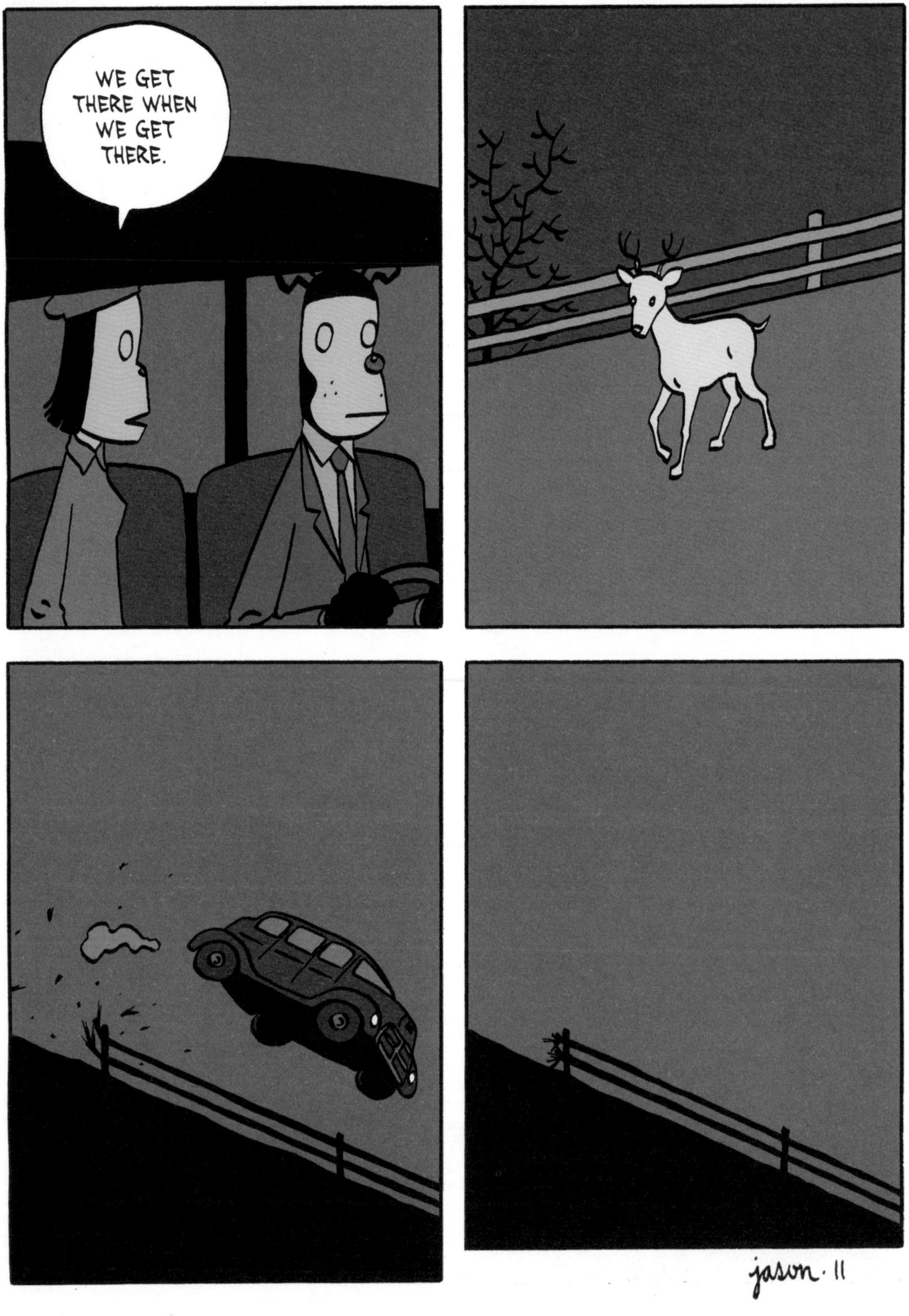
WE GET THERE WHEN WE GET THERE.
jason · 11

PRESENTING:

TOM WAITS ON THE MOON

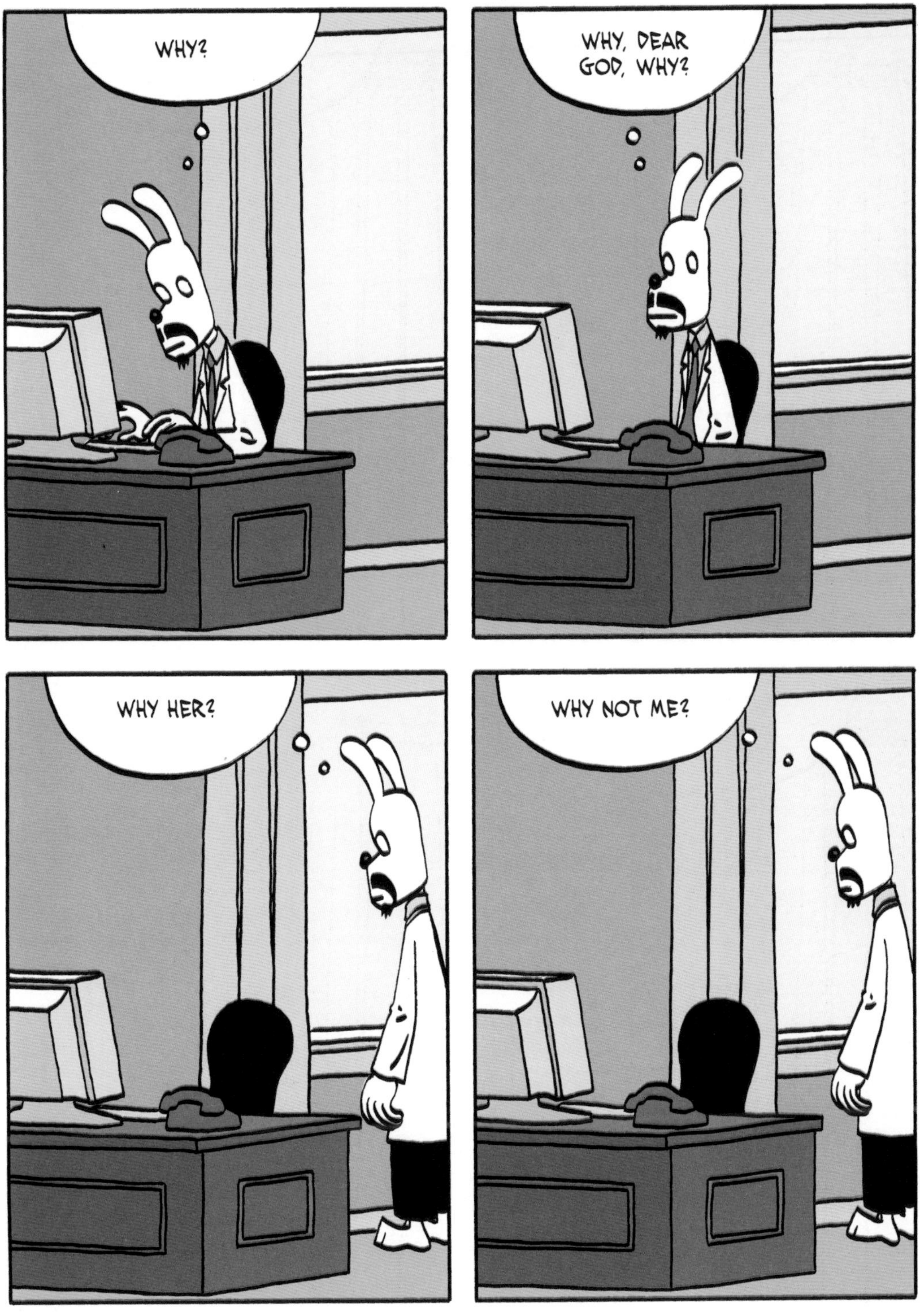
WHY?
WHY, DEAR GOD, WHY?
WHY HER?
WHY NOT ME?

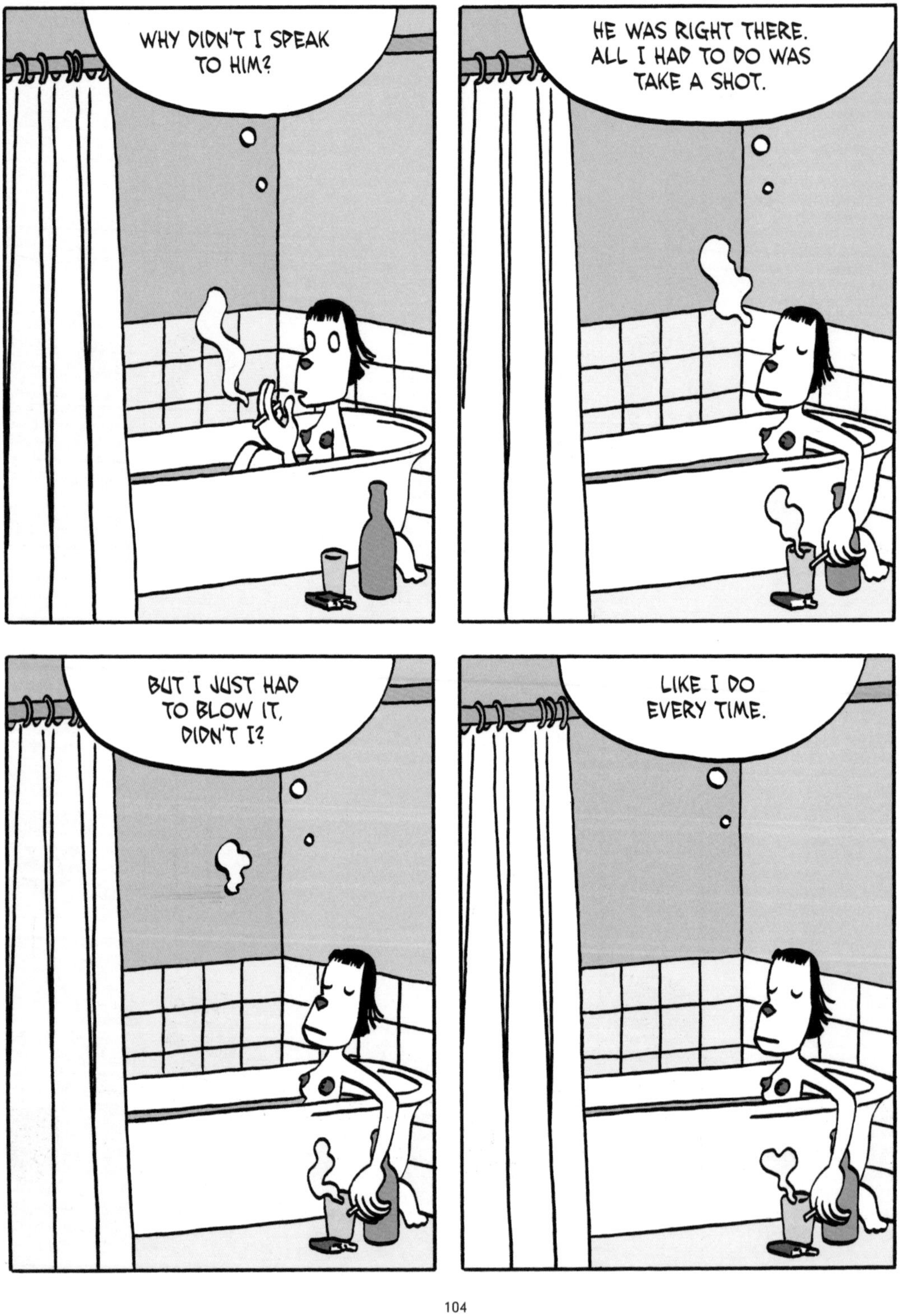
WHY DIDN'T I SPEAK TO HIM?
HE WAS RIGHT THERE. ALL I HAD TO DO WAS TAKE A SHOT.
BUT I JUST HAD TO BLOW IT, DIDN'T I?
LIKE I DO EVERY TIME.

I'M GONNA FUCK YOUR ASS. YOU LIKE THAT, DON'T YOU, BITCH?
TURN AROUND AND GET ON YOUR KNEES. 'CAUSE I SAID SO.
YEAH, YOU SUCK IT, BABY, SUCK IT GOOD. SUCK HARD AND SWALLOW.

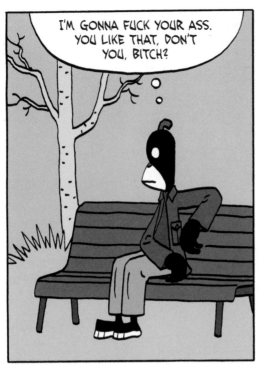

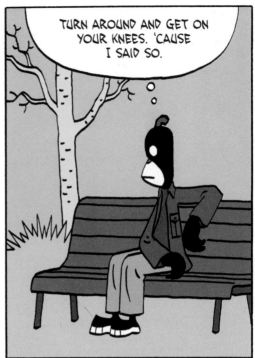

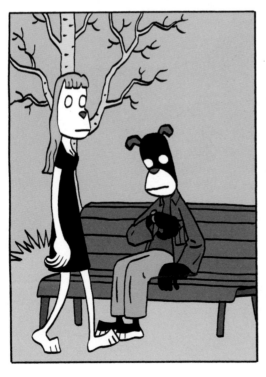

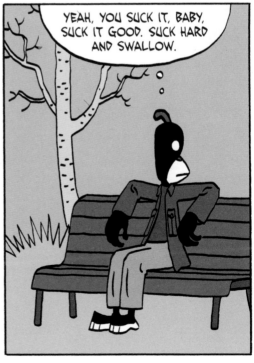

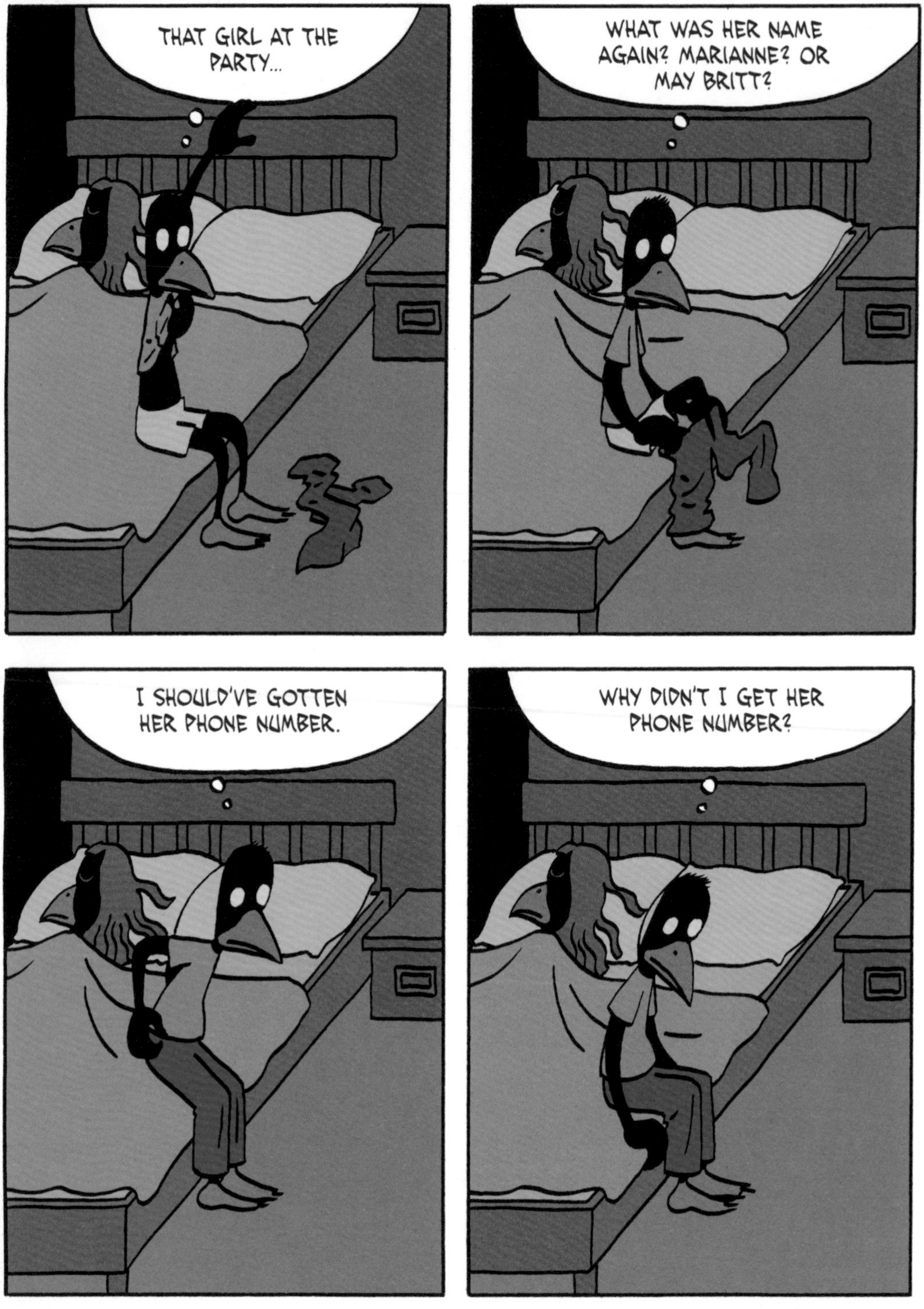
THAT GIRL AT THE PARTY...
WHAT WAS HER NAME AGAIN? MARIANNE? OR MAY BRITT?
I SHOULD'VE GOTTEN HER PHONE NUMBER.
WHY DIDN'T I GET HER PHONE NUMBER?

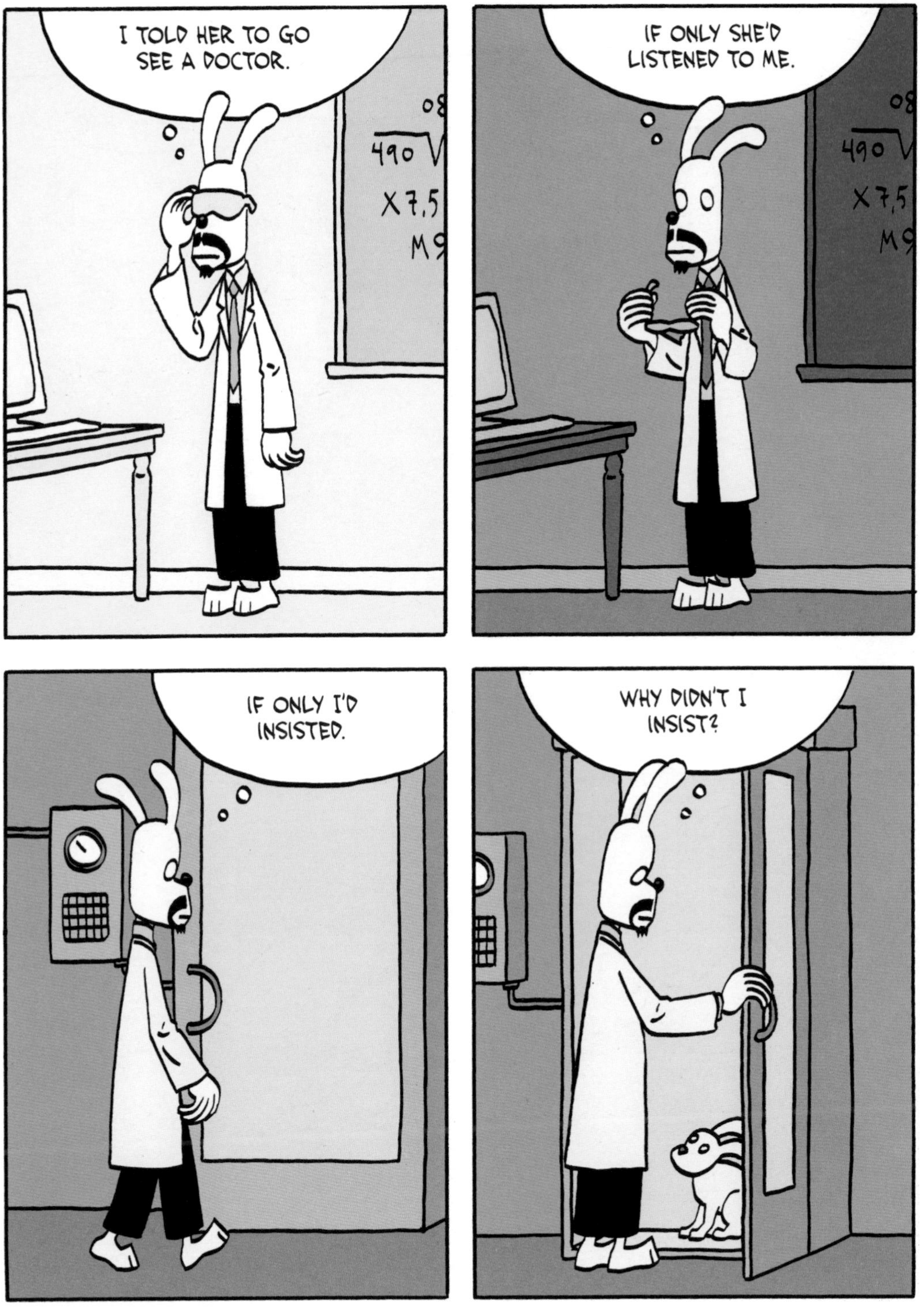
I TOLD HER TO GO SEE A DOCTOR.
IF ONLY SHE'D LISTENED TO ME.
IF ONLY I'D INSISTED.
WHY DIDN'T I INSIST?

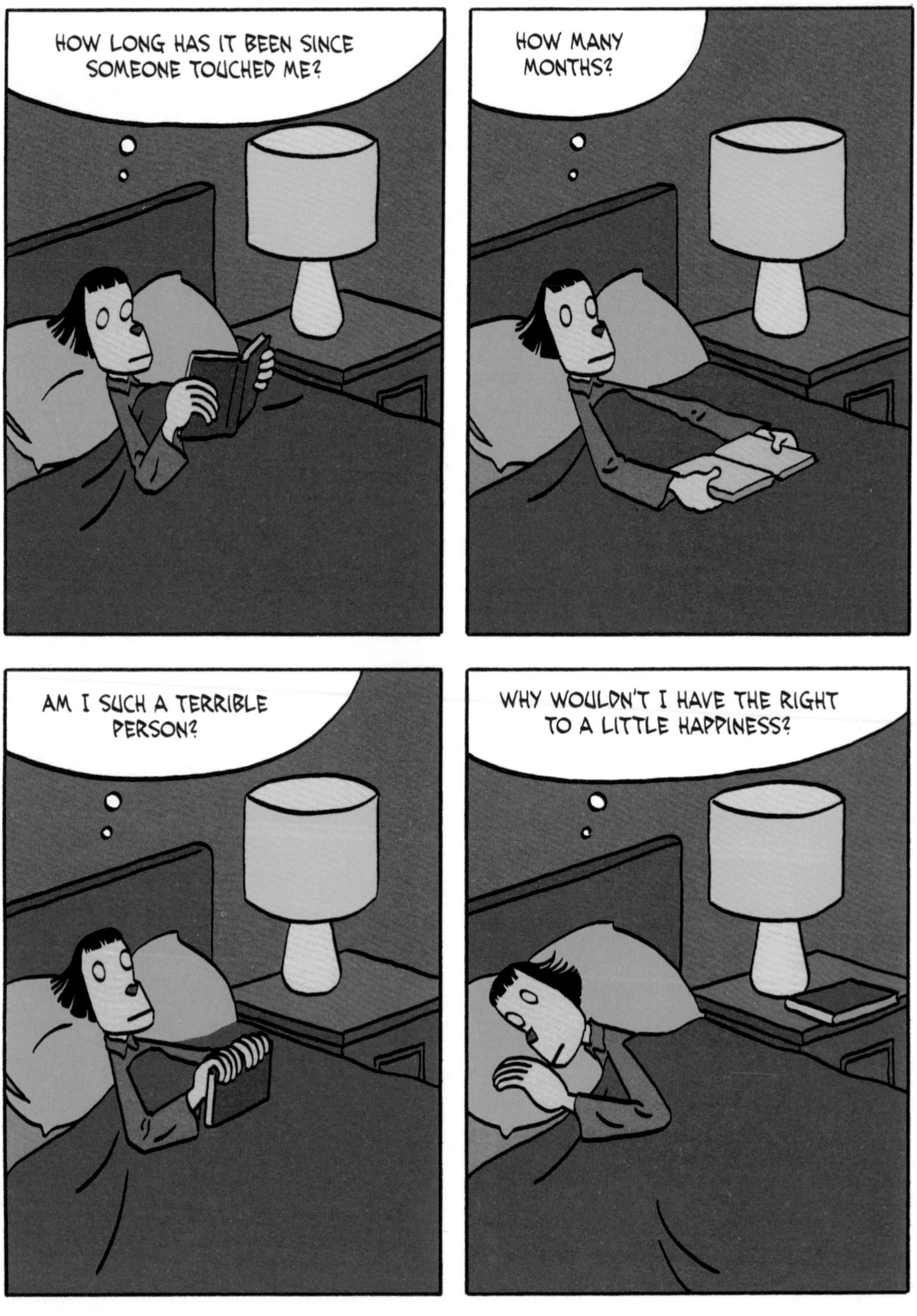
HOW LONG HAS IT BEEN SINCE SOMEONE TOUCHED ME?
HOW MANY MONTHS?
AM I SUCH A TERRIBLE PERSON?
WHY WOULDN'T I HAVE THE RIGHT TO A LITTLE HAPPINESS?

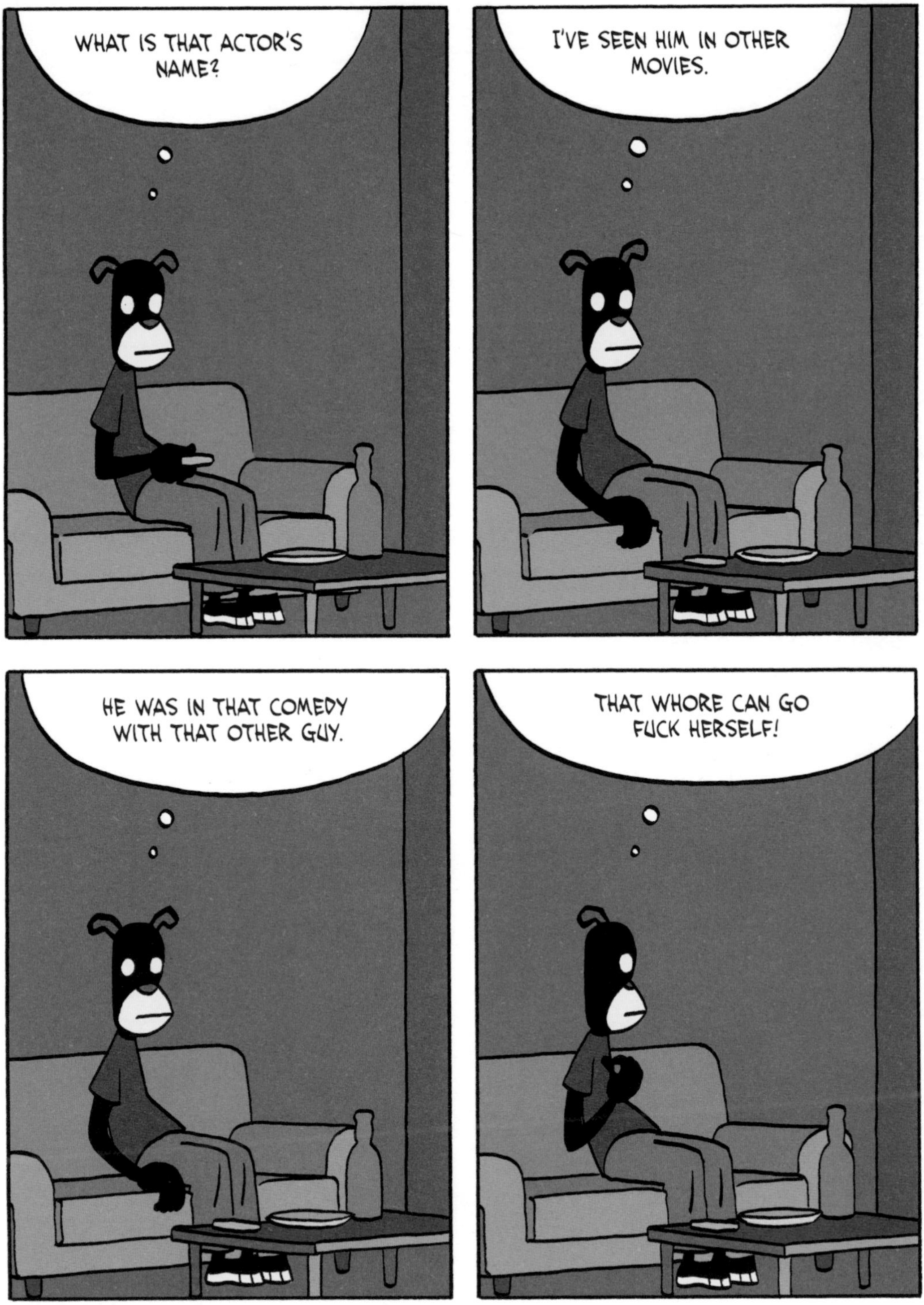
WHAT IS THAT ACTOR'S NAME?
I'VE SEEN HIM IN OTHER MOVIES.
HE WAS IN THAT COMEDY WITH THAT OTHER GUY.
THAT WHORE CAN GO FUCK HERSELF!

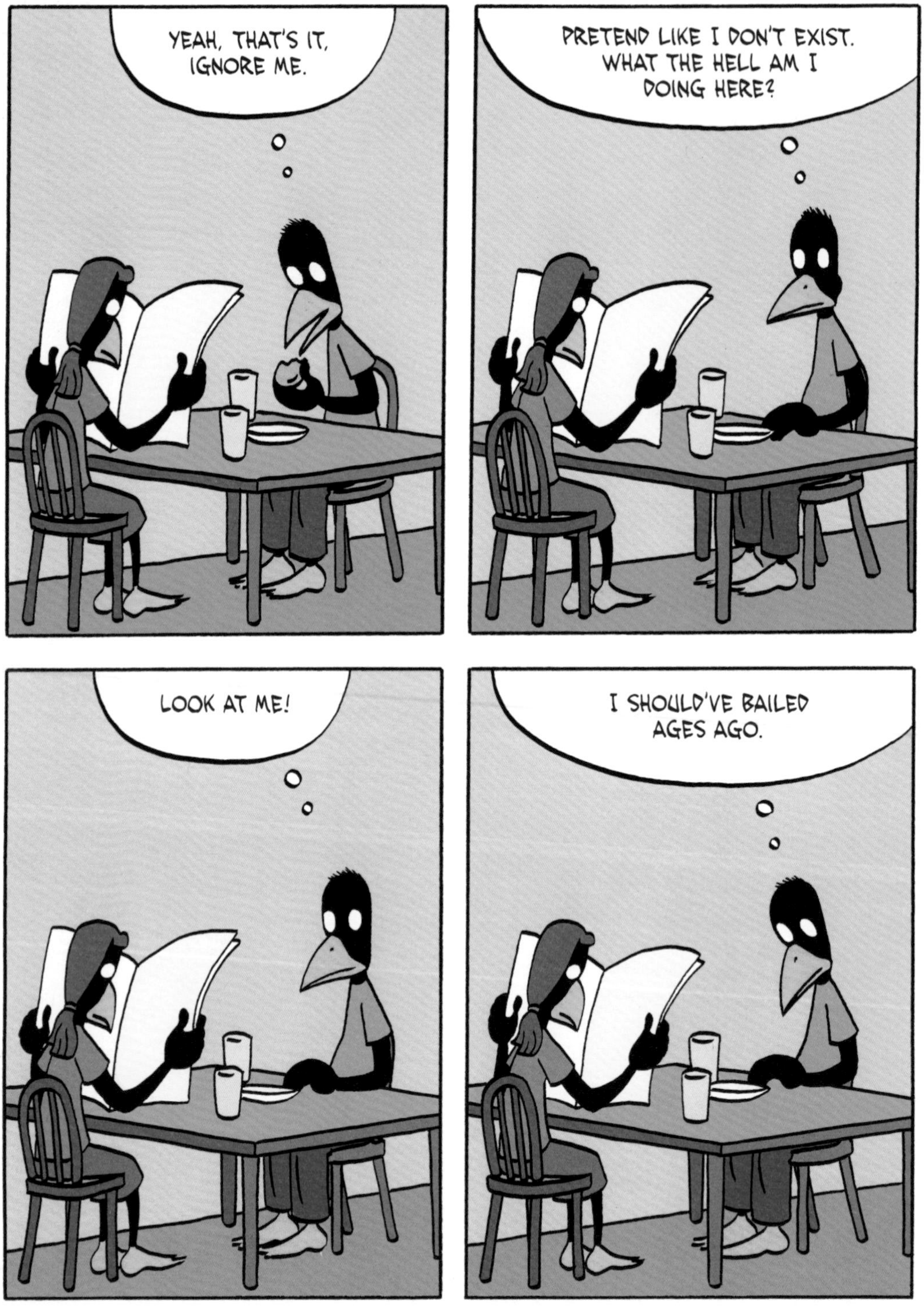
YEAH, THAT'S IT, IGNORE ME.
PRETEND LIKE I DON'T EXIST. WHAT THE HELL AM I DOING HERE?
LOOK AT ME!
I SHOULD'VE BAILED AGES AGO.

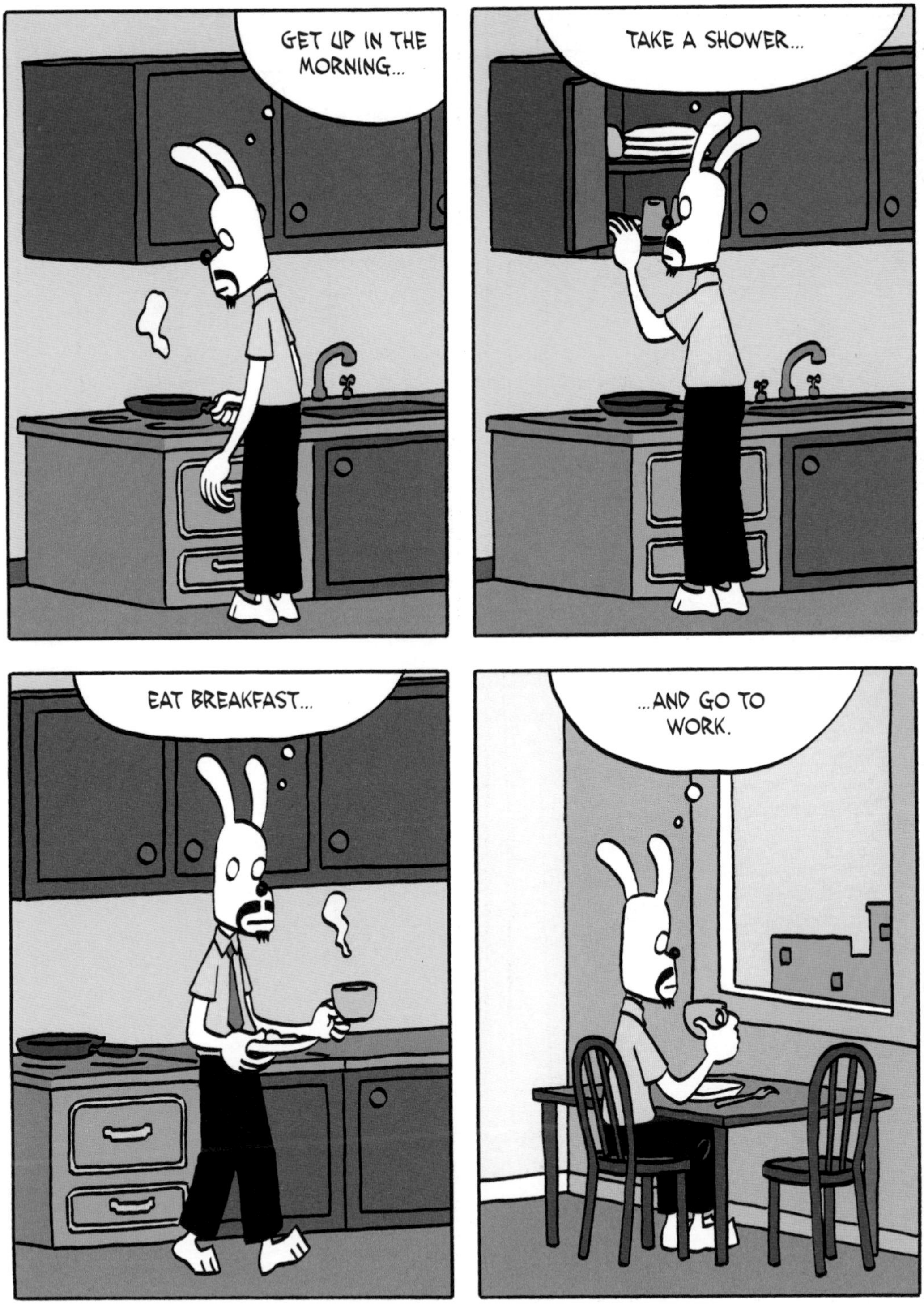
GET UP IN THE MORNING...
TAKE A SHOWER...
EAT BREAKFAST...
...AND GO TO WORK.

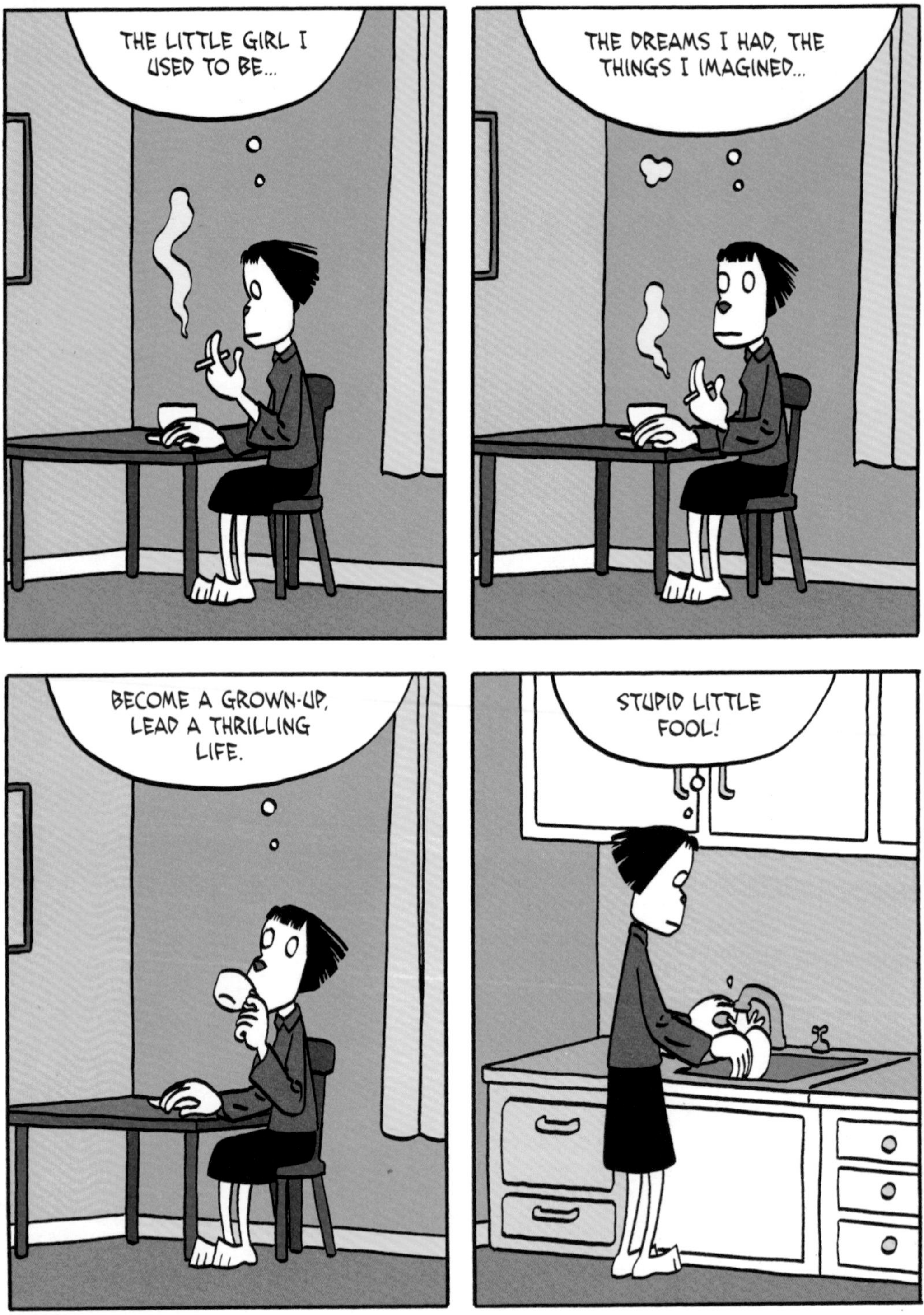
THE LITTLE GIRL I USED TO BE...
THE DREAMS I HAD, THE THINGS I IMAGINED...
BECOME A GROWN-UP, LEAD A THRILLING LIFE.
STUPID LITTLE FOOL!

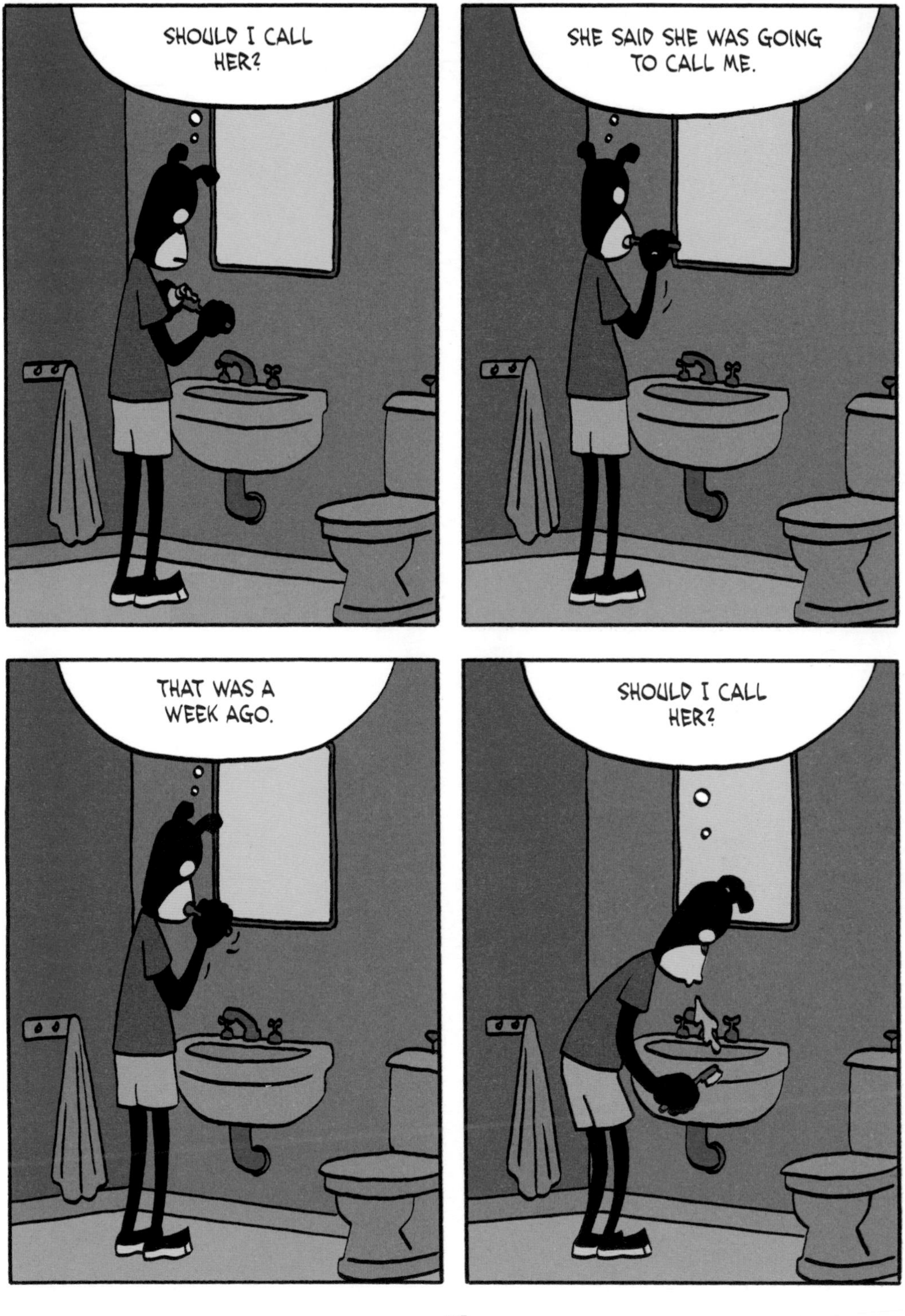
SHOULD I CALL HER?
SHE SAID SHE WAS GOING TO CALL ME.
THAT WAS A WEEK AGO.
SHOULD I CALL HER?

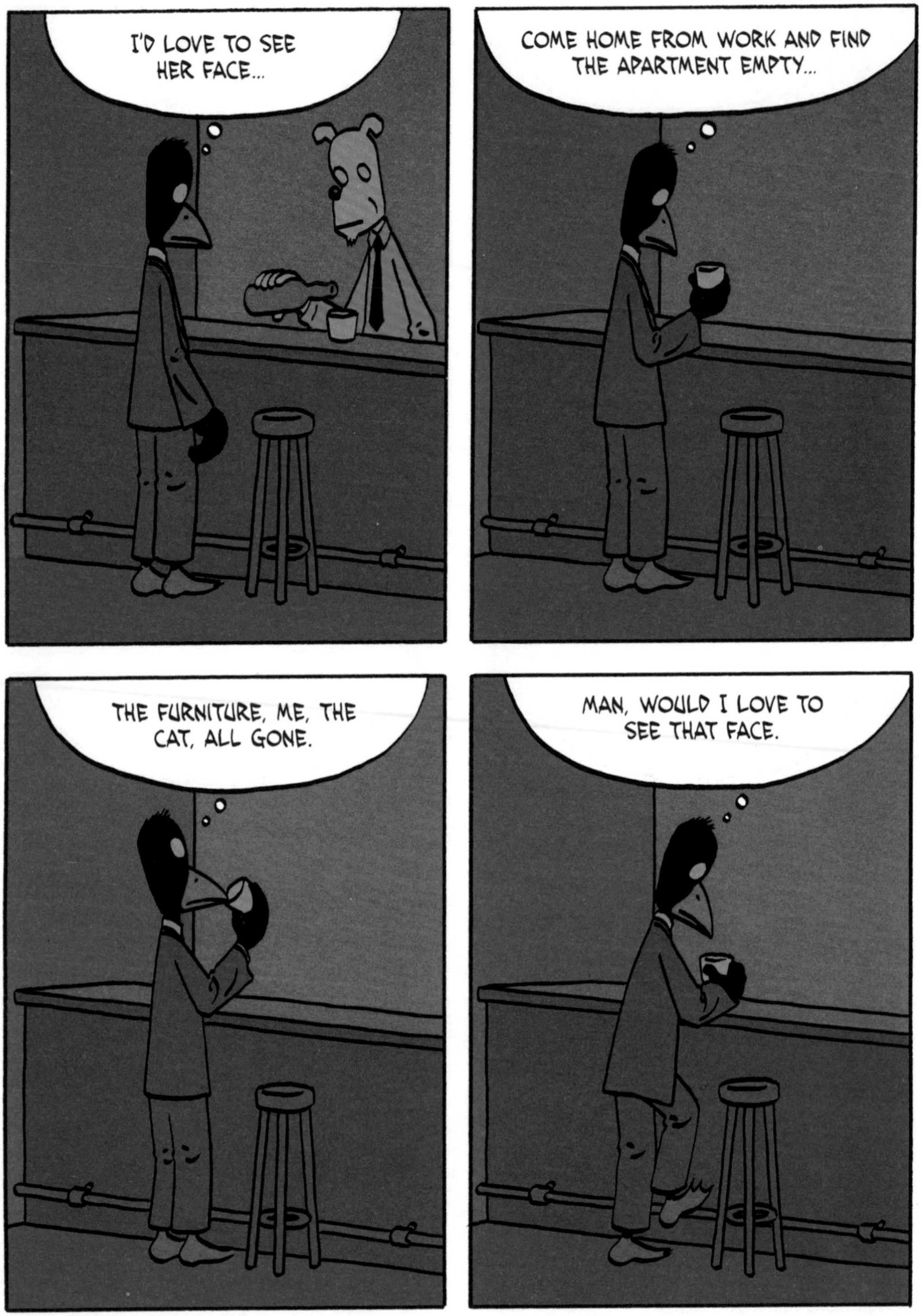
I'D LOVE TO SEE HER FACE...
COME HOME FROM WORK AND FIND THE APARTMENT EMPTY...
THE FURNITURE, ME, THE CAT, ALL GONE.
MAN, WOULD I LOVE TO SEE THAT FACE.

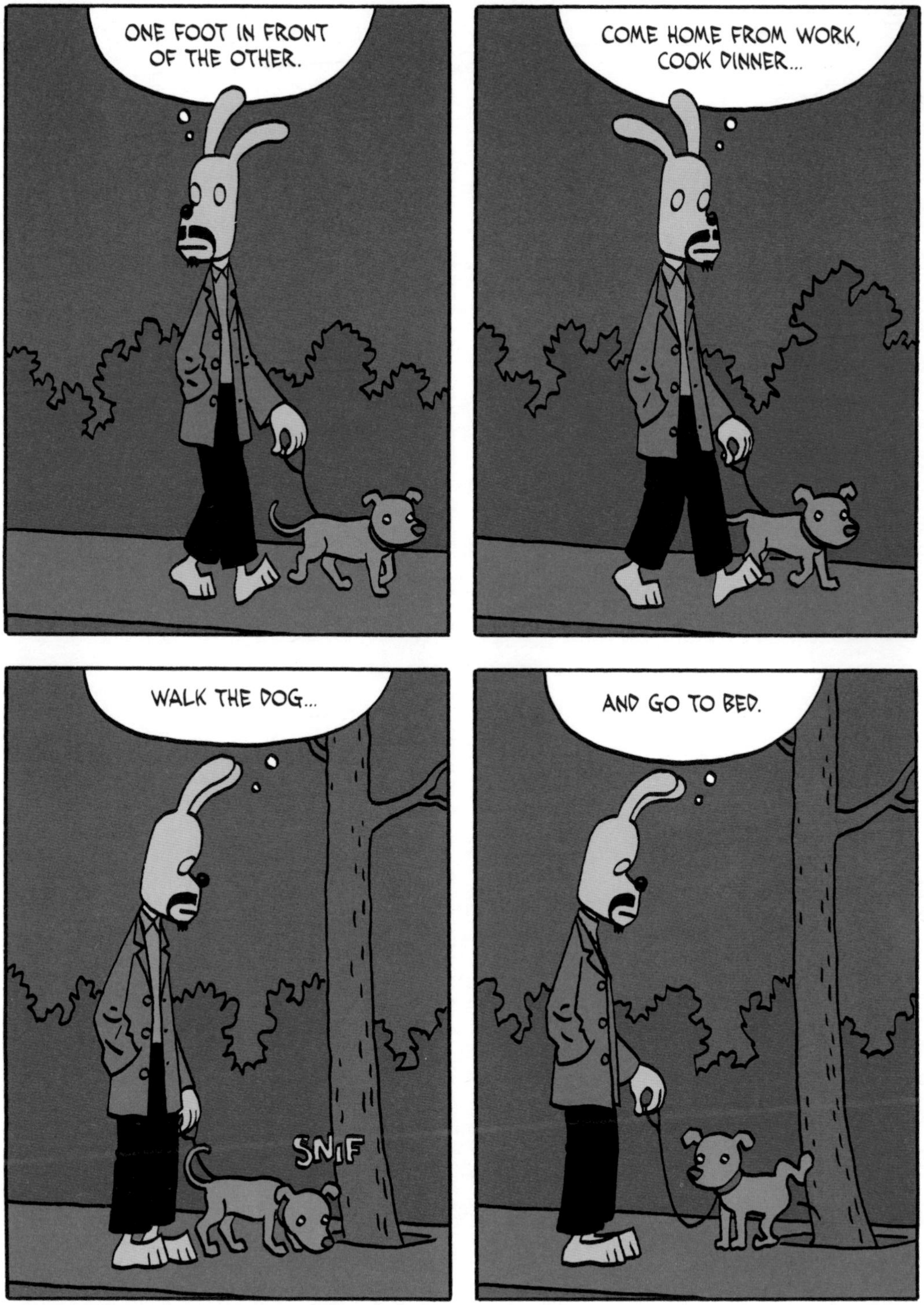
ONE FOOT IN FRONT OF THE OTHER.
COME HOME FROM WORK, COOK DINNER...
WALK THE DOG...
SNIF
AND GO TO BED.

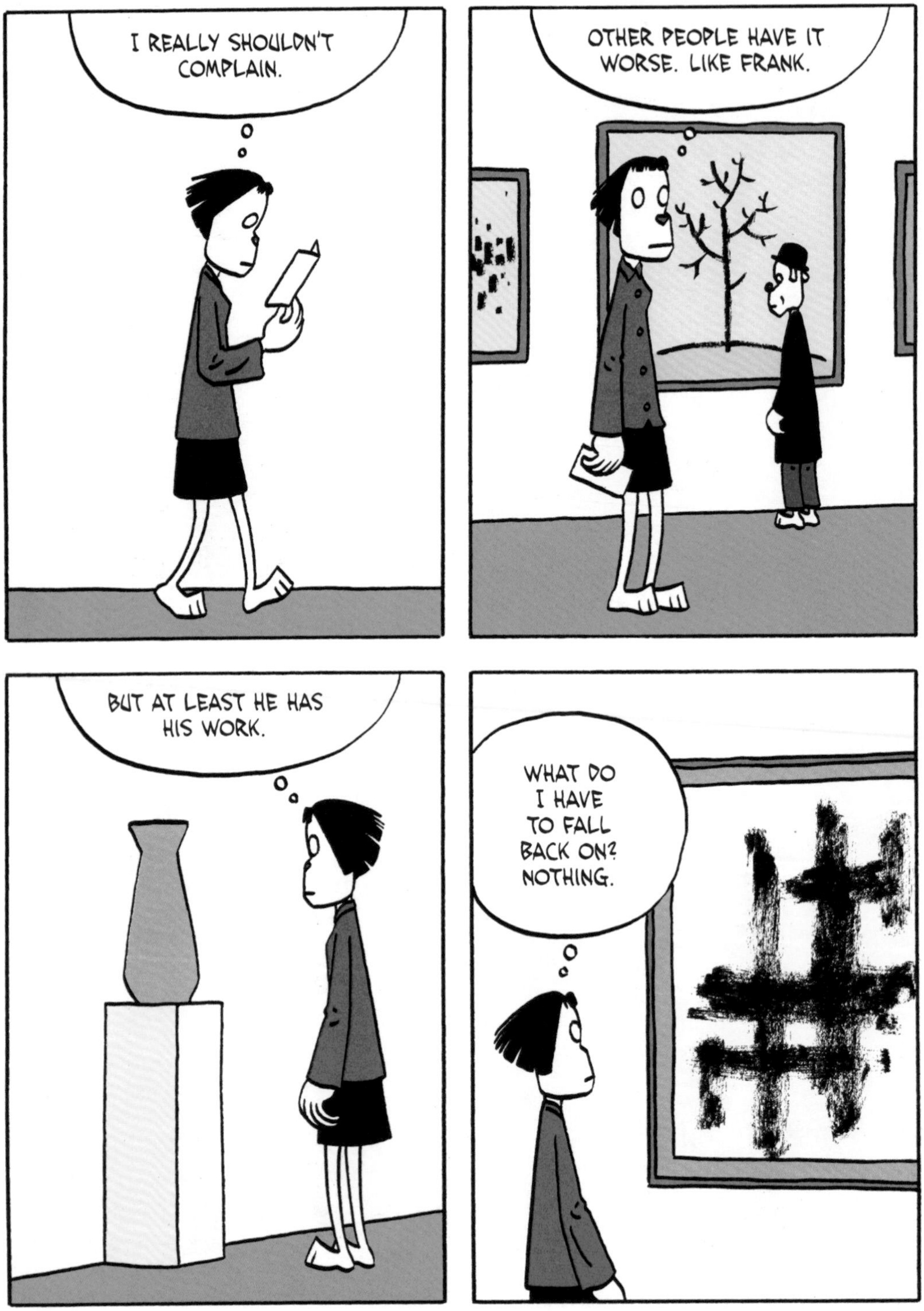
I REALLY SHOULDN'T COMPLAIN.
OTHER PEOPLE HAVE IT WORSE. LIKE FRANK.
BUT AT LEAST HE HAS HIS WORK.
WHAT DO I HAVE TO FALL BACK ON? NOTHING.

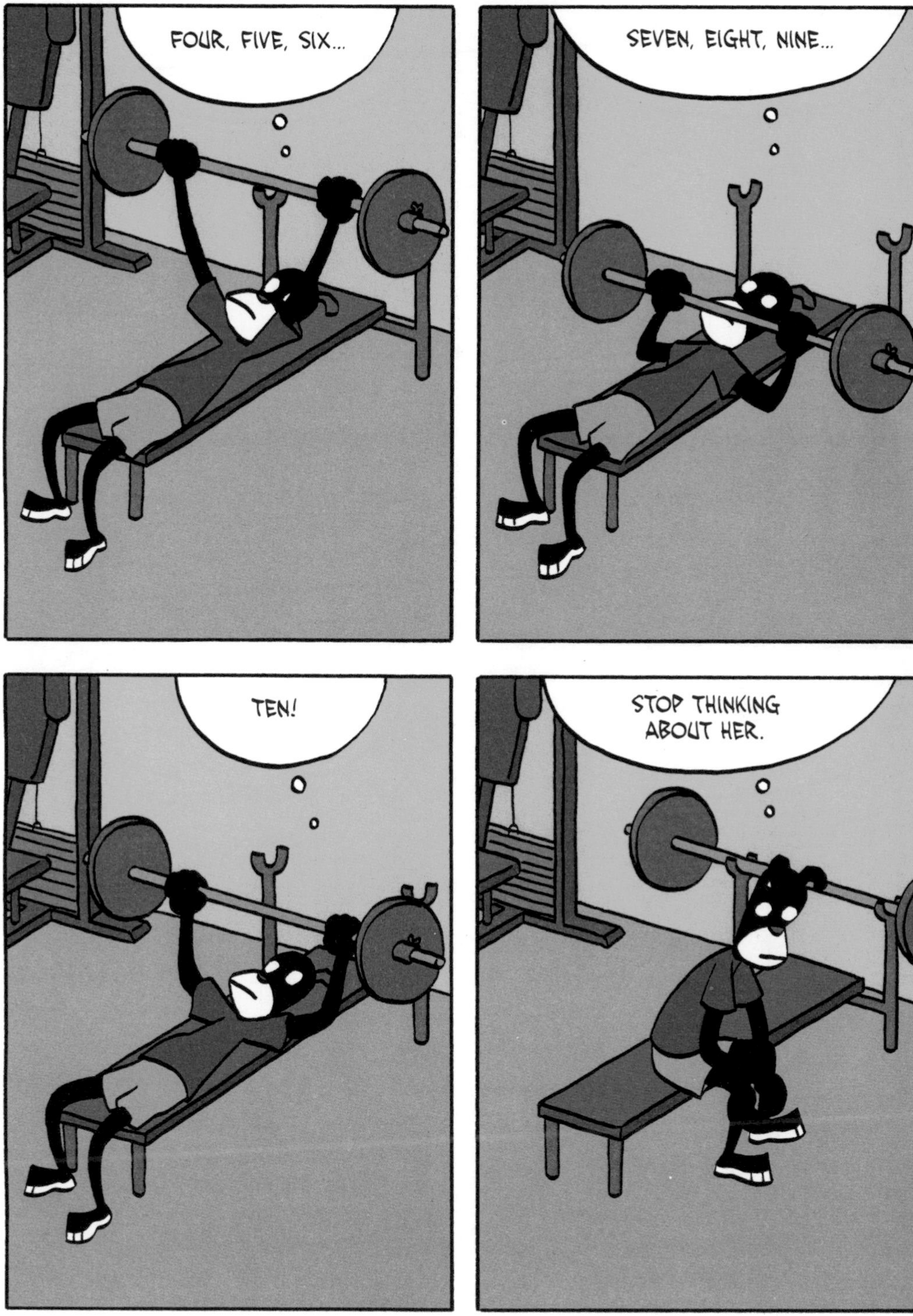
FOUR, FIVE, SIX...
SEVEN, EIGHT, NINE...
TEN!
STOP THINKING ABOUT HER.

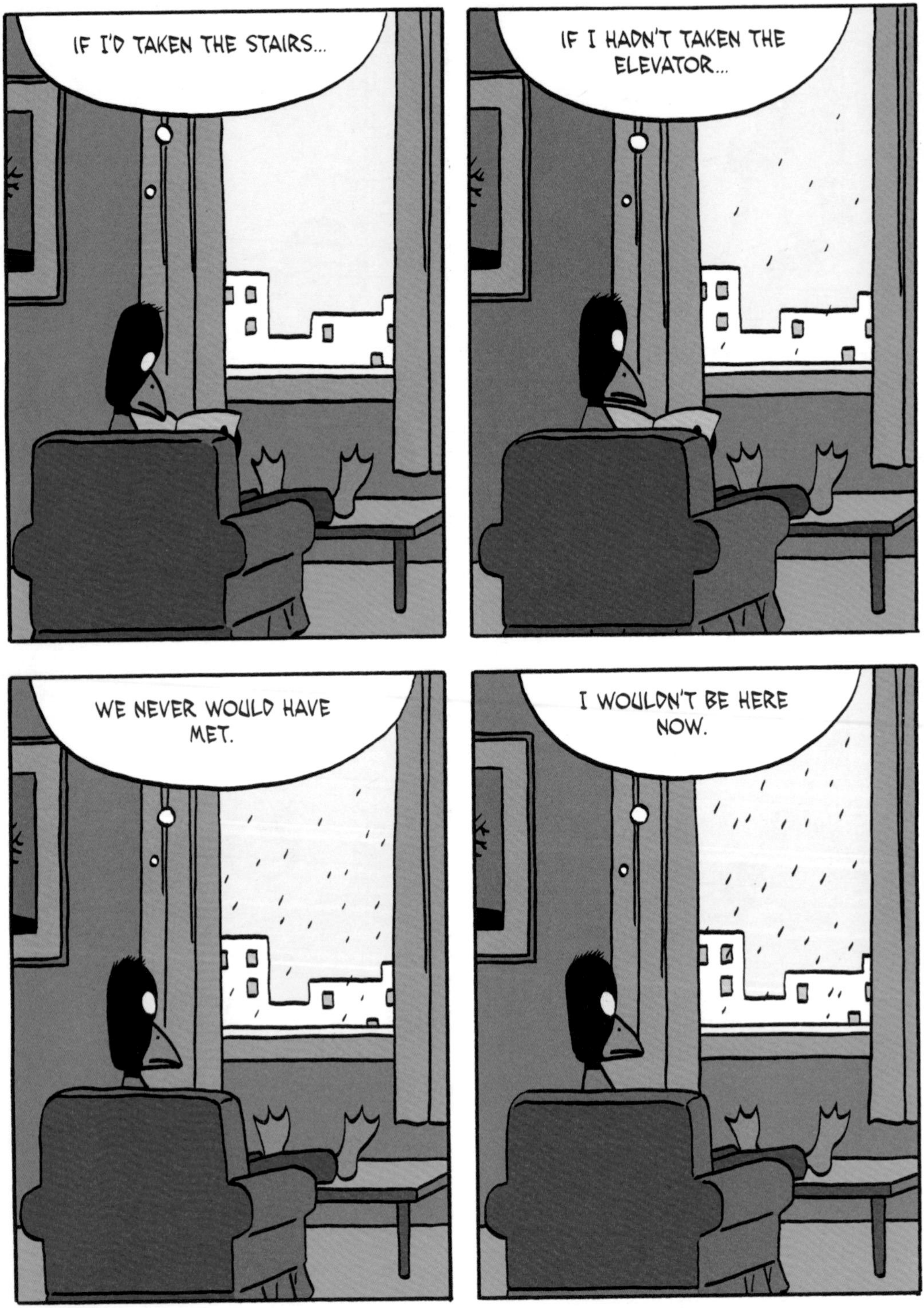
IF I'D TAKEN THE STAIRS...
IF I HADN'T TAKEN THE ELEVATOR...
WE NEVER WOULD HAVE MET.
I WOULDN'T BE HERE NOW.

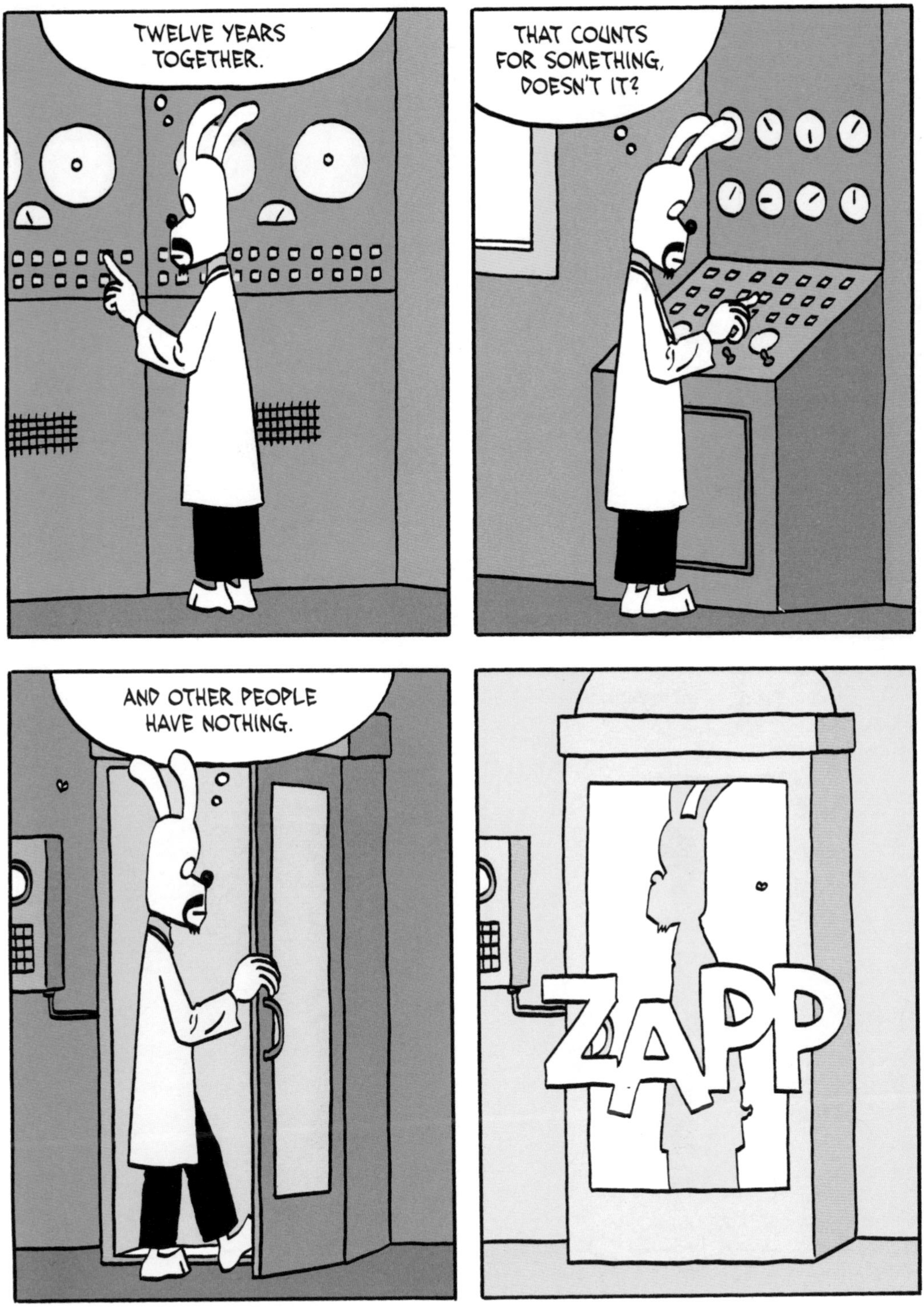
TWELVE YEARS TOGETHER.
THAT COUNTS FOR SOMETHING, DOESN'T IT?
AND OTHER PEOPLE HAVE NOTHING.
ZAPP

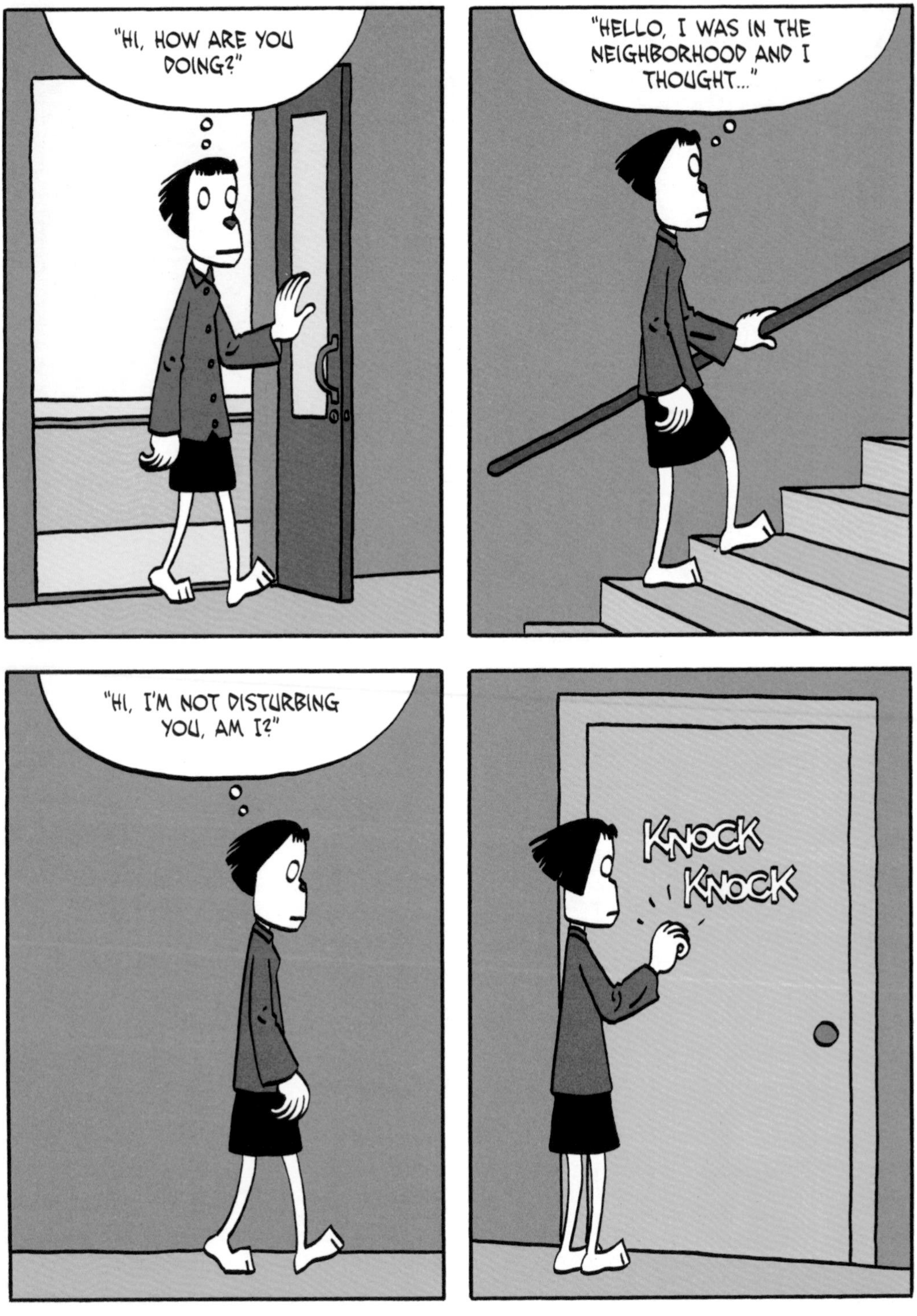
"HI, HOW ARE YOU DOING?"
"HELLO, I WAS IN THE NEIGHBORHOOD AND I THOUGHT..."
"HI, I'M NOT DISTURBING YOU, AM I?"
KNOCK
KNOCK

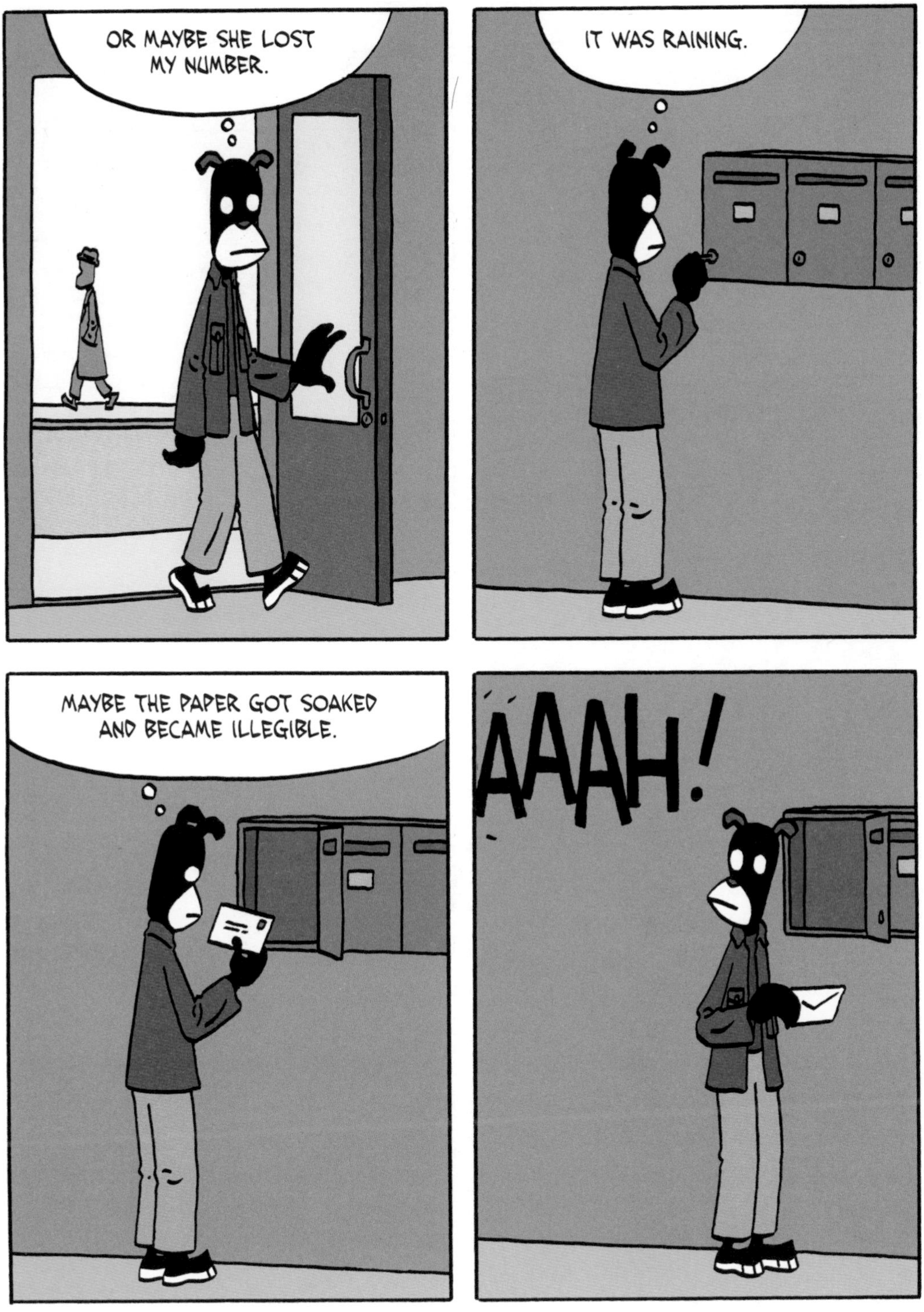
OR MAYBE SHE LOST MY NUMBER.
IT WAS RAINING.
MAYBE THE PAPER GOT SOAKED AND BECAME ILLEGIBLE.
AAAH!

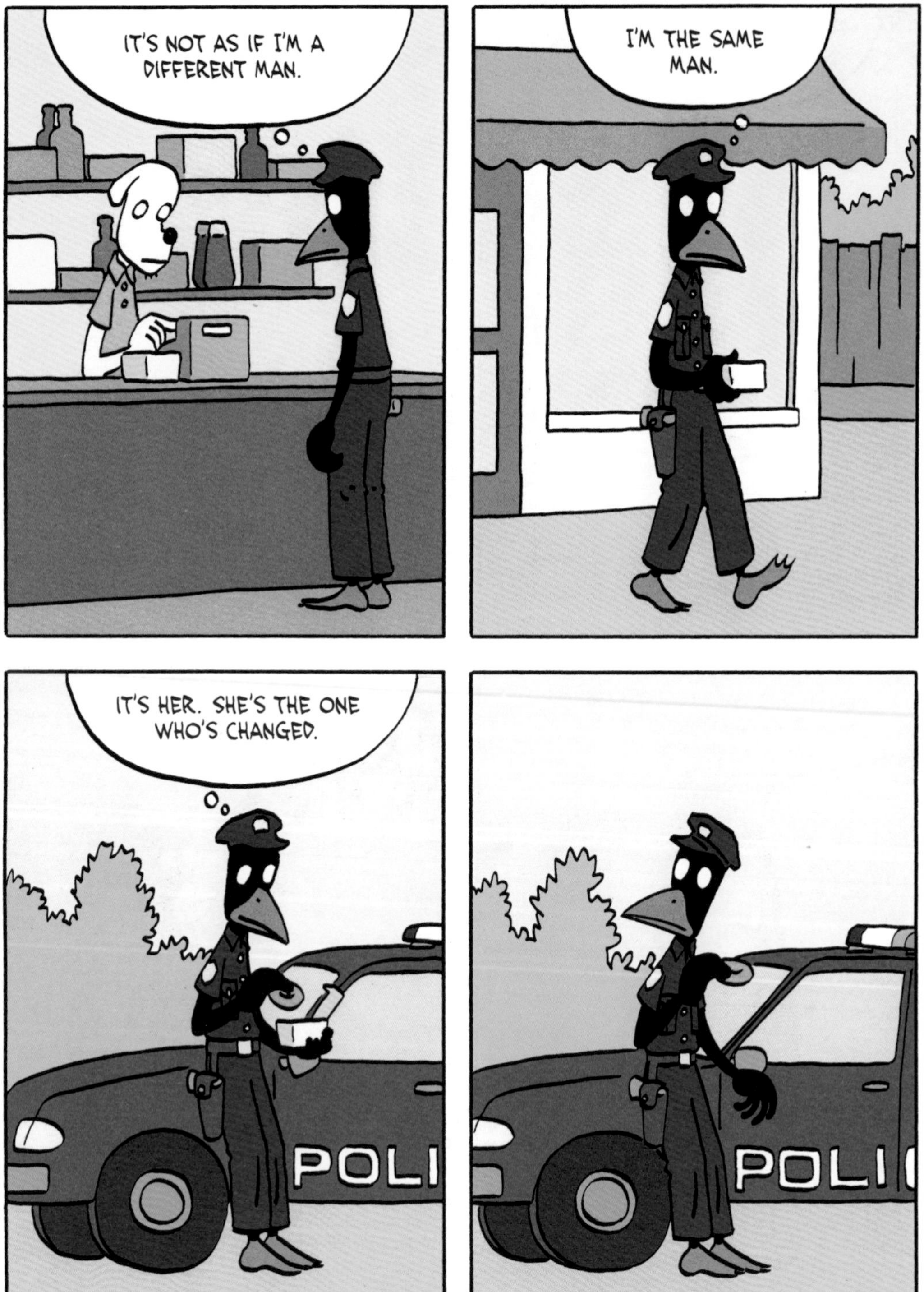
IT'S NOT AS IF I'M A DIFFERENT MAN.
I'M THE SAME MAN.
IT'S HER. SHE'S THE ONE WHO'S CHANGED.
POLI
POLI

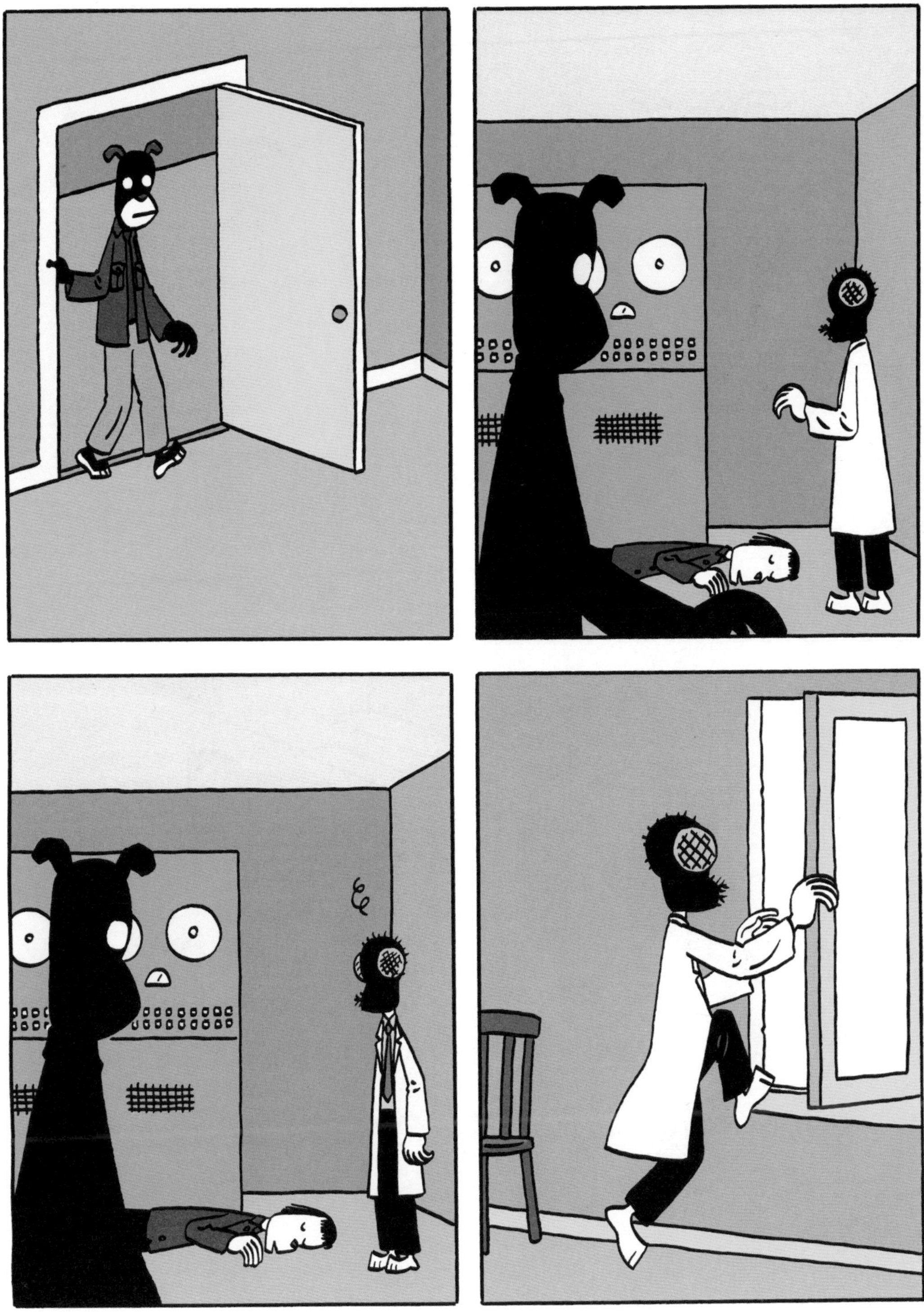

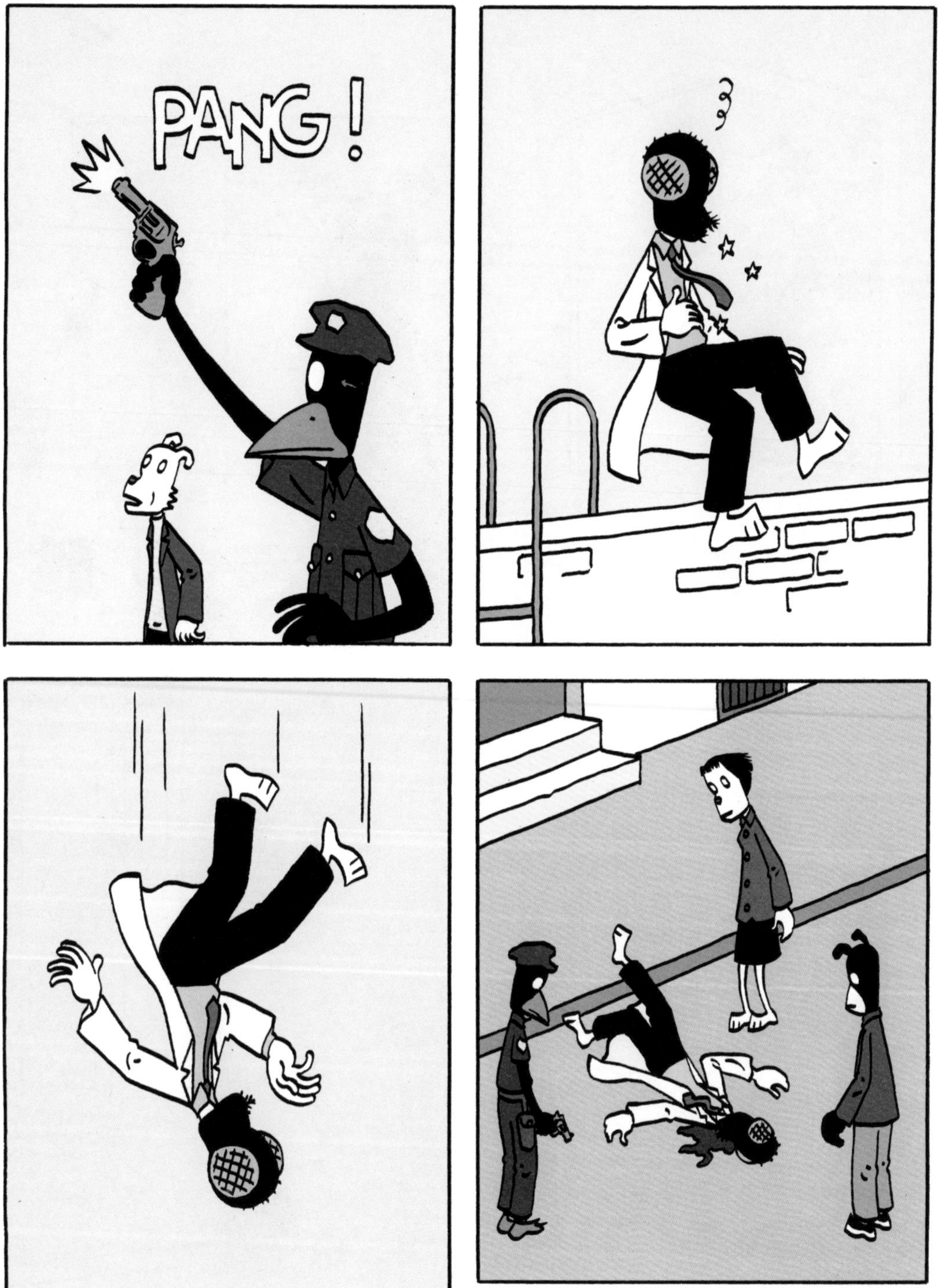
PANG!
jason · 10

PRESENTING:

SO LONG, MARY ANNE

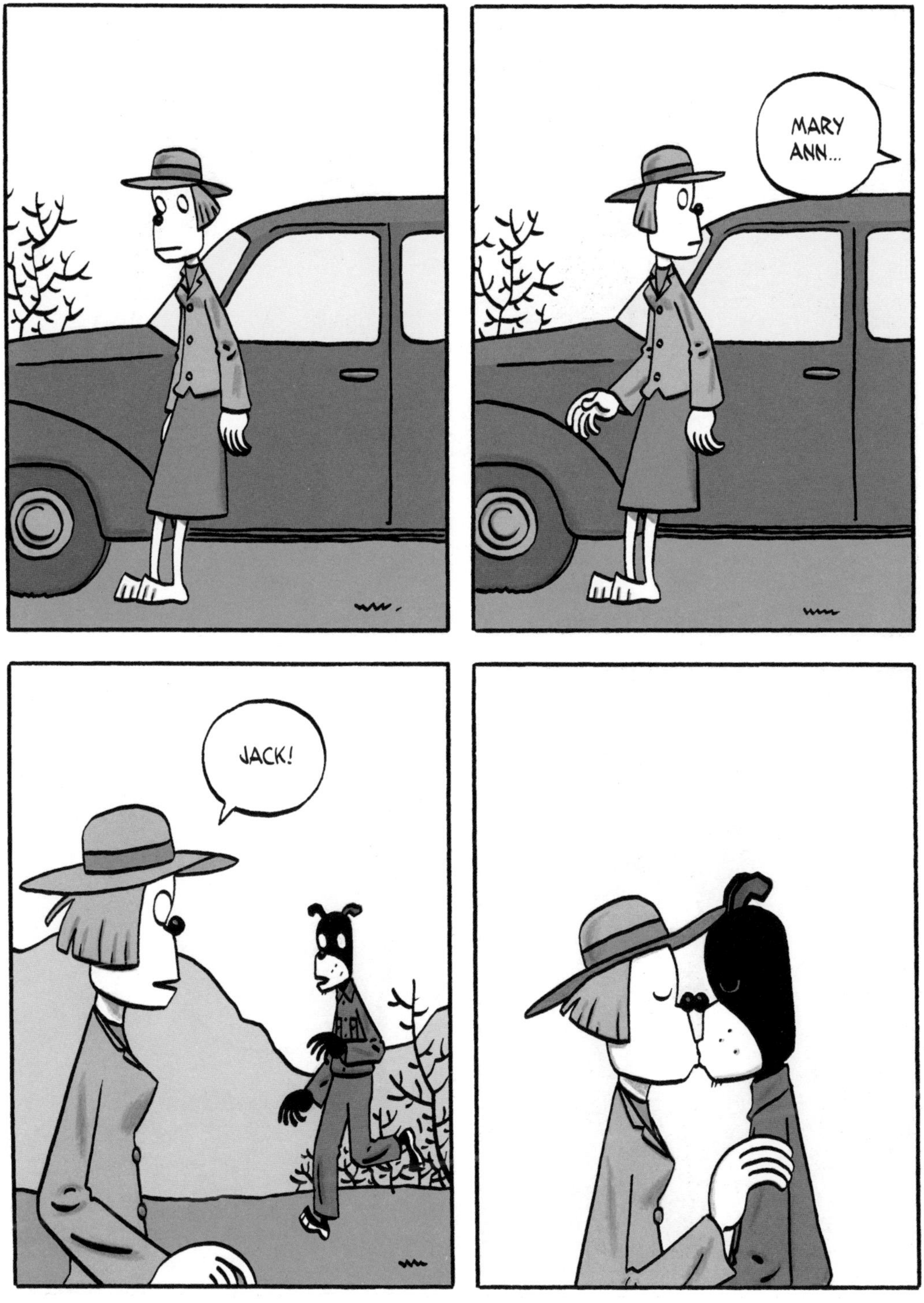
MARY ANN...
JACK!

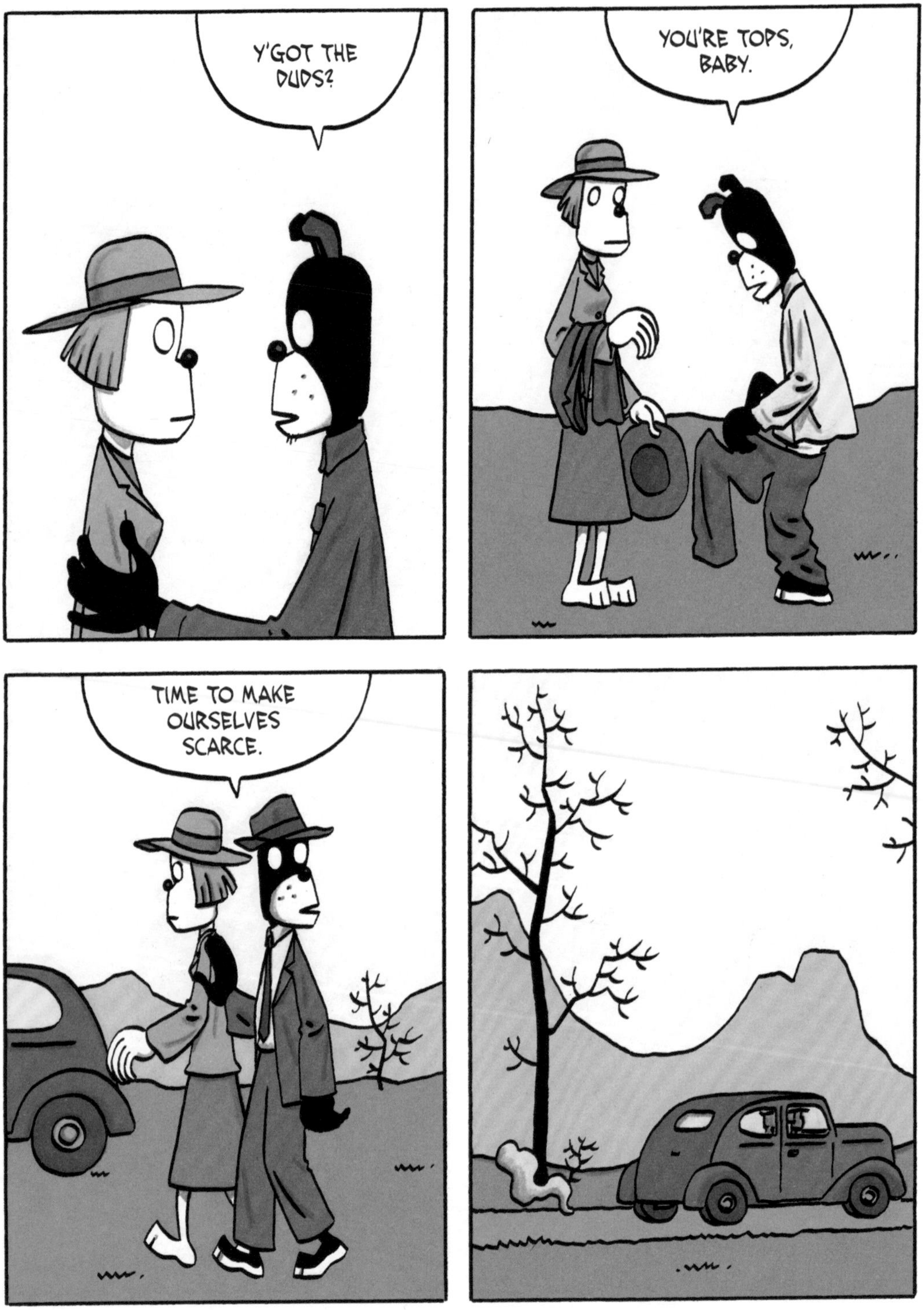
Y'GOT THE DUDS?
YOU'RE TOPS, BABY.
TIME TO MAKE OURSELVES SCARCE.

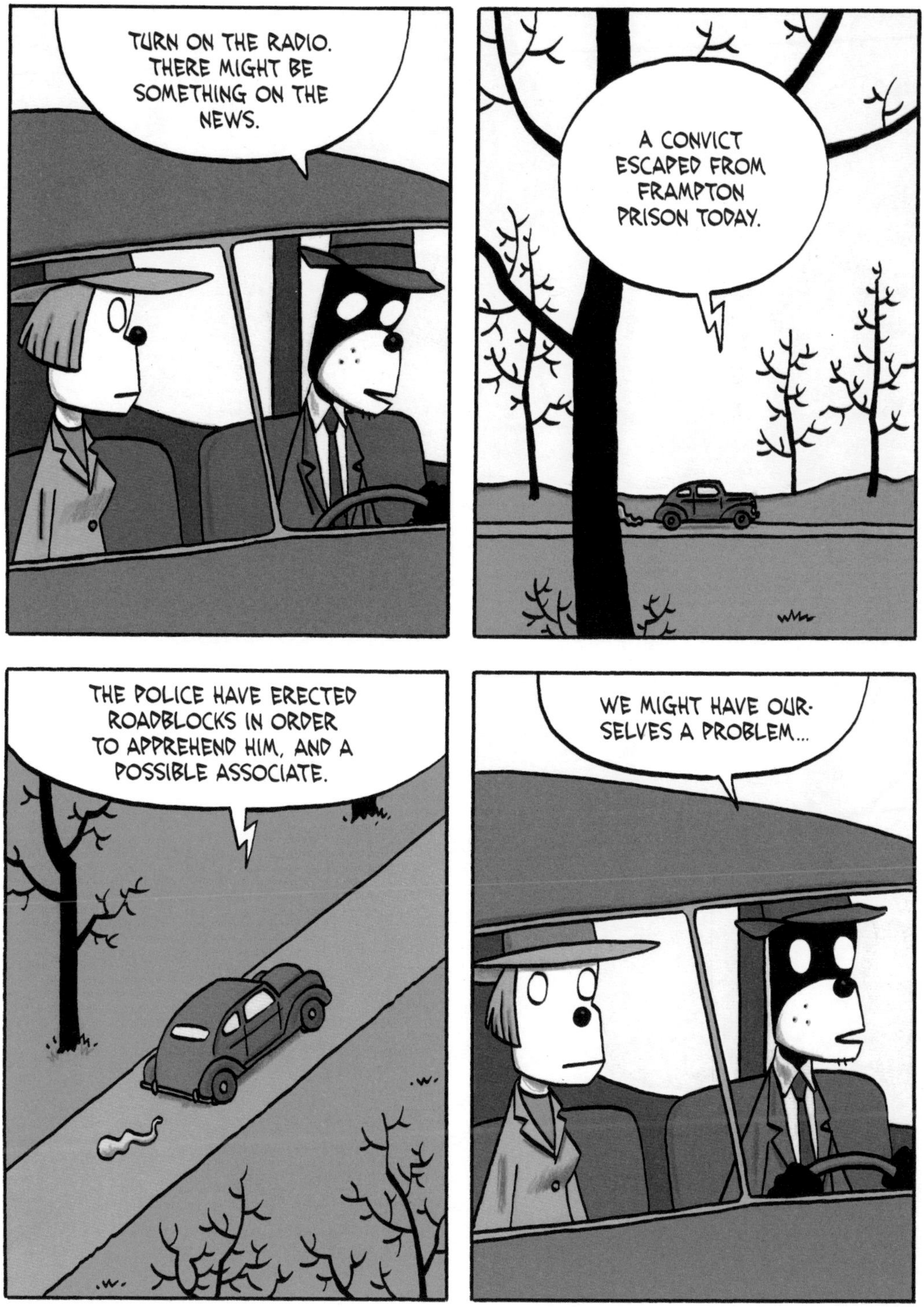
TURN ON THE RADIO. THERE MIGHT BE SOMETHING ON THE NEWS.
A CONVICT ESCAPED FROM FRAMPTON PRISON TODAY.
THE POLICE HAVE ERECTED ROADBLOCKS IN ORDER TO APPREHEND HIM, AND A POSSIBLE ASSOCIATE.
WE MIGHT HAVE OUR-SELVES A PROBLEM...

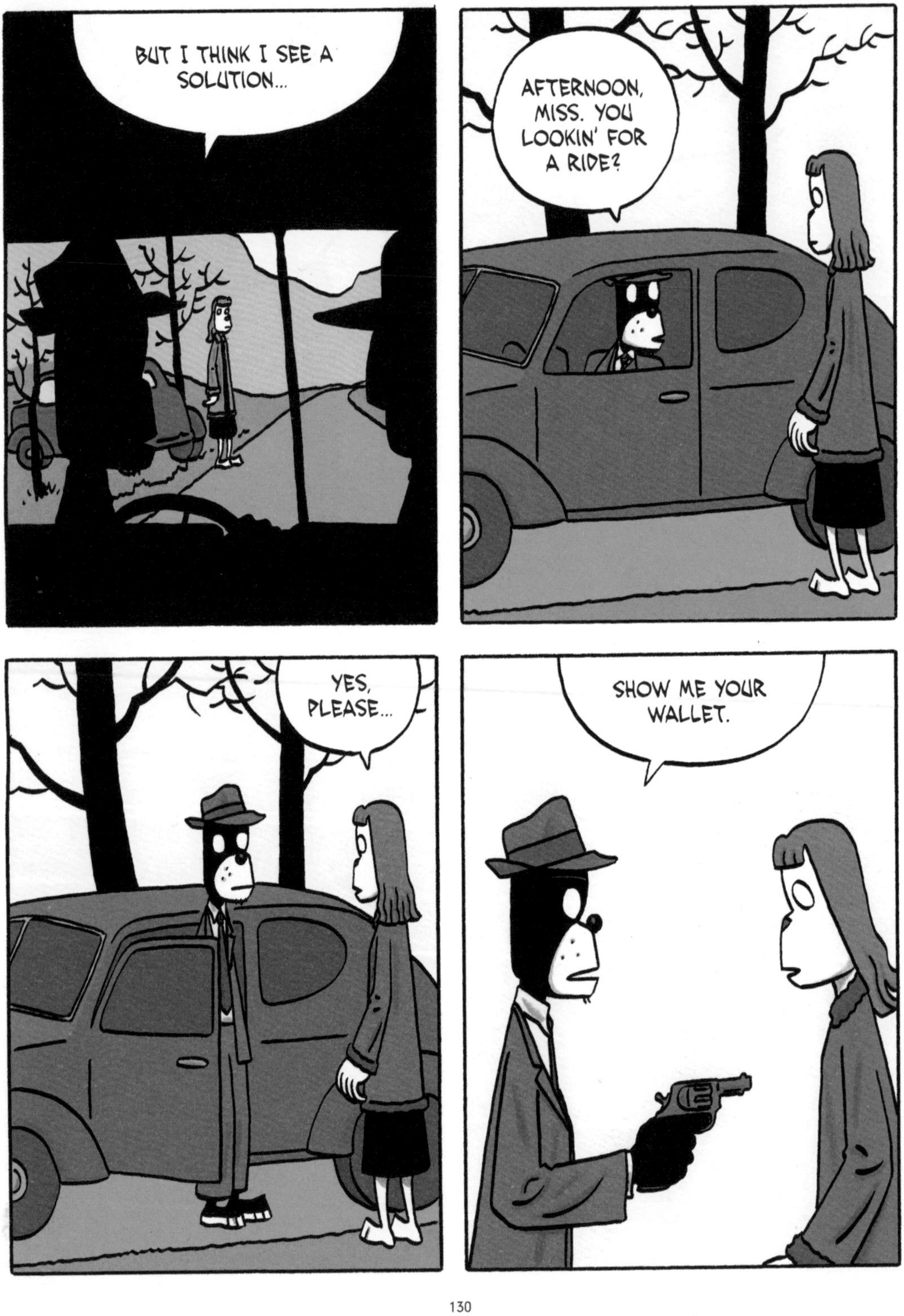
BUT I THINK I SEE A SOLUTION...
AFTERNOON, MISS. YOU LOOKIN' FOR A RIDE?
YES, PLEASE...
SHOW ME YOUR WALLET.

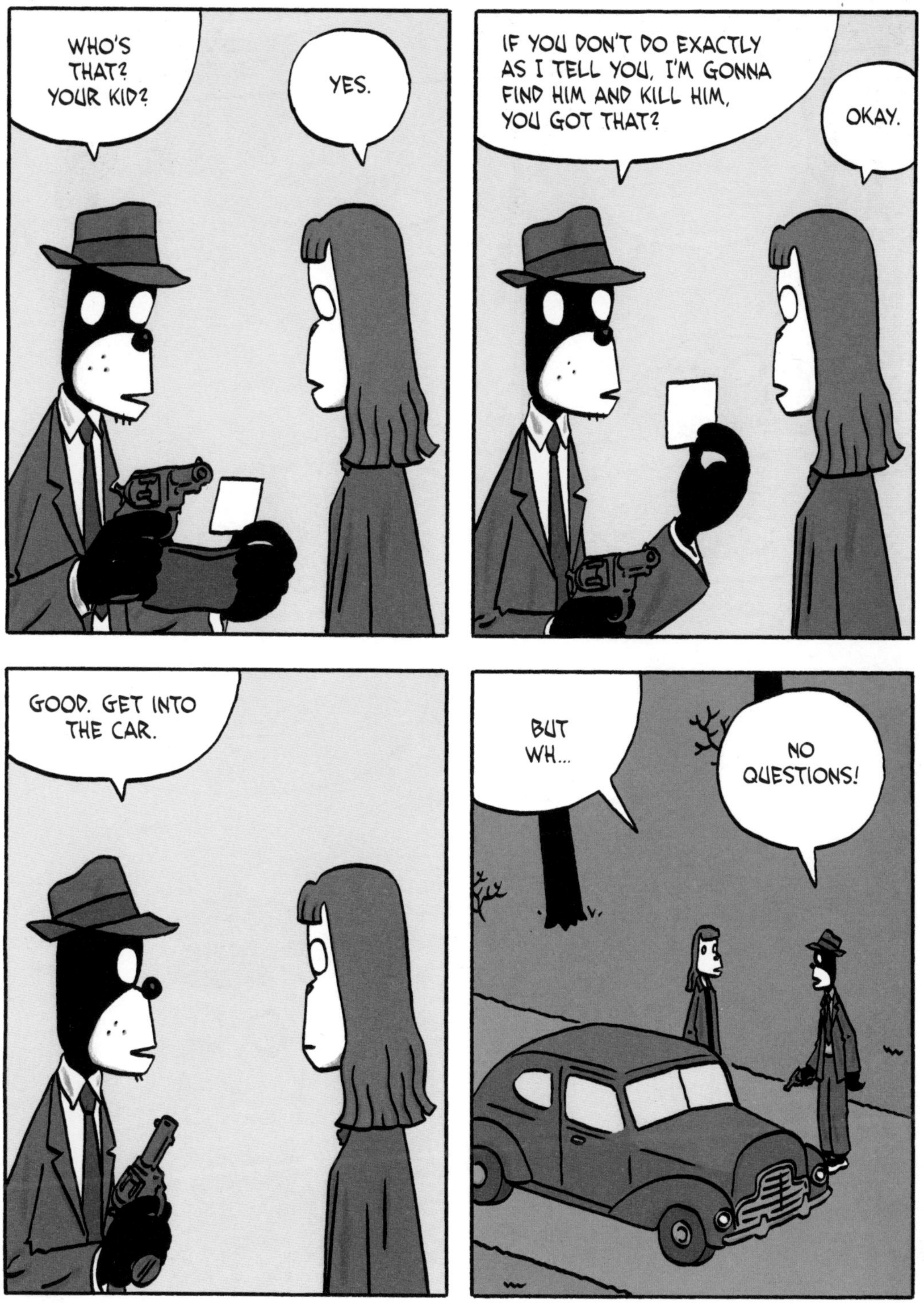
WHO'S THAT? YOUR KID?
YES.
IF YOU DON'T DO EXACTLY AS I TELL YOU, I'M GONNA FIND HIM AND KILL HIM, YOU GOT THAT?
OKAY.
GOOD. GET INTO THE CAR.
BUT WH...
NO QUESTIONS!

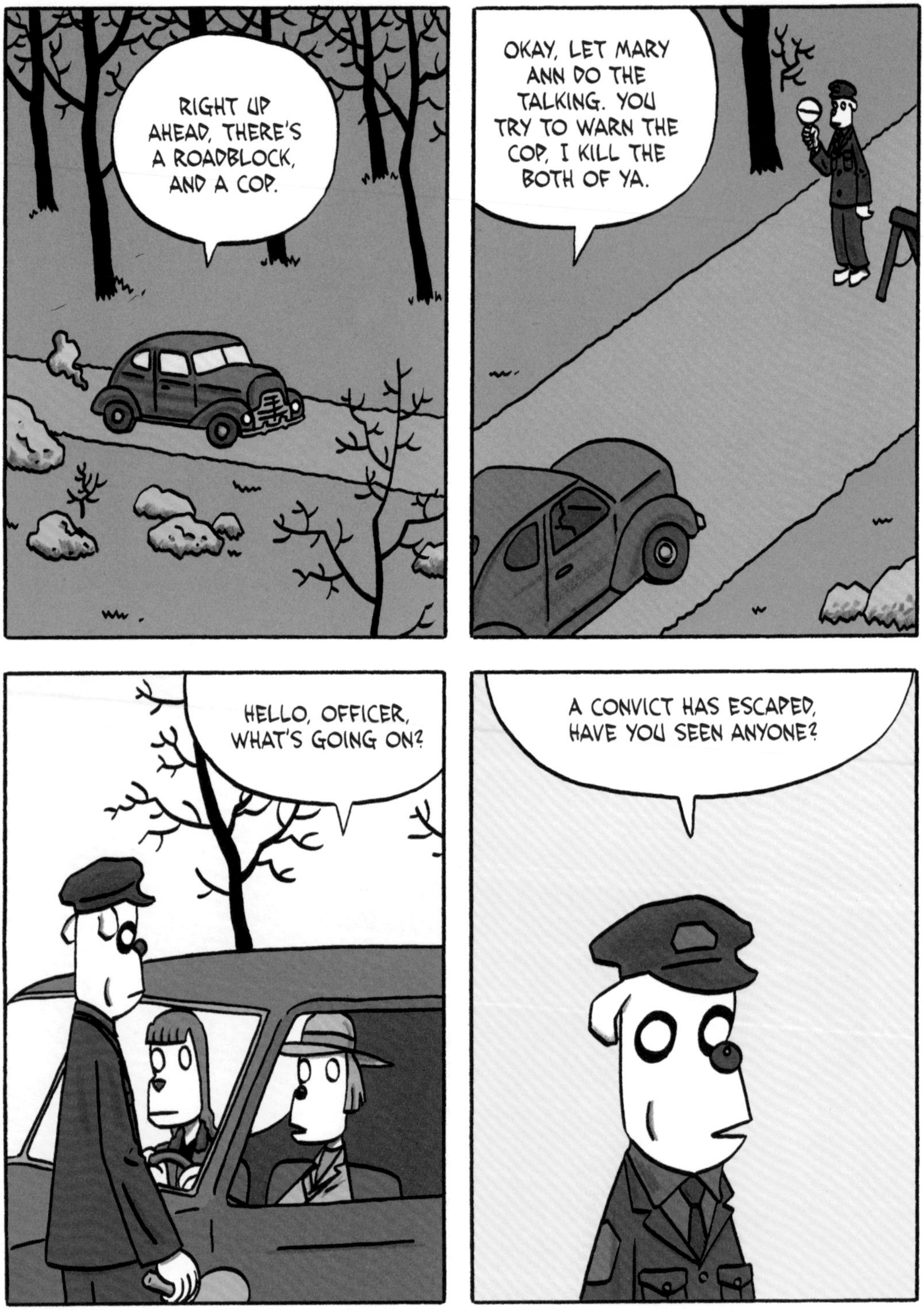
RIGHT UP AHEAD, THERE'S A ROADBLOCK, AND A COP.
OKAY, LET MARY ANN DO THE TALKING. YOU TRY TO WARN THE COP, I KILL THE BOTH OF YA.
HELLO, OFFICER, WHAT'S GOING ON?
A CONVICT HAS ESCAPED, HAVE YOU SEEN ANYONE?

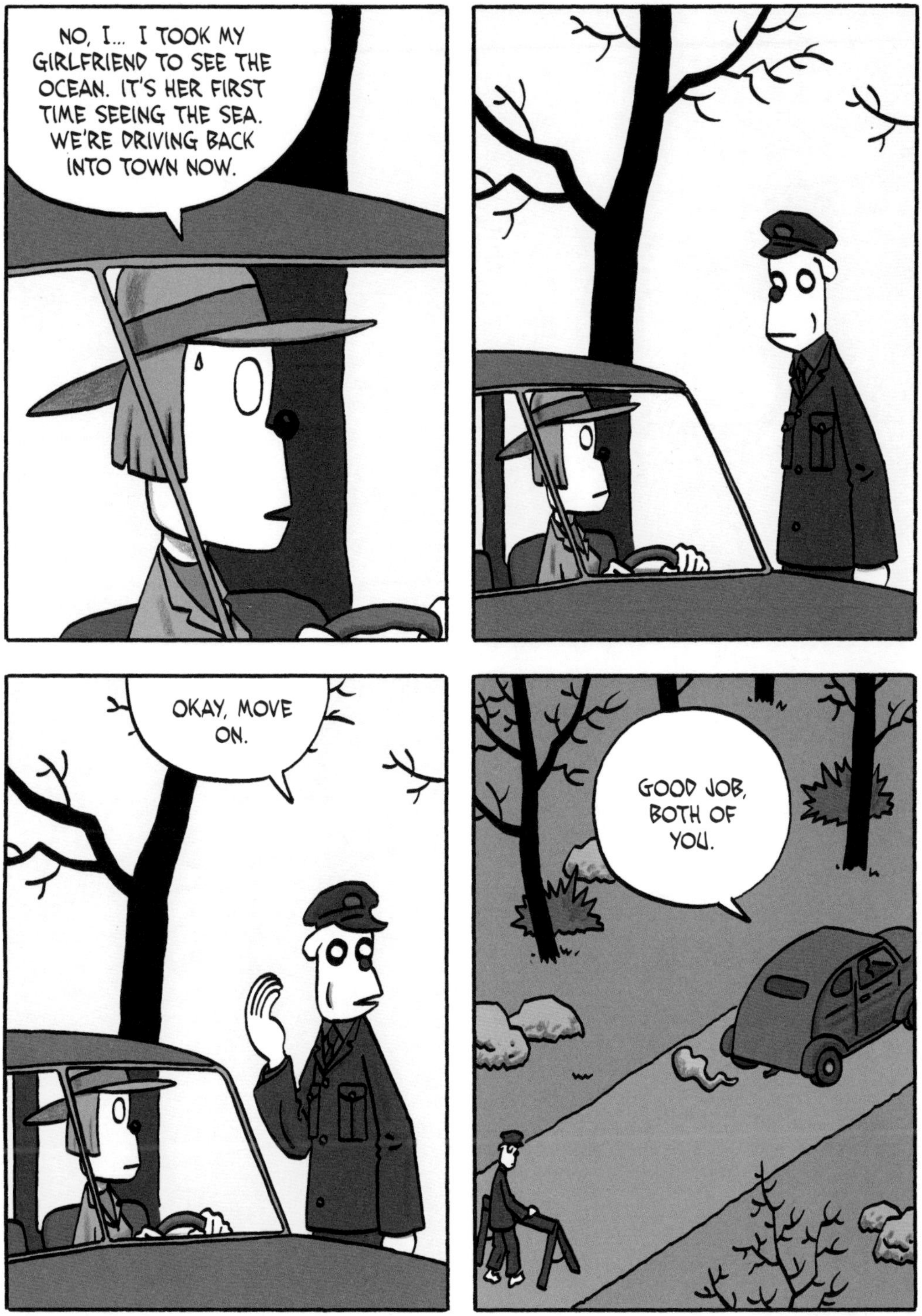
NO, I... I TOOK MY GIRLFRIEND TO SEE THE OCEAN. IT'S HER FIRST TIME SEEING THE SEA. WE'RE DRIVING BACK INTO TOWN NOW.
OKAY, MOVE ON.
GOOD JOB, BOTH OF YOU.

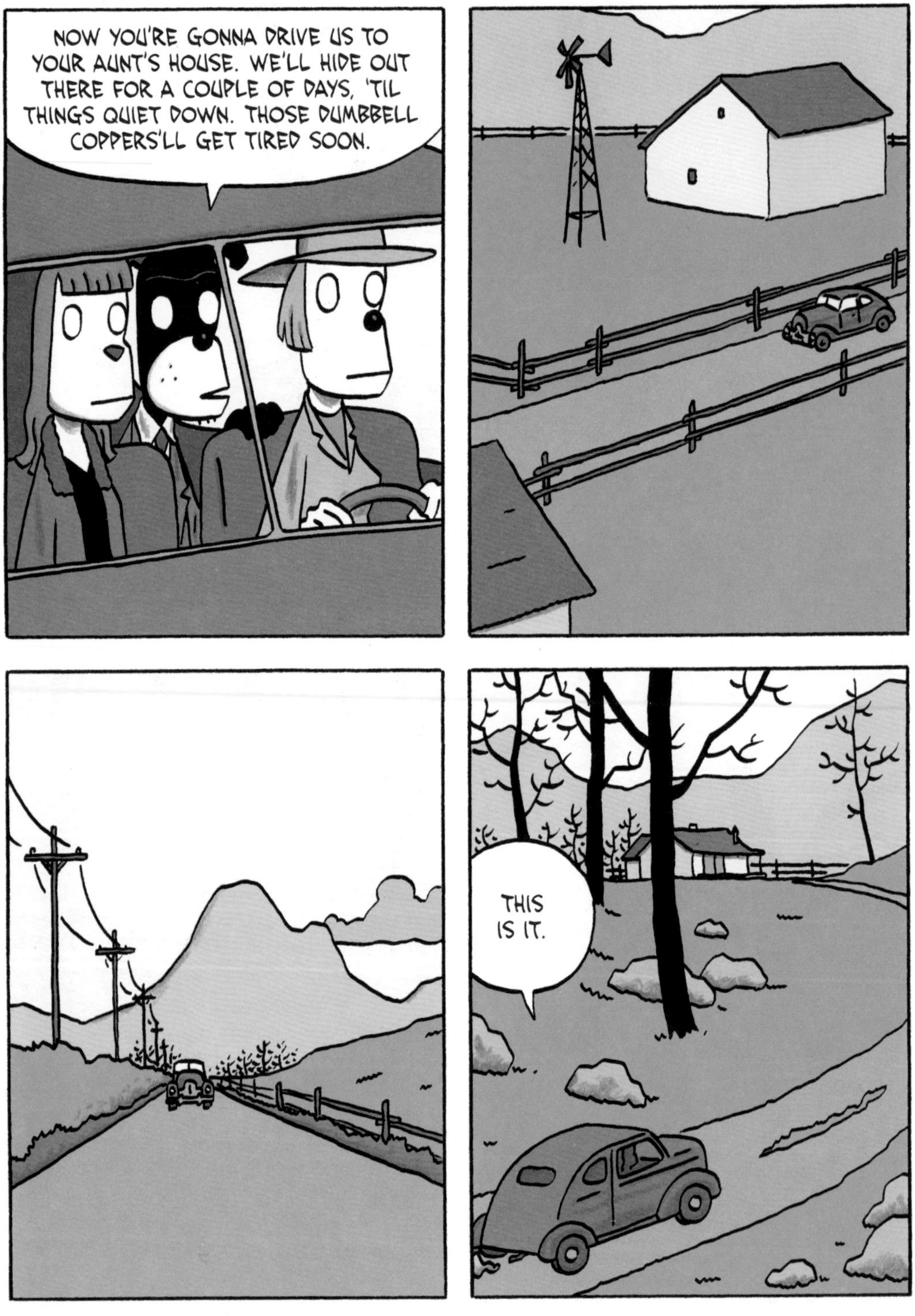
NOW YOU'RE GONNA DRIVE US TO YOUR AUNT'S HOUSE. WE'LL HIDE OUT THERE FOR A COUPLE OF DAYS, 'TIL THINGS QUIET DOWN. THOSE DUMBBELL COPPERS'LL GET TIRED SOON.
THIS IS IT.

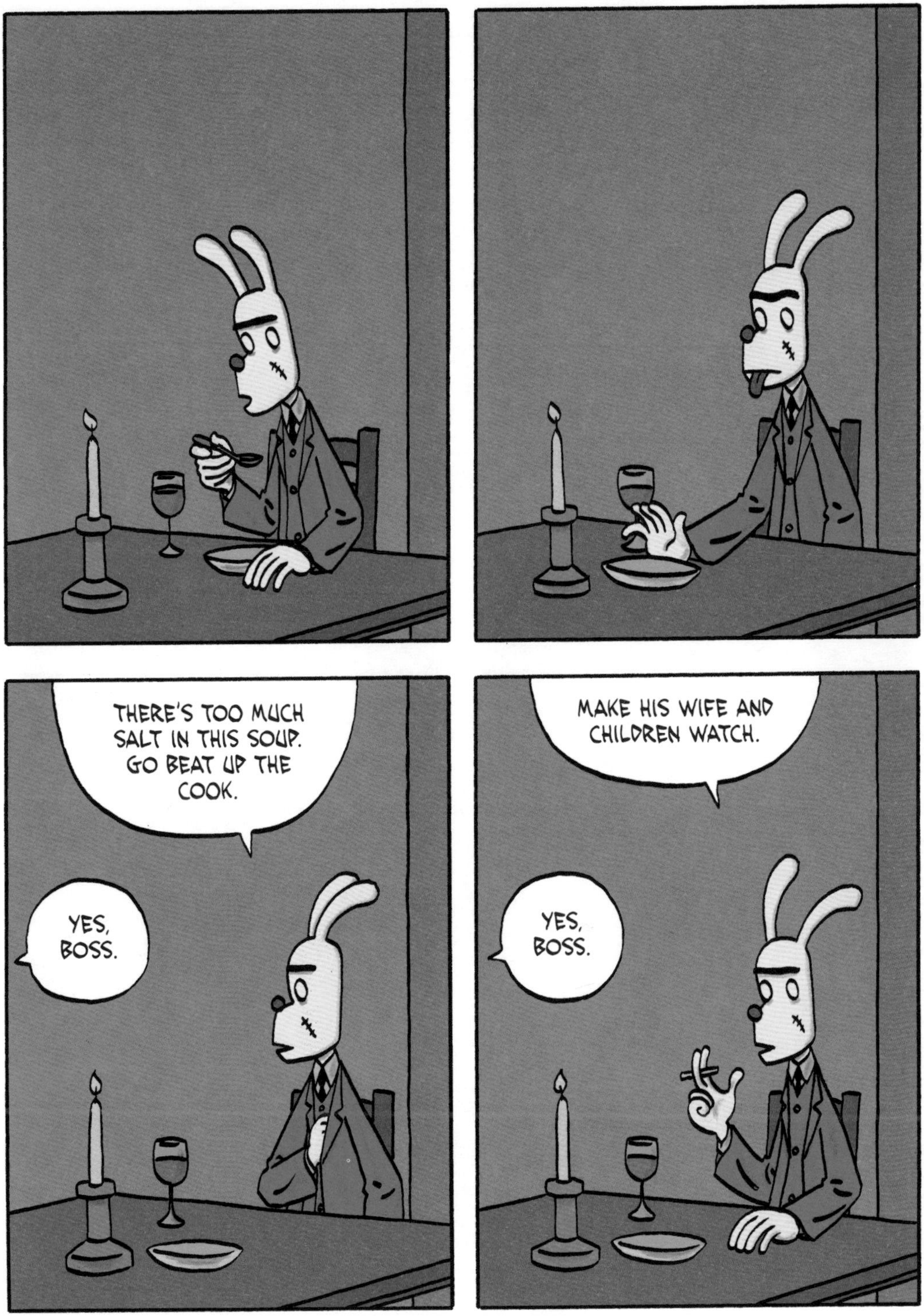
THERE'S TOO MUCH SALT IN THIS SOUP. GO BEAT UP THE COOK.
YES, BOSS.
MAKE HIS WIFE AND CHILDREN WATCH.
YES, BOSS.

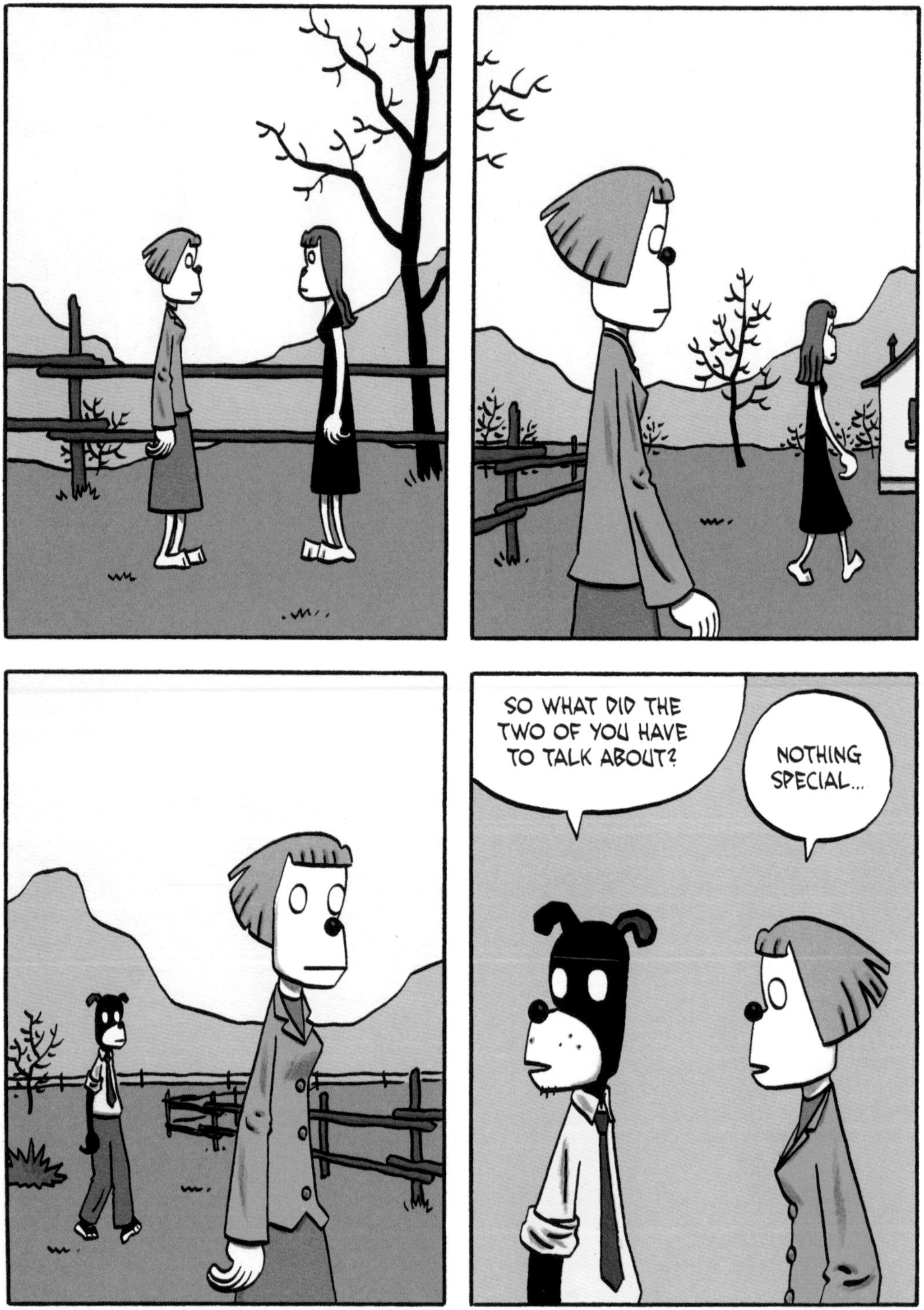
SO WHAT DID THE TWO OF YOU HAVE TO TALK ABOUT?
NOTHING SPECIAL...

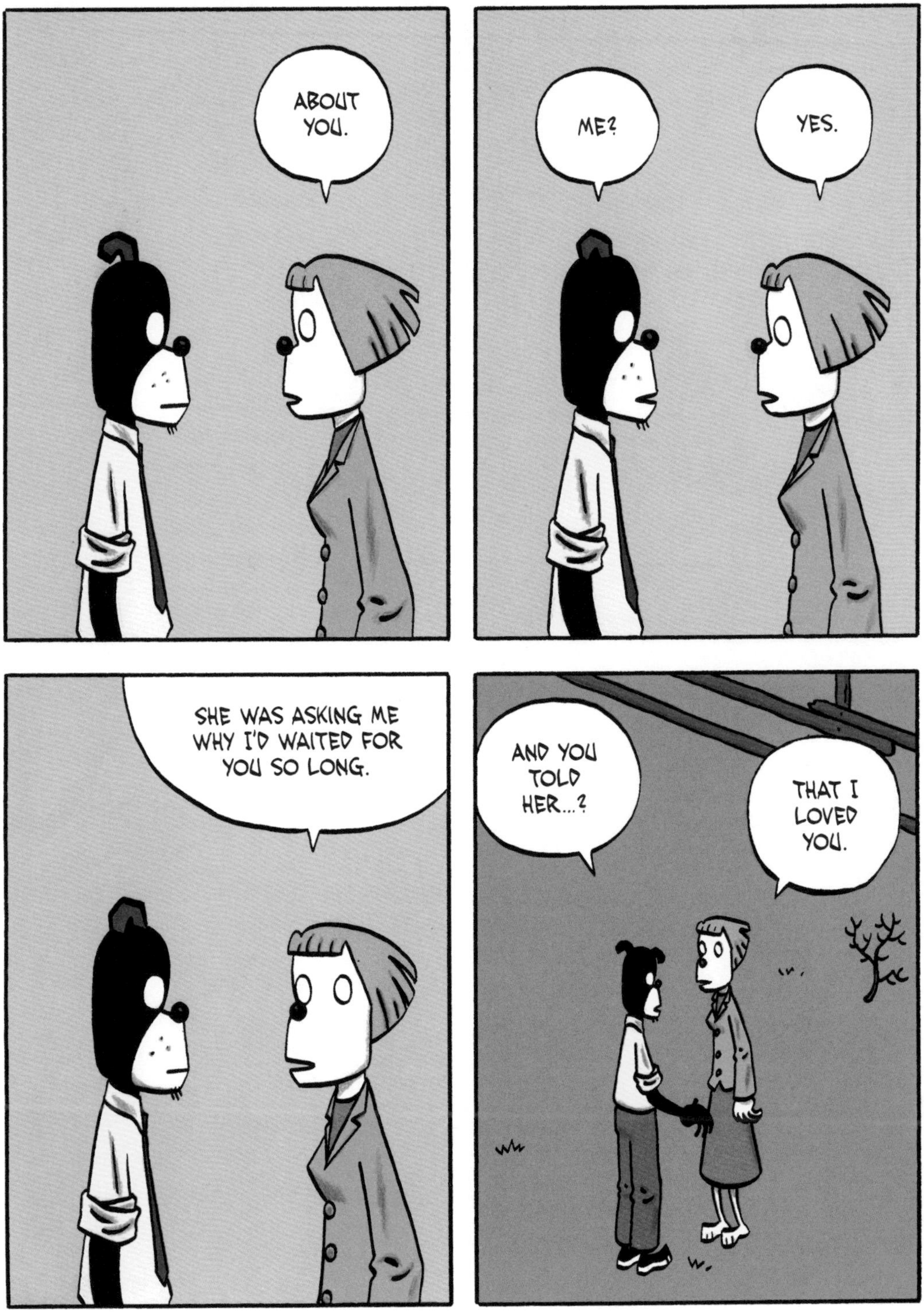
ABOUT YOU.
ME?
YES.
SHE WAS ASKING ME WHY I'D WAITED FOR YOU SO LONG.
AND YOU TOLD HER...?
THAT I LOVED YOU.

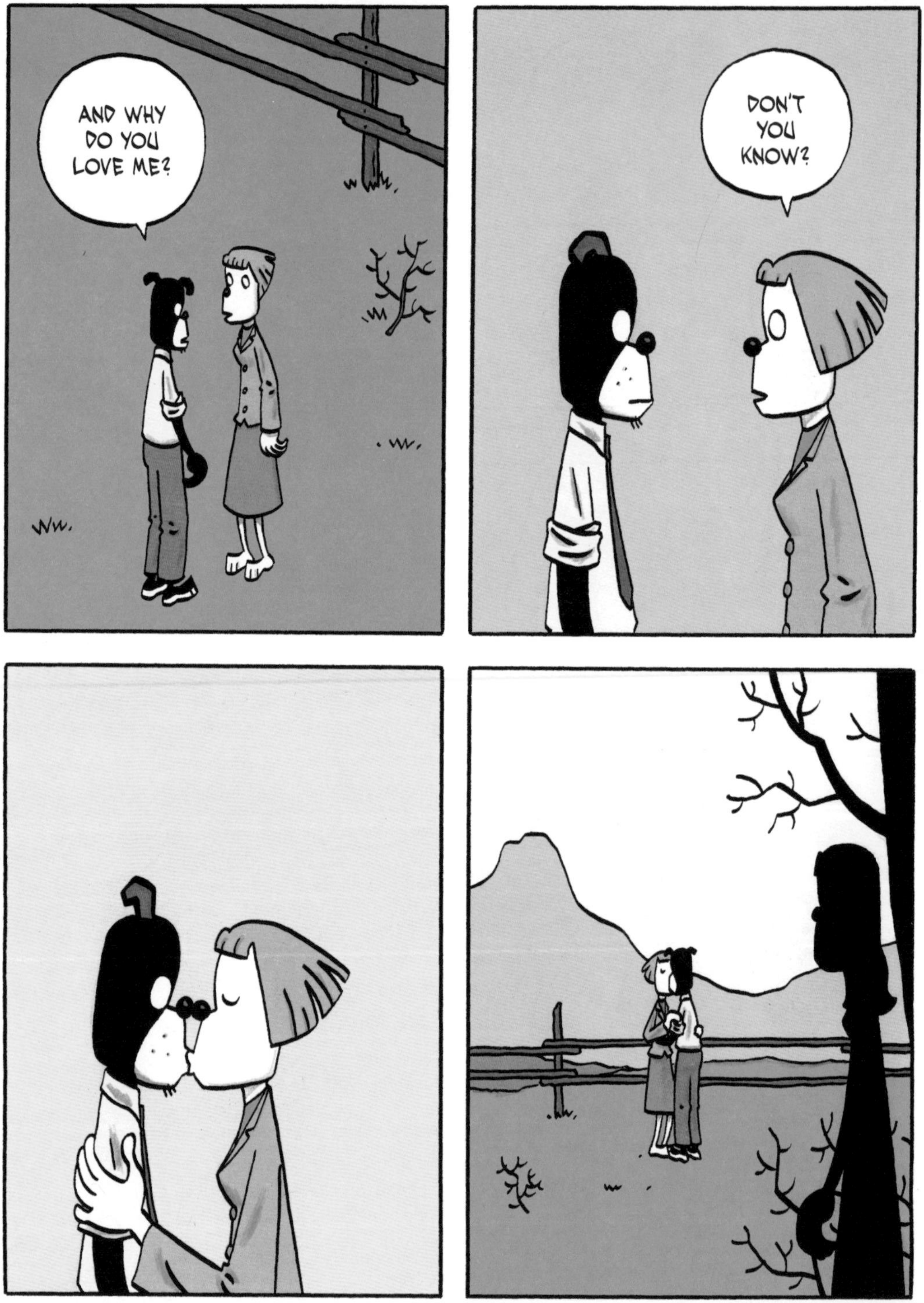
AND WHY DO YOU LOVE ME?
DON'T YOU KNOW?

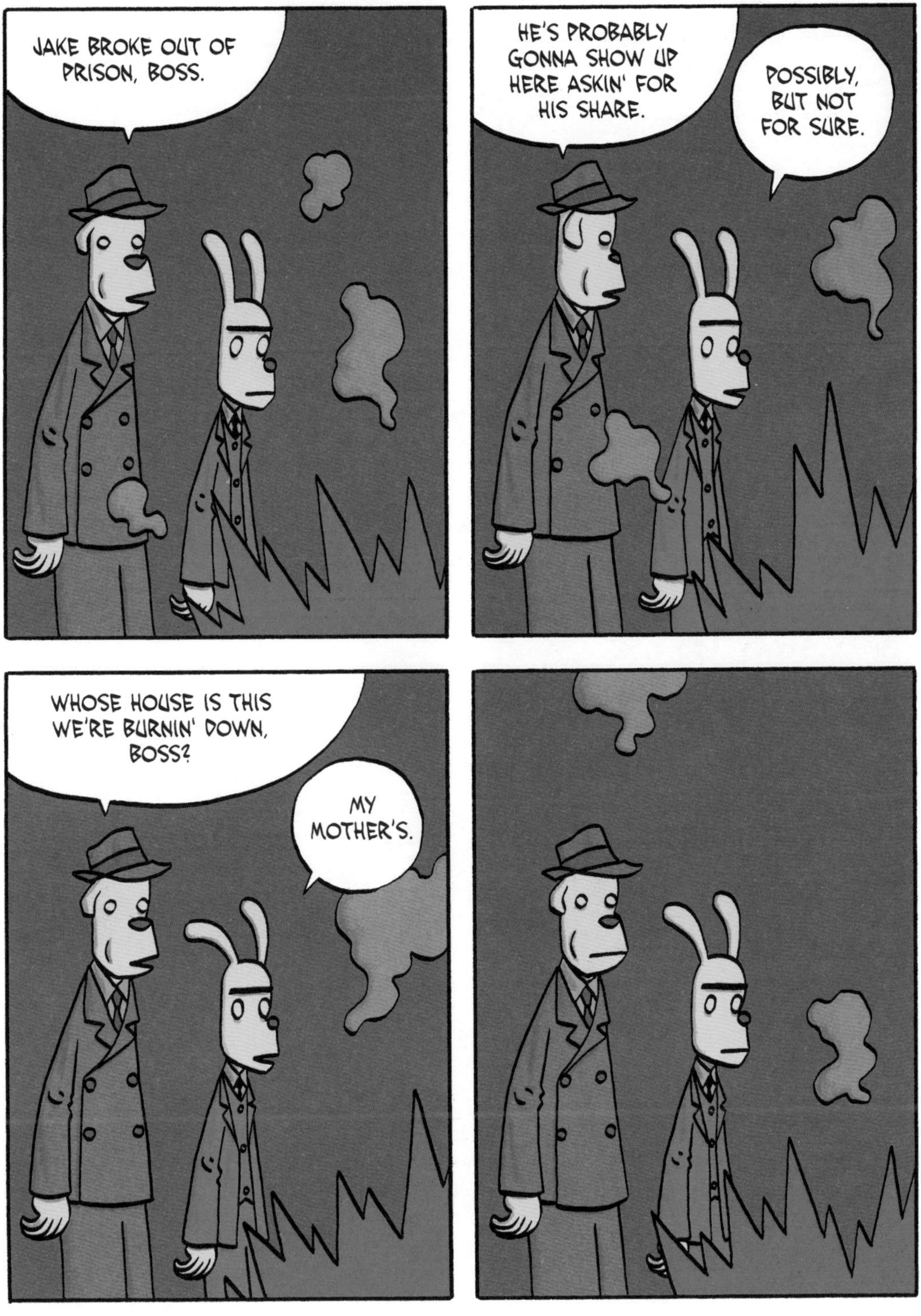
JAKE BROKE OUT OF PRISON, BOSS.
HE'S PROBABLY GONNA SHOW UP HERE ASKIN' FOR HIS SHARE.
POSSIBLY, BUT NOT FOR SURE.
WHOSE HOUSE IS THIS WE'RE BURNIN' DOWN, BOSS?
MY MOTHER'S.

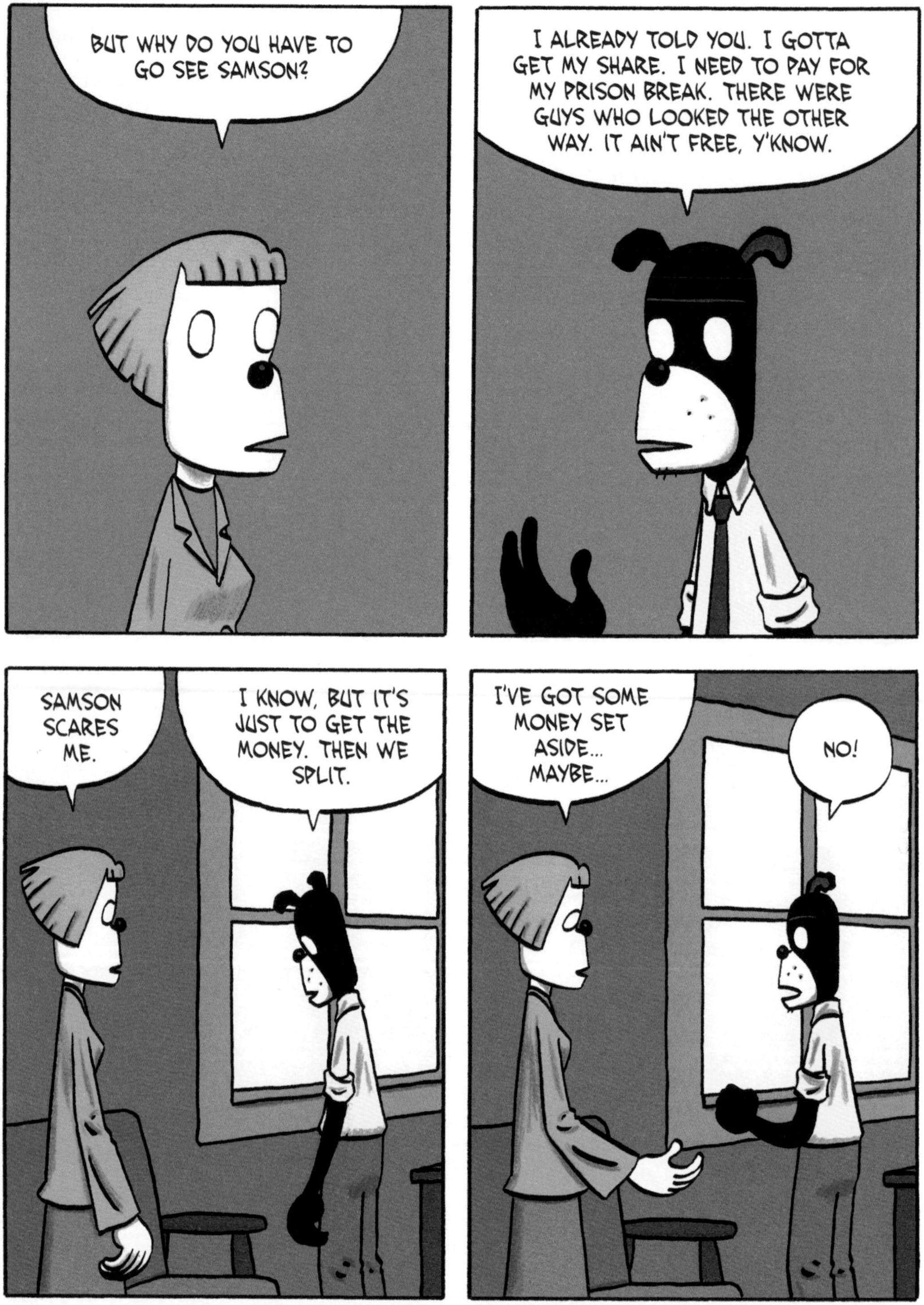
BUT WHY DO YOU HAVE TO GO SEE SAMSON?
I ALREADY TOLD YOU. I GOTTA GET MY SHARE. I NEED TO PAY FOR MY PRISON BREAK. THERE WERE GUYS WHO LOOKED THE OTHER WAY. IT AIN'T FREE, Y'KNOW.
SAMSON SCARES ME.
I KNOW, BUT IT'S JUST TO GET THE MONEY. THEN WE SPLIT.
I'VE GOT SOME MONEY SET ASIDE... MAYBE...
NO!

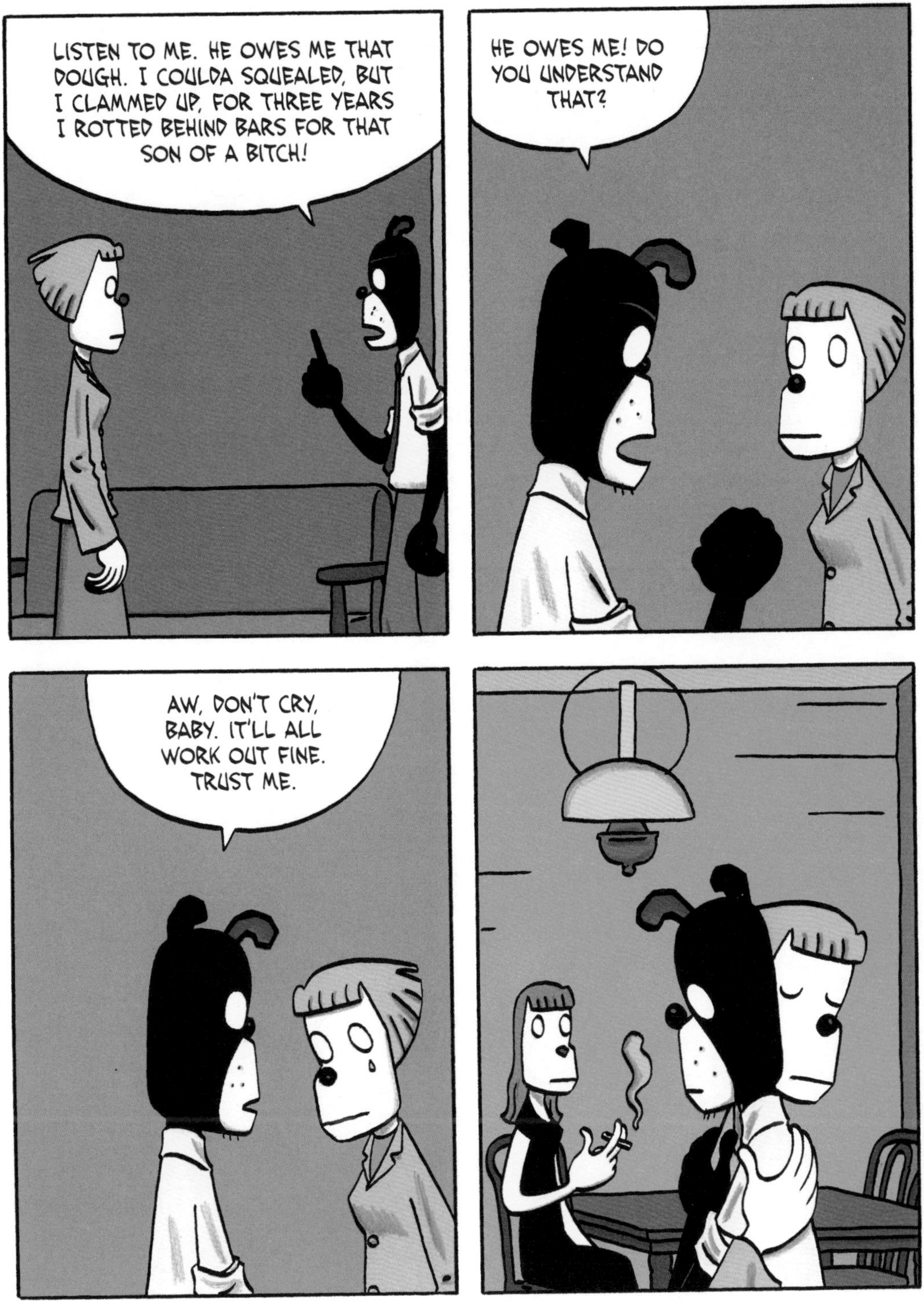
LISTEN TO ME. HE OWES ME THAT DOUGH. I COULDA SQUEALED, BUT I CLAMMED UP, FOR THREE YEARS I ROTTED BEHIND BARS FOR THAT SON OF A BITCH!
HE OWES ME! DO YOU UNDERSTAND THAT?
AW, DON'T CRY, BABY. IT'LL ALL WORK OUT FINE. TRUST ME.

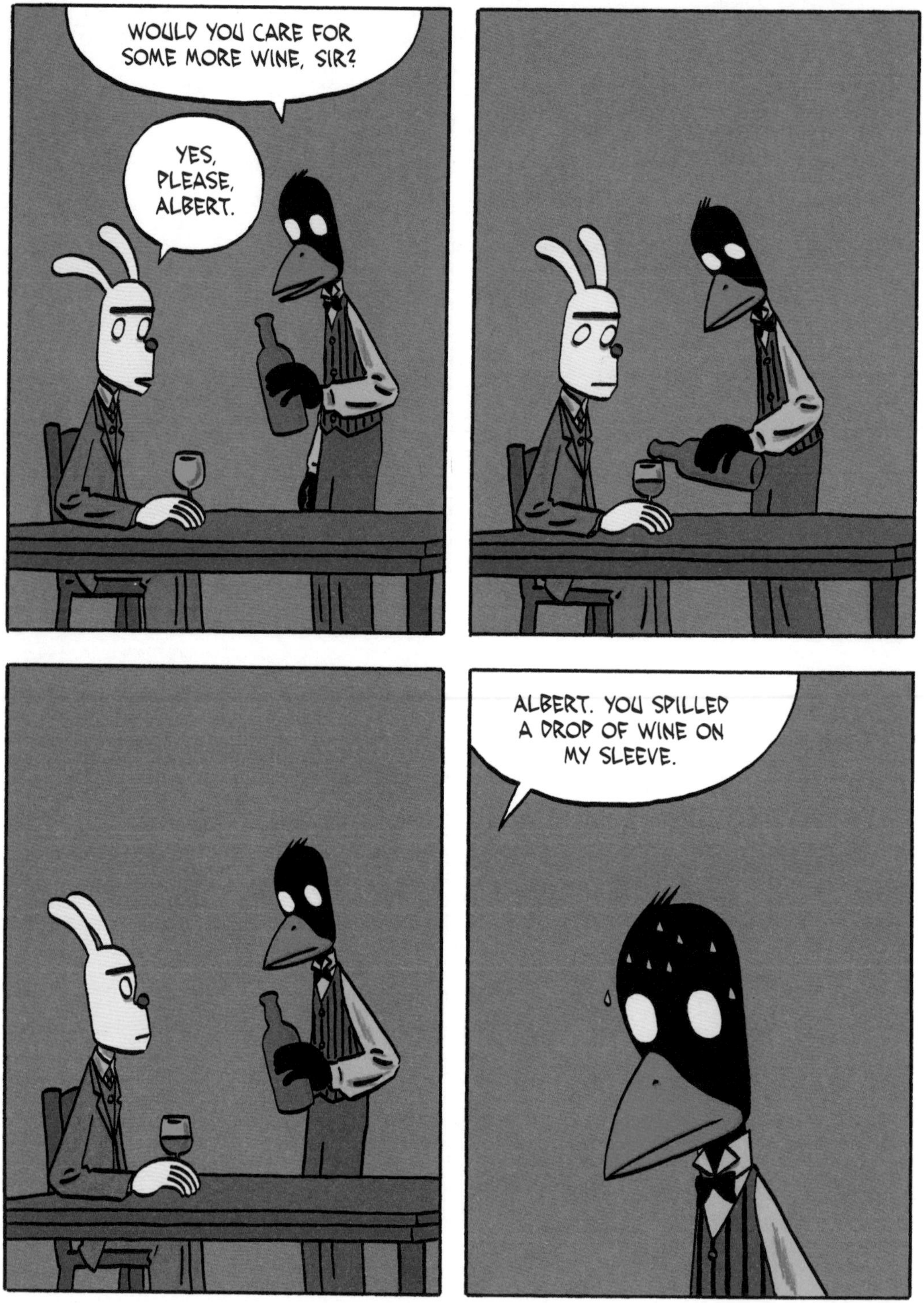
WOULD YOU CARE FOR SOME MORE WINE, SIR?
YES, PLEASE, ALBERT.
ALBERT. YOU SPILLED A DROP OF WINE ON MY SLEEVE.

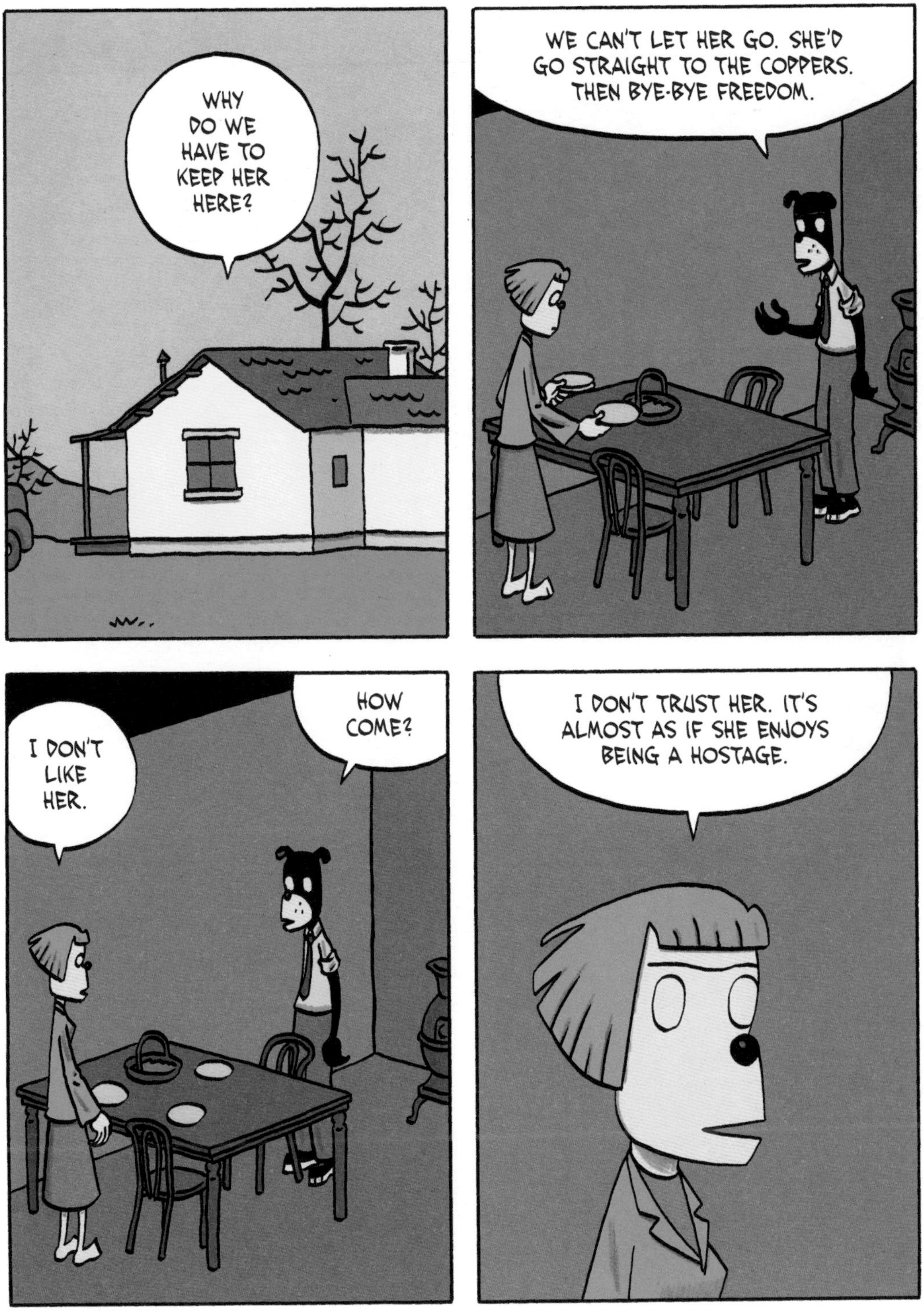
WHY DO WE HAVE TO KEEP HER HERE?
WE CAN'T LET HER GO. SHE'D GO STRAIGHT TO THE COPPERS. THEN BYE-BYE FREEDOM.
HOW COME?
I DON'T LIKE HER.
I DON'T TRUST HER. IT'S ALMOST AS IF SHE ENJOYS BEING A HOSTAGE.

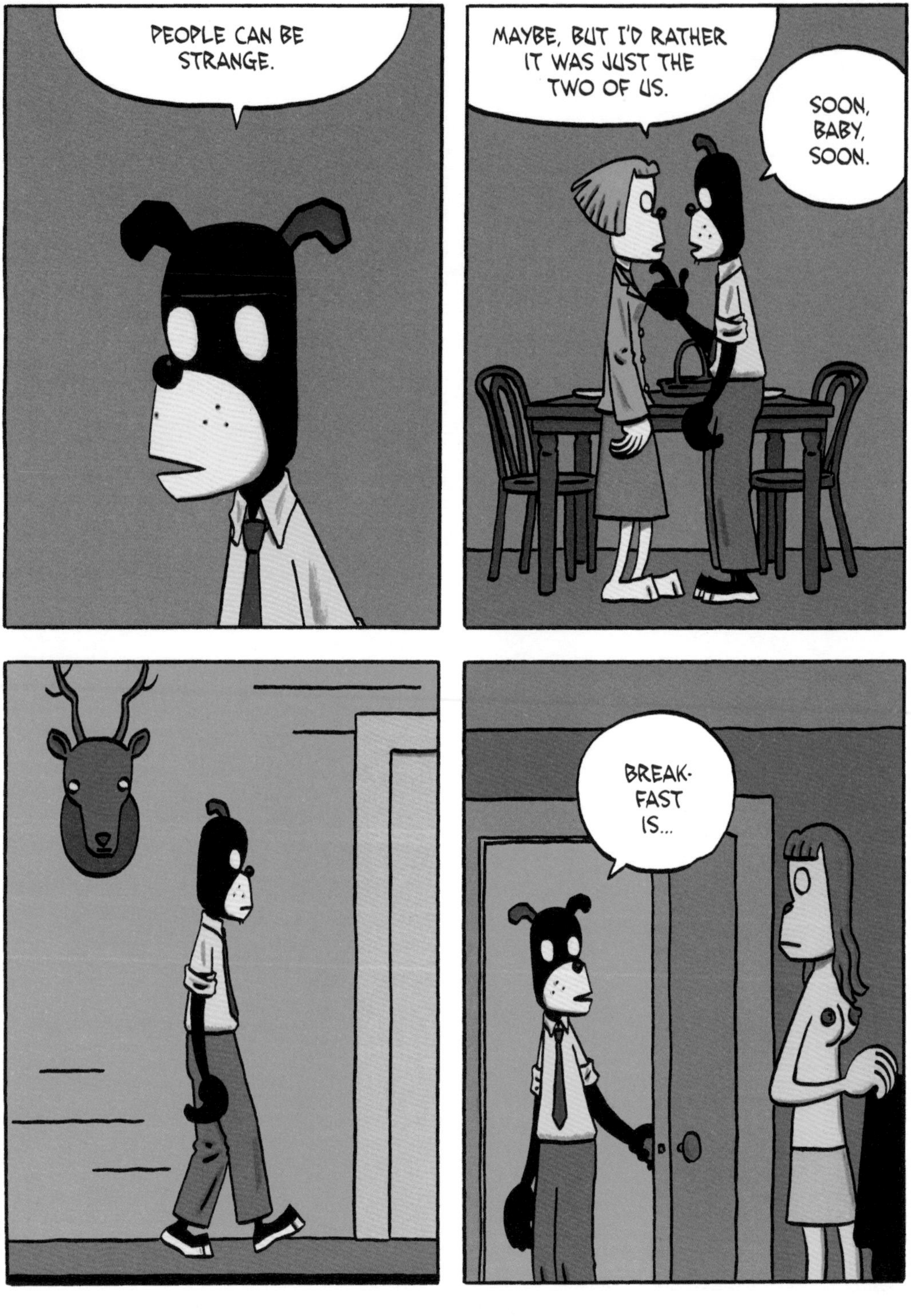
PEOPLE CAN BE STRANGE.
MAYBE, BUT I'D RATHER IT WAS JUST THE TWO OF US.
SOON, BABY, SOON.
BREAK-FAST IS...

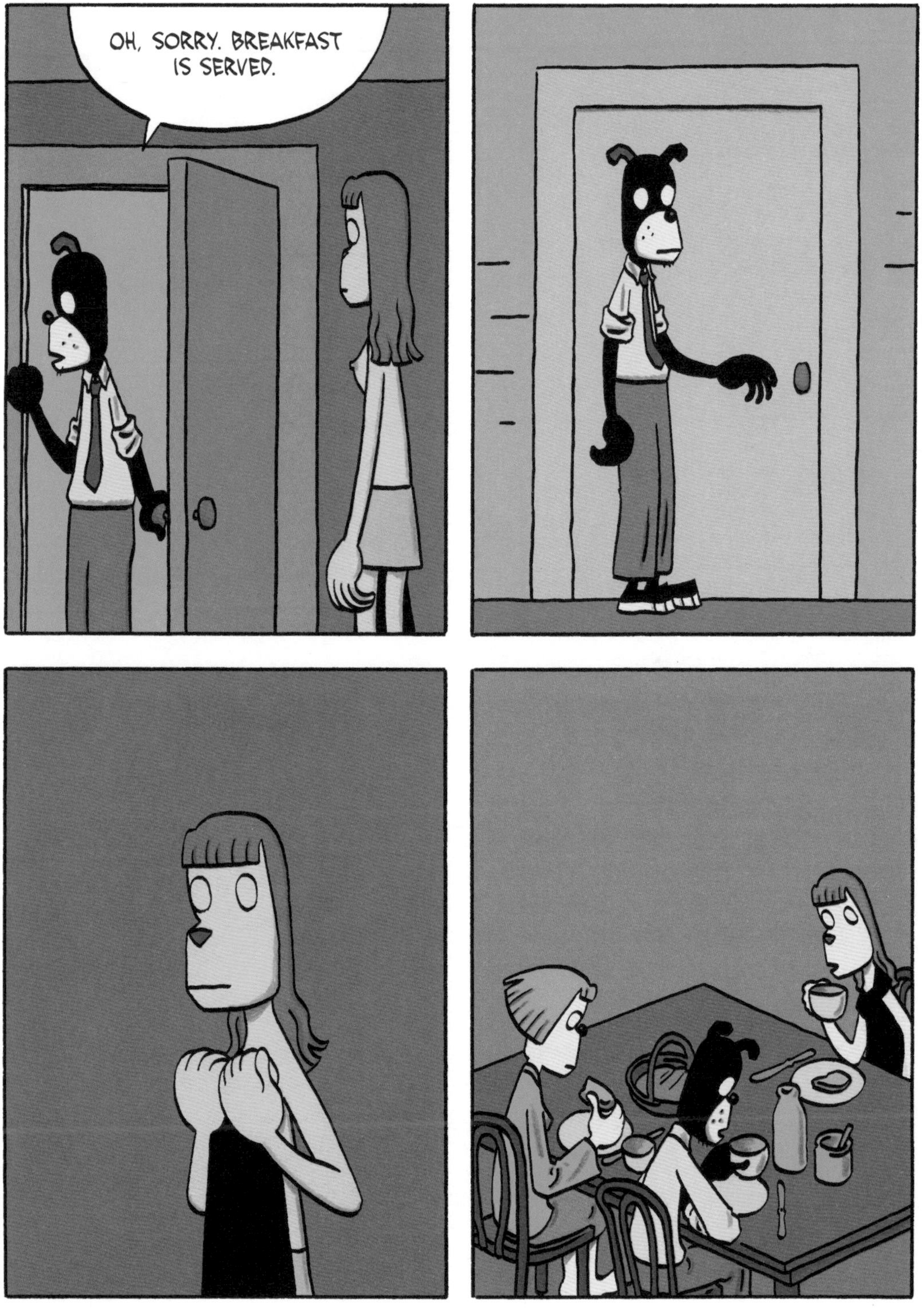
OH, SORRY. BREAKFAST IS SERVED.

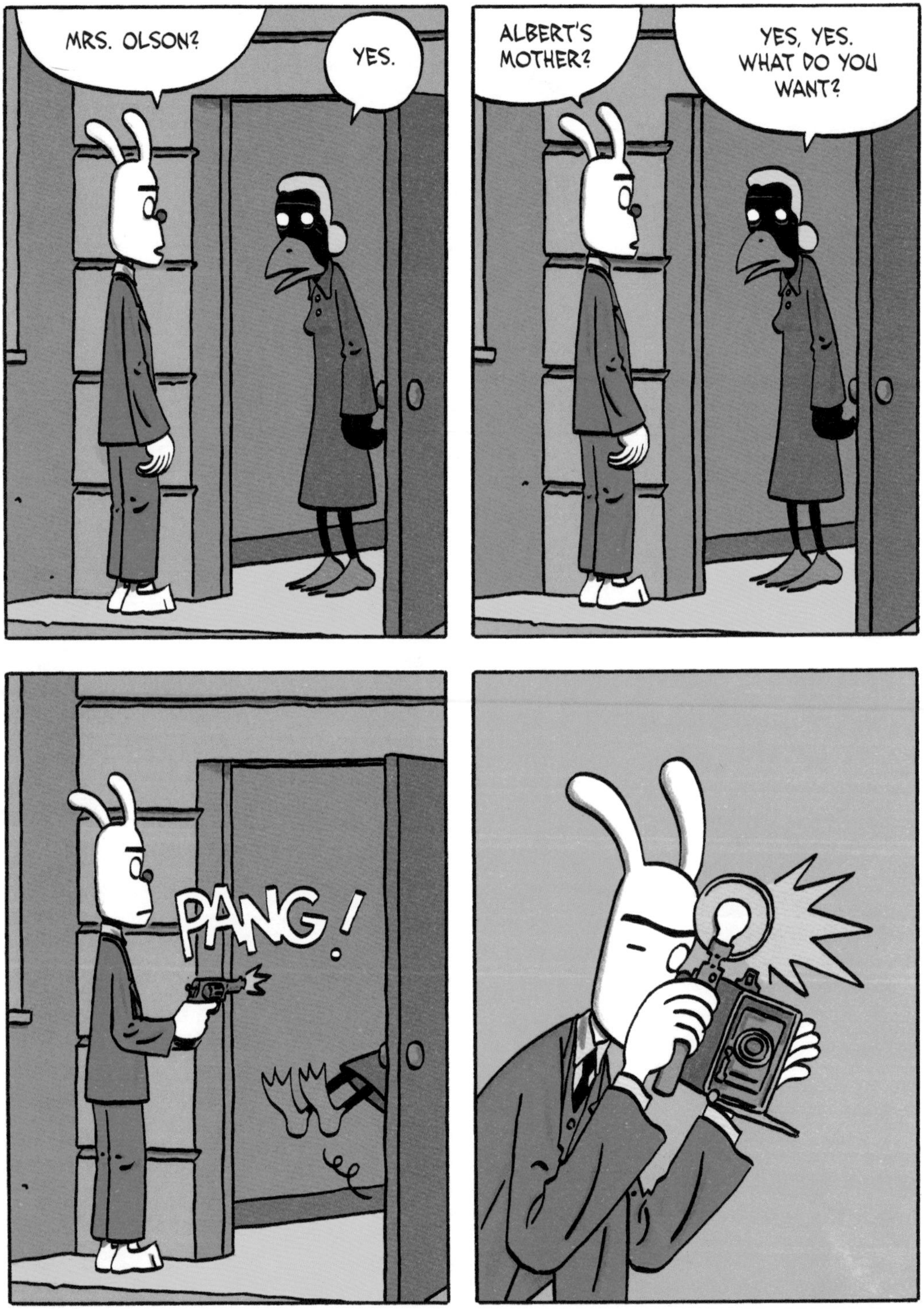
MRS. OLSON?
YES.
ALBERT'S MOTHER?
YES, YES. WHAT DO YOU WANT?
PANG!

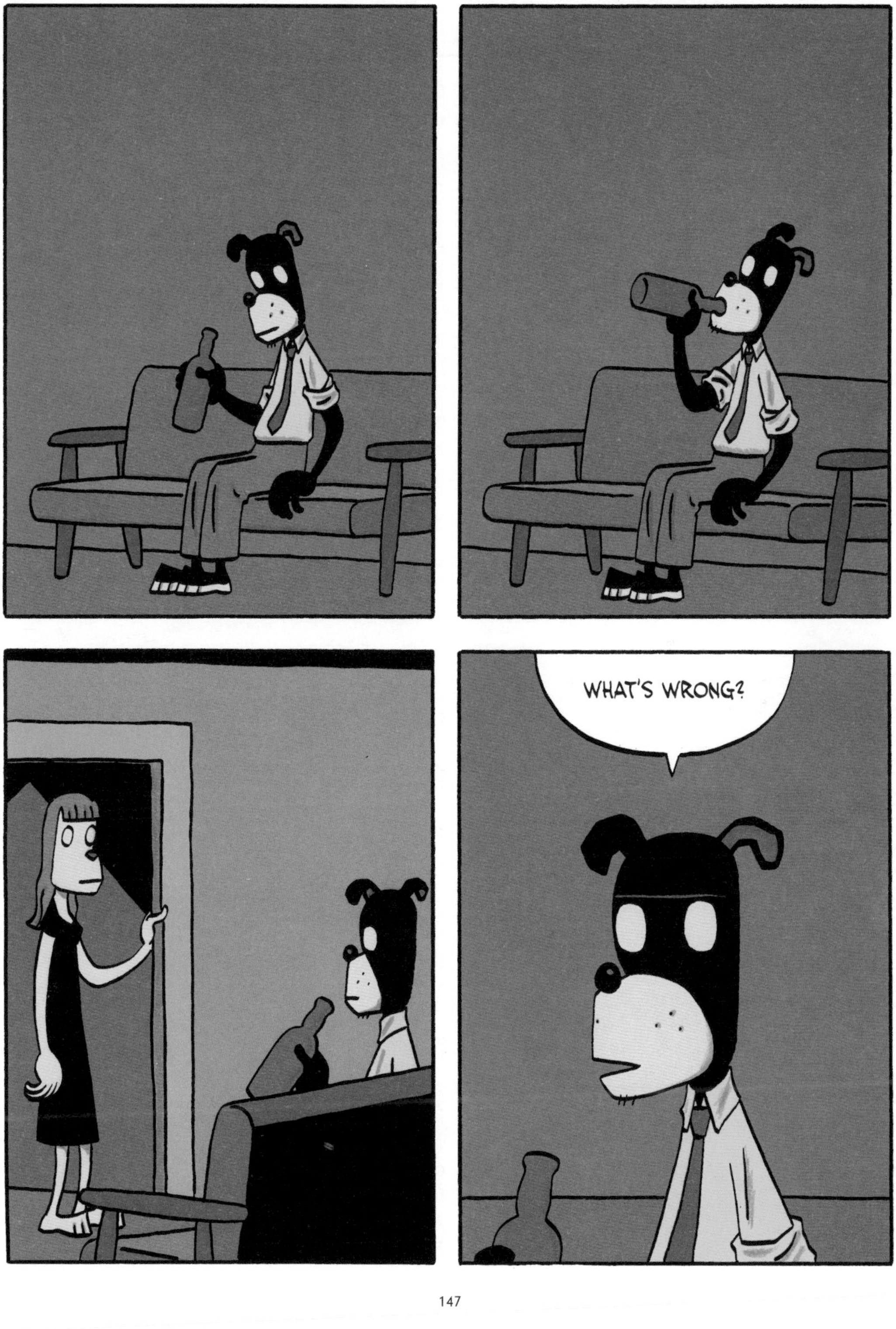
WHAT'S WRONG?

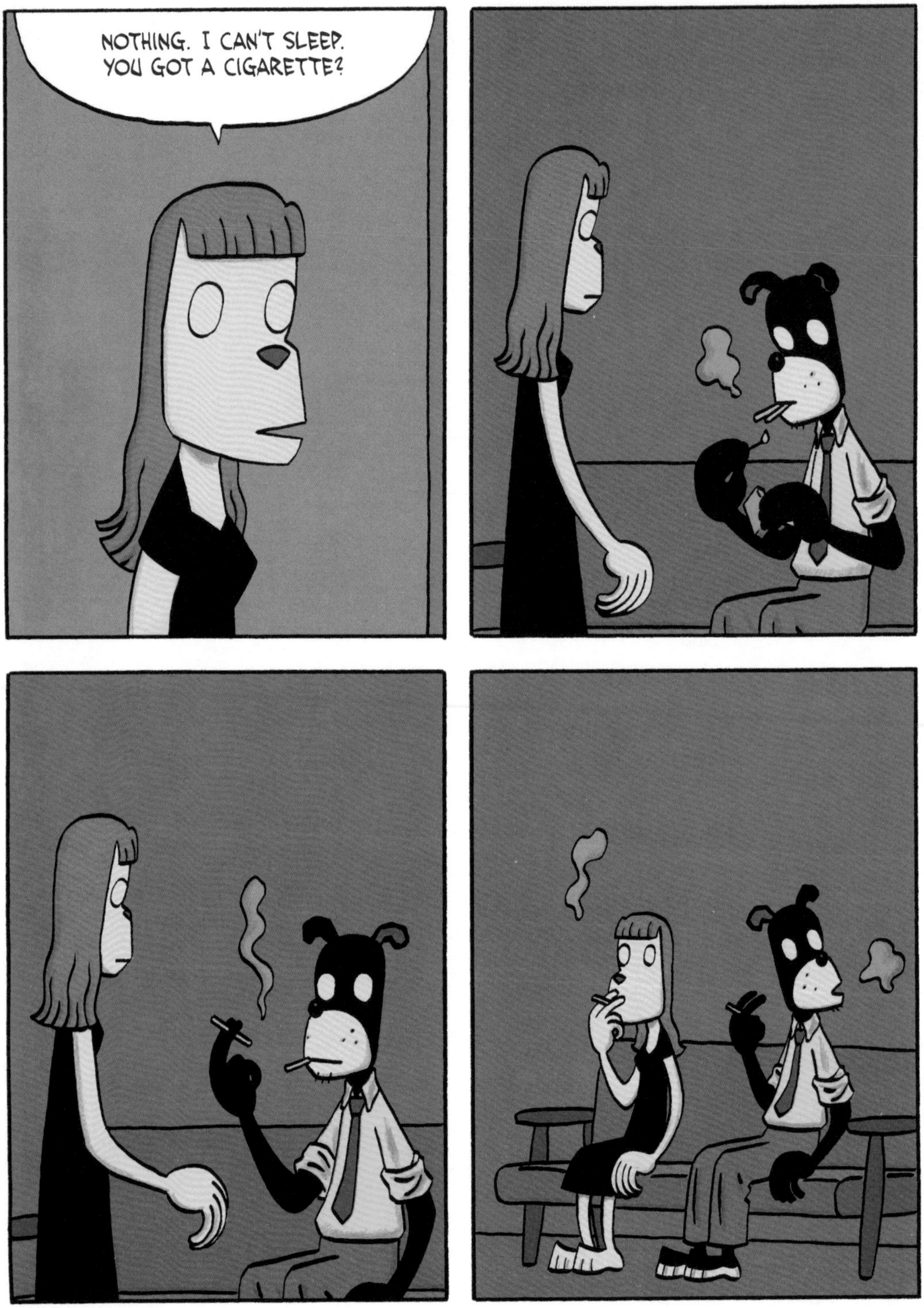
NOTHING. I CAN'T SLEEP. YOU GOT A CIGARETTE?

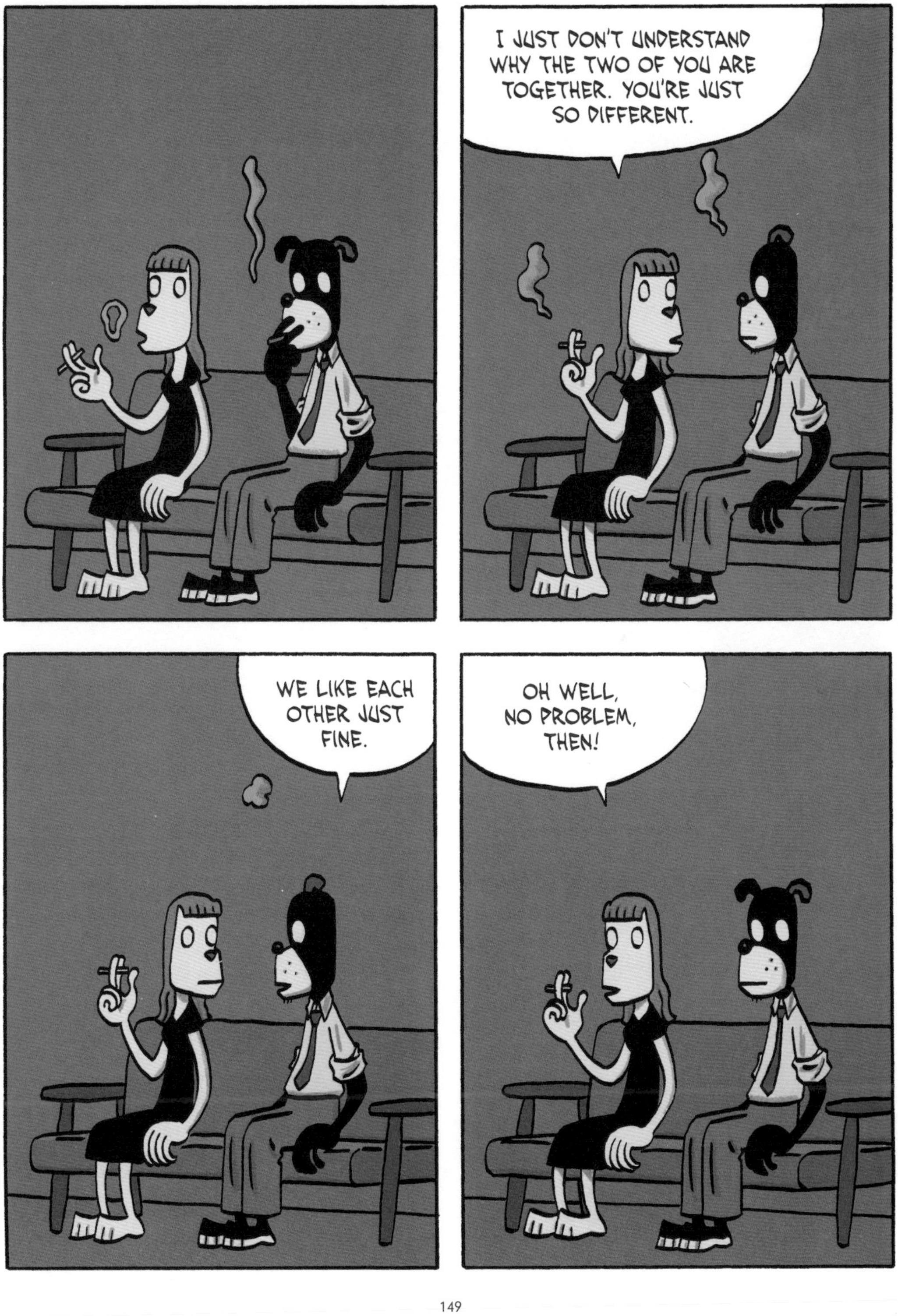
I JUST DON'T UNDERSTAND WHY THE TWO OF YOU ARE TOGETHER. YOU'RE JUST SO DIFFERENT.
WE LIKE EACH OTHER JUST FINE.
OH WELL, NO PROBLEM, THEN!

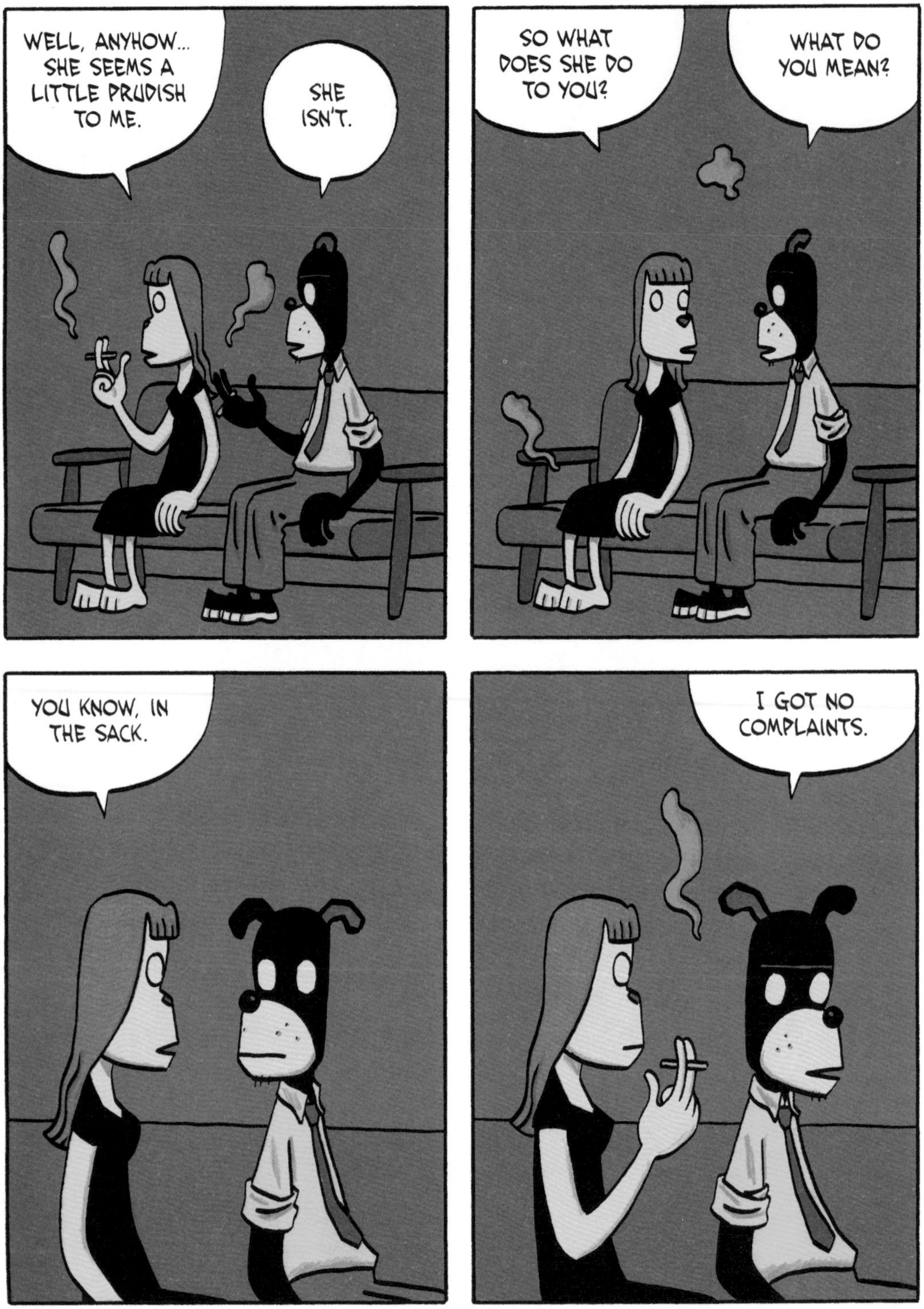
WELL, ANYHOW... SHE SEEMS A LITTLE PRUDISH TO ME.
SHE ISN'T.
SO WHAT DOES SHE DO TO YOU?
WHAT DO YOU MEAN?
YOU KNOW, IN THE SACK.
I GOT NO COMPLAINTS.

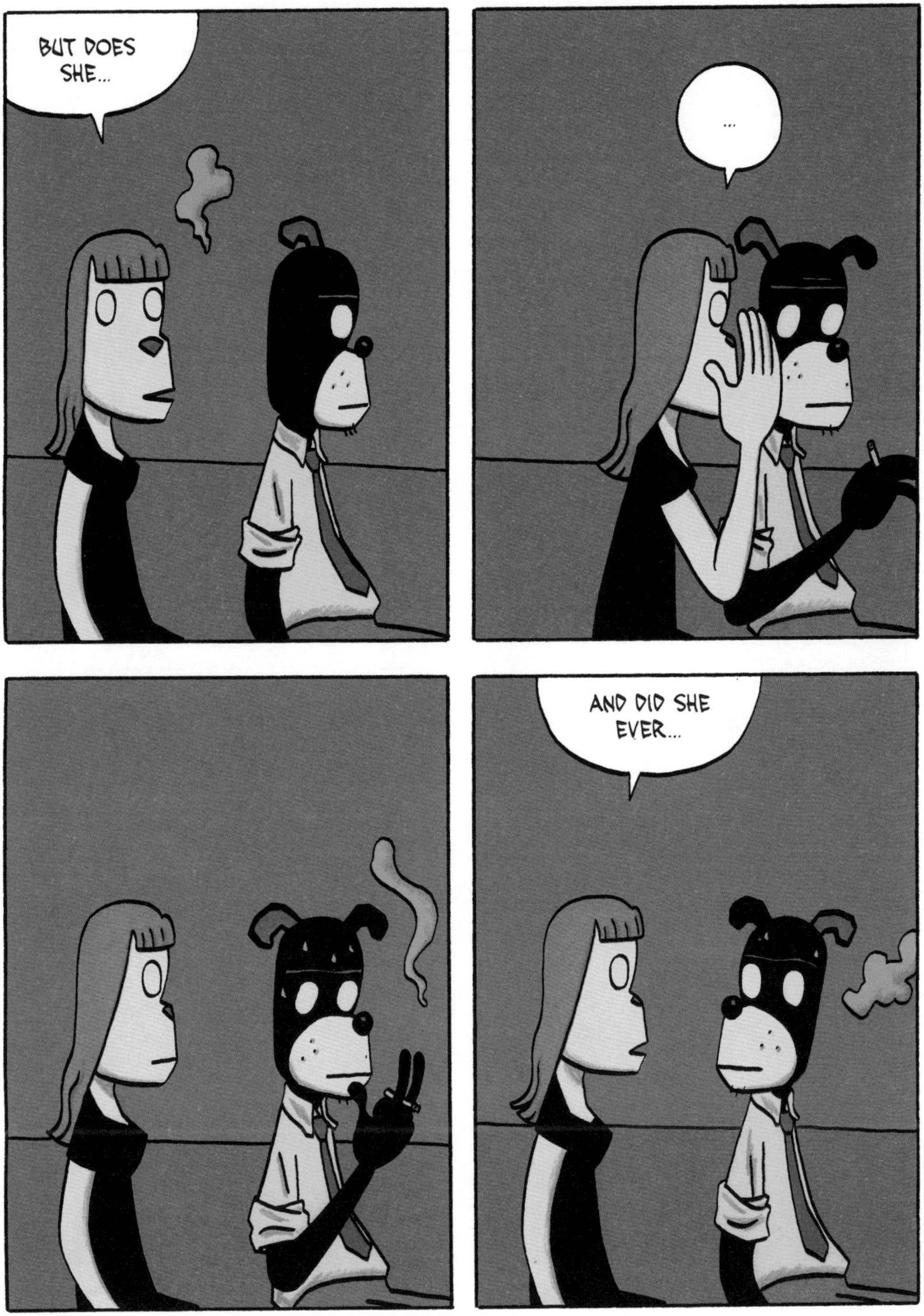
BUT DOES SHE...
...
AND DID SHE EVER...

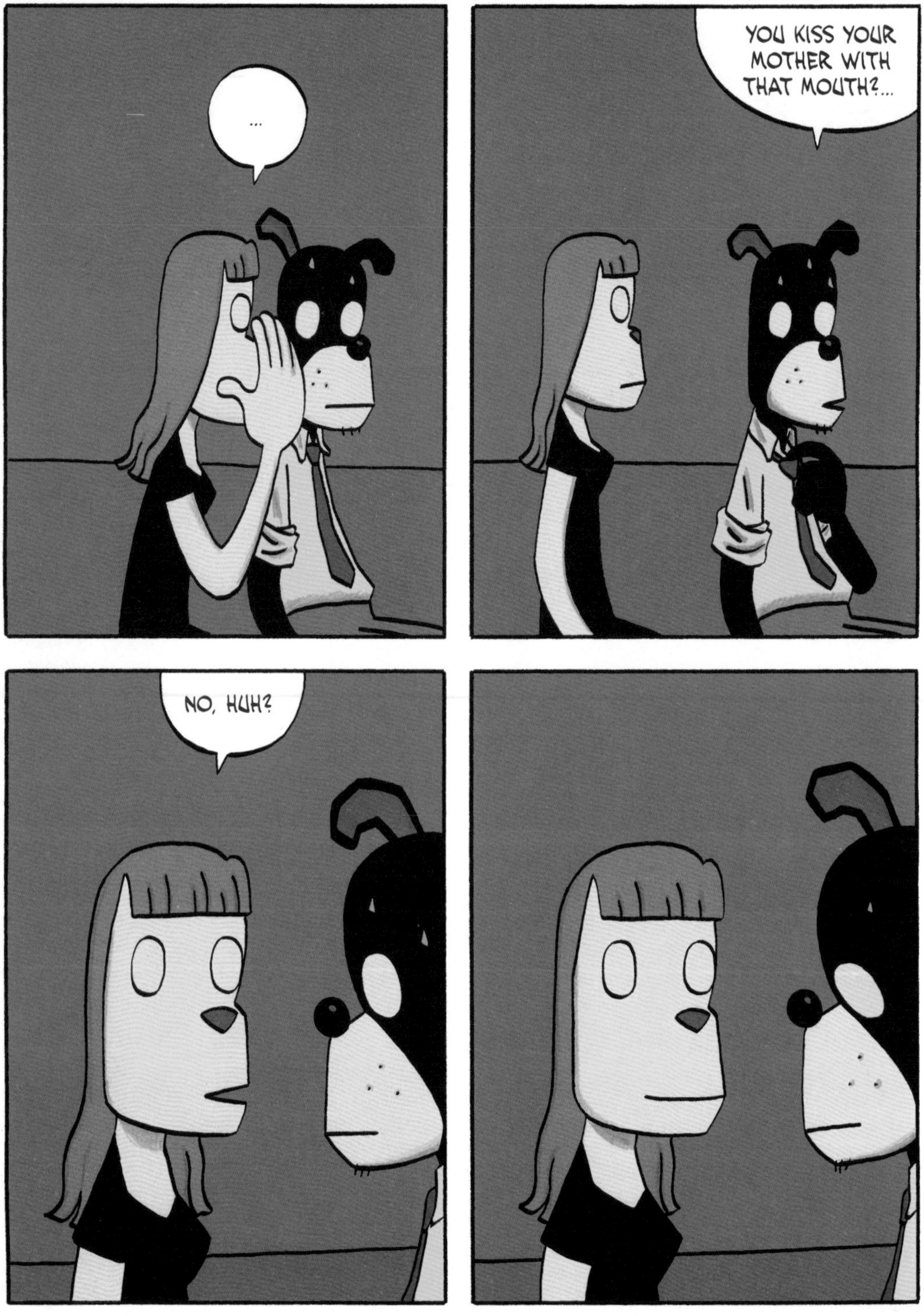
...
YOU KISS YOUR MOTHER WITH THAT MOUTH?...
NO, HUH?

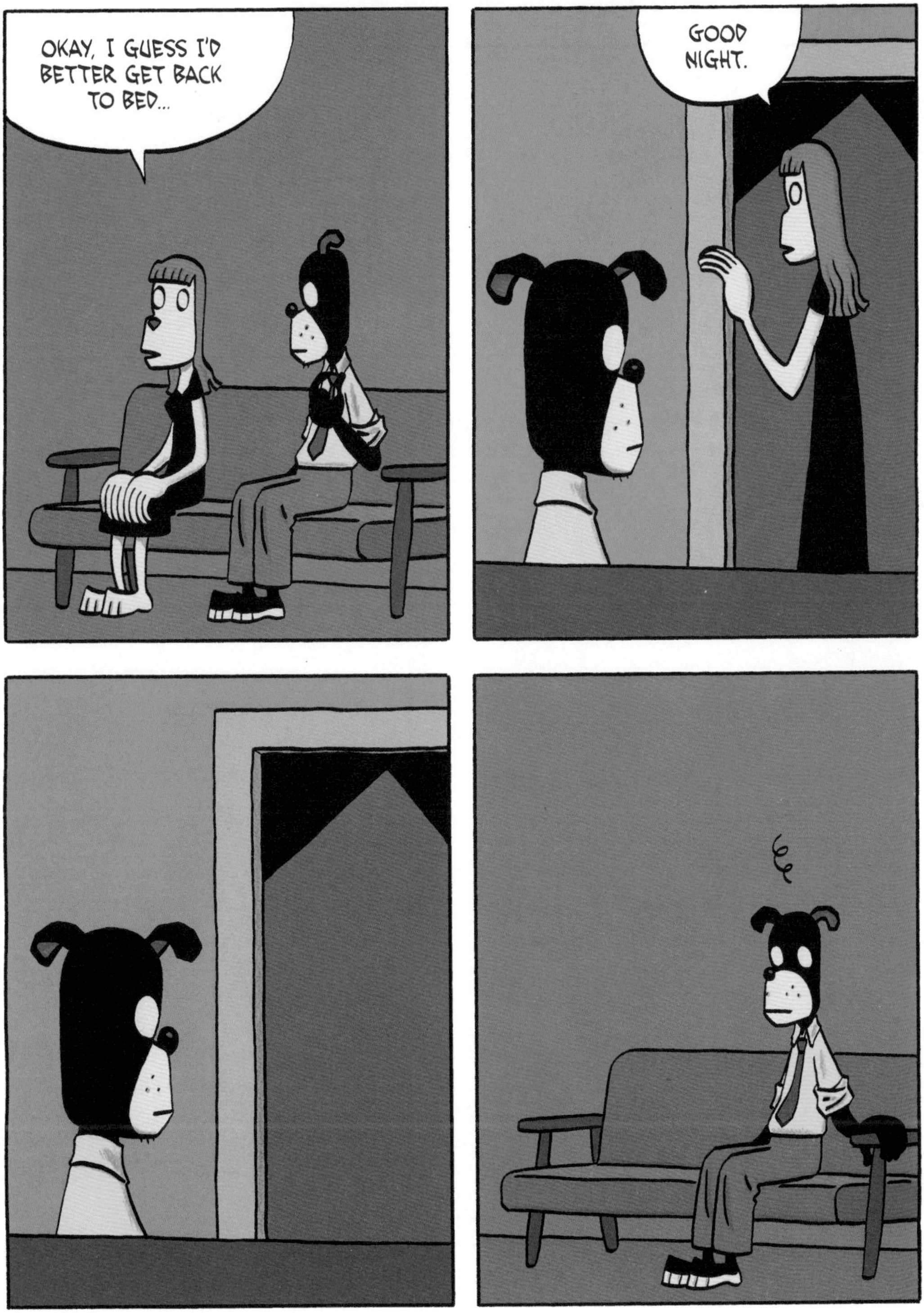
OKAY, I GUESS I'D BETTER GET BACK TO BED...
GOOD NIGHT.

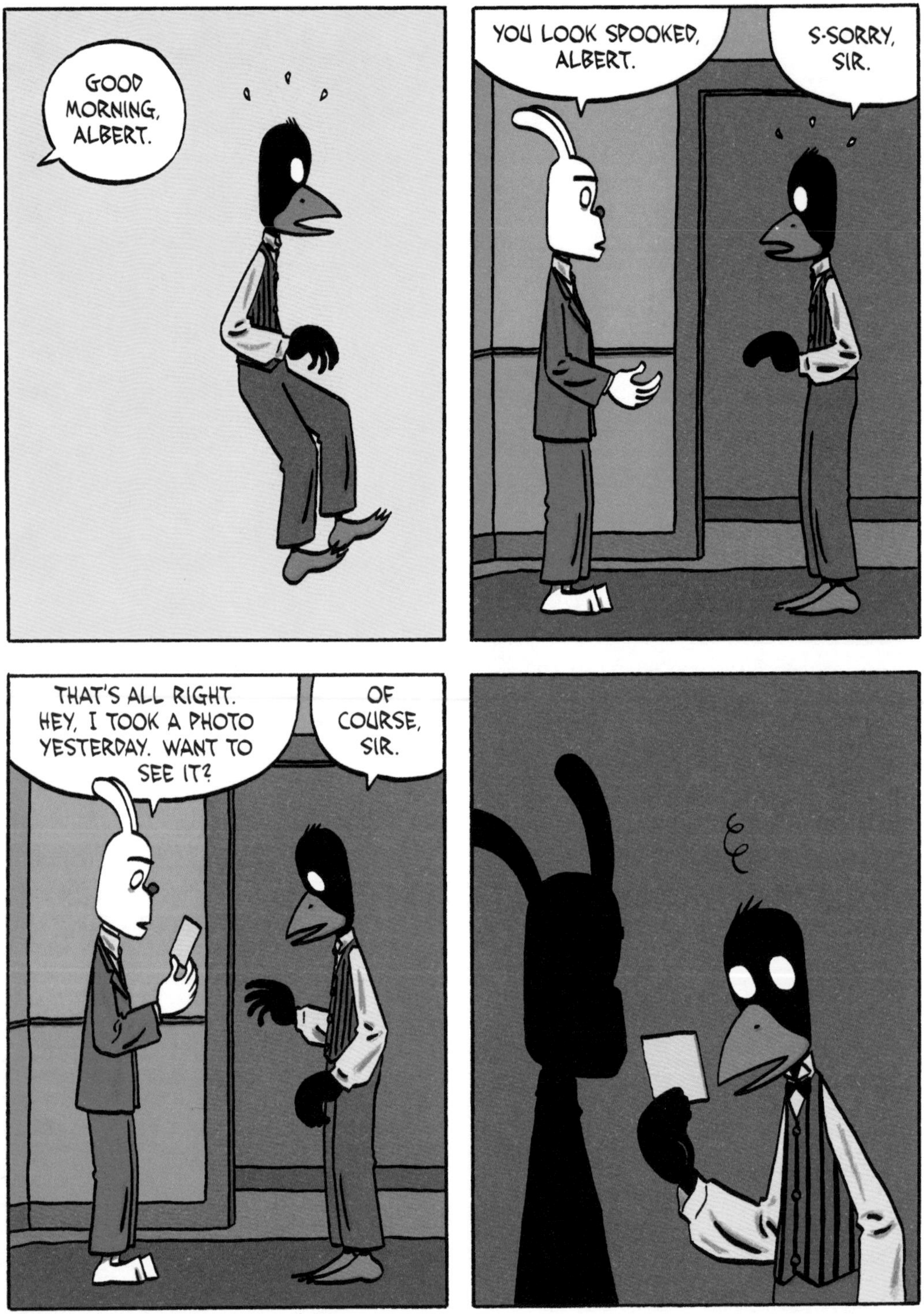
GOOD MORNING, ALBERT.
YOU LOOK SPOOKED, ALBERT.
S-SORRY, SIR.
THAT'S ALL RIGHT. HEY, I TOOK A PHOTO YESTERDAY. WANT TO SEE IT?
OF COURSE, SIR.

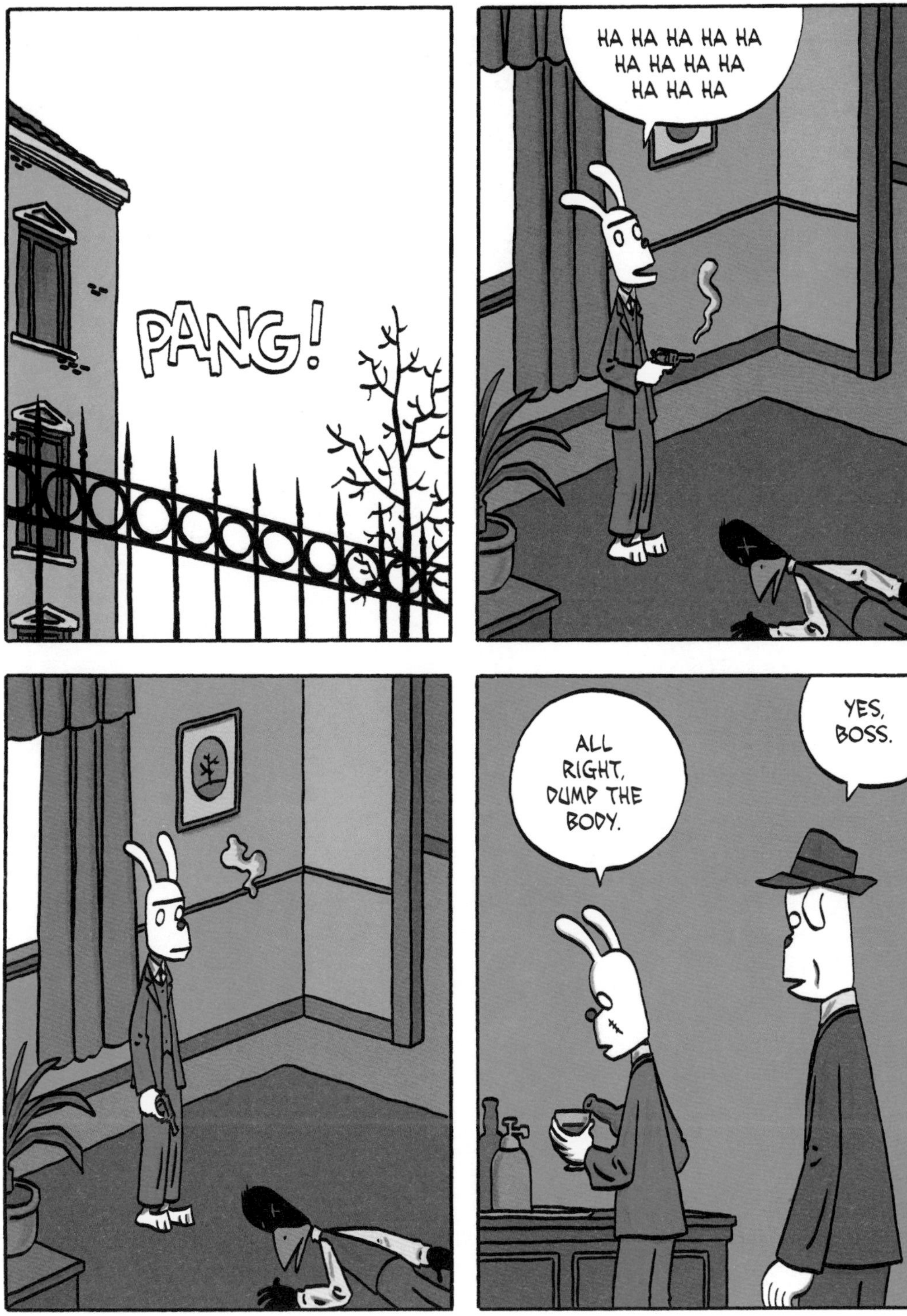
PANG!
HA HA HA HA HA HA HA HA HA HA HA HA
ALL RIGHT, DUMP THE BODY.
YES, BOSS.

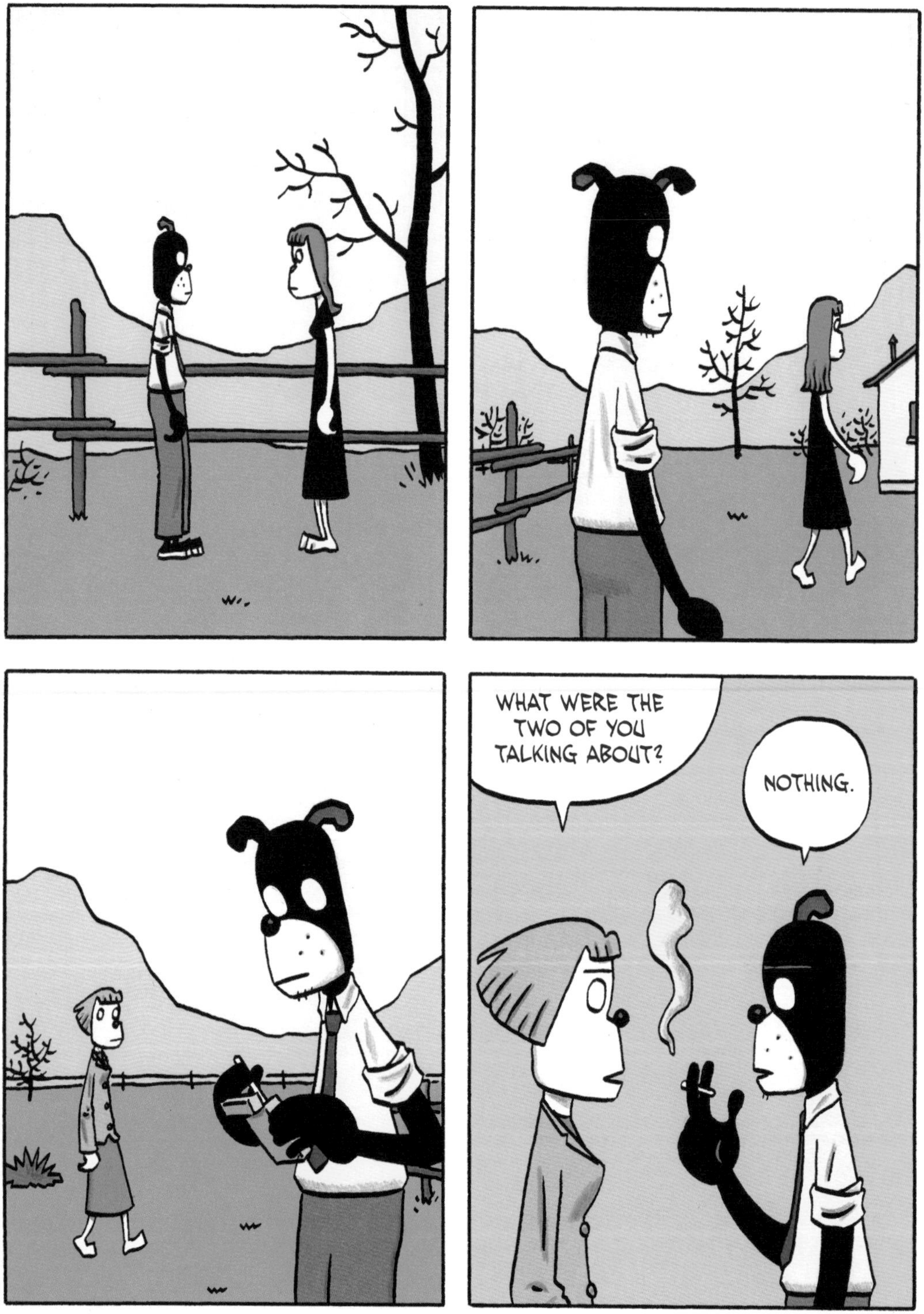
WHAT WERE THE TWO OF YOU TALKING ABOUT?
NOTHING.

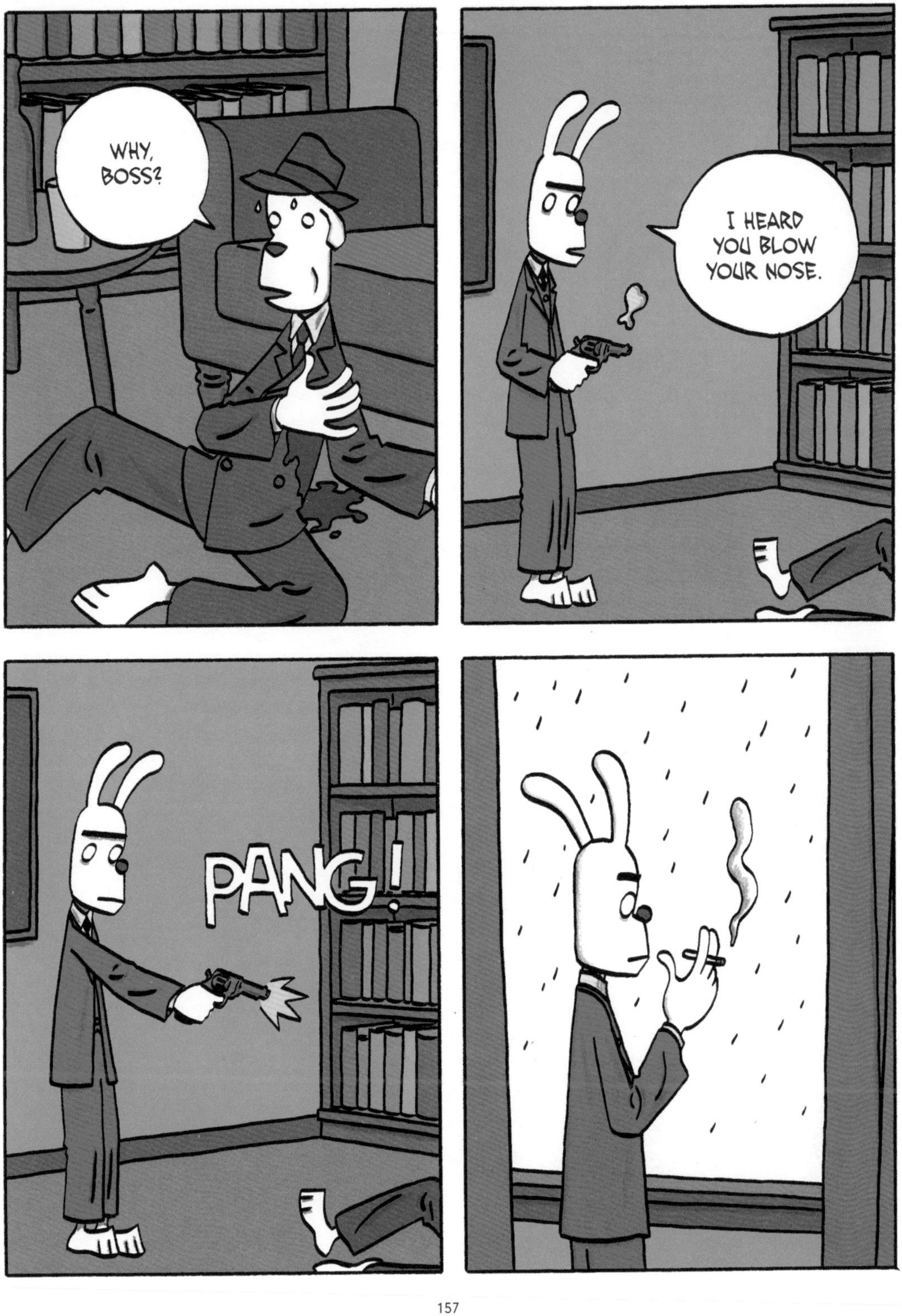
WHY, BOSS?
I HEARD YOU BLOW YOUR NOSE.
PANG!

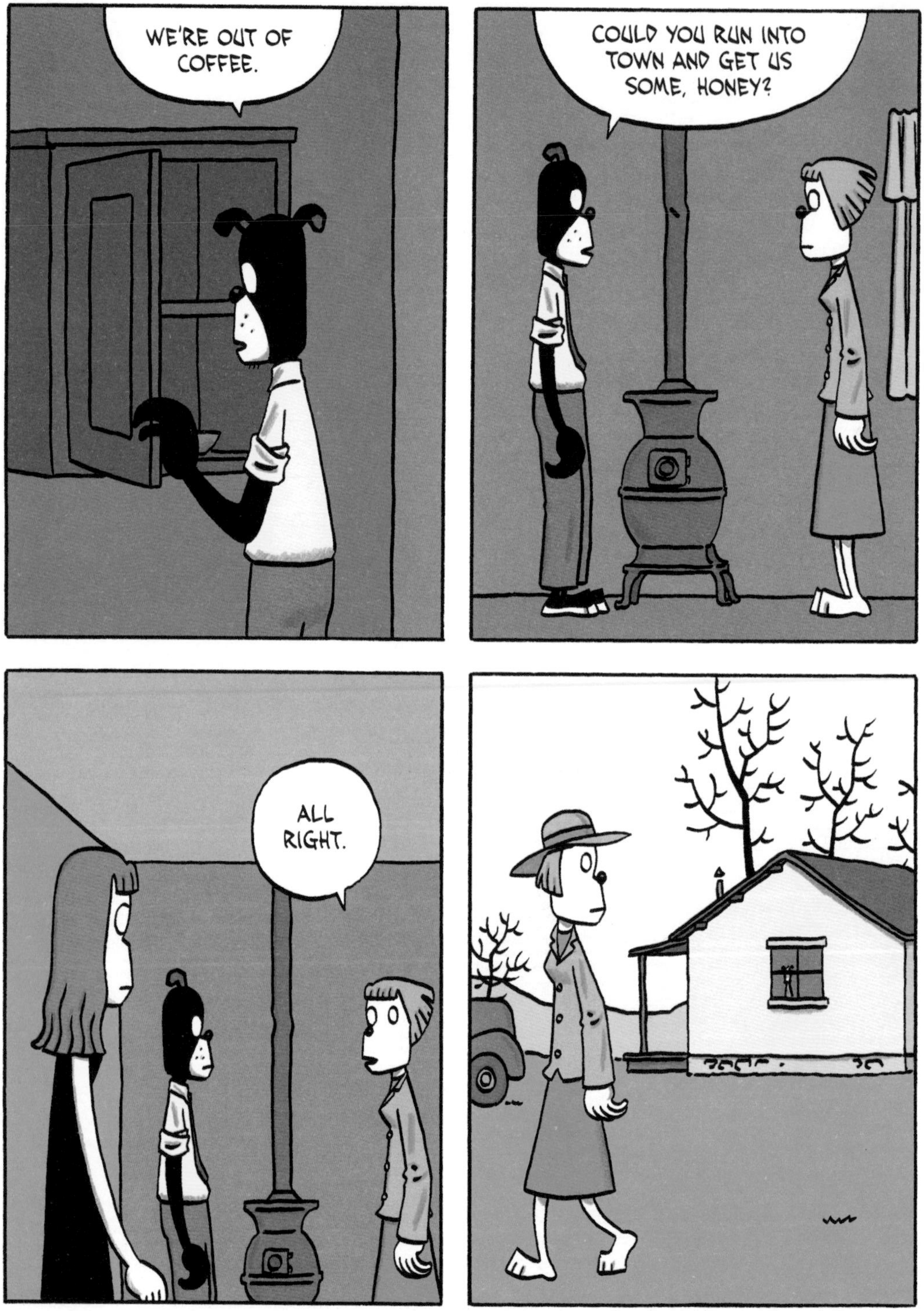
WE'RE OUT OF COFFEE.
COULD YOU RUN INTO TOWN AND GET US SOME, HONEY?
ALL RIGHT.

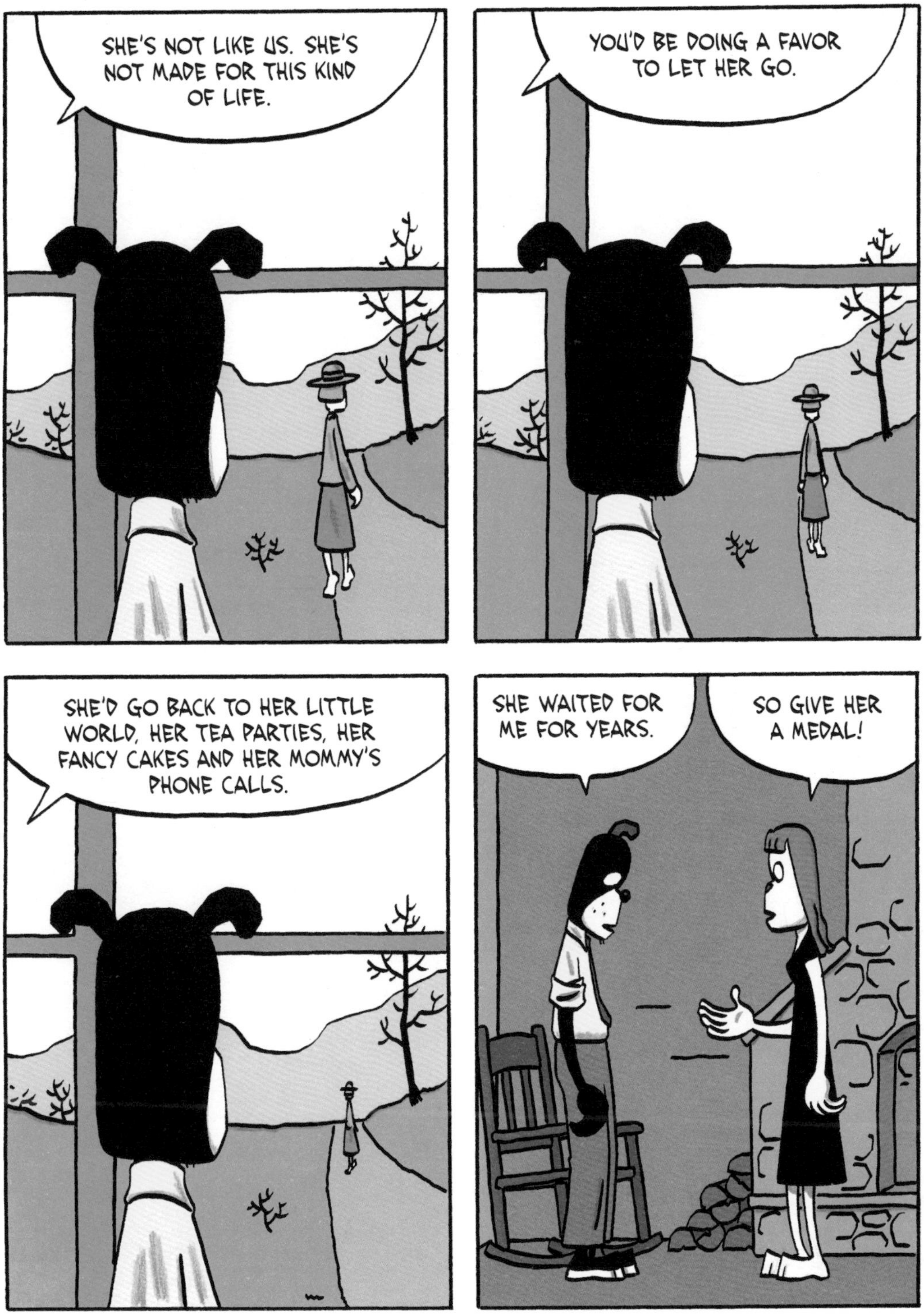
SHE'S NOT LIKE US. SHE'S NOT MADE FOR THIS KIND OF LIFE.
YOU'D BE DOING A FAVOR TO LET HER GO.
SHE'D GO BACK TO HER LITTLE WORLD, HER TEA PARTIES, HER FANCY CAKES AND HER MOMMY'S PHONE CALLS.
SHE WAITED FOR ME FOR YEARS.
SO GIVE HER A MEDAL!

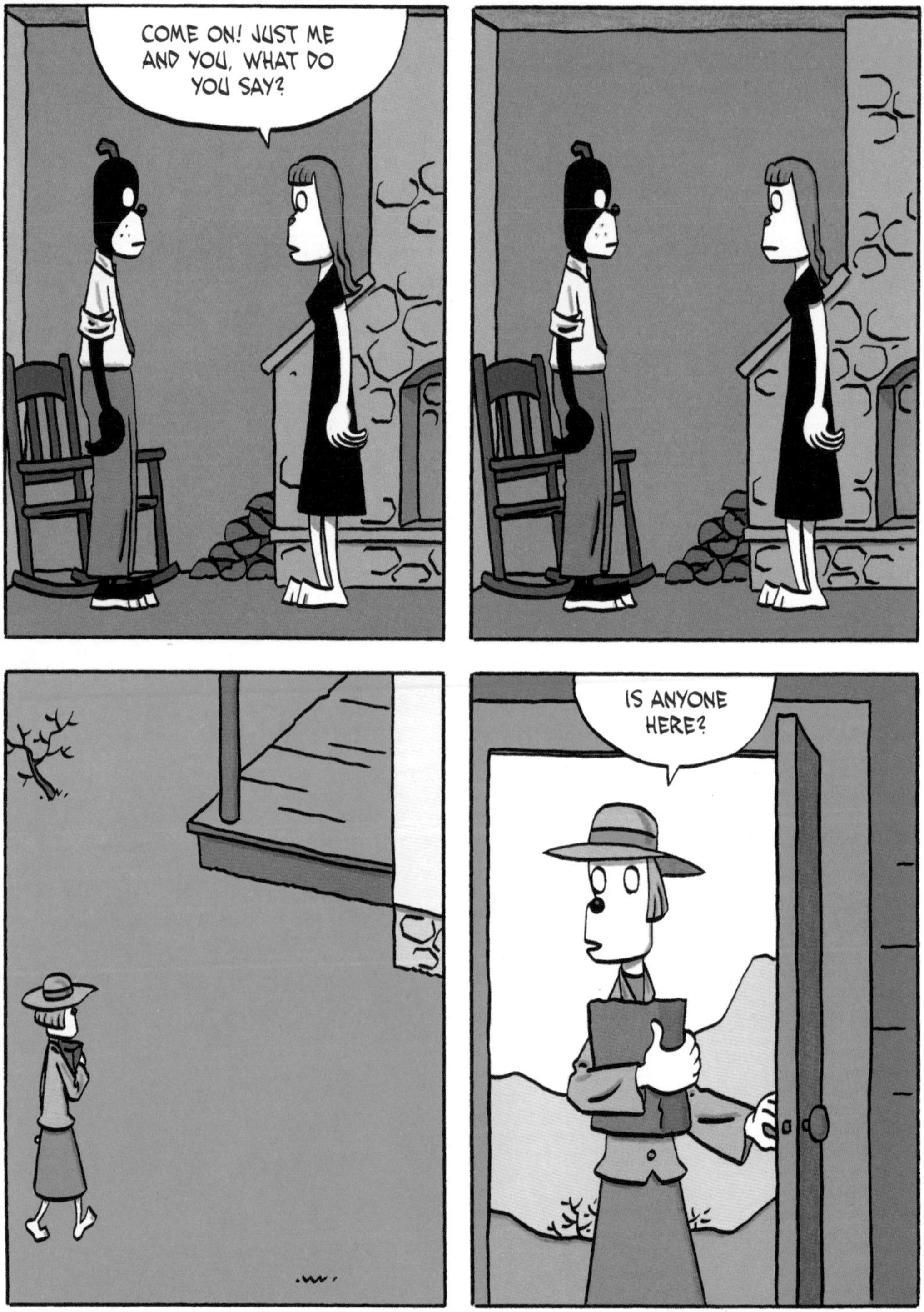
COME ON! JUST ME AND YOU, WHAT DO YOU SAY?
IS ANYONE HERE?

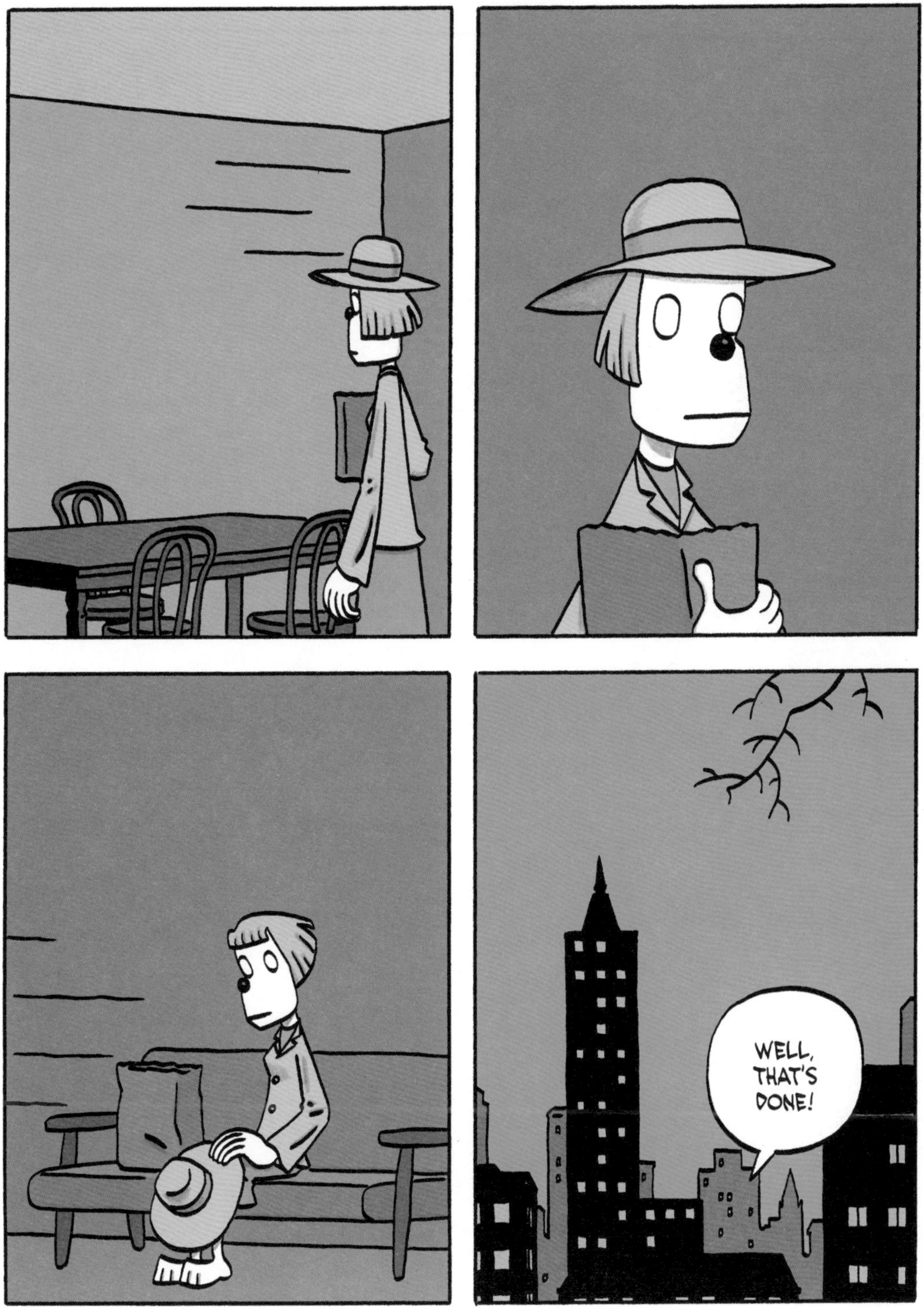
WELL, THAT'S DONE!

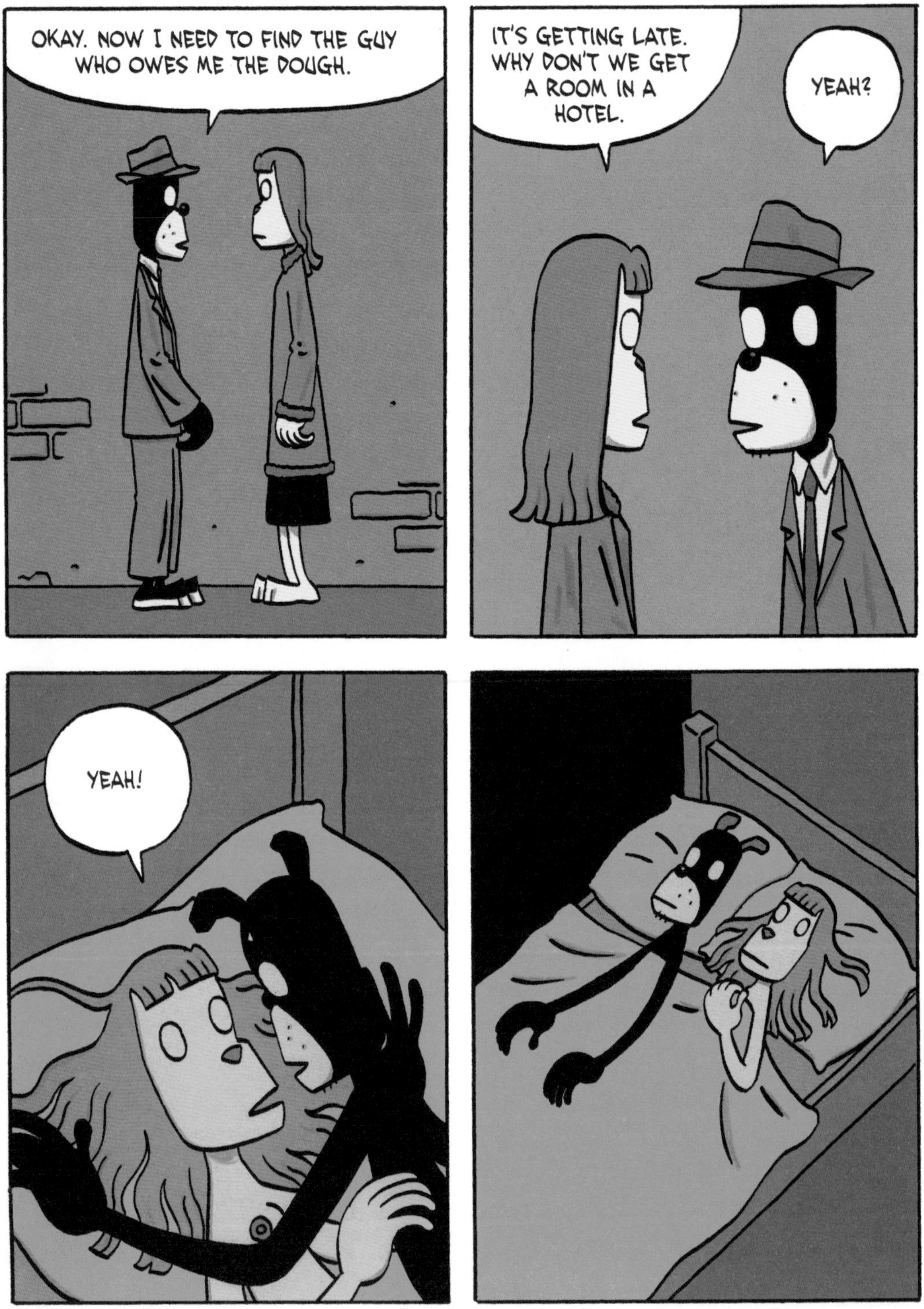
OKAY. NOW I NEED TO FIND THE GUY WHO OWES ME THE DOUGH.
IT'S GETTING LATE. WHY DON'T WE GET A ROOM IN A HOTEL.
YEAH?
YEAH!

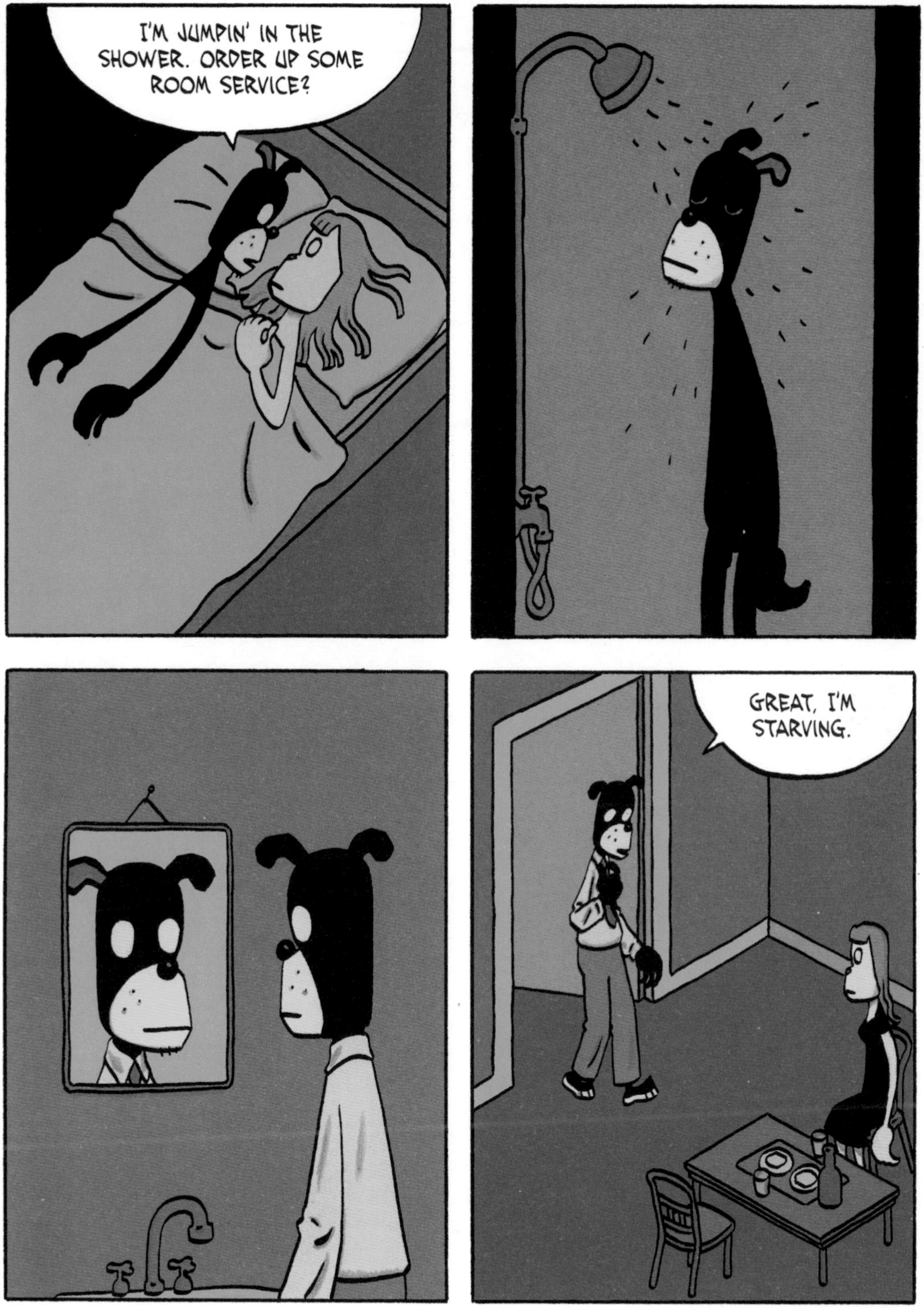
I'M JUMPIN' IN THE SHOWER. ORDER UP SOME ROOM SERVICE?
GREAT, I'M STARVING.

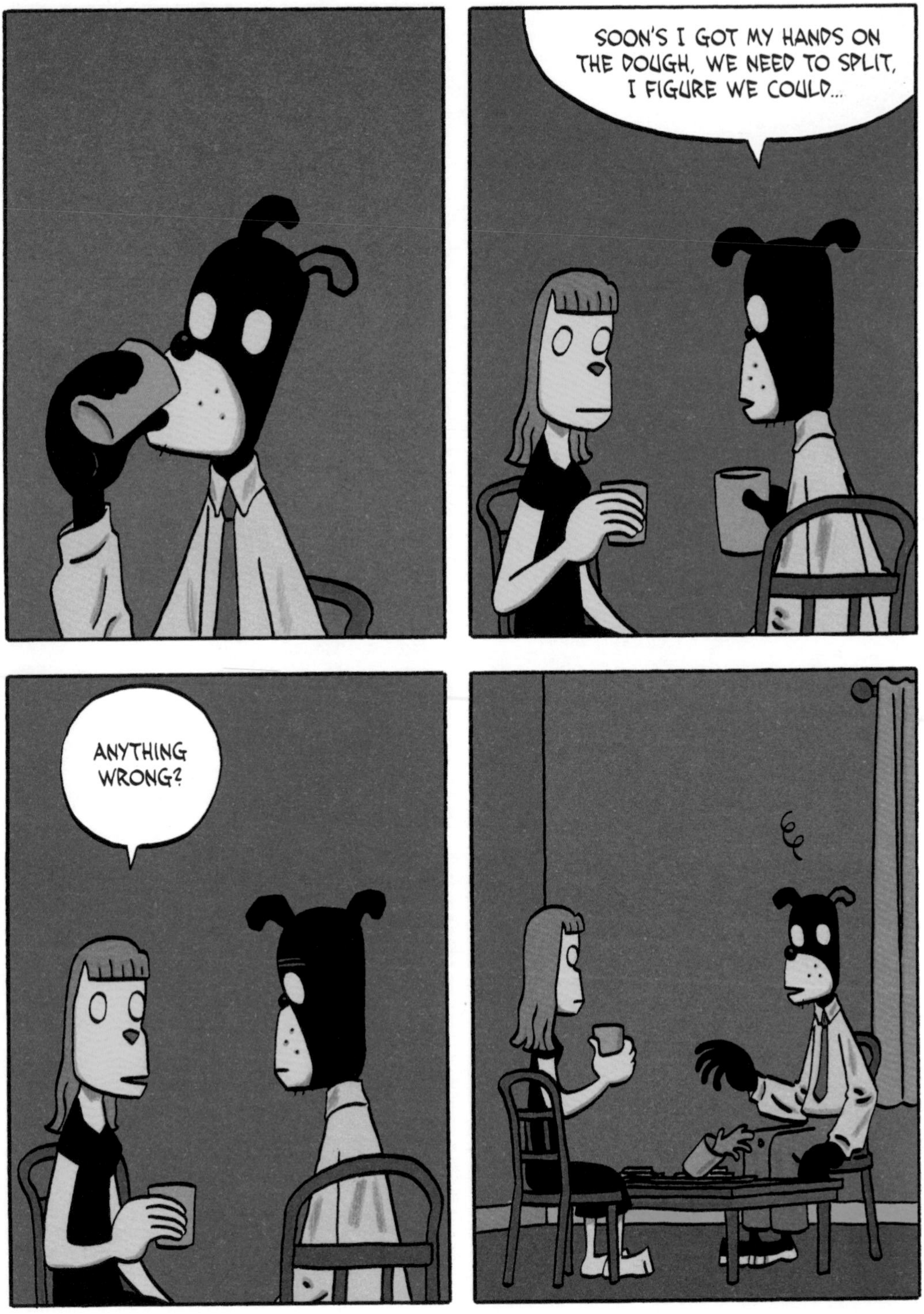
SOON'S I GOT MY HANDS ON THE DOUGH, WE NEED TO SPLIT, I FIGURE WE COULD...
ANYTHING WRONG?

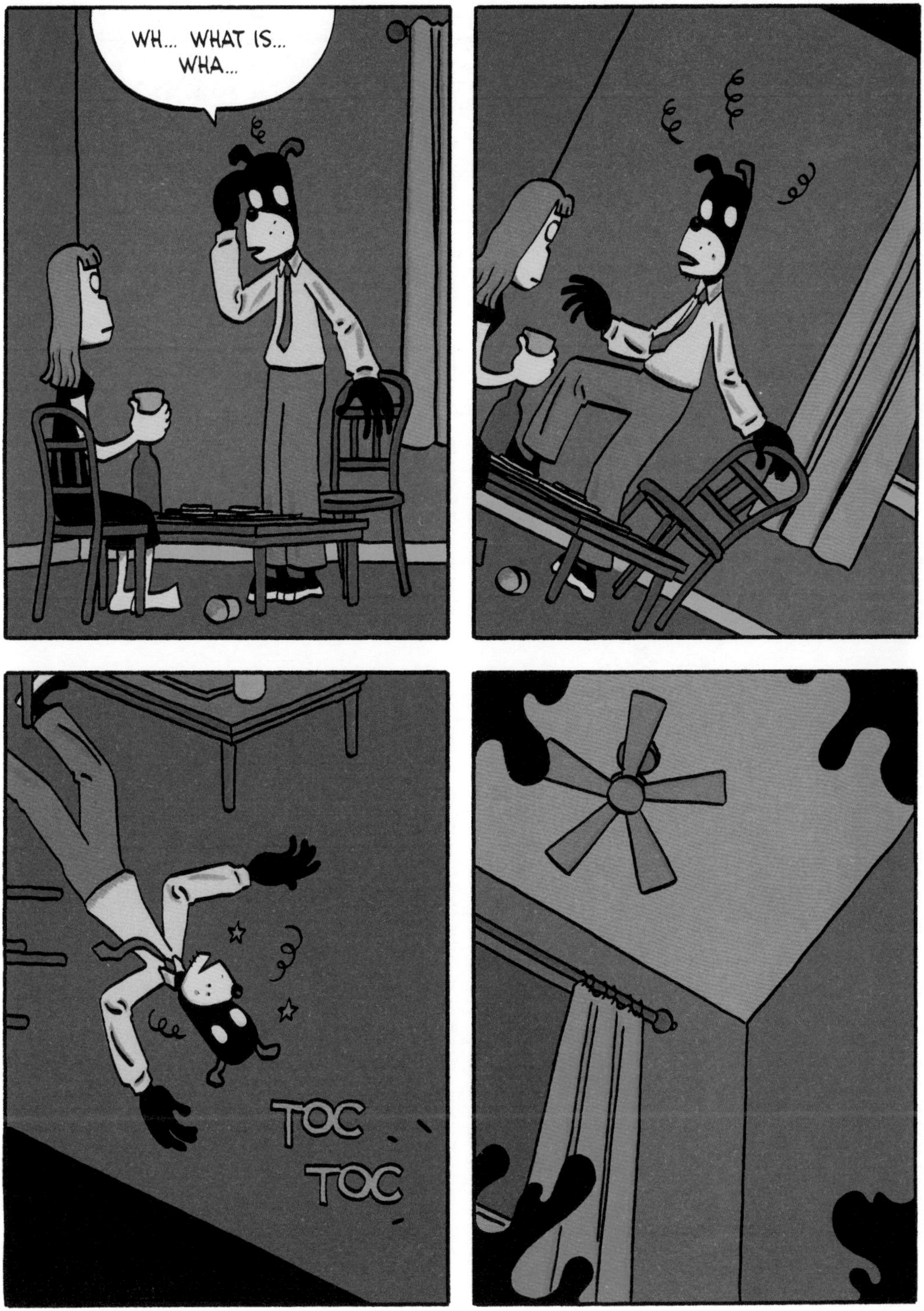
WH... WHAT IS... WHA...
TOC
TOC

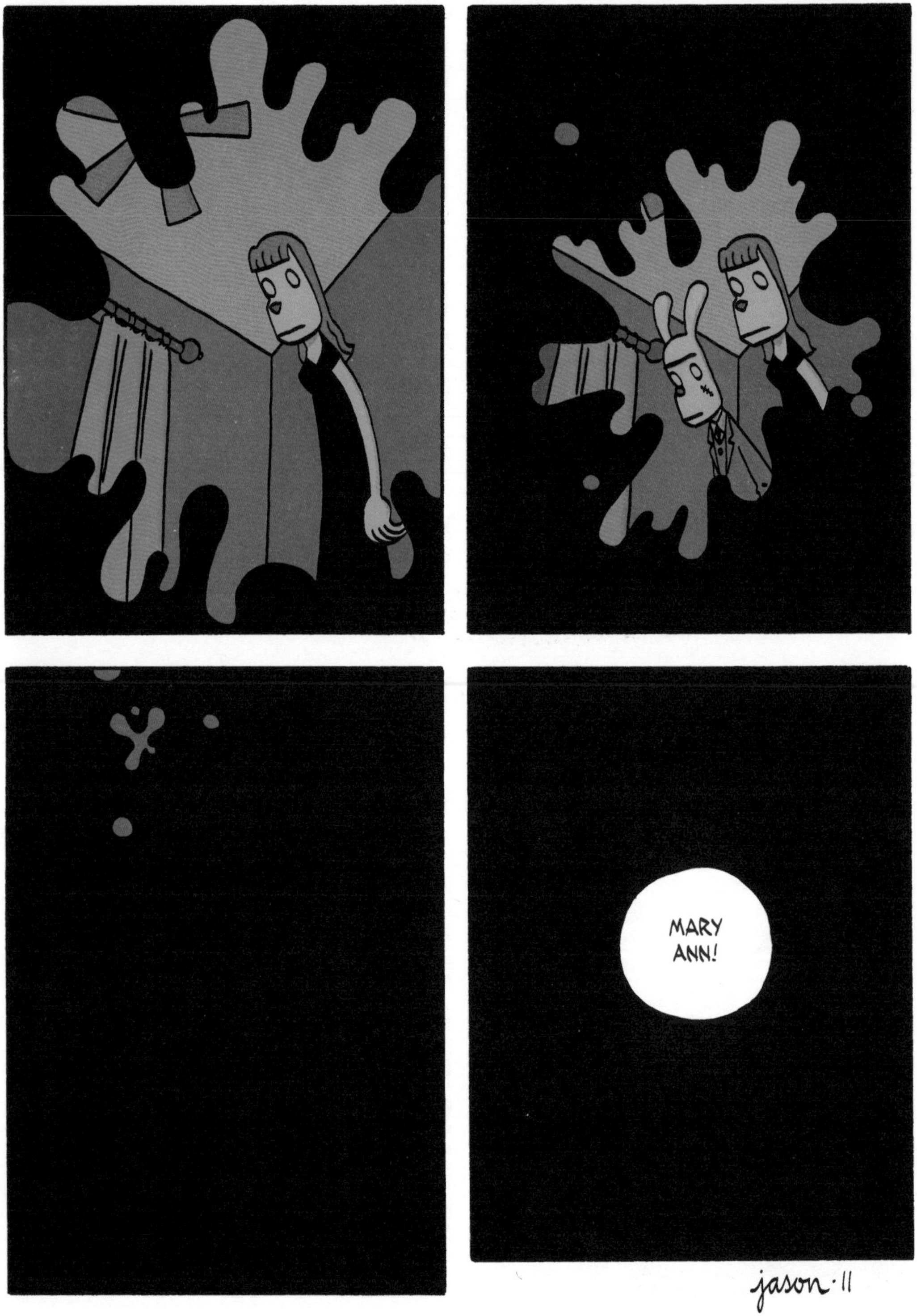
MARY ANN!

jason · 11

PRESENTING:

ATHOS IN AMERICA

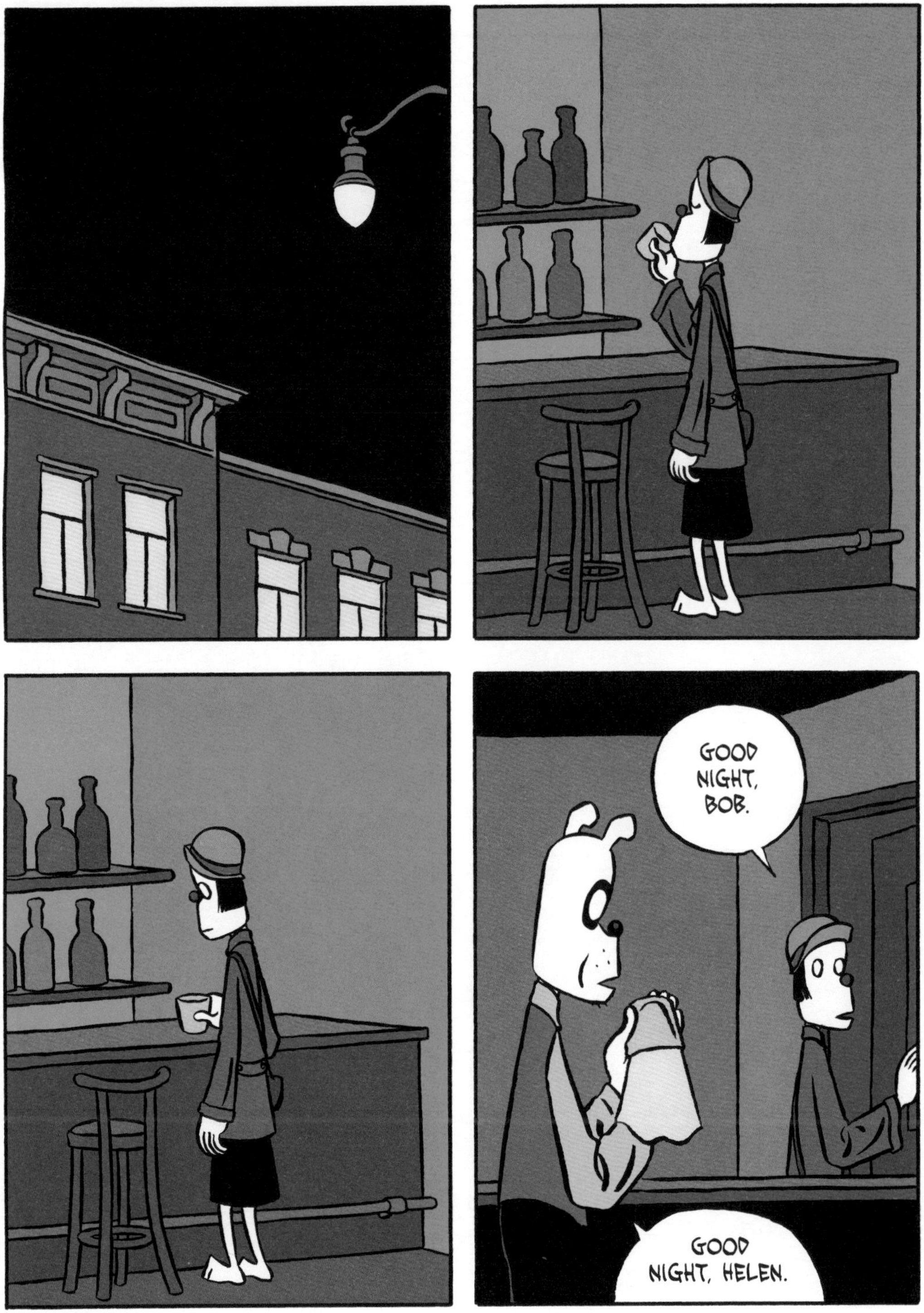
GOOD NIGHT, BOB.
GOOD NIGHT, HELEN.

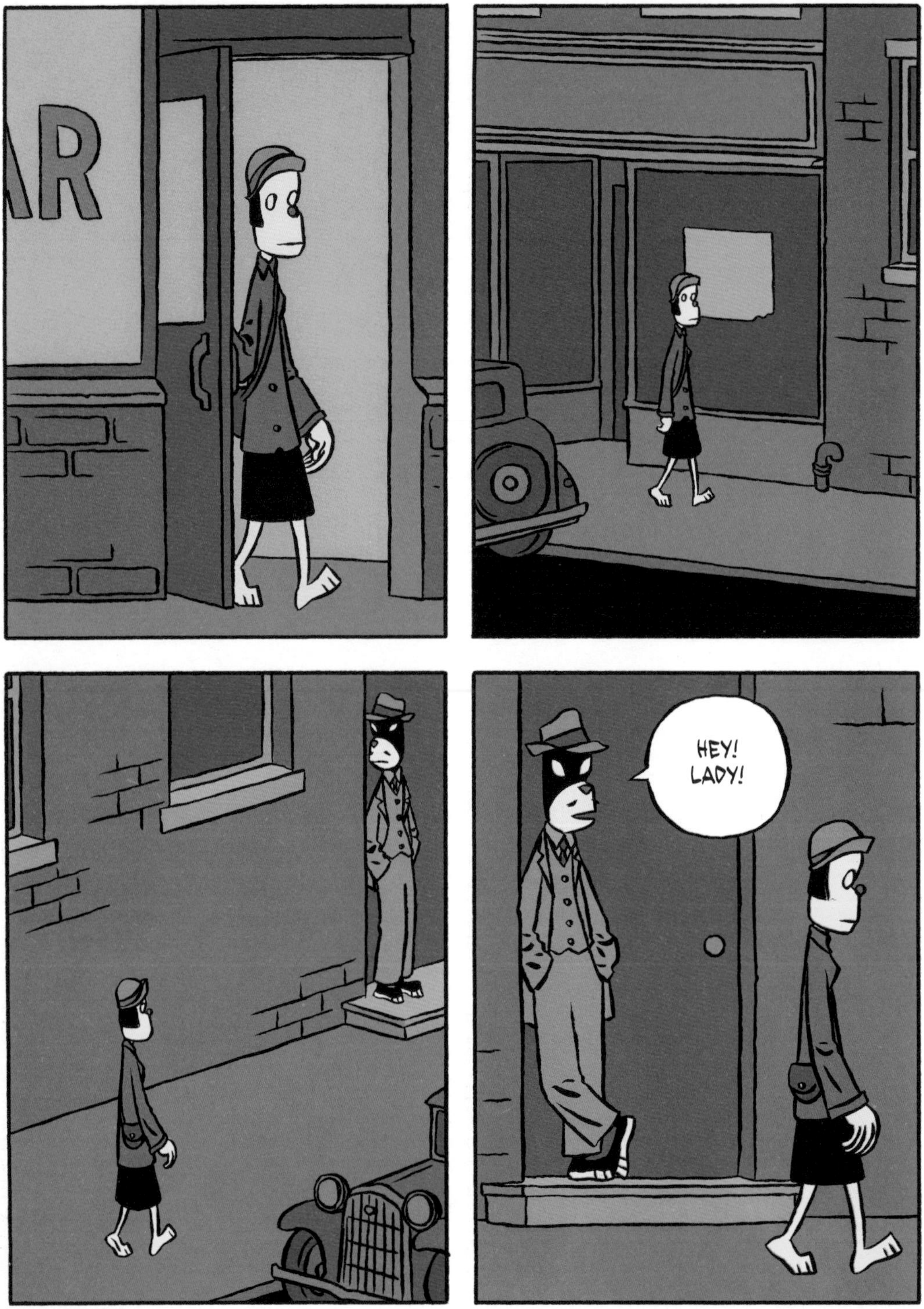
AR
HEY! LADY!

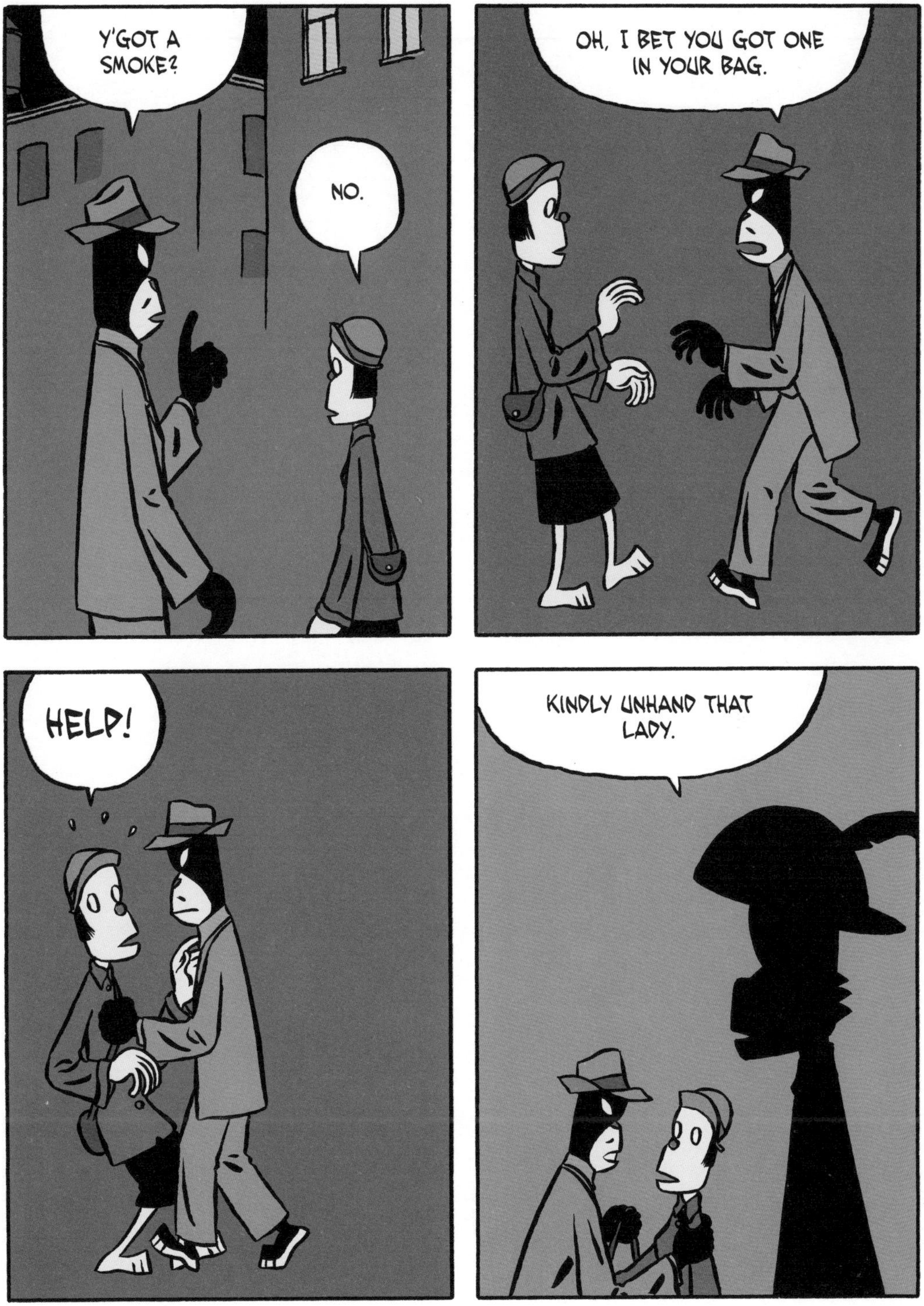
Y'GOT A SMOKE?
NO.
OH, I BET YOU GOT ONE IN YOUR BAG.
HELP!
KINDLY UNHAND THAT LADY.

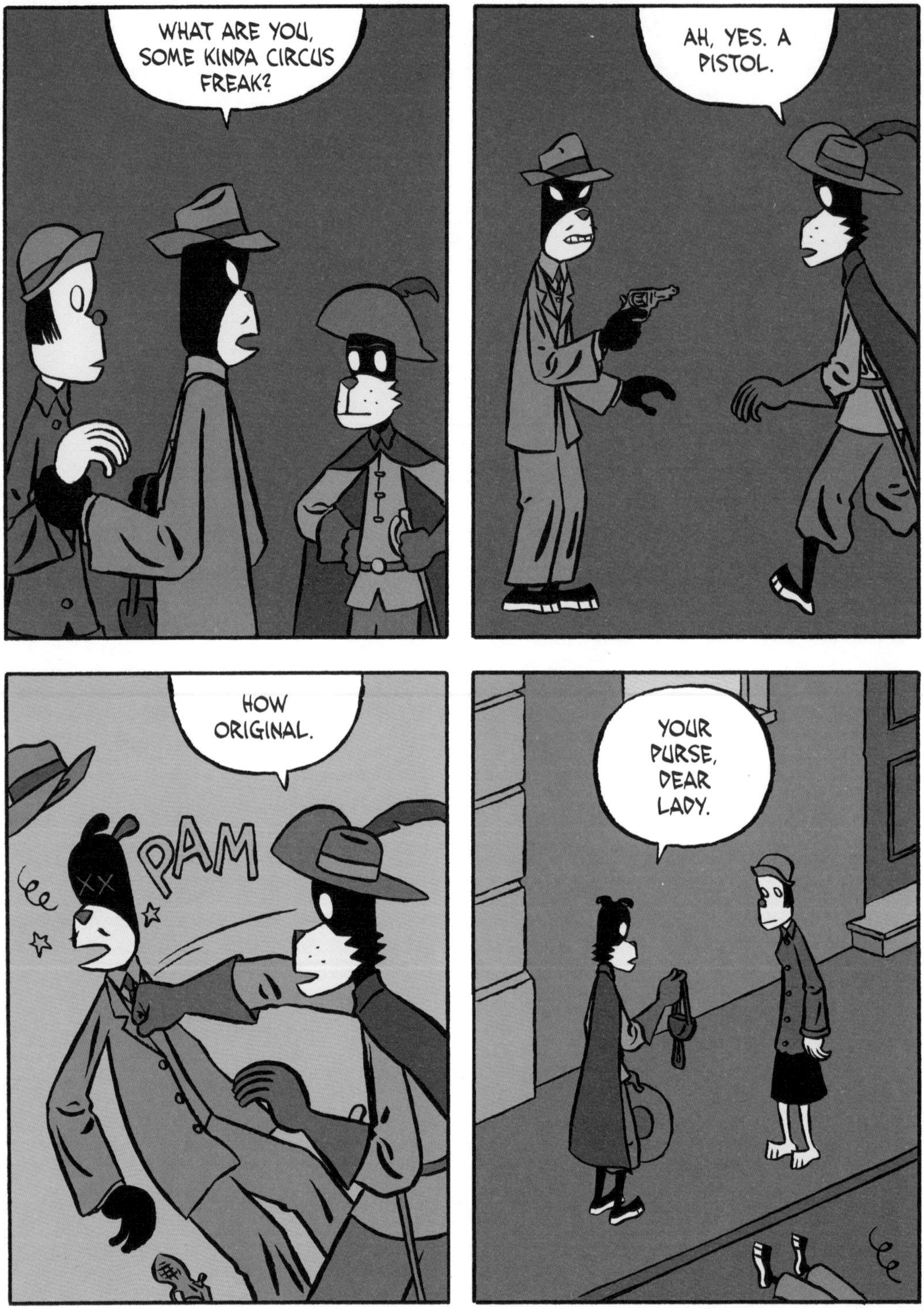
WHAT ARE YOU, SOME KINDA CIRCUS FREAK?
AH, YES. A PISTOL.
HOW ORIGINAL.
PAM
YOUR PURSE, DEAR LADY.

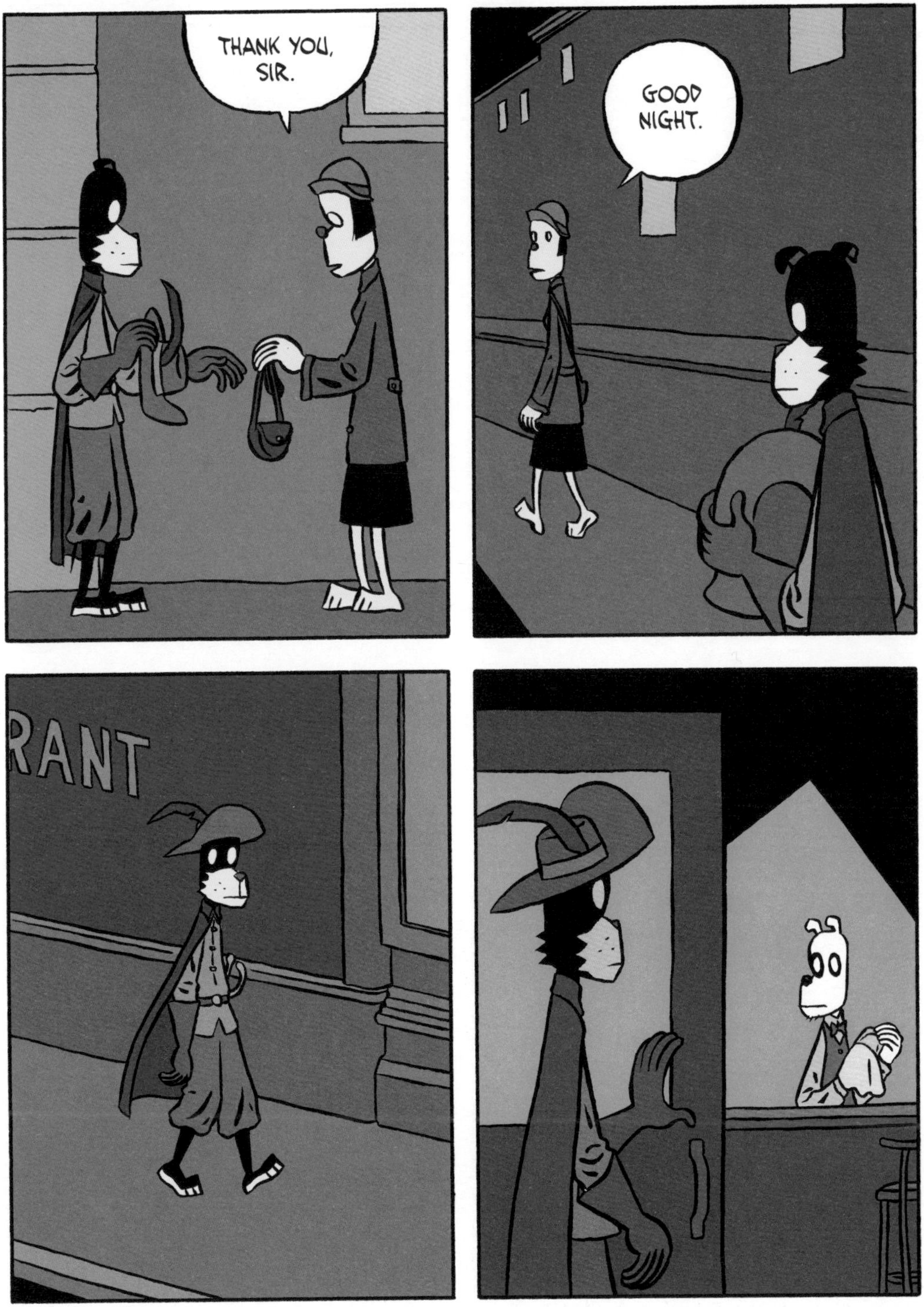
THANK YOU, SIR.
GOOD NIGHT.
RANT

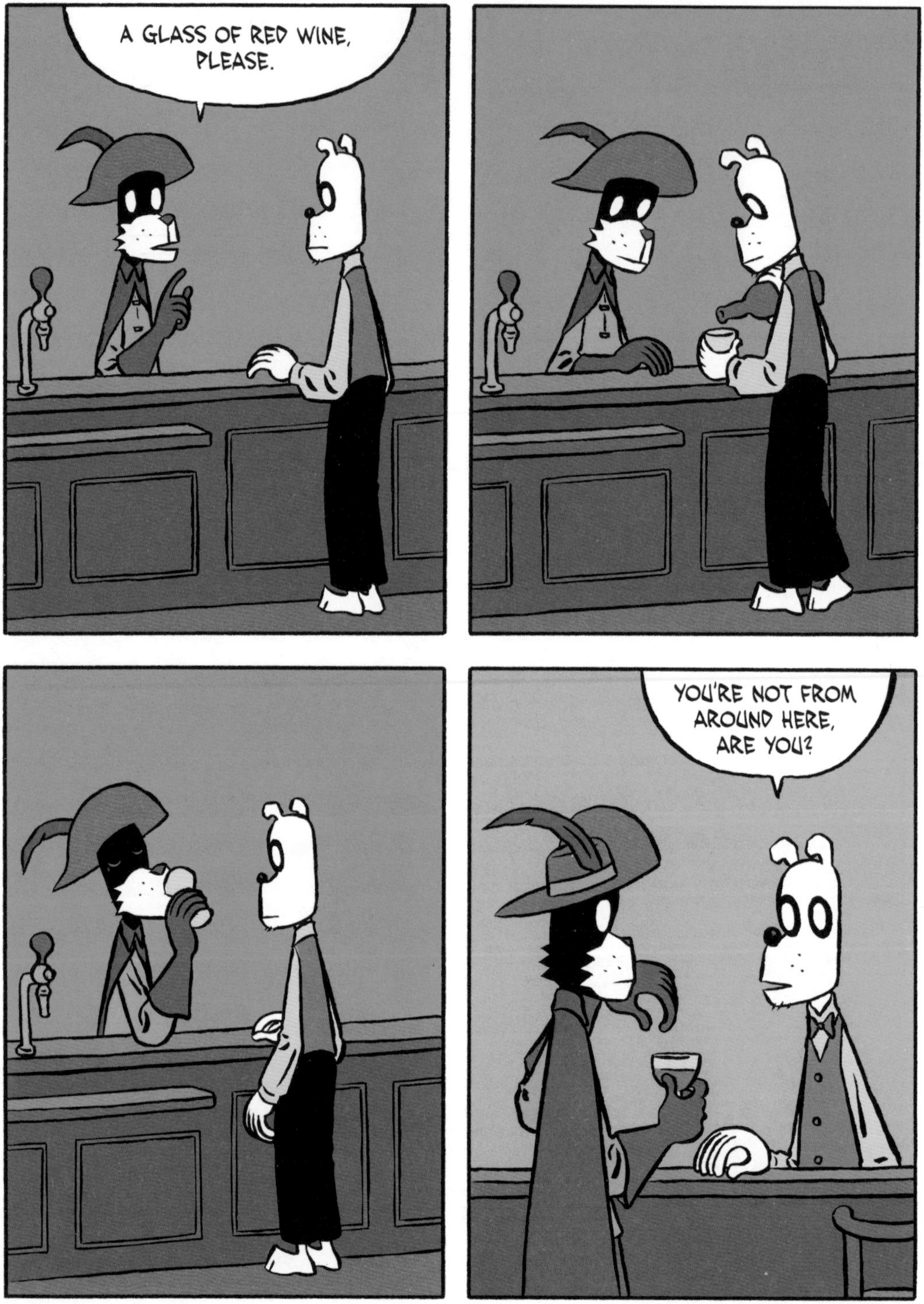
A GLASS OF RED WINE, PLEASE.
YOU'RE NOT FROM AROUND HERE, ARE YOU?

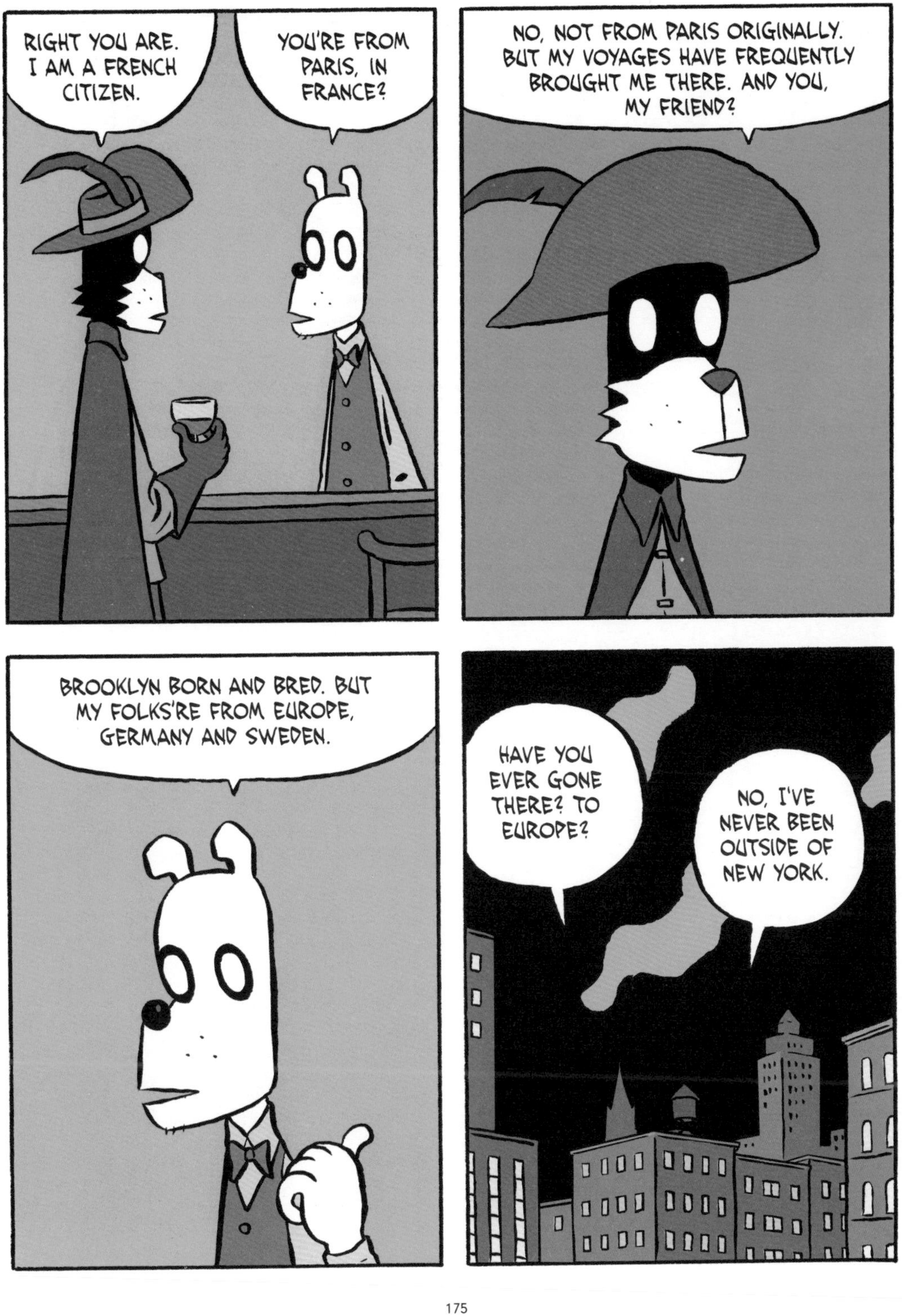
RIGHT YOU ARE. I AM A FRENCH CITIZEN.
YOU'RE FROM PARIS, IN FRANCE?
NO, NOT FROM PARIS ORIGINALLY. BUT MY VOYAGES HAVE FREQUENTLY BROUGHT ME THERE. AND YOU, MY FRIEND?
BROOKLYN BORN AND BRED. BUT MY FOLKS'RE FROM EUROPE, GERMANY AND SWEDEN.
HAVE YOU EVER GONE THERE? TO EUROPE?
NO, I'VE NEVER BEEN OUTSIDE OF NEW YORK.

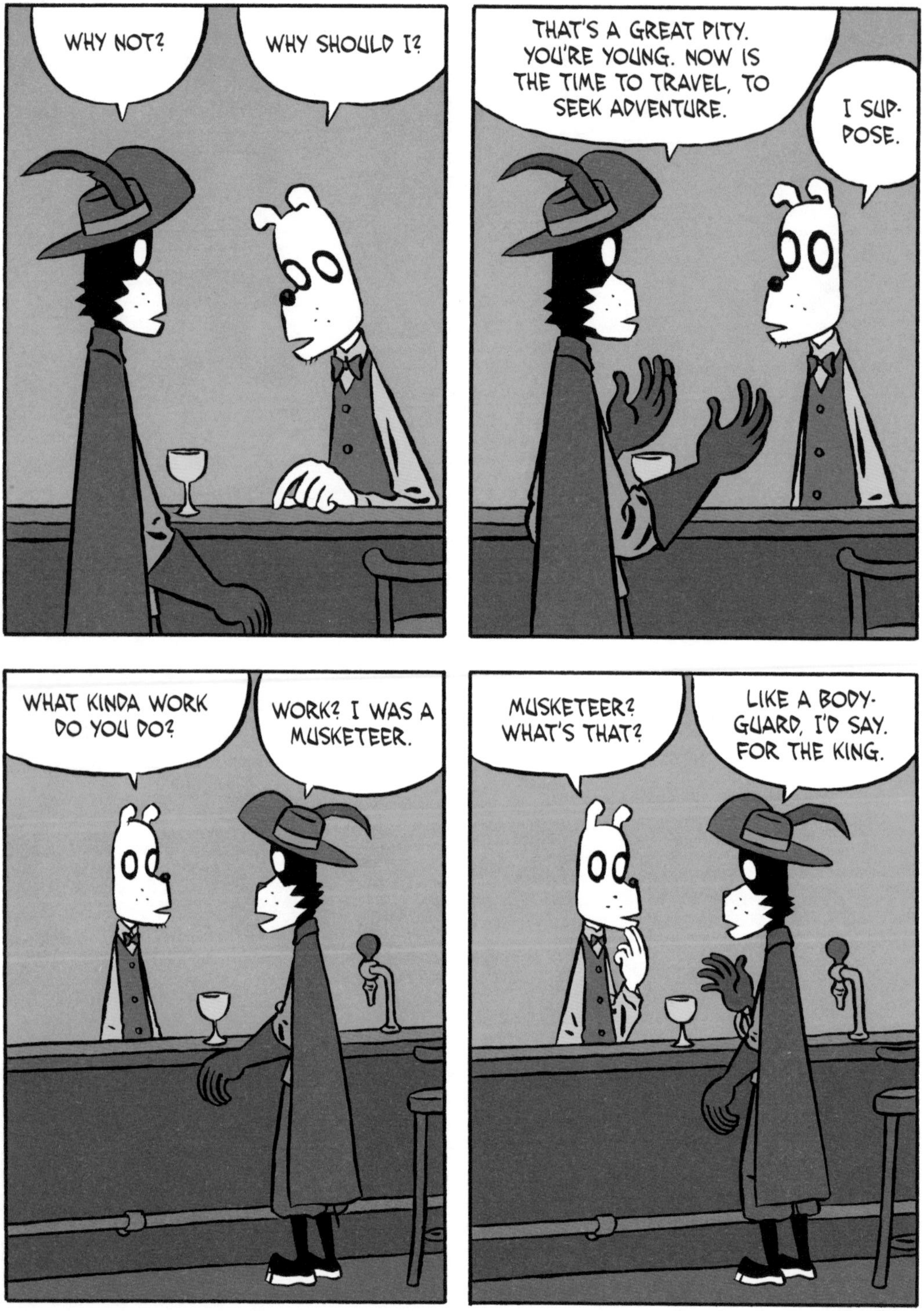
WHY NOT?
WHY SHOULD I?
THAT'S A GREAT PITY. YOU'RE YOUNG. NOW IS THE TIME TO TRAVEL, TO SEEK ADVENTURE.
I SUP-POSE.
WHAT KINDA WORK DO YOU DO?
WORK? I WAS A MUSKETEER.
MUSKETEER? WHAT'S THAT?
LIKE A BODY-GUARD, I'D SAY. FOR THE KING.

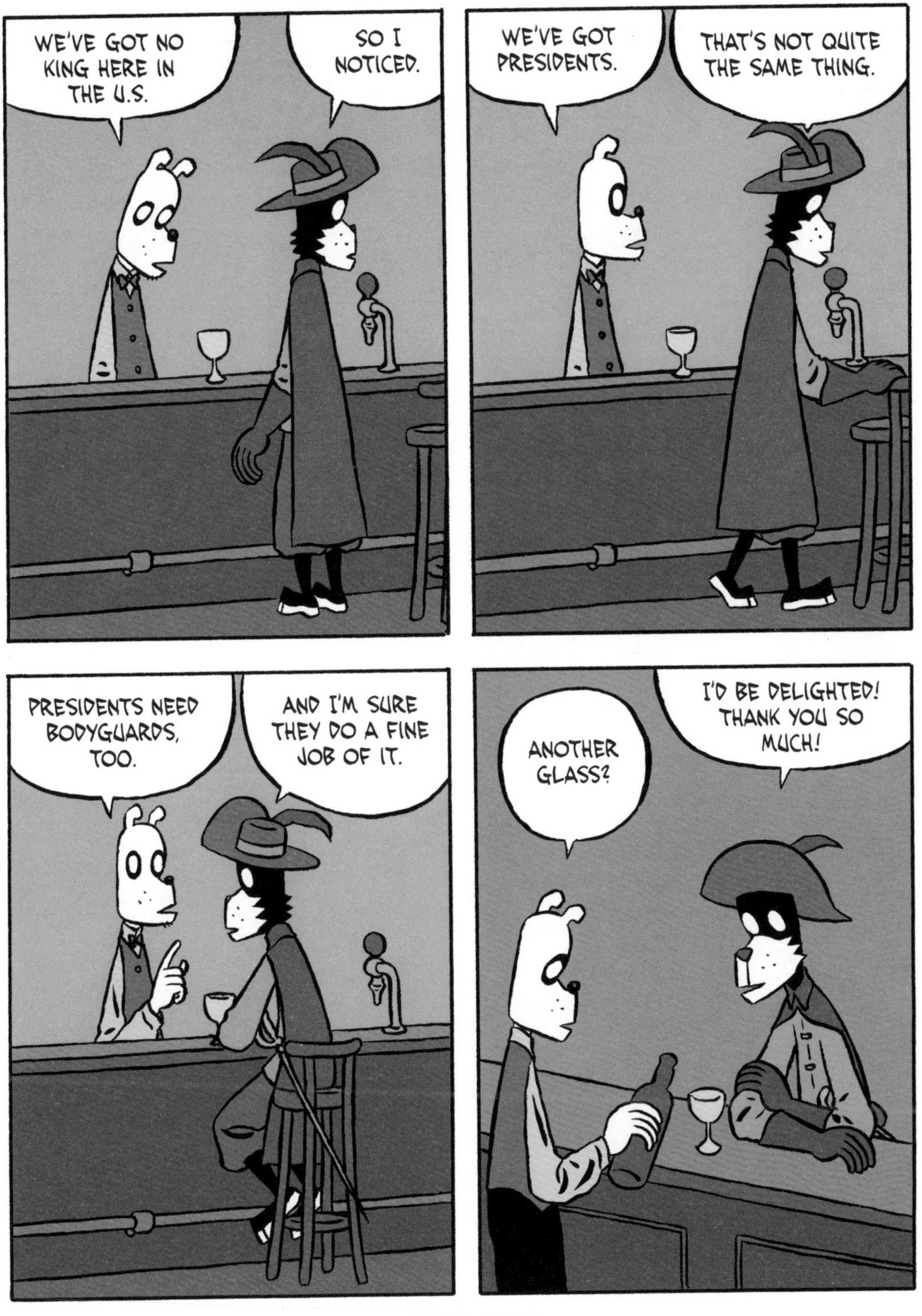
WE'VE GOT NO KING HERE IN THE U.S.
SO I NOTICED.
WE'VE GOT PRESIDENTS.
THAT'S NOT QUITE THE SAME THING.
PRESIDENTS NEED BODYGUARDS, TOO.
AND I'M SURE THEY DO A FINE JOB OF IT.
ANOTHER GLASS?
I'D BE DELIGHTED! THANK YOU SO MUCH!

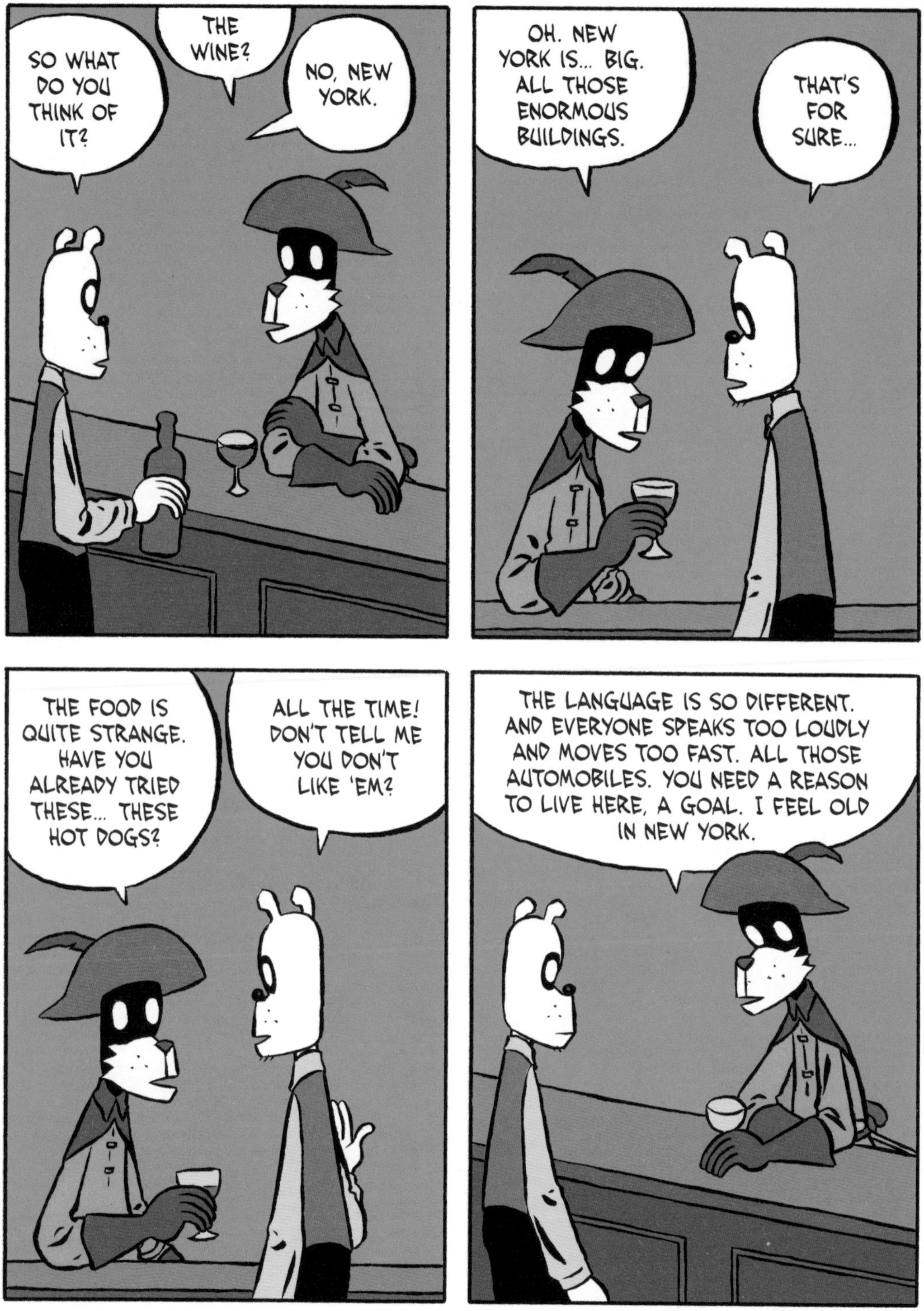
SO WHAT DO YOU THINK OF IT?
THE WINE?
NO, NEW YORK.
OH. NEW YORK IS... BIG. ALL THOSE ENORMOUS BUILDINGS.
THAT'S FOR SURE...
THE FOOD IS QUITE STRANGE. HAVE YOU ALREADY TRIED THESE... THESE HOT DOGS?
ALL THE TIME! DON'T TELL ME YOU DON'T LIKE 'EM?
THE LANGUAGE IS SO DIFFERENT. AND EVERYONE SPEAKS TOO LOUDLY AND MOVES TOO FAST. ALL THOSE AUTOMOBILES. YOU NEED A REASON TO LIVE HERE, A GOAL. I FEEL OLD IN NEW YORK.

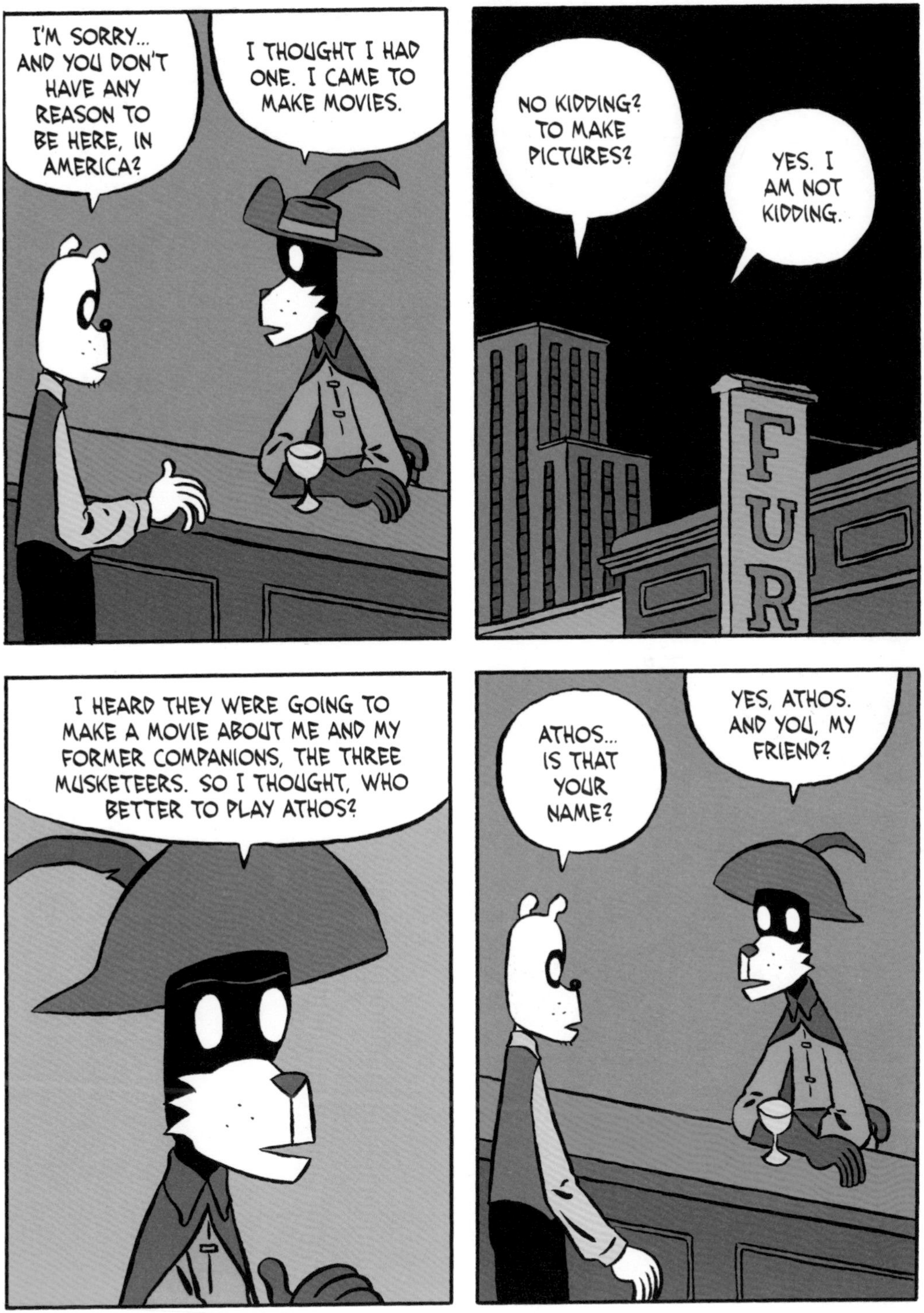
I'M SORRY... AND YOU DON'T HAVE ANY REASON TO BE HERE, IN AMERICA?
I THOUGHT I HAD ONE. I CAME TO MAKE MOVIES.
NO KIDDING? TO MAKE PICTURES?
YES. I AM NOT KIDDING.
FUR
I HEARD THEY WERE GOING TO MAKE A MOVIE ABOUT ME AND MY FORMER COMPANIONS, THE THREE MUSKETEERS. SO I THOUGHT, WHO BETTER TO PLAY ATHOS?
ATHOS... IS THAT YOUR NAME?
YES, ATHOS. AND YOU, MY FRIEND?

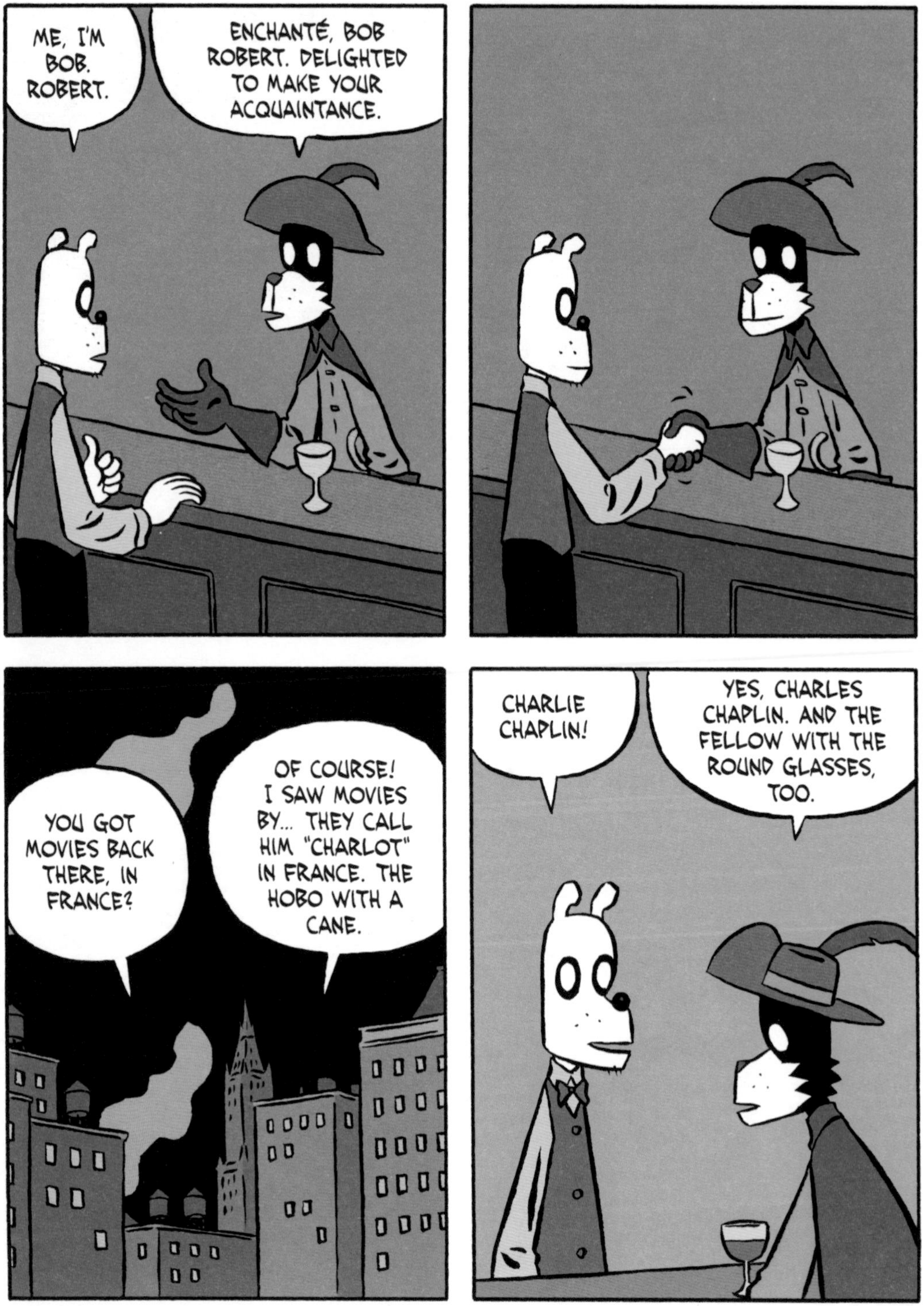
ME, I'M BOB. ROBERT.
ENCHANTÉ, BOB ROBERT. DELIGHTED TO MAKE YOUR ACQUAINTANCE.
YOU GOT MOVIES BACK THERE, IN FRANCE?
OF COURSE! I SAW MOVIES BY... THEY CALL HIM "CHARLOT" IN FRANCE. THE HOBO WITH A CANE.
CHARLIE CHAPLIN!
YES, CHARLES CHAPLIN. AND THE FELLOW WITH THE ROUND GLASSES, TOO.

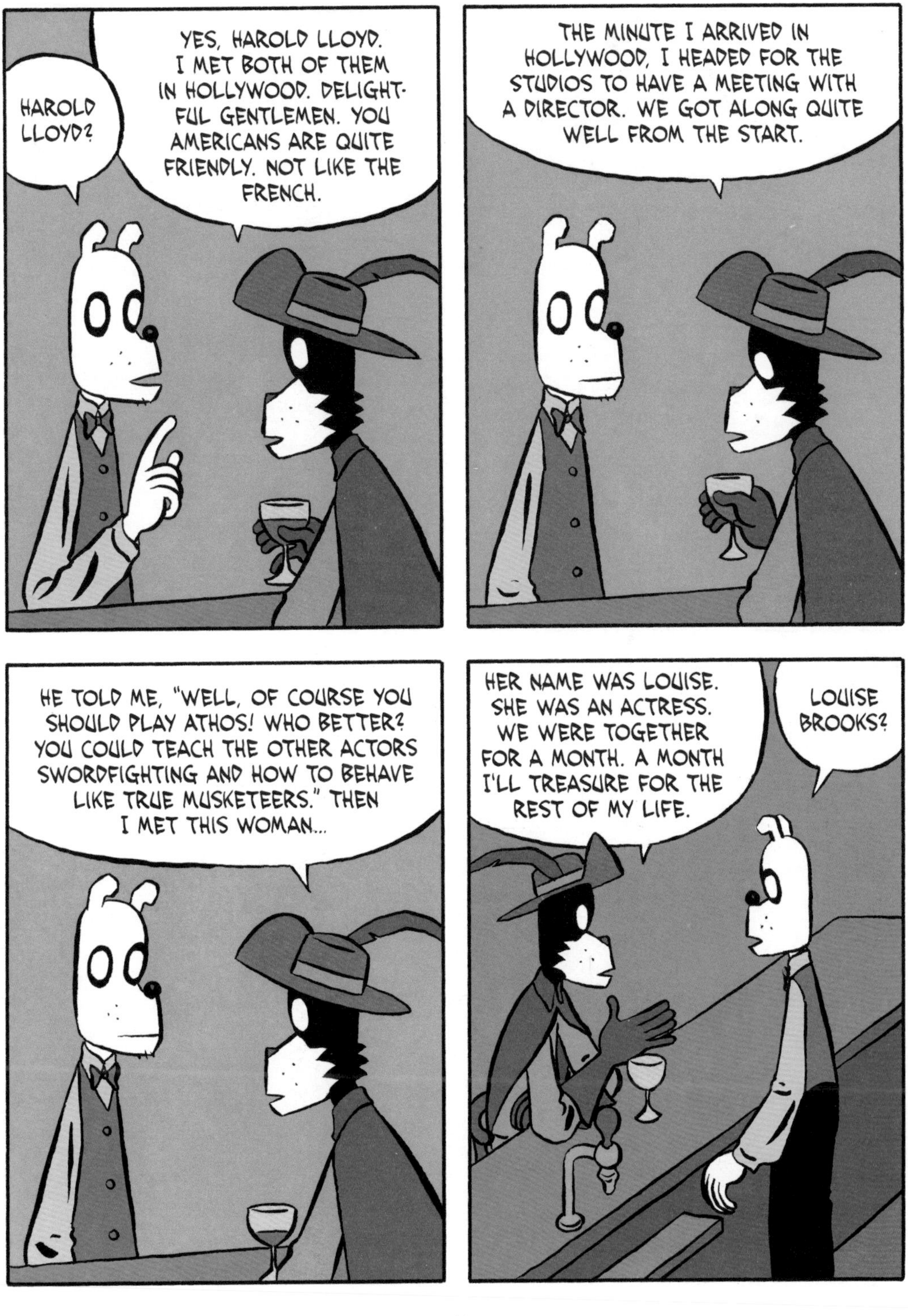
HAROLD LLOYD?
YES, HAROLD LLOYD. I MET BOTH OF THEM IN HOLLYWOOD. DELIGHTFUL GENTLEMEN. YOU AMERICANS ARE QUITE FRIENDLY. NOT LIKE THE FRENCH.
THE MINUTE I ARRIVED IN HOLLYWOOD, I HEADED FOR THE STUDIOS TO HAVE A MEETING WITH A DIRECTOR. WE GOT ALONG QUITE WELL FROM THE START.
HE TOLD ME, "WELL, OF COURSE YOU SHOULD PLAY ATHOS! WHO BETTER? YOU COULD TEACH THE OTHER ACTORS SWORDFIGHTING AND HOW TO BEHAVE LIKE TRUE MUSKETEERS." THEN I MET THIS WOMAN...
HER NAME WAS LOUISE. SHE WAS AN ACTRESS. WE WERE TOGETHER FOR A MONTH. A MONTH I'LL TREASURE FOR THE REST OF MY LIFE.
LOUISE BROOKS?

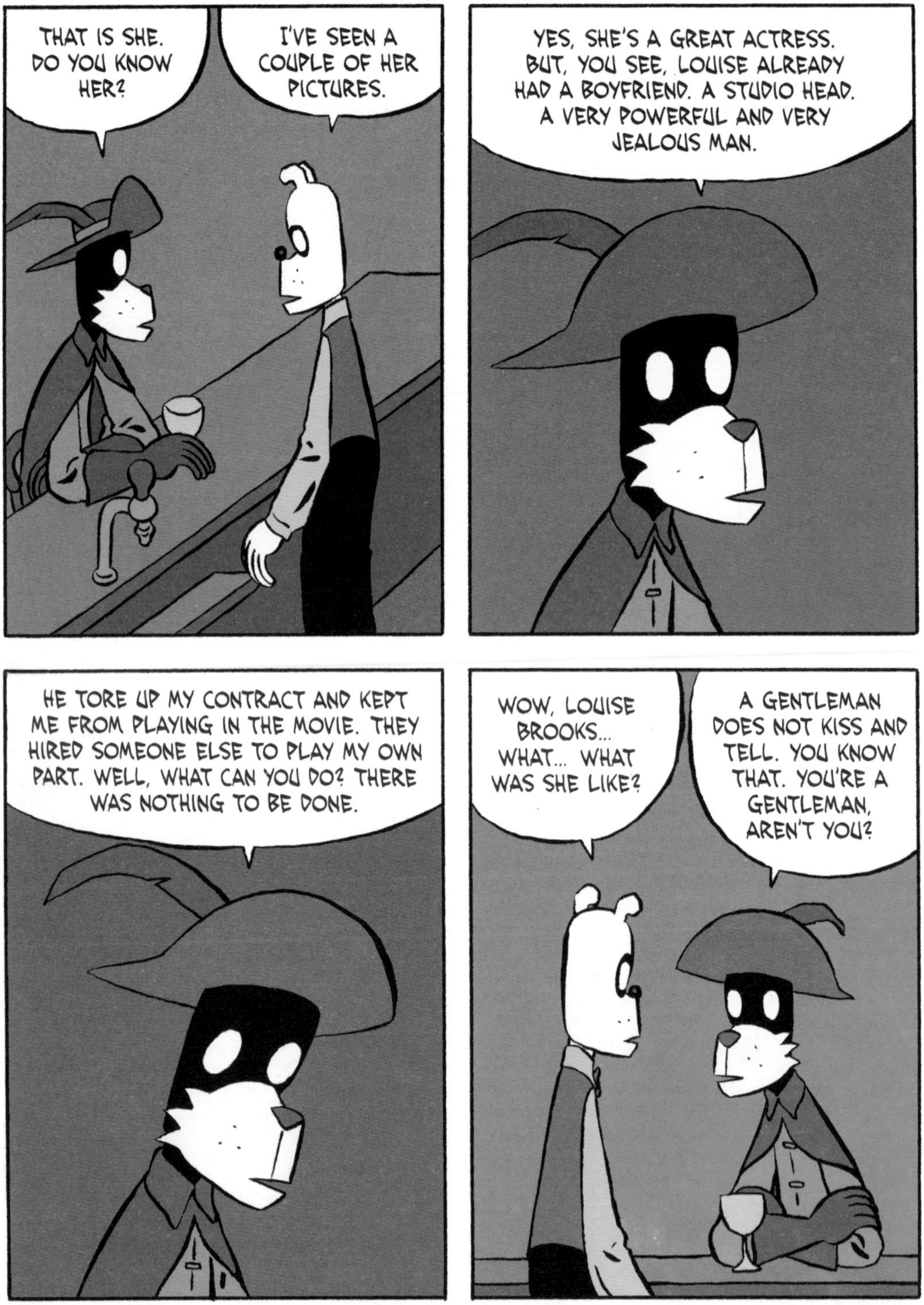

THAT IS SHE. DO YOU KNOW HER?
I'VE SEEN A COUPLE OF HER PICTURES.
YES, SHE'S A GREAT ACTRESS. BUT, YOU SEE, LOUISE ALREADY HAD A BOYFRIEND. A STUDIO HEAD. A VERY POWERFUL AND VERY JEALOUS MAN.
HE TORE UP MY CONTRACT AND KEPT ME FROM PLAYING IN THE MOVIE. THEY HIRED SOMEONE ELSE TO PLAY MY OWN PART. WELL, WHAT CAN YOU DO? THERE WAS NOTHING TO BE DONE.
WOW, LOUISE BROOKS... WHAT... WHAT WAS SHE LIKE?
A GENTLEMAN DOES NOT KISS AND TELL. YOU KNOW THAT. YOU'RE A GENTLEMAN, AREN'T YOU?

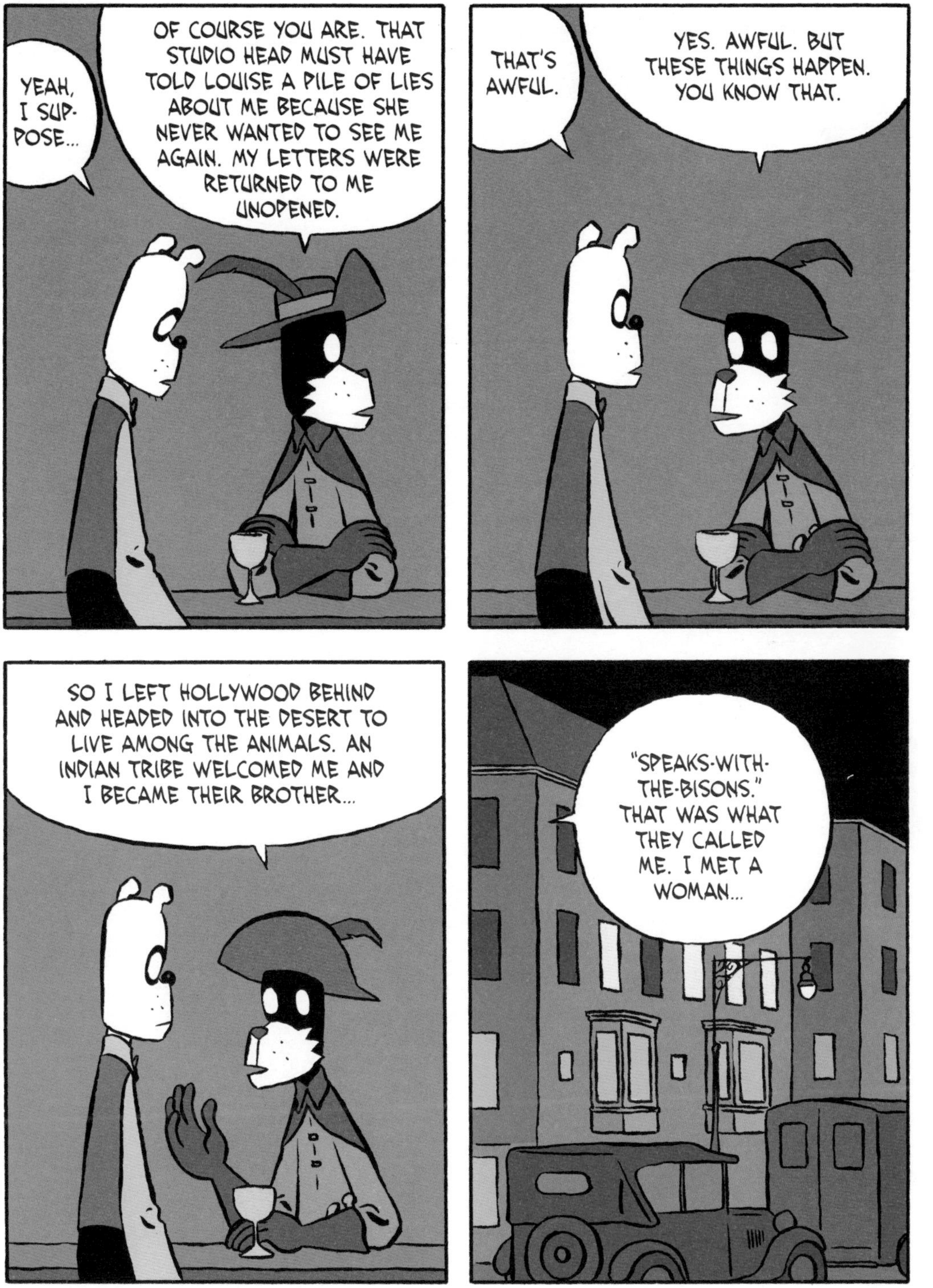
YEAH, I SUP-POSE...
OF COURSE YOU ARE. THAT STUDIO HEAD MUST HAVE TOLD LOUISE A PILE OF LIES ABOUT ME BECAUSE SHE NEVER WANTED TO SEE ME AGAIN. MY LETTERS WERE RETURNED TO ME UNOPENED.
THAT'S AWFUL.
YES. AWFUL. BUT THESE THINGS HAPPEN. YOU KNOW THAT.
SO I LEFT HOLLYWOOD BEHIND AND HEADED INTO THE DESERT TO LIVE AMONG THE ANIMALS. AN INDIAN TRIBE WELCOMED ME AND I BECAME THEIR BROTHER...
"SPEAKS-WITH-THE-BISONS." THAT WAS WHAT THEY CALLED ME. I MET A WOMAN...

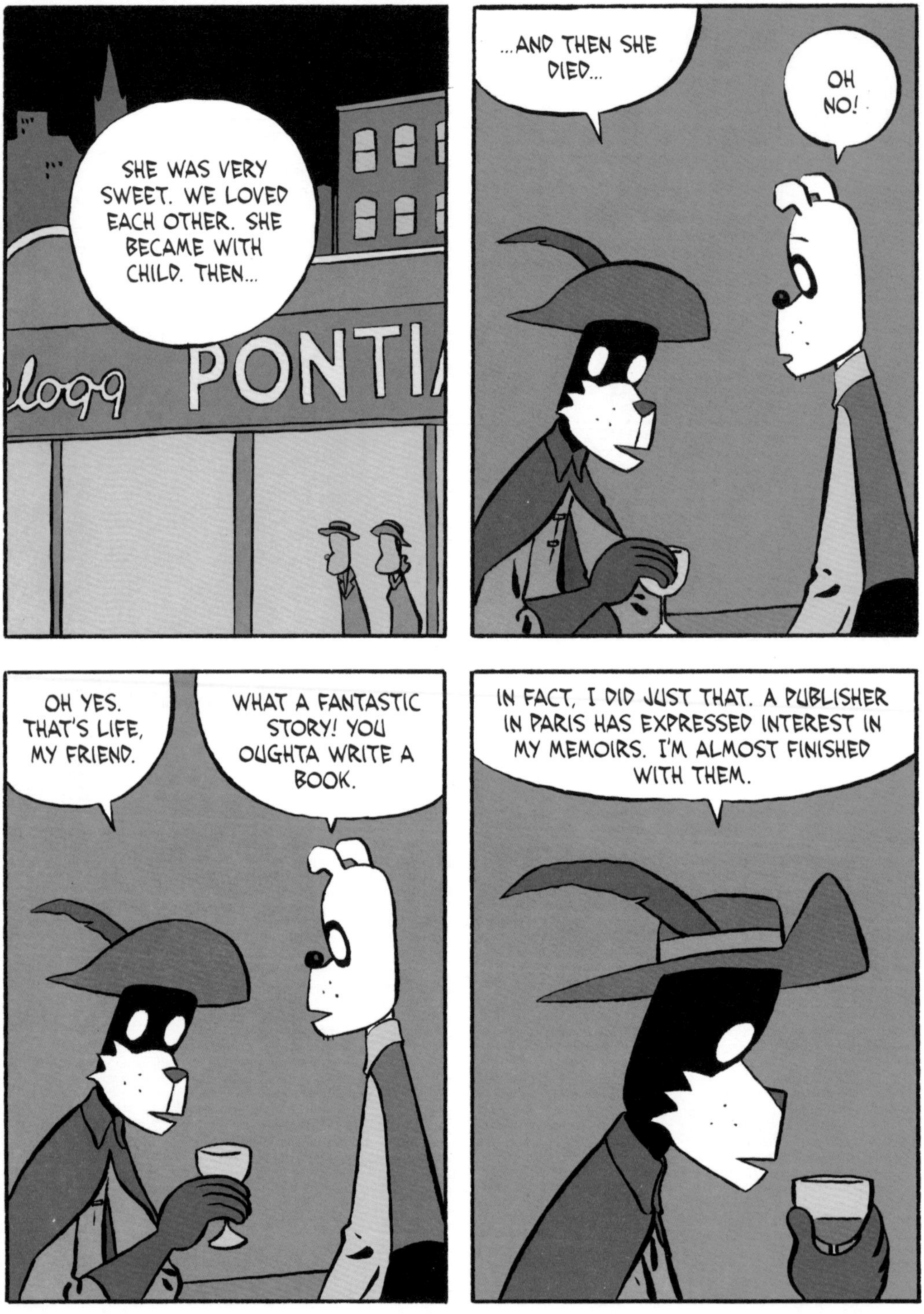
SHE WAS VERY SWEET. WE LOVED EACH OTHER. SHE BECAME WITH CHILD. THEN...
PONTI
...AND THEN SHE DIED...
OH NO!
OH YES. THAT'S LIFE, MY FRIEND.
WHAT A FANTASTIC STORY! YOU OUGHTA WRITE A BOOK.
IN FACT, I DID JUST THAT. A PUBLISHER IN PARIS HAS EXPRESSED INTEREST IN MY MEMOIRS. I'M ALMOST FINISHED WITH THEM.

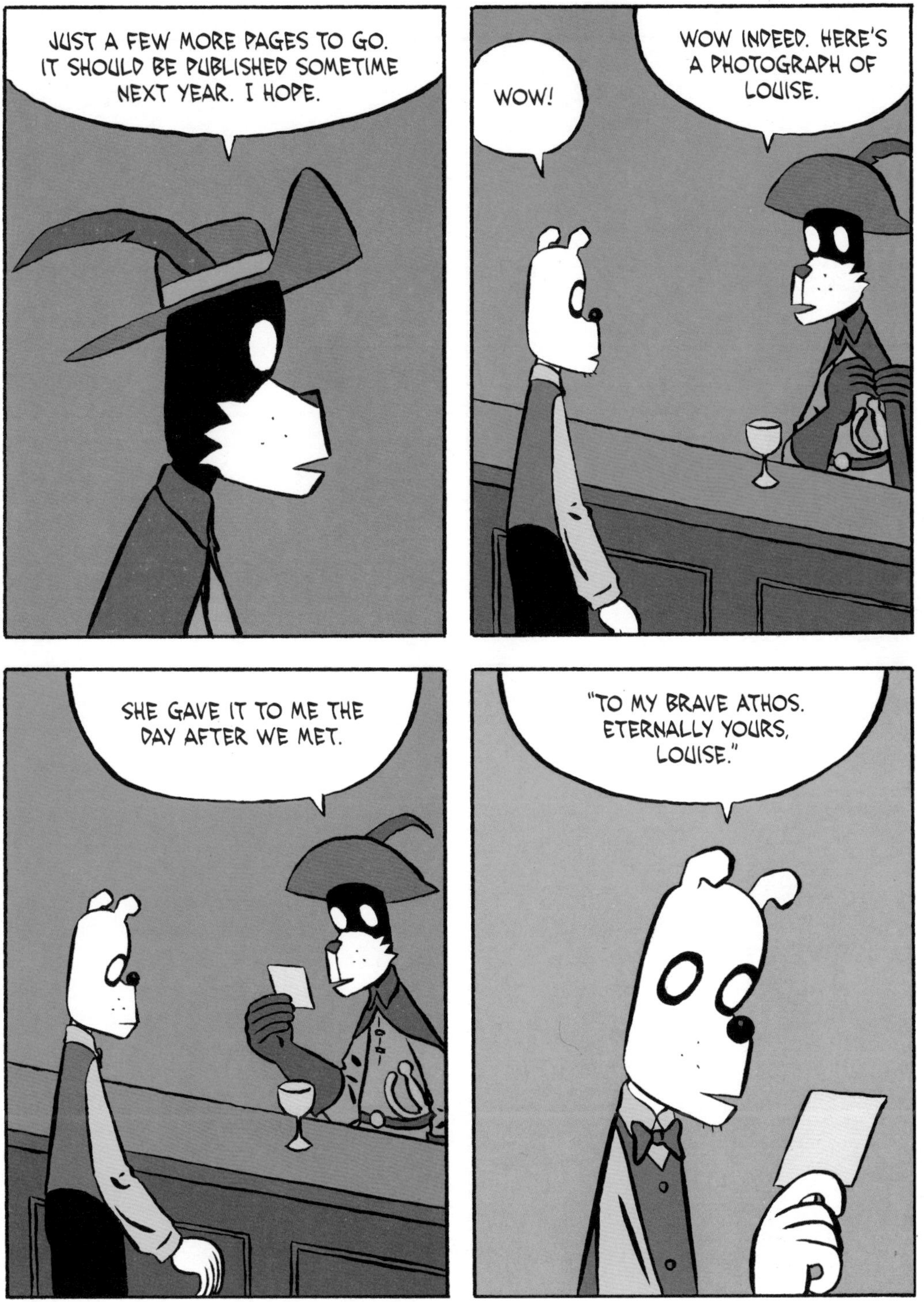
JUST A FEW MORE PAGES TO GO. IT SHOULD BE PUBLISHED SOMETIME NEXT YEAR. I HOPE.
WOW!
WOW INDEED. HERE'S A PHOTOGRAPH OF LOUISE.
SHE GAVE IT TO ME THE DAY AFTER WE MET.
"TO MY BRAVE ATHOS. ETERNALLY YOURS, LOUISE."

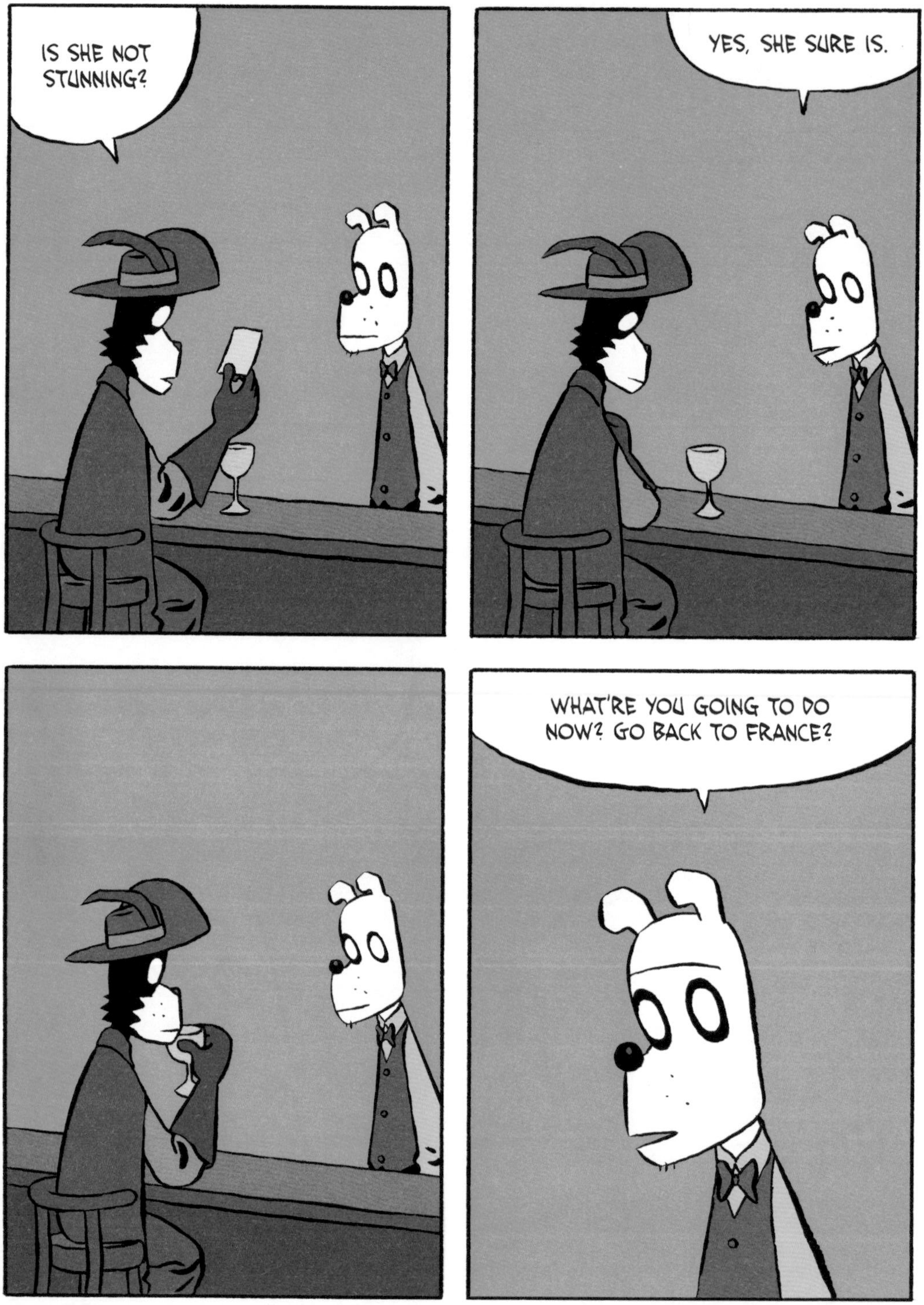
IS SHE NOT STUNNING?
YES, SHE SURE IS.
WHAT'RE YOU GOING TO DO NOW? GO BACK TO FRANCE?

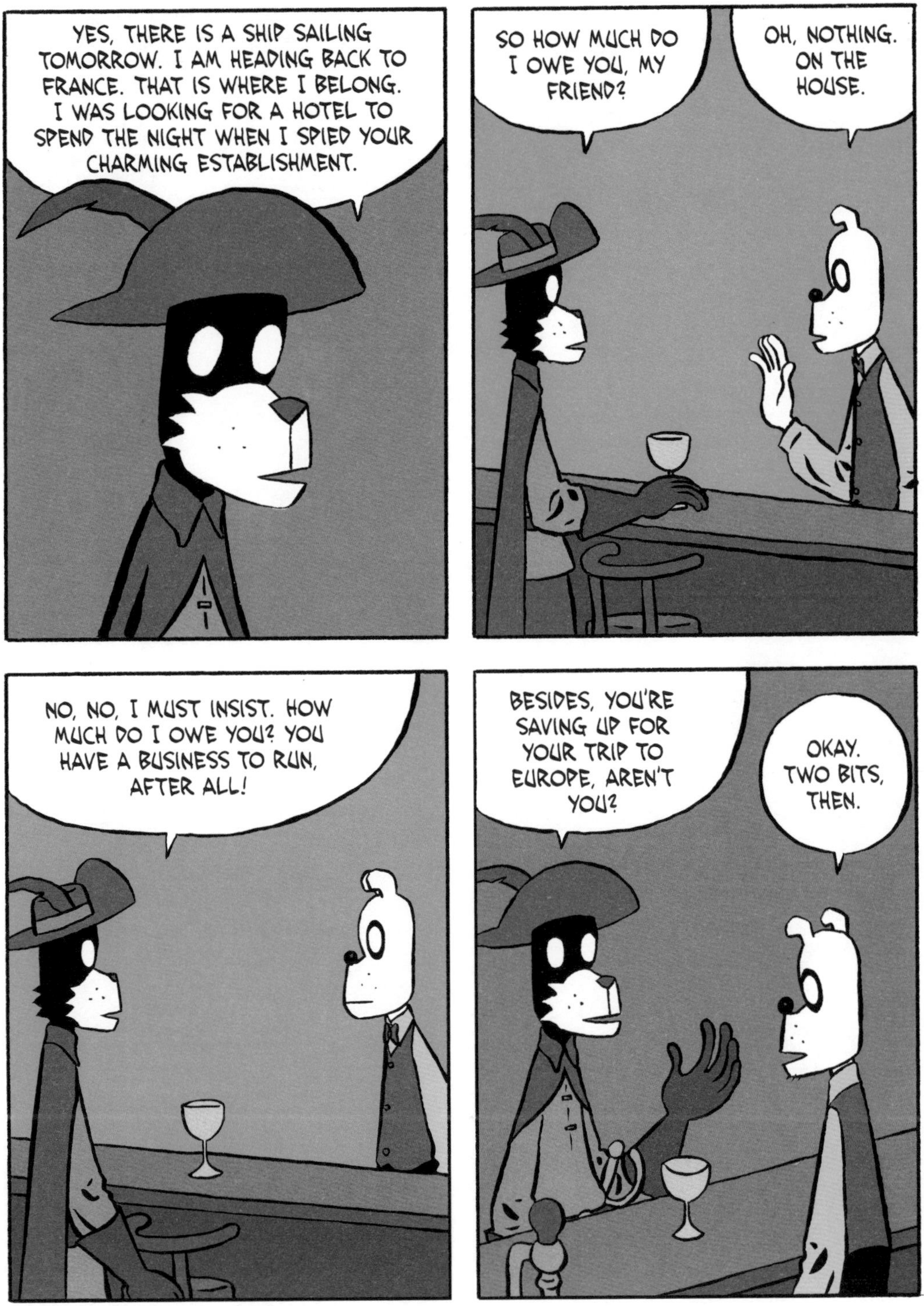
YES, THERE IS A SHIP SAILING TOMORROW. I AM HEADING BACK TO FRANCE. THAT IS WHERE I BELONG. I WAS LOOKING FOR A HOTEL TO SPEND THE NIGHT WHEN I SPIED YOUR CHARMING ESTABLISHMENT.
SO HOW MUCH DO I OWE YOU, MY FRIEND?
OH, NOTHING. ON THE HOUSE.
NO, NO, I MUST INSIST. HOW MUCH DO I OWE YOU? YOU HAVE A BUSINESS TO RUN, AFTER ALL!
BESIDES, YOU'RE SAVING UP FOR YOUR TRIP TO EUROPE, AREN'T YOU?
OKAY. TWO BITS, THEN.

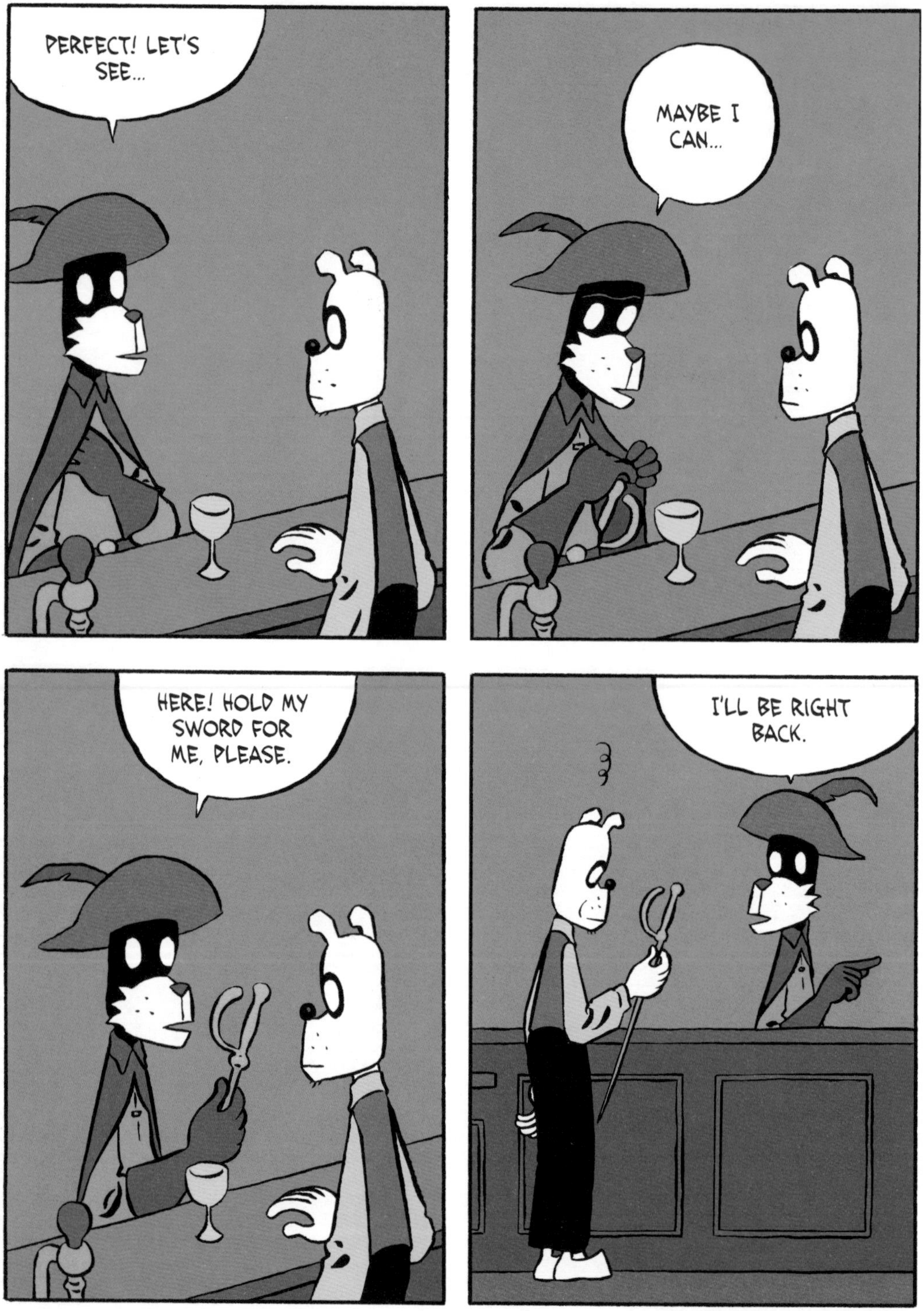
PERFECT! LET'S SEE...
MAYBE I CAN...
HERE! HOLD MY SWORD FOR ME, PLEASE.
I'LL BE RIGHT BACK.

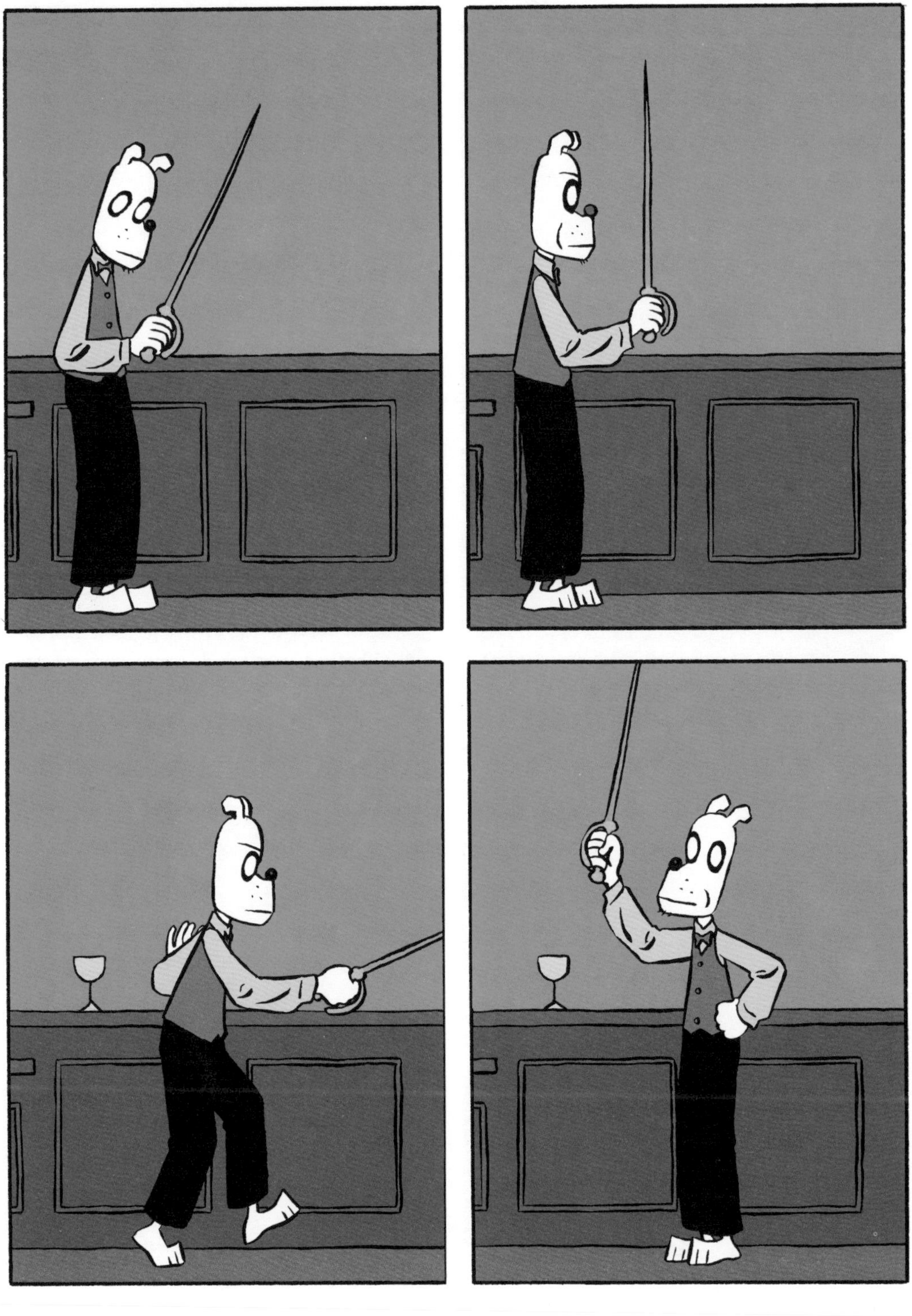

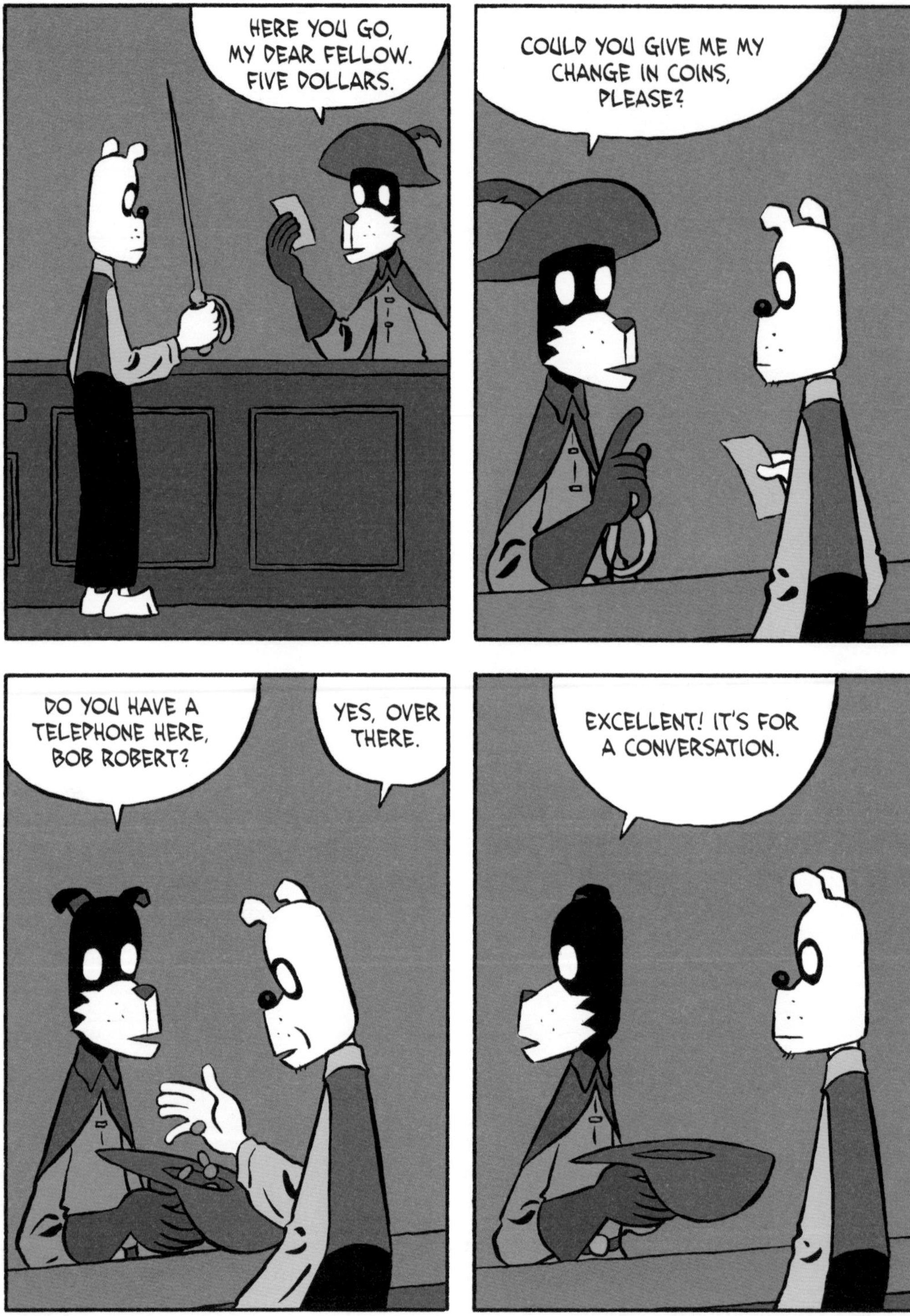
HERE YOU GO, MY DEAR FELLOW. FIVE DOLLARS.
COULD YOU GIVE ME MY CHANGE IN COINS, PLEASE?
DO YOU HAVE A TELEPHONE HERE, BOB ROBERT?
YES, OVER THERE.
EXCELLENT! IT'S FOR A CONVERSATION.

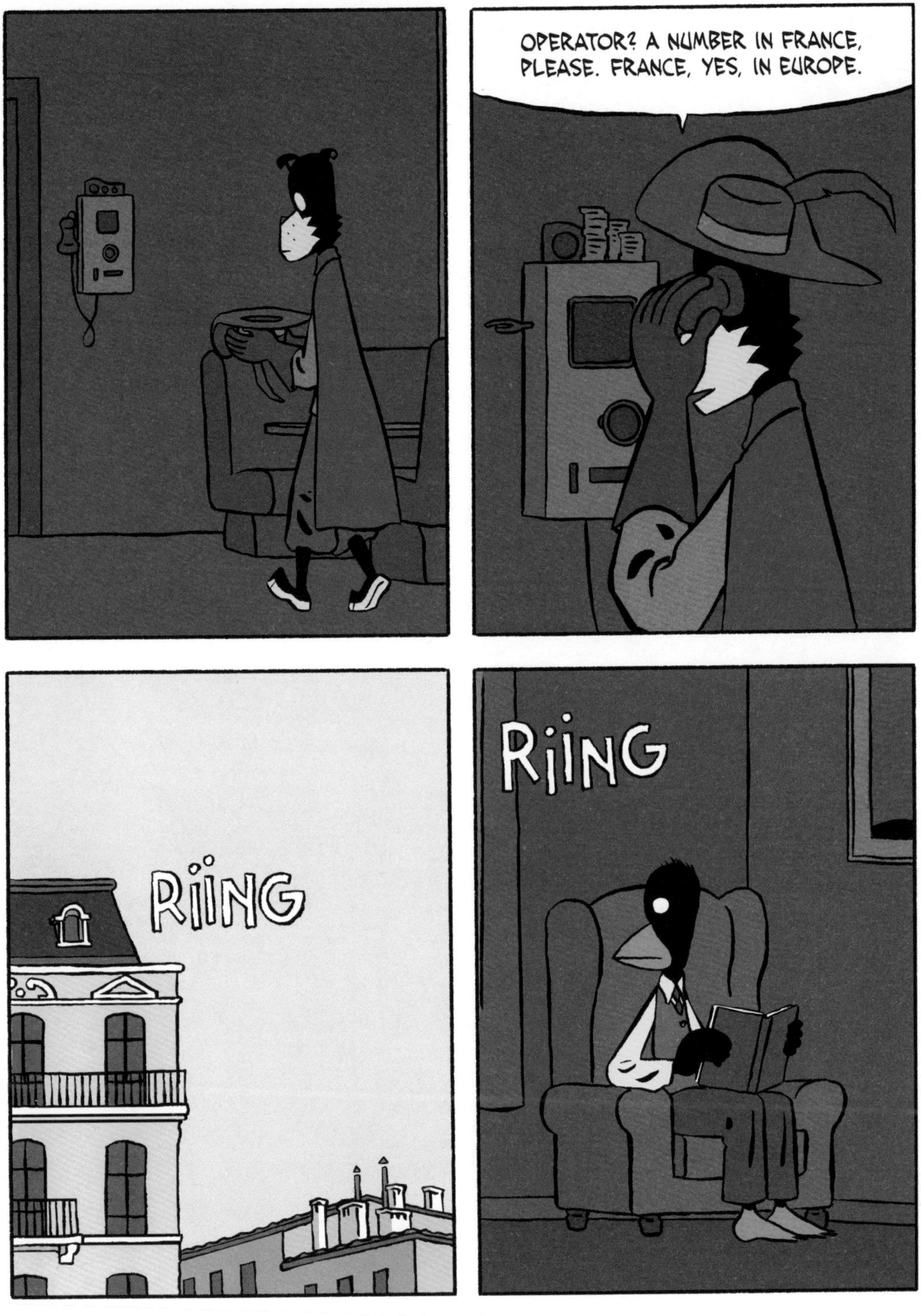
OPERATOR? A NUMBER IN FRANCE, PLEASE. FRANCE, YES, IN EUROPE.
RIING
RIING

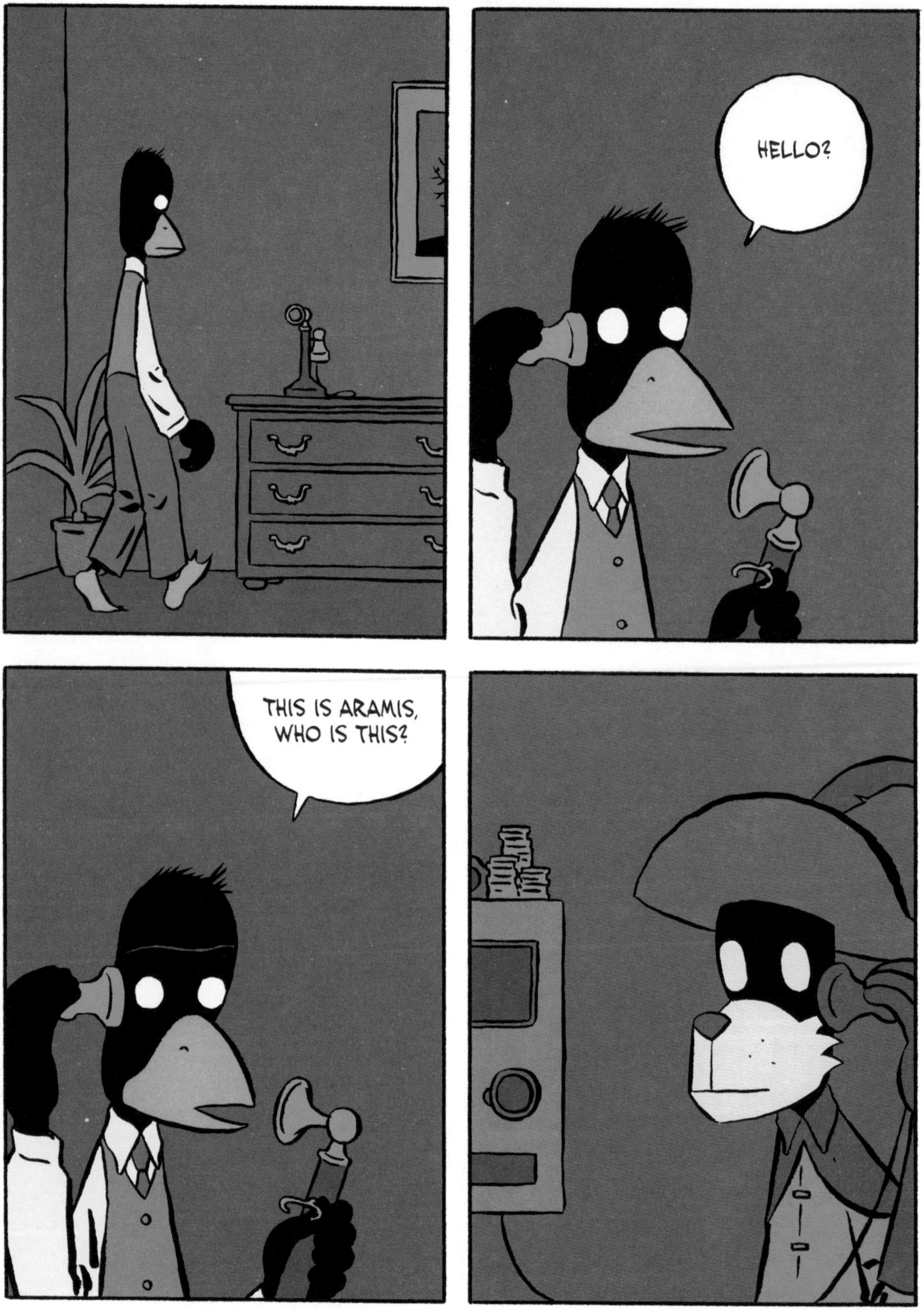
HELLO?
THIS IS ARAMIS, WHO IS THIS?

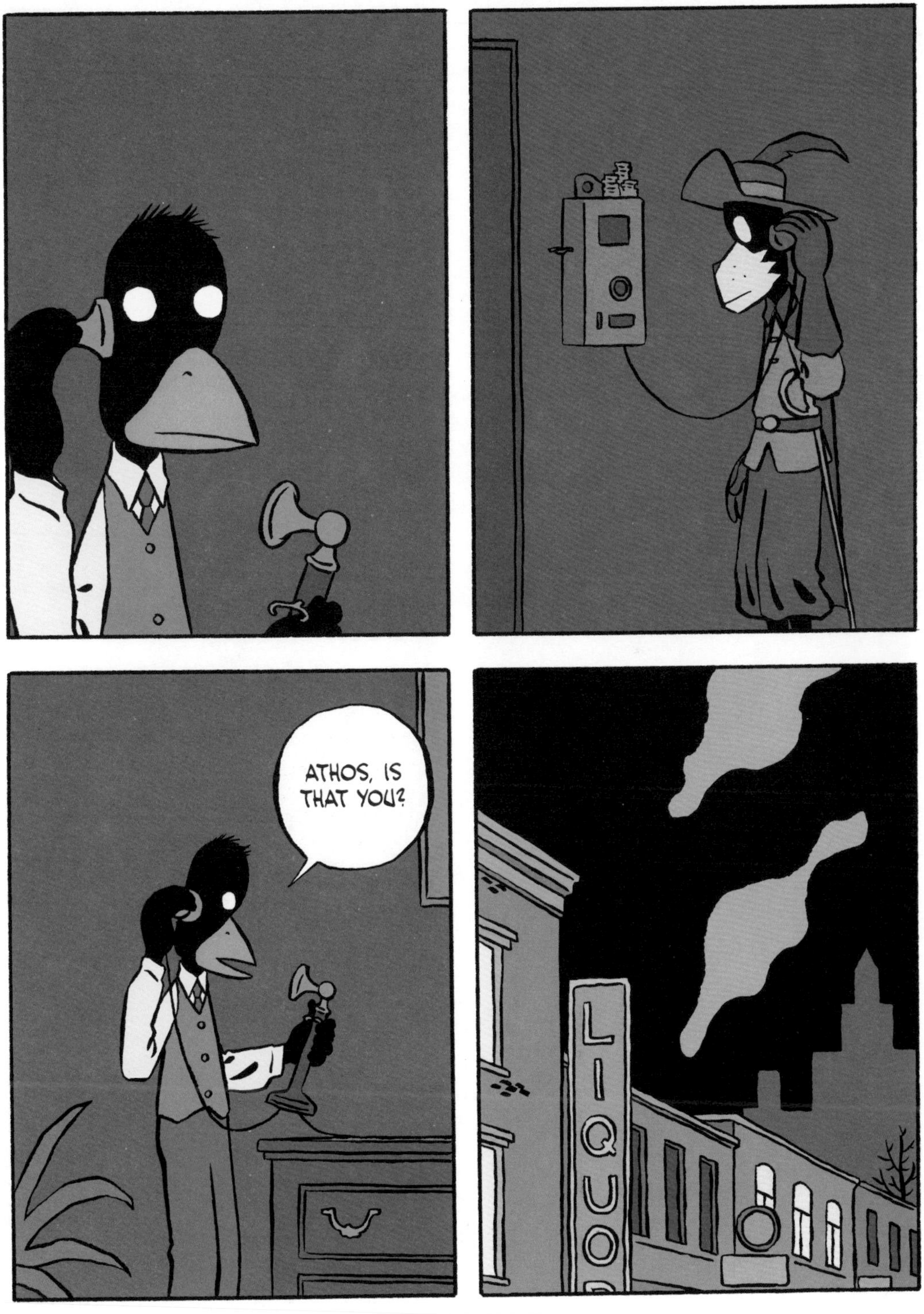
ATHOS, IS THAT YOU?
LIQUO

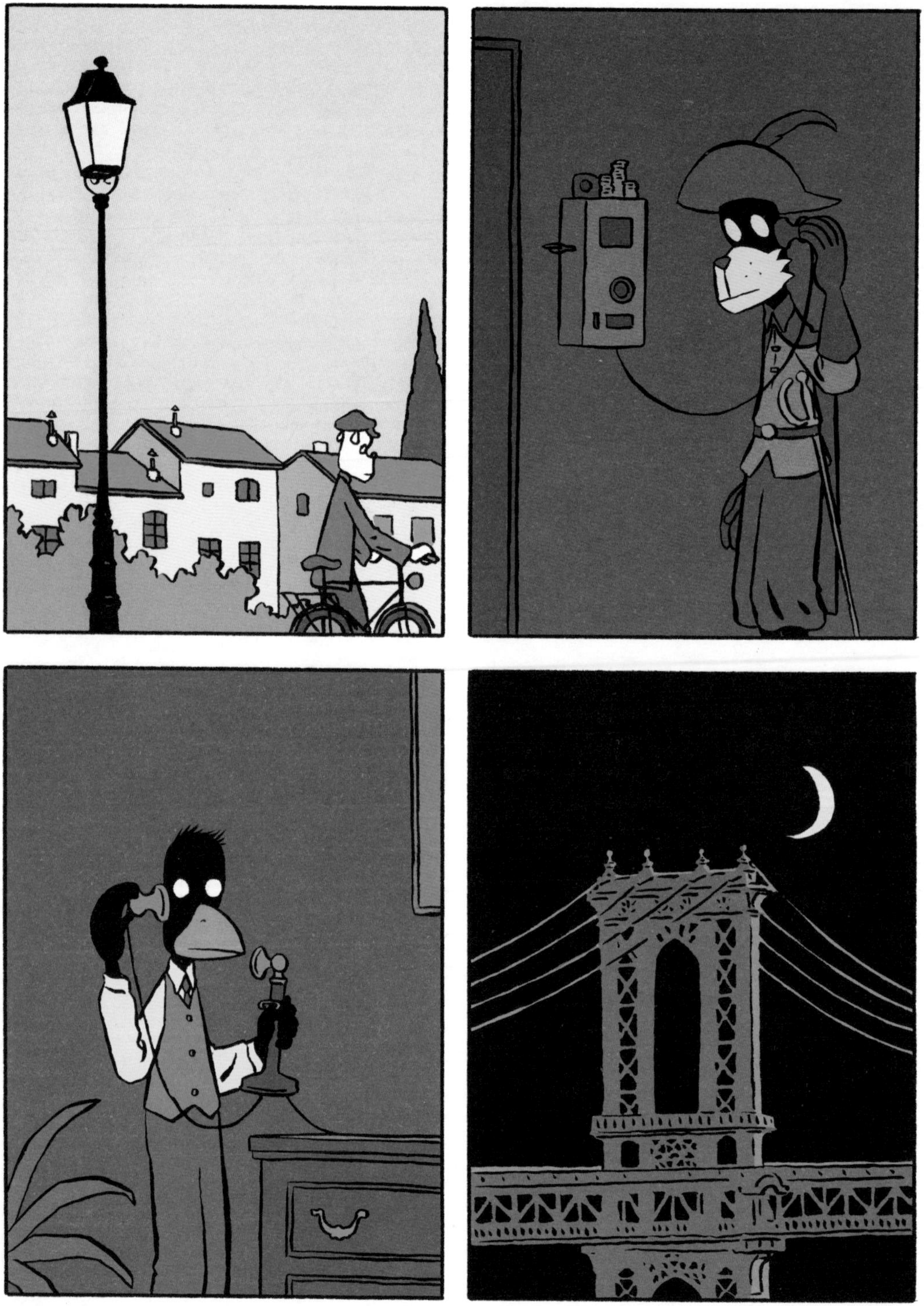

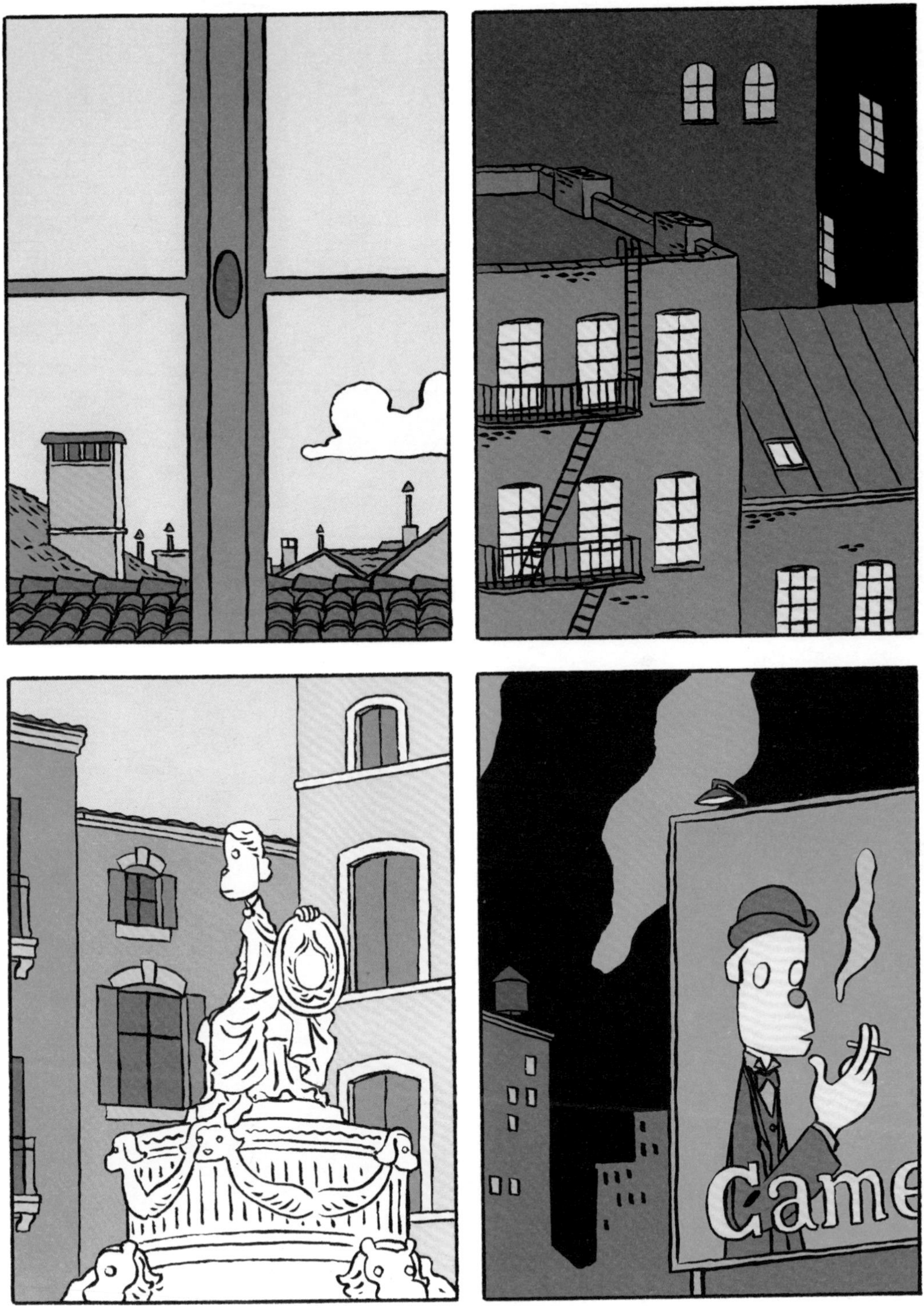
came

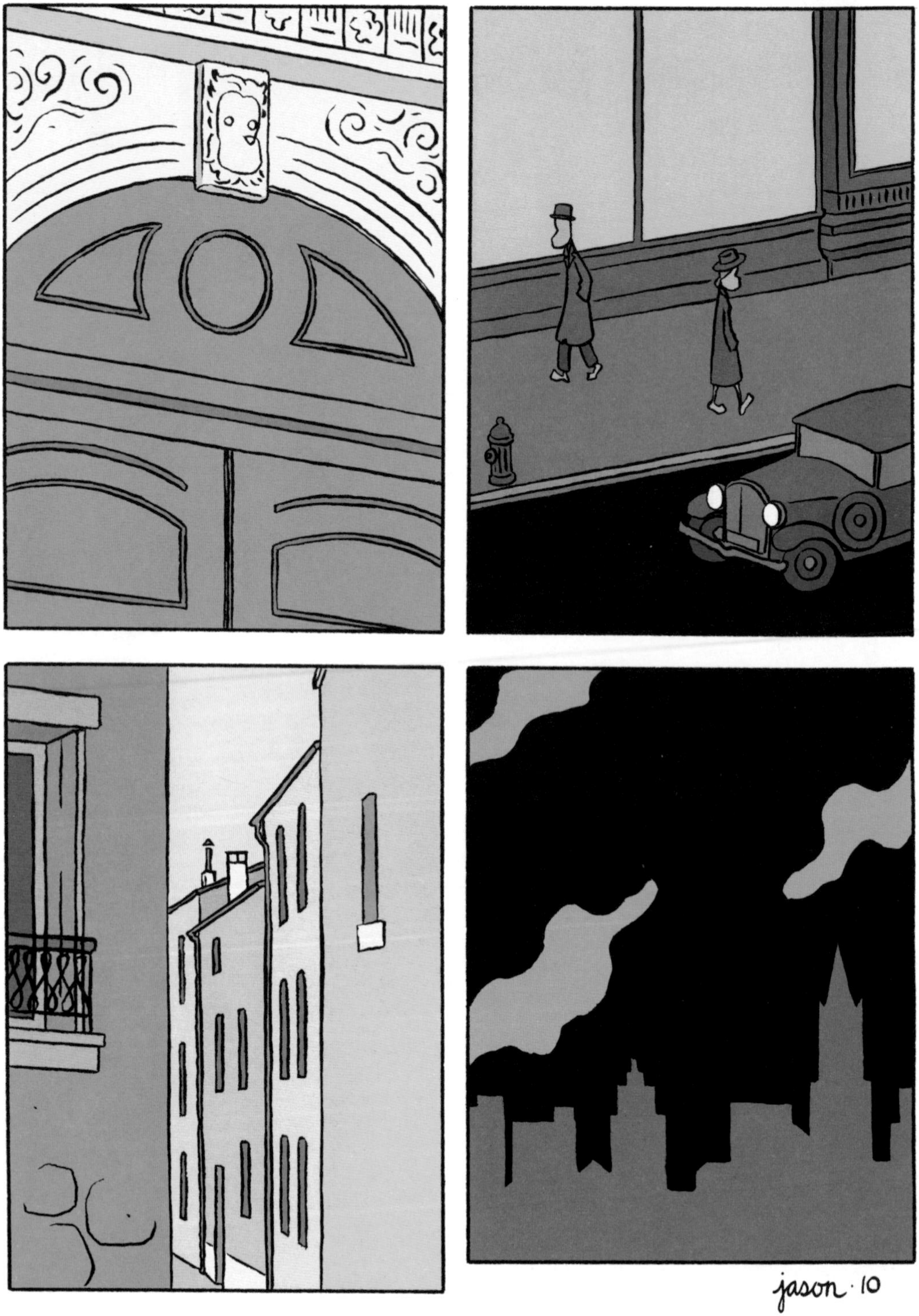
jason · 10